VENTURE CAPITAL DEVELOPMENT IN CHINA 2014

中国创业风险投资发展报告 2014

主 编 王 元 张晓原 张志宏 副主编 房汉廷 沈文京 李文雷 郭 戎

图书在版编目（CIP）数据

中国创业风险投资发展报告. 2014/王元等主编. —北京：经济管理出版社，2014.9
ISBN 978-7-5096-3403-5

Ⅰ. ①中…　Ⅱ. ①王…　Ⅲ. ①风险投资—研究报告—中国—2014
Ⅳ. ①F832.48

中国版本图书馆 CIP 数据核字（2014）第 225054 号

组稿编辑：陈　力
责任编辑：陈　力　赵晓静
责任印制：黄章平
责任校对：超　凡

出版发行：经济管理出版社（北京市海淀区北蜂窝 8 号中雅大厦 11 层　100038）
网　　址：www. E-mp. com. cn
电　　话：(010) 51915602
印　　刷：北京地大彩色印刷有限责任公司
经　　销：新华书店
开　　本：880mm×1230mm/16
印　　张：13.75
字　　数：451 千字
版　　次：2014 年 9 月第 1 版　　2014 年 9 月第 1 次印刷
书　　号：ISBN 978-7-5096-3403-5
定　　价：150.00 元

中国创业风险投资发展报告 2014

编委会

参与和支持单位（排名不分先后）

科学技术部科研条件与财务司
中国科学技术发展战略研究院
科技部火炬高技术产业开发中心
科技部科技经费监管服务中心
国家科技风险事业开发中心
商务部外国投资管理司
国家开发银行投资业务局
中国进出口银行业务开发与创新部
中国社会科学院金融研究中心
中国科技金融促进会
中国台湾创业风险投资商业同业公会
亚洲创业基金期刊集团（中国香港）
中国风险投资研究院
《中国科技投资》杂志社
北京清科创业风险投资顾问有限公司
辽宁大学工商管理学院
北京创业投资协会
天津市创业投资协会
上海市创业投资行业协会
河北省科学技术厅
河北石家庄高新技术产业开发区经济发展局
山西省科学技术厅
山西省风险投资协会
山西省科技基金发展总公司
内蒙古科技风险基金管理办公室
四川省绵阳高新技术产业开发区
四川成都创业投资协会
成都高新区金融办
成都高投盈创动力投资发展有限公司
重庆市科委
重庆市科技创业投资协会
贵州省科学技术厅
贵州高新区
贵阳高新技术创业服务中心
贵州省科技风险投资有限公司
云南省科学技术厅
云南省科技成果转化服务中心
辽宁省科技创业投资协会
辽宁科技创业投资有限公司
辽宁省沈阳市科学技术局
辽宁省沈阳科技风险开发事业中心
辽宁省大连市生产力促进中心
大连高新技术产业园区金融工作办公室
吉林省长春市科学技术局
吉林高技术创业服务中心
黑龙江省科学技术厅
黑龙江省科力高科技产业投资有限公司
哈尔滨市创业投资协会
湖北省科学技术厅
湖北省创业投资同业公会
湖北省高新技术发展促进中心
湖北省武汉市科技局
湖北省襄樊高新技术创业服务中心
河南省科学技术厅
湖南省科学技术厅
湖南省科技交流交易中心
山东省科学技术厅
山东省高新技术投资有限公司
山东省青岛市科技局
江苏省创业投资协会
无锡新区科技金融投资集团
江苏省南京市科技局
浙江省科学技术厅
浙江省风险投资协会
浙江省杭州市科技局
浙江省杭州市生产力促进中心
浙江省宁波市科学技术局
浙江省宁波市科学信息研究院
安徽省科学技术厅
安徽省科技成果转化服务中心
江西省科学技术厅
江西省科技金融促进会
福建省高新技术创业服务中心
福建省厦门市科技局
福建省厦门火炬高技术产业开发区管委会
广东省风险投资促进会
广东省佛山高新区管委会
广东省佛山高新区经济发展和科技局
广州风险投资促进会
广东省珠海高新技术创业服务中心
珠海高新区科经局
深圳市创业投资同业公会

海南省科学技术厅
甘肃省科技风险投资公司
甘肃省兰州高科创业投资担保有限公司
宁夏回族自治区科学技术厅
宁夏回族自治区科学技术厅生产力促进中心
陕西省科学技术厅
陕西省宝鸡高新区高技术创业服务中心
陕西省杨凌农业高新技术产业示范区管委会金融办
陕西省西安高新技术产业开发区管理委员会金融服务办公室
新疆维吾尔自治区科学技术厅
新疆维吾尔自治区科技生产力促进中心
青海省国有科技资产经营管理有限公司
广西壮族自治区科学技术厅
广西壮族自治区科技情报所
广西分析测试协会

目 录

摘 要

2013年中国创业风险投资业呈现十大特征①

全国创业风险投资调查写作分析组②

2013年，尽管我国A股市场低迷不振，但整个资本市场改革取得重大进展，市场活力进一步增强，中国创业风险投资行业呈现增长趋势；同时业内出现深度盘整，行业发展趋于理性。本文结合2013年度统计调查数据，对我国创业风险投资行业年度发展的现状、特点及未来发展进行了初步研究。

1 2013年度我国创投行业呈现的显著特征

1.1 机构数量和募资呈现增长态势

2013年，中国创业风险投资各类机构数达到1408③家，较2012年增加225家，增长19.0%。其中，创业风险投资企业（基金）1095家，较2012年增加153家，增幅9.5%；创业风险投资管理企业313家，较2012年增加72家，增幅29.9%（见图1）。当年新募基金215家，逼近2010年水平；随着行业竞争进一步加剧，全年有30多家基金正常或不正常清盘。

① 2014年1~5月，科技部、商务部、国家开发银行联合开展了第12次“全国创业风险投资机构统计调查”，依据《中华人民共和国统计法》的有关规定，该专项统计工作（国统制〔2012〕111号）组织全国31个省（市、自治区）58个调查机构进行协同工作，通过“中国创业风险投资信息系统”（www.ivcc.cn）进行网上统计。系统设置了信息核查与校验功能，可实现填报单位、调查员与调查管理员对数据样本的多层级甄别与审核，主要包括：标准化创业风险投资机构，对信托公司、综合性投资公司、产业基金、担保公司等非专业创投机构的样本进行有效剔除；对创投管理公司与创投企业（基金）进行分类统计；剔除基金管理公司与基金间、母基金与子基金间的重复管理资本等。

② 中国科学技术发展战略研究院2014年“全国创业风险投资调查写作分析组”成员包括：郭戎、李希义、张俊芳、魏世杰、付剑峰、周伶、王秋颖、薛薇、张明喜等，写作组成员分别完成各章执笔。本报告总撰：张明喜、郭戎。

③ 为实际存量机构数，主要包括：创业投资企业（基金）、创业投资管理企业以及少量从事政府创业投资业务的事业单位。该数据已剔除不再经营创投业务或注销的机构数。

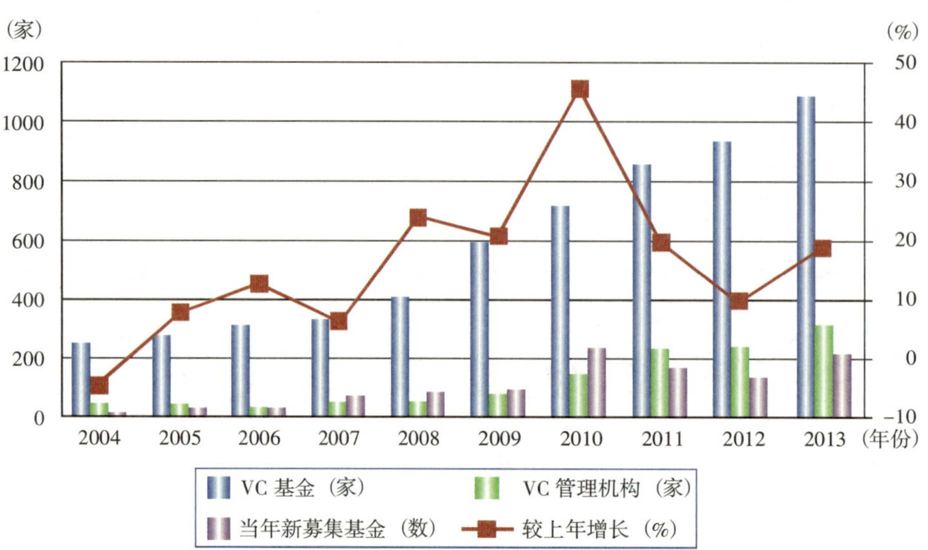

图 1 中国创业风险投资企业（基金）总量、增量（2004~2013）

2013 年，全国创业风险投资管理资本总额达 3573.9 亿元，较 2012 年增加 261 亿元，增幅 7.9%；基金平均管理资本规模为 3.26 亿元，较上年有所减小（见图 2）。创投行业管理逐渐去投机化，走向复杂化和专业化的道路，采用委托与外包管理的方式，全国共有 65 家母基金，受托管理 229 家创业风险投资基金，其中最大母基金管理的 45 家子基金，资金规模达 102 亿元。

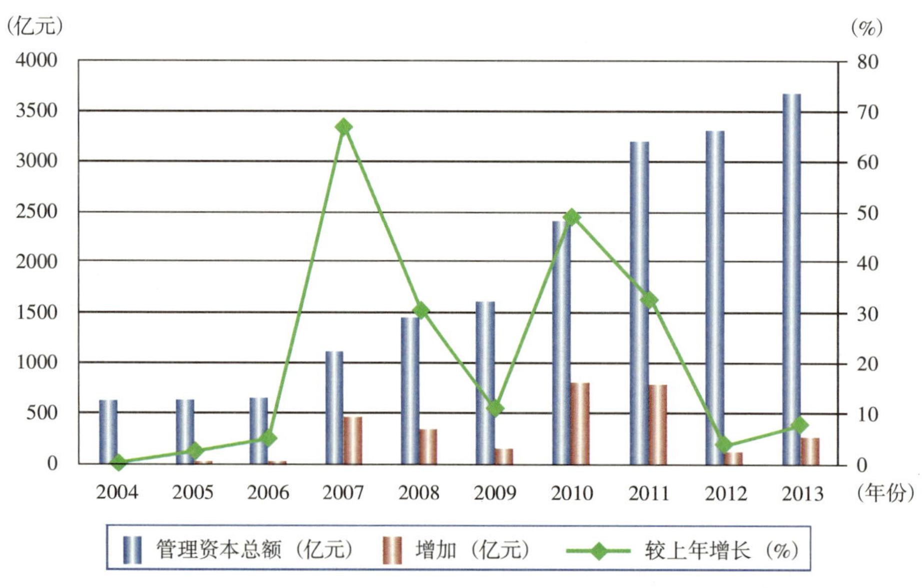

图 2 中国创业风险投资管理资本总额（2004~2013）

1.2 未上市公司占据资本来源主要位置，国有出资大幅下降

从中国创业风险投资的资本来源结构看，2013 年仍以未上市公司为主体，占总资本的 42.81%，较 2012 年上升 8.78 个百分点；政府与国有独资合计占比 29.18%，较 2012 年下降 11.41 个百分点（见图 3）。

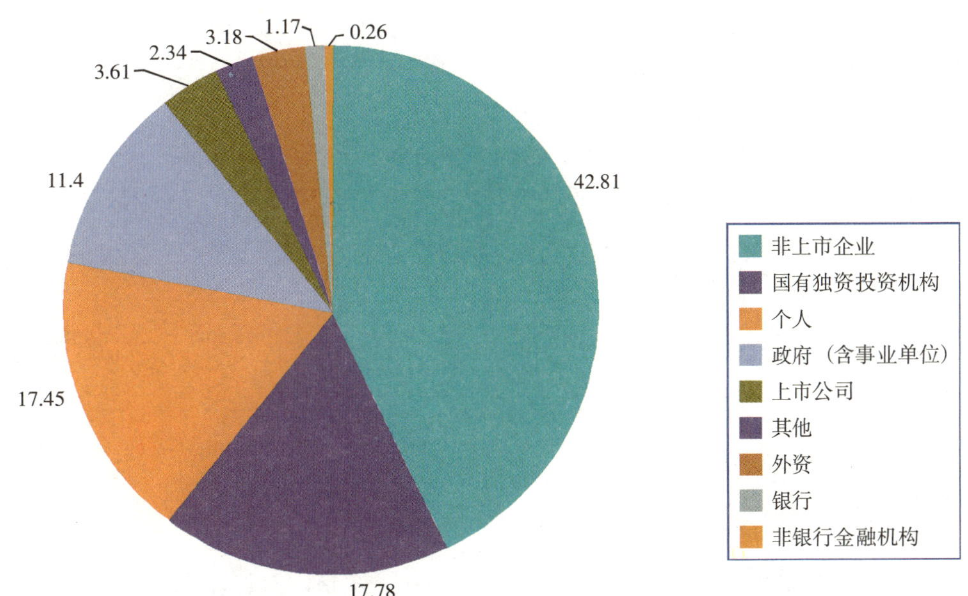

图 3 中国创业风险投资资本来源（2013）

1.3 投资项目和投资金额放缓

无论是在投资项目还是投资金额，2013 年均较去年有小幅度减少；对高新技术企业项目投资相对增加，但平均投资强度有所降低，投资更趋于小规模、早前期企业。2013 年，已披露的中国创业风险投资机构当年投资项目 1501 项，与 2012 年大体相当；投资金额为 279.0 亿元，较 2012 年减少 11.1%；项目平均投资额为 1858.5 万元。其中，投资于高新技术企业项目数为 590 家，较 2012 年减少 9.5%；投资金额 109.0 亿元，较上年减少 26.3%；项目平均投资额为 1846.9 万元。

截至 2013 年底，全国创业风险投资机构累计投资项目数 12149 项，较 2012 年增加 1037 项[①]，增长 9.3%；其中投资高新技术企业项目数 6779 项，占比 55.8%，累计投资 2634.1 亿元，较 2012 年增长 11.8%；其中投资高新技术企业 1302.1 亿元，占比 49.4%（见表 1）。

表 1 截至 2013 年底中国创业风险投资累计投资情况（2010~2013）

年度	累计投资项目总数（个）	投资高新技术企业/项目数（个）	累计投资金额（亿元）	投资高新技术企业/项目金额（亿元）
2010	8693	5160	1491.3	808.8
2011	9978	5940	2036.6	1038.6
2012	11112	6404	2355.1	1193.1
2013	12149	6779	2634.1	1302.1

① 由于创业风险投资项目为多轮投资，因此，在计算当年投资时后续投资项目也计为当年投资项目数，但在计算累计投资时，多轮投资项目仅为一个项目投资，因此实际累计项目数的增加值小于当年项目数。

1.4 医药保健、新材料等行业表现活跃，网络产业等继续引领投资

2013 年，中国创业风险投资年度投资金额最为集中的五个行业是医药保健、新材料工业、新能源与高效节能技术、金融保险业和传统制造业，累计占比 36.9%；投资项目最为集中的五个行业是金融保险业、医药保健、新能源与高效节能技术、传统制造业以及新材料工业，累计占比 43.2%。总体而言，2013 年我国创投行业的投资行业集中度略有下降，投资重点由过去制造业为主开始偏向于医疗保健、互联网金融等新兴产业，新能源、高效节能技术和新材料产业依然受投资者追捧。从趋势上看，因移动互联网的兴起，涌现出大量投资机会，网络产业/IT 服务业投资快速增加；医药保健/生物科技具有较强的抗周期性，显现出较高的投资价值（见表 2）。

表 2 中国创业风险业投资项目的前十大行业分布（2012~2013）　　单位：%

行业划分（代码）		年度	2013		2012	
			投资金额	投资项目	投资金额	投资项目
C9	新能源和环保业	新能源、高效节能技术	18.88	18.60	18.10	19.50
		新材料工业				
		环保工程				
		核应用技术				
C8	医药生物业	医药保健	12.31	14.16	7.70	11.0
		生物科技				
J6	金融保险业		10.12	6.54	5.40	4.20
C7	计算机、通信和其他电子设备制造业	通信设备	9.81	11.78	9.70	10.40
		计算机硬件产业				
		半导体				
		光电子与光机电一体化				
I	信息传输、软件和信息服务业	网络产业	7.86	14.24	9.30	11.30
		IT 服务业				
		软件产业				
		其他 IT 产业				
CA	传统制造业		7.19	6.03	10.10	8.80
L	文化、体育和娱乐业（传播与文化娱乐业）		6.16	5.24	6.40	5.30
A	农林牧副渔		6.33	3.66	6.10	4.70
H	住宿和餐饮业（消费产品和服务业）		5.00	3.45	6.30	3.50
O	其他行业		2.65	3.74	7.60	7.30

1.5 投资呈现前端化和早期化，首轮投资占主流

2013 年，中国创业风险投资机构的投资重心相比 2012 年有所前移，对种子期的投资金额增加至 12.22%，投资数占比 18.36%；对起步期的投资无论从金额占比还是项目占比均有较大幅度上升（见表 3）。从投资轮次上看，首轮投资和后续投资分别占 77.5%和 22.5%，首轮投资仍然占主导地位，但后续投资的比例不断上升。

表 3 中国创业风险投资项目所处阶段的总体分布（按投资项目占比） 单位：%

成长阶段 \ 年份	2006	2007	2008	2009	2010	2011	2012	2013
种子期	37.40	26.60	19.30	32.20	19.90	9.70	12.30	18.36
起步期	21.30	18.90	30.20	20.30	27.10	22.70	28.70	32.46
成长（扩张）期	30.00	36.60	34.00	35.20	40.90	48.30	45.00	38.21
成熟（过渡）期	7.70	12.40	12.10	9.00	10.00	16.70	13.20	10.00
重建期	3.60	5.40	4.40	3.40	2.20	2.60	0.80	0.97

1.6 江苏、广东、浙江最活跃，中西部部分省市增长迅猛

江苏、广东、浙江管理资本总量位居前三甲，前十个省市的管理资本总额占全国管理资本总量的 86.1%，呈现集聚现象，地区差异仍十分明显。同时，福建、安徽、四川、湖北等地区的创业风险投资发展势头强劲，例如安徽省管理资金规模达到了 117.08 亿元（见图 4）。

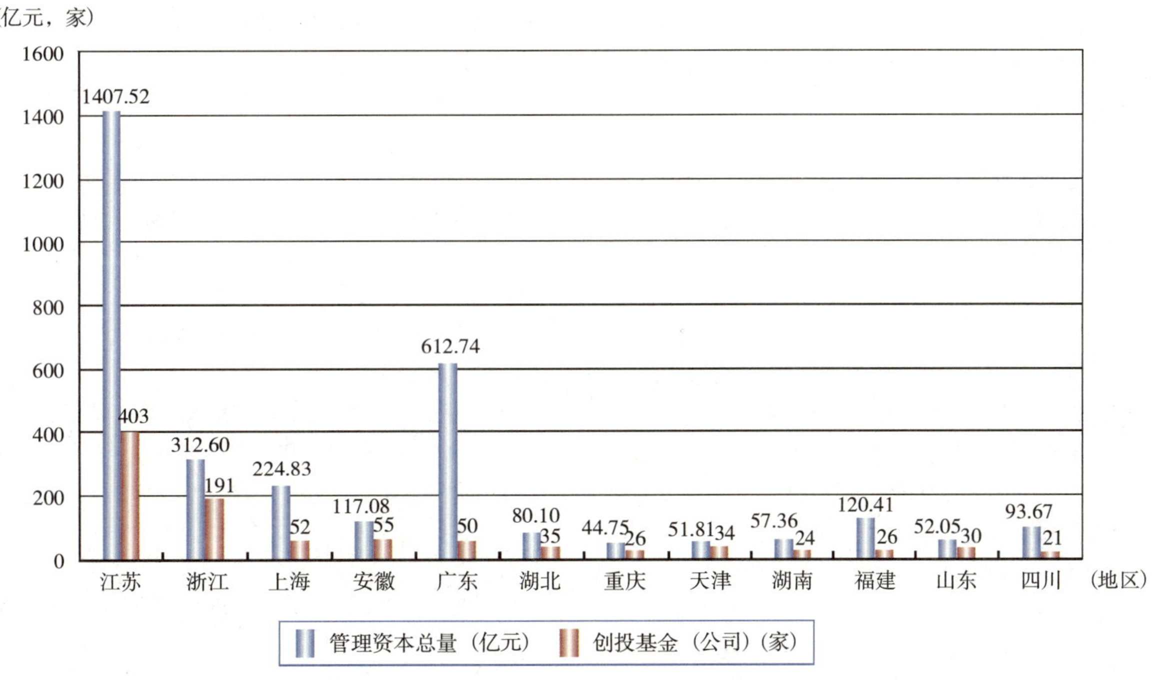

图 4 部分地区创业风险投资管理资本和机构数量（2013）

1.7 多元化退出格局凸显，回报率有所下滑

2013 年，受国内资本市场 IPO 暂停、海外上市渠道狭窄等持续利空因素影响，中国企业在全球资本市场的活跃程度呈现持续下降态势，全年仅有 66 家中国企业在境内外资本市场上市，其中 27 家获得创投支持①。按照退出渠道划分，回购退出占比达 44.83%，为最主要方式；上市退出占比出现自 2008 年以来的首次下滑，并购退出占比为 26.25%（见表 4）。

2013 年，全行业的退出绩效较上年有所下滑。上市退出收益持续下滑，仅为平均账面回报的 4.48 倍；并购退出

① 清科研究中心. 2013 年 66 家中企上市 A 股市场喜迎开闸［R］. 2014-01-02.

的项目收益率有所提高，达 24.09%。此外，回购与清算的收益率均比过去有较大幅度增加，创业风险投资机构的项目管理能力得以提升。

表 4 中国创业风险投资的退出方式分布（2007~2013） 单位：%

年份 \ 退出方式	上市	并购	回购	清算	其他
2007	24.20	29.00	27.40	5.60	13.70
2008	22.70	23.20	34.80	9.20	10.10
2009	25.30	33.00	35.30	6.30	0.00
2010	29.80	28.60	32.80	6.90	1.90
2011	29.40	30.00	32.30	3.20	5.10
2012	29.41	18.93	45.01	6.65	0.00
2013	24.33	26.25	44.83	4.60	0.00

1.8 政府引导基金不断发力

截至 2013 年底，科技型中小企业创业投资引导基金累计投入财政资金 30.59 亿元；其中，通过阶段参股方式，共出资 20.09 亿元，参股了 71 家重点投资于科技型中小企业的创业投资企业，累计注册资本约 150 亿元；通过风险补助和投资保障方式共立项 1411 项，累计安排补助资金 10.5 亿元。中央财政投入 70.5 亿元实施国家新兴产业创投计划，支持设立了 141 只国家参股创投基金，总规模近 390 亿元，间接带动银行贷款和社会资金 638 亿元。

从全国范围看，截至 2013 年底，获得各级政府创业风险投资引导基金参股支持的创业风险投资机构累计达 252 家，政府创业风险投资引导基金累计出资 326.91 亿元，引导带动创业风险投资管理资金规模超过 1600 亿元。

1.9 政策环境日益优化

近年来，中央及地方出台了一系列政策措施支持创业风险投资发展。调查显示，22.0%的创业风险投资机构享受到政府资金支持，25.0%的机构享受所得税减免优惠，28.2%的机构获得信息交流支持，12.2%的机构获得人员培训帮助。可以看出，政府对创投机构的直接支持在减少，但提供的间接服务在不断完善。

2013 年，《国务院办公厅关于金融支持经济结构调整和转型升级的指导意见》、《国务院办公厅关于金融支持小微企业发展的实施意见》等一系列政策的出台，明确提出加强对科技型、创新型、创业型小微企业的金融支持力度，积极引导创业投资企业投资于小微企业，建立科技金融服务体系，细化科技型小微企业标准，完善对各类科技成果的评价机制；中国（上海）自由贸易试验区挂牌成立，在自贸区的先行先试政策中，提出鼓励股权投资发展的诸多举措。上述支持创新创业企业、中小微企业和科技成果转化的政策不断为创投行业的发展释放新的改革红利。

同年 12 月，《国务院关于全国中小企业股份转让系统有关问题的决定》出台，标志着“新三板”扩大至全国取得实质性进展，对于增加创业风险投资机构投资机会，缓解中小微企业融资难，拓宽创业风险投资机构退出渠道具有重要意义。截至 2013 年底，355 挂牌企业家全年完成 60 次发行融资，募集资金 10.02 亿元。

1.10 行业自律逐步构建

修订后的《证券投资基金法》于 2013 年 6 月 1 日正式实施，在加大基金持有人保护力度的同时，首次将非公开募集基金纳入调整范围，私募证券投资基金获得合法地位；值得肯定的是，该法并未将创业风险投资纳入，符合该行业发展的特定规律。在中央层面，中国科技金融促进会风险投资专业委员会、中国投资协会股权和创业投资专业委员会等组织推动创业风险投资业界交流，加强创业风险投资行业规范和自律管理。在地方层面，江苏、浙江、北京、上海、深圳、广东、重庆、安徽等各自成立创业风险投资协会（同业公会），使其成为服务型行业自律组织，指导、协调、帮助会员更好地从事创业投资活动，维护会员合法权益，对创业风险投资事业的发展起到重要作用。

2 风险投资家对行业的评价与预测

2013 年的调查统计工作，细化了风险投资家对自身发展、全行业发展、未来投资前景状况的评价，同时要求创业投资机构负责人填写有关选项，提高了调查结果的科学性。

2.1 对自身发展状况持乐观态度

1026 家创业风险投资机构对当年自身发展状况持乐观评价的机构占比明显高于悲观评价的机构，超过一半的创业风险投资机构认为自身发展较为乐观，其中包括 3.31%认为自身发展状况非常好，11.79%认为自身发展状况好，36.06%认为自身发展状况较好，总体评价远高于 2012 年。

2.2 对全行业发展的判断略有改善

创业风险投资机构对全行业发展情况做出的评价是：持乐观态度的机构占比高于持悲观态度的机构，认为全行业整体发展非常好、好以及较好的机构占比达到 30.67%，高于上年 19 个百分点；认为全行业发展非常差、差和较差的机构占比为 21.23%。

2.3 对 2014 年投资预期向好

对于 2014 年投资前景，创业风险投资机构给出了较为乐观的预测，超过一半的机构看好未来前景，其中 2.0%的机构认为前景非常好，11.3%的机构认为前景好，43.3%的机构认为前景较好，认为前景较不好的机构占 3.3%，认为不好的仅为 1.9%。

3 促进我国创投行业发展的初步思考

2014 年 5 月，国务院为加快推动我国创投行业发展提出了进一步要求，回顾历史和剖析现状，创投行业发展还存在现行制度不能完全满足发展需求、募资较困难、天使支持力度有待加大、退出渠道不畅通等问题。为加快推动我国创投行业的健康持续发展，培育发展战略性新兴产业，支撑和引领发展方式转变，根据创投行业发展特征、面临问题和国际经验，进行了以下初步思考。

3.1 逐步回归创业风险投资的本质

我国创投行业要取得长足的进展，从“名似”、“形似”阶段进入“神似”阶段，应该回归创业风险投资的本质——技术创新风险的经营能力，对“技术高、年龄小”的项目进行投资。创业风险投资不同于其他金融资本，其服务的目标对象是高强度研发的创新企业，加速研发产生的知识产权化、资本化和产业化，实现“惊险的一跃”。创业风险投资机构越是以“技术高、年龄小”的项目入手，越是能锻炼出技术风险经营能力，也就越是发挥了信号“放大器”、“筛选器”的功能，对社会技术路线的优化功能也就越强，彰显创业风险投资“高能资本”的特性。

3.2 鼓励和支持天使投资发展

不断培育天使投资人队伍，形成多层次的天使投资群体；在中小企业发展专项资金中增设天使资本引导基金，对符合条件的天使投资进行风险代偿；借鉴美国州政府给予天使投资税收优惠的做法，允许天使投资机构和个人向符合条件早期项目的投资抵免其应纳税所得额；加强对天使投资机构和个人的备案登记及动态管理，加强服务跟踪；营造宽容失败的社会环境，引导由普遍关注成功者和成功投资向鼓励宽容失败的创业精神转变。

3.3 引导民间资本进入创业风险投资领域

推动以有限合伙形式成立创业风险投资机构，将中关村国家自主创新示范区有限合伙制创业投资企业法人合伙人企业所得税试点政策完善后推广至全国；引导和规范创业风险投资机构采取众筹模式进行募资，突破募资对象超过 200 人的限制；大力支持创业风险投资机构及其股东或有限合伙人发行债券，不断扩大资本来源。

3.4 发挥国有创投和引导基金的重要作用

按照公共财政原则，重新制定国有创业投资机构和政府性创业投资引导基金绩效考核办法，确保国有创投和引导基金所引导的创投机构主要投向科技型、创新型企业早前期阶段；稳妥推进国有创投混合所有制改革，建立经营者的激励约束机制，实现国有创投政府责任与市场化运作的有机结合。

3.5 扫清创业风险投资向早前端投资的相关障碍

支持符合条件的创业风险投资所投资企业在全国中小企业股份转让系统挂牌；将科技成果处置权、收益权等权利赋予科研项目承担单位，简化科技成果处置程序，加大对科技成果完成人和为科技成果转化作出重要贡献人员的激励力度；简化初创期企业股权登记、变更和转让的相关制度。

3.6 加快推进场外市场建设

在区域性产权交易市场基础上，以中国技术交易所为核心，建立全国技术产权交易机构联盟；建立信息化、网络化的技术交易系统和展示平台，开展线上和线下相结合的综合服务，促进技术产权资本化；在清理整顿的基础上，将区域性股权市场纳入多层次资本市场体系，推进以科技成果交易、中小微企业股权流转为核心的场外市场建设；建立场外市场与创业风险投资机构的良性互动机制，为创业风险投资提供多元化的退出渠道。

Abstract

10 Features of Chinese Venture Capital Industry in 2013①

National Venture Capital Survey Writing & Analysis Team②

Although 2013 saw a slump in Chinese A share market, major progress had been made in the reform of capital market. The market' vitality was further enhanced and Chinese venture capital industry showed a growth trend. Meanwhile, the industry underwent a deep restructuring, ensuring more reasonable development. This paper conducts a preliminary study concerning the current conditions, features and future development of Chinese venture capital industry according to the results of statistical survey in 2013.

1 Noteworthy features of Chinese venture capital industry in 2013

1.1 Quantity of institutions and fundraising showed a growth trend

The venture capital institutions in China was up to 1408③ in 2013, a growth of 19.0% as compared to 225 in 2012. Among them, 1095 are venture capital enterprises (funds), up by 9.5% in comparison to 153 in 2012; 313 are venture capital management enterprises, a rise of 29.9% as compared to 72 in 2012 (See Fig.1). 215 new funds were created, almost as many as that in 2010. With the competition in this industry becoming more and more tense, more than 30 funds went into liquidation in 2013 normally or abnormally.

① From Jan. to Apr. in 2013, the Ministry of Science and Technology, the Ministry of Commerce, the National Development Bank jointly launched "National Venture Capital Survey". In accordance with the relevant provisions of " China Statistics Law", they organized 58 investigation agencies in 31 provinces (municipalities and autonomous regions) to work together on the special statistics (State Statistics 〔2012〕 111), and carried out online statistics through "China Venture Capital Information System". The system has information verification and validation functions which enable reporting units, investigators and survey administrators to conduct multi-level screening and audit of the data sample, mainly including: standardizing venture capital institutions, effectively removing the samples of trust companies, integrated investment companies, industry funds, security companies and other non-professional venture capital organizations, carrying out classified statistics of venture capital management companies and venture capital companies (unds), excluding the repeat management capital between fund management companies and the funds as well as between the parent funds with sub-funds and so on.

② China Science and Technology Development Strategy Research Institute's 2013 "National Venture Capital Survey Writing & Analysis Team" members include: Guo Rong, Li Xiyi, Zhang Mingxi, Zhang Junfang, Fu Jianfeng, Wei Shijie, Zhou Ling, Wang Qiuying and so on. The authors of the report are Zhang MIingxi and Guo Rong.

③ It is the actual number of stock agencies, including venture capital enterprises (funds) , venture capital management companies as well as a small amount of undertaking institutions engaged in government venture capital operations. The data exclude Institutions no longer engaged in venture capital operations or canceled institutions.

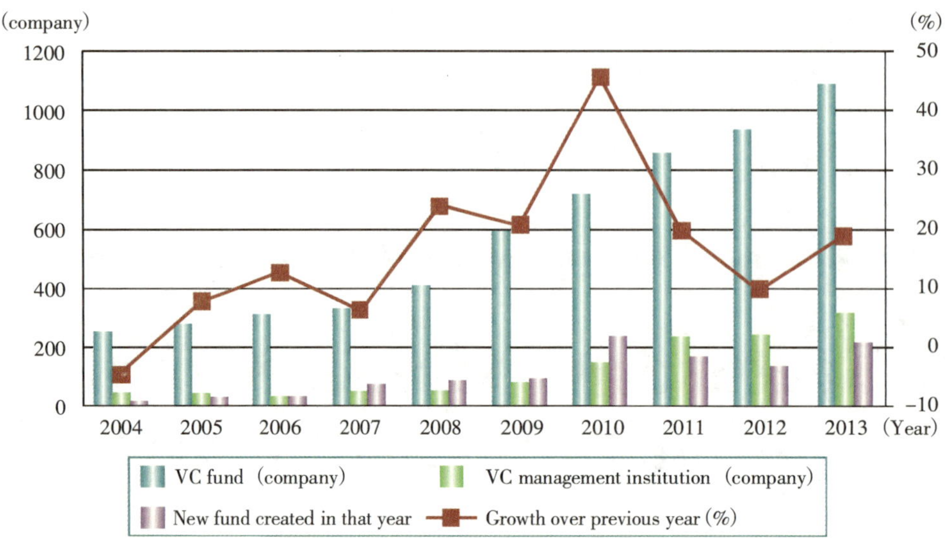

Fig.1 Total and Increase of Chinese Venture Capital Enterprises (Funds) (2004–2013)

The management capital of venture capital industry in 2013 totaled RMB 357.39 billion, an increase of RMB 26.1 billion and 7.9% over 2012; the average management capital of fund was RMB 326 million, a decrease in comparison to last year (See Fig. 2). The management for venture capital industry was on the way to become increasingly less speculative and more complex and professional. Mandatory management and outsourcing management were employed. There were 65 funds of funds (FOF) nationwide, which were entrusted to manage 229 venture capital funds. Among them, the largest FOF manages 45 Sub-funds, with its capital scale up to RMB 10.2 billion.

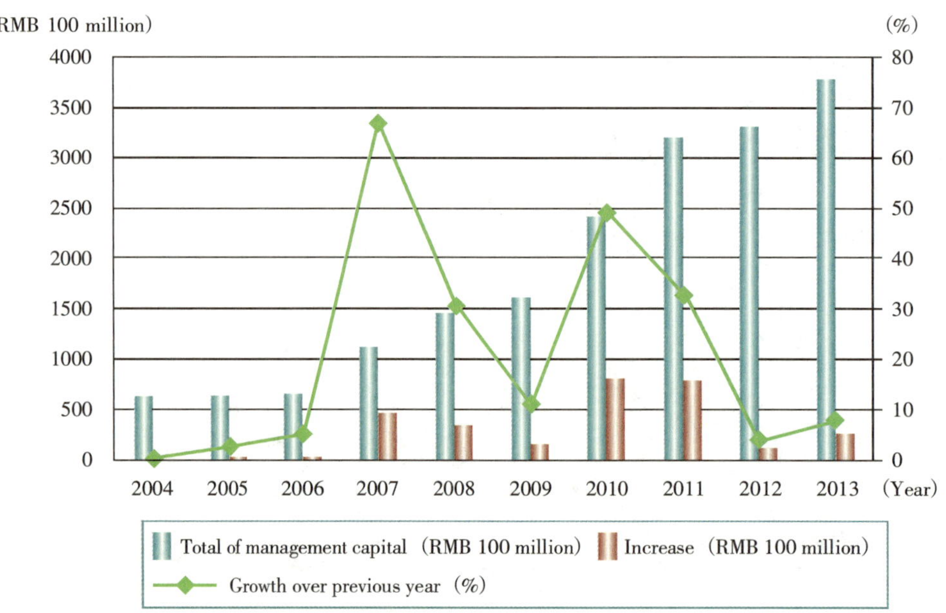

Fig.2 Total of Management Capital of Venture Capital Industry in China (2004–2013)

1.2 Unlisted companies dominated the capital resources; state capital contributions decreased largely

The structure of capital resources for Chinese venture capital industry shows that unlisted companies still dominated the capital resources in 2013, accounting for 42.81% of total capital, and up by 8.78 percent point in comparison to 2012; the government and solely state-owned capital contribution totaled 29.18%, down by 11.41 percent point in comparison to 2012 (See Fig. 3).

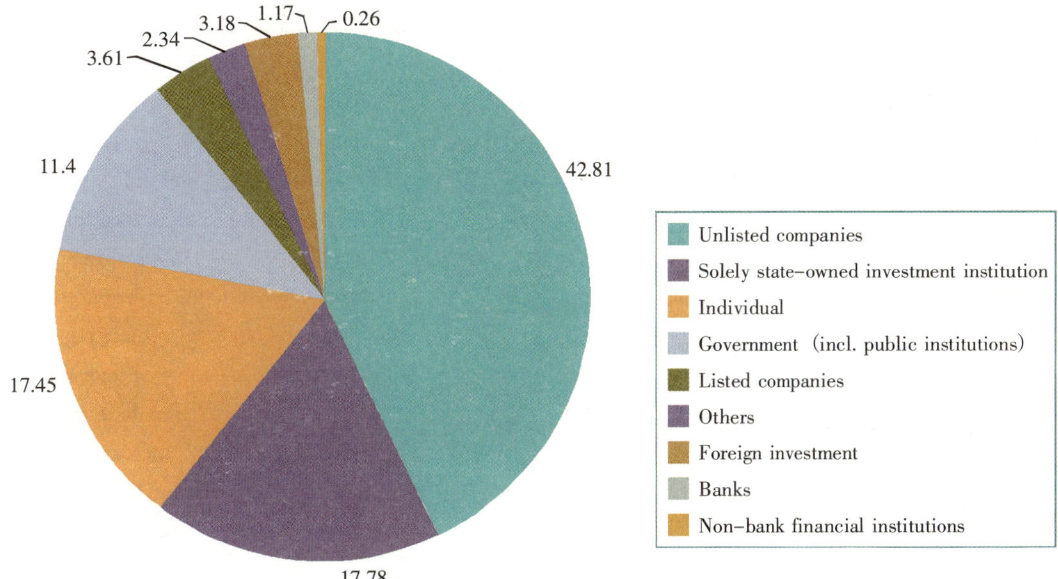

Fig.3 Capital Resources for Chinese Venture Capital Industry (2013)

1.3 Investment projects and investment amounts dropped

Both investment projects and investment amounts reduced slightly in 2013 in comparison to 2012. The investment in high-tech enterprises increased relatively, however the investment intensity at average was decreased. The investment favored small-scale enterprises at its earlier development stage. The investment projects by Chinese venture capital institutions exposed in 2013 were 1501, substantially the same as that in 2012; the investment amount was RMB 27.9 billion, down by 11.1% in comparison to 2012. The average investment per project was RMB 18.585 million. 590 high-tech enterprises were invested, down by 9.5% in comparison to 2012; the investment amount was RMB 10.9 billion, down by 26.3% over last year; and the average investment per project was RMB 18.469 million.

By the end of 2013, the projects invested by venture capital institutions nationwide totaled 12149, an increase of 1037[①] and up by 9.3% in comparison to 2012; 6779 high-tech enterprises were invested, accounting for 55.8%. The accumulative investment totaled RMB 263.41 billion, an increase of 11.8% over 2012, among which, RMB 130.21 billion were invested in high-tech enterprises, accounting for 49.4% of the total investment (see Table 1).

① Since venture capital projects are of multi-round investment, when calculating the current year's investment, the subsequent investment projects shall also be included. However, when calculating accumulated investment, multi-round investment is only one project investment, therefore, the increase of actually accumulated projects is less than the current year projects.

Table 1 Accumulated investment of China's venture capital at the end of 2013 (2010-2013)

Year	Cumulative total investment projects	Investment in high-tech enterprise / projects	Cumulative investment (100 million Yuan)	Investment in high-tech enterprises / projects (100 million Yuan)
2010	8693	5160	1491.3	808.8
2011	9978	5940	2036.6	1038.6
2012	11112	6404	2355.1	1193.1
2013	12149	6779	2634.1	1302.1

1.4 Medical & health care and new materials industry were active in capital attraction and the Internet industry continued to take the lead in investment attraction

In 2013, investment amounts of Chinese venture capital industry were concentrated on five major industries, i.e., medical& health care, new materials industry, new energy an efficient energy-saving technology, finance and insurance industry, and traditional manufacturing industry, taking up 36.9%. The investment projects were concentrated on five major industries, i.e., finance and insurance industry, medical& health care, new energy and efficient energy-saving technology, traditional manufacturing industry and new materials industry, accounting for 43.2%. In general, the industry invested by Chinese venture capital industry in 2013 was less centralized. The investment preferred emerging industries such as medical & health care and Internet finance over the manufacturing industry. New energy, efficient energy-saving technology and new materials industry remain popular among the investors. As the trend tells, a variety of investment opportunities comes up due to the rise of mobile Internet, and the investment in Internet/IT service increases rapidly. As medical & health-care/biotechnology have strong resistance to periodicity, they have higher investment value (see Table 2).

Table 2 Top 10 industries invested by China's venture capital (2012-2013) Unit: %

<table>
<tr><th colspan="3" rowspan="2">Industry sectors (code) / Year</th><th colspan="2">2013</th><th colspan="2">2012</th></tr>
<tr><th>Investment amount</th><th>Investment projects</th><th>Investment amount</th><th>Investment projects</th></tr>
<tr><td rowspan="4">C9</td><td rowspan="4">New energy and environmental protection industry</td><td>New energy, energy efficient technologies</td><td rowspan="4">18.88</td><td rowspan="4">18.60</td><td rowspan="4">18.10</td><td rowspan="4">19.50</td></tr>
<tr><td>New materials industry</td></tr>
<tr><td>Environmental engineering</td></tr>
<tr><td>Nuclear applied technology</td></tr>
<tr><td rowspan="2">C8</td><td rowspan="2">Pharmaceutical and biotech industry</td><td>Healthcare</td><td rowspan="2">12.31</td><td rowspan="2">14.16</td><td rowspan="2">7.70</td><td rowspan="2">11.00</td></tr>
<tr><td>Biotech</td></tr>
<tr><td>J6</td><td colspan="2">Finance and insurance industry</td><td>10.12</td><td>6.54</td><td>5.40</td><td>4.20</td></tr>
<tr><td rowspan="4">C7</td><td rowspan="4">Computer, communications and other electronic equipment Manufacturing</td><td>Communication equipment</td><td rowspan="4">9.81</td><td rowspan="4">11.78</td><td rowspan="4">9.70</td><td rowspan="4">10.40</td></tr>
<tr><td>Computer hardware industry</td></tr>
<tr><td>Semiconductor</td></tr>
<tr><td>Optoelectronics and mechatronics</td></tr>
<tr><td rowspan="4">I</td><td rowspan="4">Information transmission, software and information services</td><td>Internet industry</td><td rowspan="4">7.86</td><td rowspan="4">14.24</td><td rowspan="4">9.30</td><td rowspan="4">11.30</td></tr>
<tr><td>IT service industry</td></tr>
<tr><td>Software industry</td></tr>
<tr><td>Other IT industry</td></tr>
</table>

Industry sectors (code) / Year		2013		2012	
		Investment amount	Investment projects	Investment amount	Investment projects
CA	Traditional manufacturing industry	7.19	6.03	10.10	8.80
L	Culture, Sports and Entertainment (Communication and cultural entertainment)	6.16	5.24	6.40	5.30
A	Farming, forestry, animal husbandry, side-line production and fishery	6.33	3.66	6.10	4.70
H	Accommodation and catering industry (consumer products and services)	5.00	3.45	6.30	3.50
O	Others	2.65	3.74	7.60	7.30

1.5 The investment favored enterprises at earlier stages; first round investment dominated

The Chinese venture capital institutions more favored the enterprises at earlier stages in 2013. The investment for enterprises at seed stage was up to 12.22%, accounting for 18.36% of total investment. The investment for initial stage increased significantly both in ratio in the total investment and ratio in total investment projects (see Table 3). From the investment round, the first round investment and subsequent investment take up 77.5% and 22.5%, respectively. The first round investment remained in the leading position; however, the proportion of subsequent investment rises increasingly.

Table 3 Overall stage distribution of investment projects of China Venture Investment (by the percentage of investment projects)

Unit: %

Growth stage / Year	2006	2007	2008	2009	2010	2011	2012	2013
Seed stage	37.40	26.60	19.30	32.20	19.90	9.70	12.30	18.36
Initial stage	21.30	18.90	30.20	20.30	27.10	22.70	28.70	32.46
Growth (expansion) stage	30.00	36.60	34.00	35.20	40.90	48.30	45.00	38.21
Mature (transition) stage	7.70	12.40	12.10	9.00	10.00	16.70	13.20	10.00
Rebuilding stage	3.60	5.40	4.40	3.40	2.20	2.60	0.80	0.97

1.6 Jiangsu, Guangdong and Zhejiang had the most active market; provinces and cities in Central and West China saw a rapid growing market

Of the total management capital, Jiangsu, Guangdong and Zhejiang were the top three; the total management capital of top ten provinces (cities) accounted for 86.1% of the total national management capital, centralized to certain extent. The regional difference remains remarkably obvious. In the meantime, the venture capital industry in Fujian, Anhui, Sichuan, Hubei and other regions experienced a vigorous development momentum, for example, the management capital of Anhui Province was up to RMB 11.708 billion (see Fig. 4).

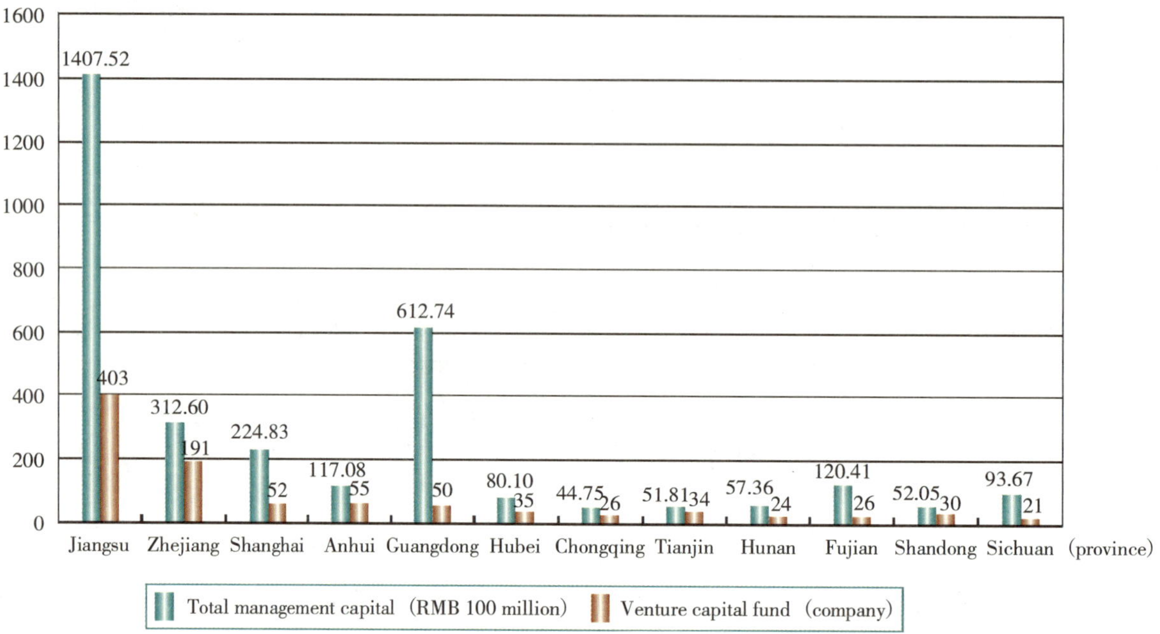

Fig. 4 Management Capital and Quantity of Venture Capital Institutions in Some Regions (2013)

1.7 Diversified exit patterns formed; rate of return declined

The presence of Chinese enterprises in the global capital market continued to decline in 2013 due to bearish factors such as the suspension of IPO in the national capital market and narrow channel for overseas listing. Only 66 Chinese enterprises were listed in both domestic and overseas capital markets throughout the year, among which 27 obtained VC support①. According to the exit ways, repurchasing exit was the main exit way, up to 44.83%; listing exit experienced a decline the first time since 2008; and M&A exit accounted for 26.25% (see Table 4).

The industry saw a decline in exit return in 2013 as compared to that in 2012. The listing exit return continued to fall, only 4.48 times of average return on book value; the rate of return from M&A exit project increased to 24.09%. Besides, the rate of return on repurchasing and liquidation increased greatly as compared to previous years, indicating that the project management ability of venture capital institutions was improving.

Table 4 Exit methods of China's venture capital investment (2007-2013) Unit: %

Year \ Exit methods	IPO	M&A	Repurchase	Liquidation	Others
2007	24.20	29.00	27.40	5.60	13.70
2008	22.70	23.20	34.80	9.20	10.10
2009	25.30	33.00	35.30	6.30	0.00
2010	29.80	28.60	32.80	6.90	1.90
2011	29.40	30.00	32.30	3.20	5.10
2012	29.41	18.93	45.01	6.65	0.00
2013	24.33	26.25	44.83	4.60	0.00

① Zero2IPO Research. 66 medium-sized enterprises were listed in 2013 A share market embraced a good start [R]. January 2, 2014.

1.8 Government-guided fund remained active

By the end of 2013, RMB 3.059 billion financial fund was raised for venture capital-guided fund of small and medium-sized high-tech enterprises. Of which, a total of RMB 2.009 billion was contributed for participation in 71 venture capital enterprises focusing on investment in small and medium-sized high-tech enterprises by means of staged participation, with the total registered capital up to about RMB 15 billion. 1411 projects were approved in the manner of subsidy for VC and investment guarantee, and subsidy of RMB 1.05 billion was allocated. The central government allocated RMB 7.05 billion to implement a national VC proposal for emerging industry, and to support the creation of 141 VC funds that the government owns direct stake. The total amount is close to RMB 39 billion, which created RMB 63.8 billion of bank loan and social fund indirectly.

252 venture capital institutions were supported and participated by VC-guided fund from all levels of government nationwide by the end of 2013; the contribution by government-guided VC fund totaled RMB 32.691 billion. This has created a scale of management capital of venture capital over RMB 160 billion.

1.9 Policy environment increasingly optimized

In recent years, central and local governments have issued a series of policies and measures to support the development of venture capital. Survey shows that 22.0% of venture capital institutions have enjoyed the financial support from the governments; 25.0% of the institutions have enjoyed the income tax relief; 28.2% of the institutions have obtained the in formation exchange support and 12.2% of the institutions have received the assistance in terms of training. It can be seen that, the direct support from the governments for the venture capital institutions declines, but the indirect services given thereby continuously improve.

In 2013, *the Guiding Opinions of the General Office of the State Council on Financial Support to Economic Restructuring and Transformation and Upgrading, the Implementing Opinions of the General Office of the State Council on Financial Support to the Development of Small and Micro Enterprises* and a series policies clearly strengthen the financial support for the science and technology, innovative, entrepreneurial small and micro enterprises, and actively guide the venture capital companies to invest in small and micro enterprises, establish technology and financial services system, refine the standards of science and technology small and micro enterprises, and improve the evaluation mechanism for all kinds of scientific outcomes; China (Shanghai) Pilot Free Trade Zone was set up; among the trial policies thereof, there are a plenty of measures encouraging the development of equity investment. The abovementioned policies for supporting the innovative start-ups, small and micro enterprises and conversion of scientific and technological achievements continue releasing new reform bonus for the development of the venture capital industry.

In December of the same year, the promulgation of the Decisions of the State Council on Several Issues concerning the National SME Share Transfer System reflects the substantial progress of the nationwide expansion of the "new three board", which is of great significance for increasing the investment opportunities of venture capital institutions, easing the financing difficulties of small and micro enterprises and broadening the exist channels of the venture capital institutions. As at the end of 2013, 355 listed companies had completed financing for 60 times throughout the year, raising funds of RMB1.002 billion.

1.10 Industry self-regulation was gradually established

The revised *Law on the Securities Investment Fund* formally took effect on June 1, 2013, which for the first time, includes the private funds into the adjustment scope while increasing the efforts for protecting the holders of funds and thus the legal status of the private securities investment funds has been admitted. Fortunately, that law does not incorporate the venture capital investment, which is in line with the specific laws of development of the industry. In terms of the central government, China Science and Technology Financial Promo tion Committee and Venture Capital Professional Committee, China Venture Capital & Private Equity Association and other professional lead to promote the exchanges within the venture capital investment industry and strengthen the norms and self-management thereof. Local authorities in Jiangsu, Zhejiang, Beijing, Shanghai, Shenzhen,

Guangdong, Chongqing, Anhui and other places respectively set up Venture Capital Associations (industrial associations), which has become service-oriented industry self-regulatory organizations to guide, coordinate and help members better engage in the venture capital activities and safeguard the legitimate rights and interests of members, playing an important role in the development of venture capital industry.

2 Venture capitalists' evaluation and forecast of the industry

The statistic survey in 2013 subdivided the venture capitalists' evaluation on their own development, the development of the whole industry, and future investment prospects, and at the same time, required the persons in charge of the venture capital institutions to make decisions among relevant options to make the survey results more scientific.

2.1 Optimistic about their own development

Among the 1026 venture capital institutions, the number of those remaining optimistic about their own development is significantly higher than those remaining pessimistic, More than half of venture capital institutions believe they embrace more optimistic self-development. Among others, 3.31% believe that their development is very good; 11.79% think their development is good and 36.06% comparatively favorable, which is much higher than in 2012 as a whole.

2.2 Comment on the industry development improved slightly

Evaluation of the venture capital institutions on the development of the whole industry is: The institutions holding optimistic attitude are more than those to the opposite; 30.67% institutions think the overall development of the whole industry is very good, good and comparatively favorable, 19% higher than the previous year and those think that the development of the whole industry is very poor, poor and comparatively poor account for 21.23%.

2.3 Good investment expectation for 2014

In terms of the investment prospects for 2014, the venture capital institutions have made a more optimistic forecast, More than half of agencies are positive about the future prospects, of which 2.0% believe that the prospects will be very good; 11.3% believe good prospects and 43.3% think that the prospects will be comparatively favorable. However, the institutions holding relatively poor prospects account for 3.3% and those holding poor ones only take up for 1.9%.

3 Preliminary thoughts on the promotion of the development of venture capital industry

In May 2014, the State Council further put forward requirements to accelerate and promote the development of venture capital industry. Reviewing the history and analysis of the status quo, there are several issues in the development of the venture capital industry, including the failure of the current system to fully meet the development needs, the relatively difficult fund-raising, the to-be-increased angel support and the blocked exit channel. To speed up the promotion of the healthy and sustainable development of the venture capital industry, foster the development of strategic emerging industries, support and lead the transformation of the development pattern, the following preliminary considerations are hereby put for ward based on the characteristics, challenges and international experience in the development of the venture capital industry.

3.1 Stepwise regression to the nature of venture capital

Our venture capital industry is to be considerably developed and shall return to the essence of venture capital-the management ability of risks in technology innovation, namely, from the "similarity in name" and "similarity in form" stage to the "similarity in spirit" stage to invest in "high technology and emerging projects". Venture capital investment is different from other financial funds and is aimed at the innovative enterprises investing strength in research and development to accelerate the development of the intellectual property, capitalization and industrialization thereof for the purpose of "breathtaking leap". The increasing "high technology and emerging projects" chosen by the venture capital institutions may exercise their capabilities to manage the technology risks and thereby play their role as a signal "amplifier" and "filter", which means that they have stronger function to optimize the social technology roadmap, highlighting the "energy capital" features of the venture capital.

3.2 Encourage and support the development of angel investment

Continue to nurture the team of angel investors to form multi-level angel investment groups; add guiding angel capital fund in development funds specific for SMEs and make risk compensation for qualified angel investor; by making reference to the practice of the state government of the United State, i.e., giving tax preferences to angel investment, allow angel investment institutions and individuals to credit their taxable income by using the investment in the early projects; strengthen the registration and dynamic management over the angel investment institutions and individuals to enhance ser vice tracking; create a tolerant social environment to guide the transformation from focus on the winners and successful investment to the encouragement for the entrepreneurial spirit of failure tolerance.

3.3 Guide private capital to enter the field of venture capital

Promote the establishment of the venture capital institutions in the form of limited partnership, extend the enterprise income tax pilot policy on the legal person of venture capital of Zhongguancun National Innovation Demonstration Zone of limited partnership to the whole country, guide and regulate the venture capital institutions to raise funds by applying the crowdfunding mode, break the limit of over 200 contributors and vigorously support the venture capital institutions and its shareholders or limited partners to issue bonds, so as to continuously expand the sources of capital.

3.4 Give play to the important role of the state-owned venture capital and guidance fund

In accordance with the principles of public finance, re-enact the measures for the performance assessment of the state-owned venture capital institutions and government venture capital guidance fund so as to ensure that the venture capital institutions dominated by the state-owned venture capital fund and guidance funds mainly invest in the early stages of high-tech and innovative enterprises. Steadily push forward the mixed ownership reform of the state-owned venture capital and establish the incentive and restraint mechanisms for the operators to achieve the combination of government responsibility of the state-owned venture capital with the market-oriented operation.

3.5 Clear away the related obstacles hindering the venture capital's investment in early front-end process

Support qualified investee of the venture capital to list on the National Equities Exchange and Quotations, entitle the right to dispose of the technological achievements, the income right and other rights to units undertaking the research projects, simplify the handling procedures for technological achievements, increase the incentives on the person creating the scientific and technological achievements and that making important contribution to the transformation thereof and simplify the equity registration, change and transfer of start-ups and the related system.

3.6 Accelerate the construction of the OTC market

On the basis of the regional property market, establish the national union of technology property institutions with China technology exchanges as the core; establish an information and network-oriented technology trading system and display platform, to provide comprehensive services with the combination of online and offline methods for the purpose of promoting the technological property capitalization; in addition to the rectification, include the regional equity markets in the multi-level capital market system, and promote the OTC market construction with the scientific and technological achievements trading and the equity transfer of small and micro enterprises as the core and establish a favorable interaction mechanism between the OTC market and the venture capital institutions to provide multiple exit channels for the venture capital.

1 中国创业风险投资机构与资本

1.1 2013 年度调查概述

2013 年 12 月，科技部、商务部、国家开发银行等单位联合启动了第 12 次全国创业风险投资年度调查，统计工作由科技部专门下发调查通知，依据国家科技专项统计标准（国统制〔2012〕111 号），组织全国 31 个省（市、自治区）、58 个调查实施机构和 132 名调查员进行网上填报①。各类创业风险投资机构对调查工作给予了大力的配合，本次调查工作在 5 月结束。经过 10 余年的努力，本项统计调查工作为我国许多重要政策的出台提供了有力支撑，也为创业风险投资评奖和引导基金的申报工作提供了有效的数据支持，成为我国科技金融工作的重要组成部分。

2014 年度报告所调查的创业投资机构包括以下三类：①创业投资企业，即创业风险投资基金，也包括创业投资引导基金（俗称“母基金”）。②创业投资管理企业，其受创业投资企业委托，筛选投资项目，提出投资决策建议，并受托进行投资后管理。③少量从事政府创业风险投资业务的事业单位，有的直接以政府资金对项目进行投资，有的则具有创业风险投资引导资金的作用，参股创业风险投资企业，或对创业风险投资企业的投资给予某种形式的补助。

截至 2013 年底，“中国创业风险投资信息系统”（www.ivcc.cn）中共有 2965 家机构参加过调查（包括已注销或转业企业）。根据创业风险投资的标准概念，我们对样本进行了剔除：①信托公司等不属于创业风险投资范畴的金融机构。②不属于创业风险投资的某些行业性和综合性投资公司，如电力投资、工交投资集团、某些投资主业较为模糊不清的投资类公司等，对以大项目为投资主业的产业投资基金也给予了剔除。③主要从事担保业务的担保公司，但持续地开展了创业风险投资业务的担保公司除外。④转业而不再从事创业风险投资业务的机构。⑤所填信息过少且所填报数据之间严重不匹配的机构。⑥随着我国创业风险投资的业态不断复杂化，很多大型创业风险投资机构纷纷参与了商业性母子基金模式，如果简单相加则会带来管理资本的重复计算，同时，政府引导基金的设立也带来类似问题。因此在调查过程中，剔除了相关资本的重复计算。⑦创业风险投资企业与创业风险投资管理机构，当存在委托与受托关系时，剔除了相关资本和项目的重复计算。⑧在境外注册设立、在境内仅以办公室形式开展商业活动的私募股权机构。

1.2 创业风险投资机构和管理资本

2013 年，受全球经济缓慢复苏、制造业投资调整充分、投资消费结构转换和微观企业效益改善等因素影响，中国经济由需求衰退周期逐渐转换为供给调整周期，由高速增长向中高速增长转换。发达国家经济和金融稳定与新兴市场国家动荡的趋势使得全球资本市场呈现两极分化。

尽管我国 A 股市场低迷不振，但整个资本市场改革取得重大进展，市场活力进一步增强，中国创业风险投资行业呈现增长趋势，当年募资、投资增速均较上一年度有所增加。

2013 年，中国创业风险投资各类机构数达到 1408

① 根据我们对全美创业投资协会（NVCA）、欧洲私募股权投资协会（EVCA）等年度数据披露情况的观察，当年的数据公布一般在次年的 4~6 月。从 2010 年起，统计数据纳入《中国科技统计年鉴》。

家①，较 2012 年增加 225 家，增长 19.0%。其中，创业风险投资企业（基金）1095 家，较 2012 年增加 153 家，增幅 16.2%；创业风险投资管理企业 313 家，较 2012 年增加 72 家，增幅 29.9%；2013 年新募集基金 215 家（见表 1-1、图 1-1）。

表 1-1 中国创业风险投资企业（基金）总量、增量（2004~2013）② 单位：%

项目＼年份	2004	2005	2006	2007	2008	2009	2010	2011	2012	2013
VC 基金（家）	257	277	312	331	410	495	720	860	942	1095
较上年增长（%）	-4.8	7.7	12.6	6.09	23.9	20.7	45.5	19.4	9.5	19.0
VC 管理机构（家）	47	42	33	52	54	81	147	236	241	313
较上年增长（%）	—	-10.6	-21.4	57.6	3.8	50.0	81.5	60.5	2.1	29.9
当年新募集基金（家）	17	27	35	76	88	99	238	171	136	215

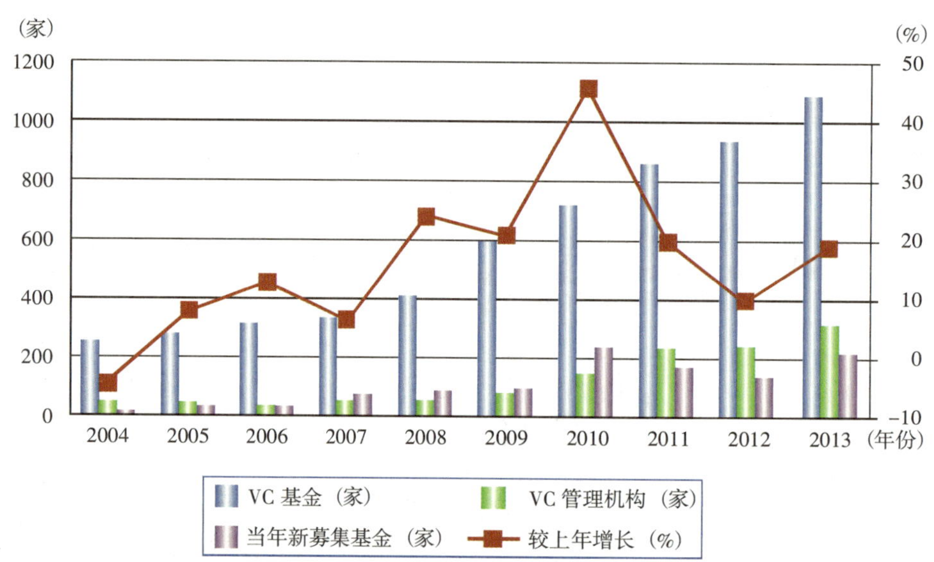

图 1-1 中国创业风险投资企业（基金）总量、增量（2004~2013）

2013 年，全国创业风险投资管理资本总量达到 3573.9 亿元，较 2012 年增加 261 亿元，增幅为 7.9%；基金平均管理资本规模为 3.26 亿元，较 2012 年有所减小（见表 1-2、图 1-2）。

全国共有 65 家母基金，受托管理了 229 家创业风险投资基金，最大母基金管理的子基金数达 45 家，管理资金规模 102 亿元。

① 为实际存量机构数，主要包括：创业投资企业（基金）、创业投资管理企业以及少量从事政府创业投资业务的事业单位。该数据已剔除不再经营创投业务或注销的机构数。

② 由于我国创投行业的迅猛发展，基金形态的日趋复杂，从 2010 年起，按照国际惯例进行统计，区分基金和基金管理公司，并对前期数据进行了追溯调整。

表 1-2 中国创业风险投资管理资本总额（2004~2013） 单位：%

项目＼年份	2004	2005	2006	2007	2008	2009	2010	2011	2012	2013
管理资本总额（亿元）	617.5	631.6	663.8	1112.9	1455.7	1605.1	2406.6	3198.0	3312.9	3573.9
较上年增长（%）	0.2	2.3	5.1	67.7	30.8	10.3	49.9	32.9	3.6	7.9
基金平均管理资本规模（亿元）	2.4	2.28	2.13	3.36	3.55	3.24	3.34	3.72	3.52	3.26

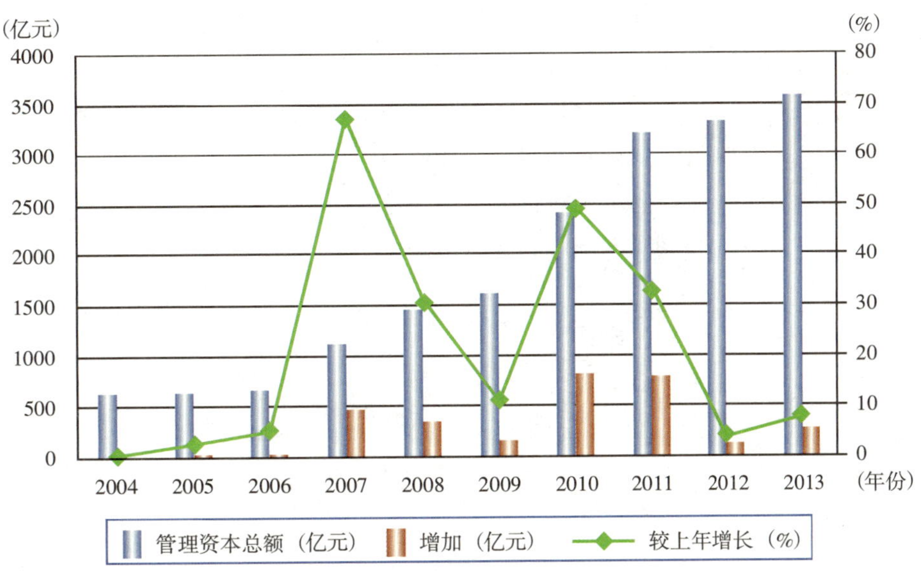

图 1-2 中国创业风险投资管理资本总额（2004~2013）

1.3 创业风险投资的资本来源

依据资本来源结构，本报告将创业风险投资资本分为两大类：外资和内资。外资包括境内和境外两个部分。境内外资是指通过已在中国大陆境内注册并运作的外商独资（含港、澳、台）和合资合作企业取得的创业风险投资资本；境外资金是指境外机构获得的创业风险投资资本。本报告统计的外资资本主要是境外和境内外资机构向注册在中国大陆地区的创业风险投资企业所注入的资本额，不包括以离岸形式向中国大陆地区直接投资的外资量。

内资创业风险投资资本分类如下：①政府资金，包括各级政府（包括事业单位）对创业风险资本的直接资金支持。②国有独资公司资金，指国有独资公司直接提供的资金。③非上市公司资金，包括非上市股份有限公司和有限责任公司投入的创业风险投资资本。④上市公司资金，主要指在境内证券市场公开上市的公司投入创业风险投资的资本。⑤金融机构资金，包括银行和保险公司、证券公司、信托公司等非银行金融机构的各类资金投入。⑥自然人及其他出资。

2013 年，中国创业风险投资的构成如图 1-3 所示，资本来源结构仍以非上市公司为主体，占总资本的 42.81%，较 2012 年上升 8.78 个百分点，上升幅度较大；政府与国有独资投资机构合计占比 29.18%，较 2012 年下降 11.41 个百分点，绝对出资额基本持平。与 2012 年相比，个人占比略有下降，外资资本下降明显，银行资本占比略有增加（见图 1-4）。

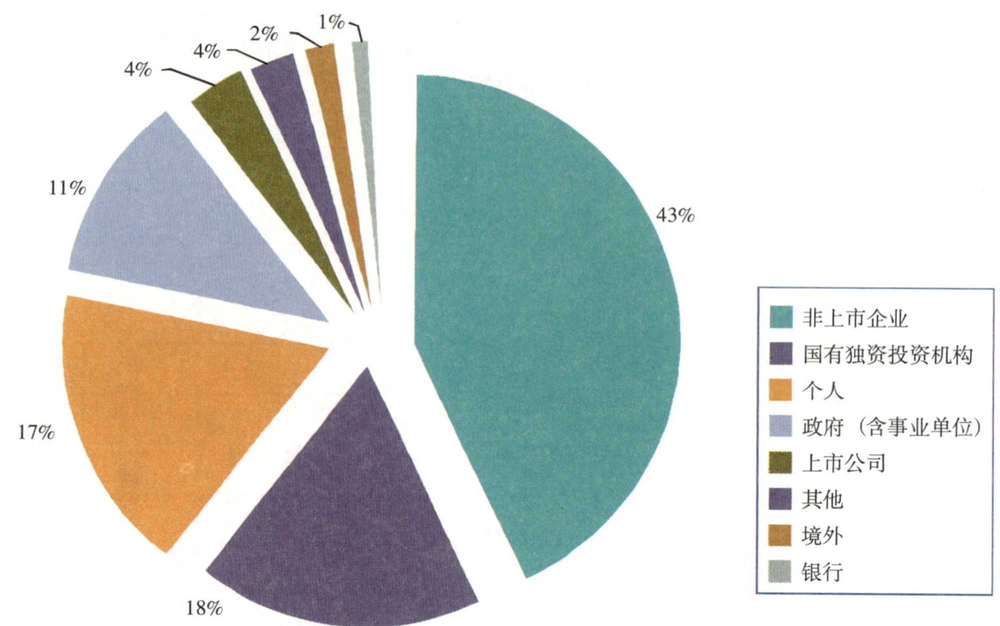

图 1-3 中国创业风险投资资本来源（2013）

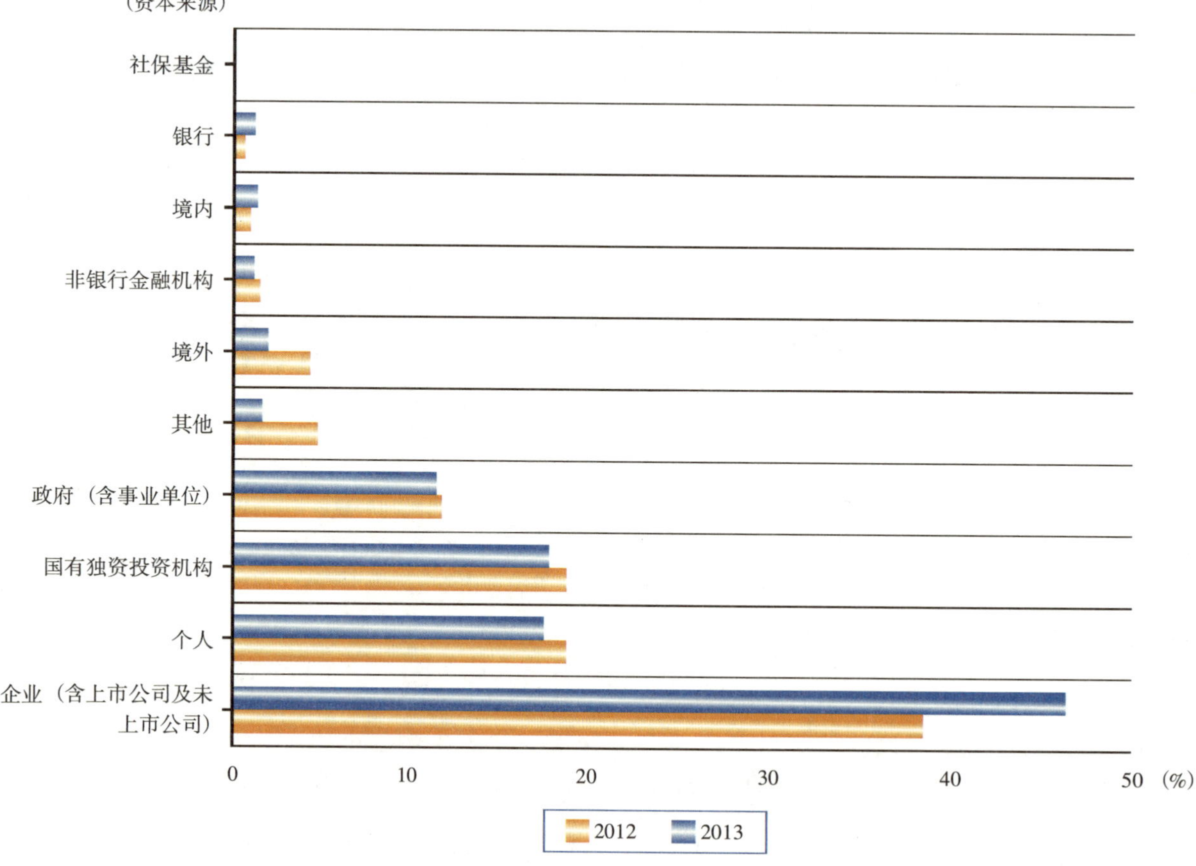

图 1-4 中国创业投资资本来源变化（2012~2013）

1.4 创业风险投资机构的资本规模及分布

总体而言，2013 年创业风险投资机构的管理规模与 2012 年基本持平，管理机构的管理资金规模大多集中在 5000 万~2 亿元。从资金分布情况看，管理资金在 5000 万以下的创业风险投资机构占机构总数的 22.5%，管理资金在 5000 万~1 亿元的机构占比为 24.4%，与 2012 年相比上升；管理资金在 1 亿~2 亿元的机构占比为 22.1%，较 2012 年有所上升；2 亿~5 亿元的机构占比为 19.8%，与 2012 年相比略有下降；而规模在 5 亿元以上的管理资金占比为 10.1%，较 2012 年下降 1.9 个百分点（见图 1-5）。

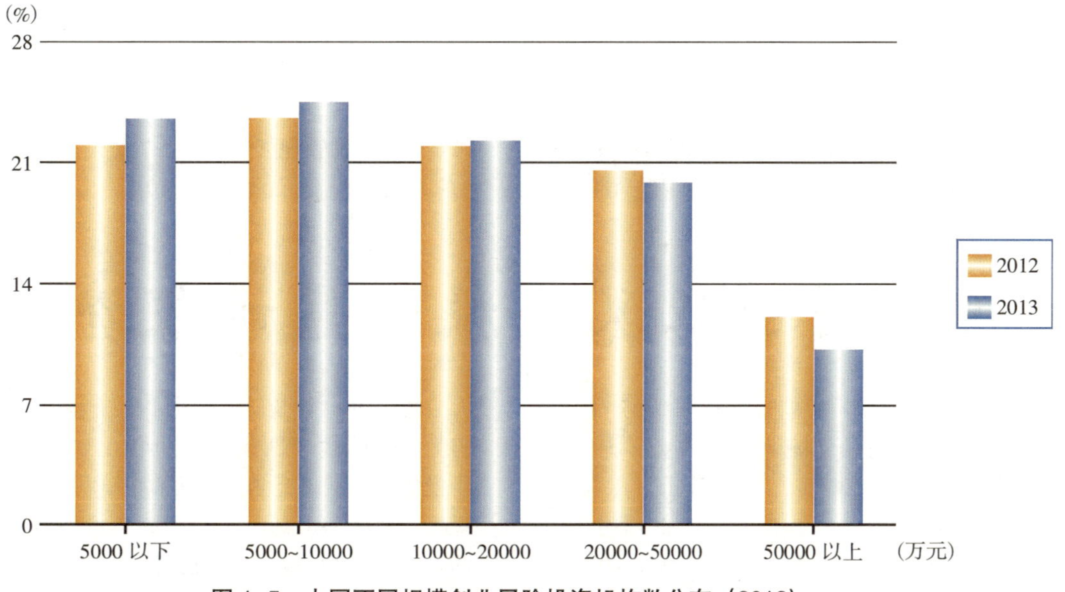

图 1-5 中国不同规模创业风险投资机构数分布（2013）

按管理资金规模划分，2013 年，管理资金规模在 5000 万元以下的机构掌握着中国创业风险投资总资本的 2.1%，规模在 5000 万~1 亿元的机构掌握了 5.9%的份额，规模在 1 亿~2 亿元的机构掌握了 9.7%的总资金，规模在 2 亿~5 亿元的机构所占管理资本的份额为 17.7%，均比 2012 年有所提升。64.6%的管理资本掌握在规模在 5 亿元以上的机构手中（见图 1-6）。可见，2013 年，受国内外环境影响，我国创业风险投资机构的规模略有缩小。

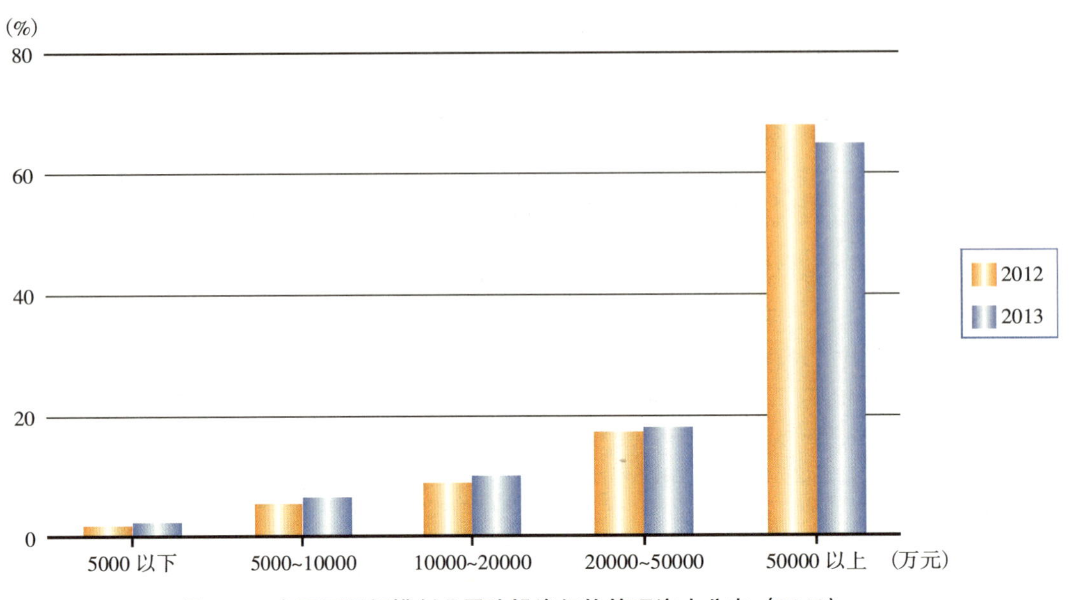

图 1-6 中国不同规模创业风险投资机构管理资本分布（2013）

2013 年，国内创业风险投资管理机构中，最大管理资金为 130 亿元，超过 50 亿元的有 7 家；在创业风险投资基金中，最大管理资金规模 287 亿元，超过 100 亿元的有 5 家，超过 50 亿元的有 4 家。

1.5 中国创业风险投资累计投资情况

2013 年，中国创业风险投资机构当年投资项目 1501 项，与去年基本持平；投资金额为 278.96 亿元，较 2012 年减少 12.7%，项目平均投资额为 1865 万元。其中，投资于高新技术企业项目数为 590 家，较 2012 年减少 12.07%；投资金额为 108.97 亿元，较上年减少 29.47%，项目平均投资额为 1846.96 万元。

截至 2013 年底，全国创业风险投资机构累计投资项目数 12149 项，较 2012 年增加 1037 项，[①] 增长 9.3%，其中投资高新技术企业项目数 6779 项，占比 55.8%；累计投资金额 2634.1 亿元，较 2012 年增长 11.8%，其中投资高新技术企业金额 1302.1 亿元，占比 49.4%（见表 1-3）。

表 1-3 截至 2013 年底中国创业风险投资累计投资情况（2010~2013）

年度	累计投资项目总数（项）	投资高新技术企业/项目数（项）	累计投资金额（亿元）	投资高新技术企业/项目金额（亿元）
2010	8693	5160	1491.3	808.8
2011	9978	5940	2036.6	1038.6
2012	11112	6404	2355.1	1193.1
2013	12149	6779	2634.1	1302.1

① 由于创投投资项目为多轮投资，因此，在计算当年投资时后续投资项目也计为当年投资项目数，但在计算累计投资时，多轮投资项目仅为一个项目投资，因此实际累计项目数的增加值少于当年项目数。

2 中国创业风险投资的投资分析

2.1 中国创业风险投资的行业特征

2.1.1 中国创业风险投资的行业分布

2013 年，中国创业风险投资年度投资金额主要集中在医药保健、新材料工业、新能源/高效节能技术、金融保险业和传统制造业五个行业，36.92%以上的资金投资在这五个行业，其集中度较 2012 年上升了 1.55 个百分点。中国创业风险投资年度投资项目主要集中在金融保险业、医药保健、新能源/高效节能技术、传统制造业以及新材料工业五个行业，集中了当年 43.17%以上的项目，其集中度较 2012 年上升了 8.01 个百分点（见表 2–1、图 2–1、图 2–2）。

表 2–1 中国创业风险投资项目的行业分布：投资金额与投资项目（2012~2013）[①] 单位：%

行 业	2013 年		2012 年	
	投资金额	投资项目	投资金额	投资项目
医药保健	9.99	10.04	4.85	6.18
新材料工业	7.61	7.13	7.81	8.76
新能源、高效节能技术	6.75	8.69	7.19	7.20
金融保险业	6.54	10.12	5.42	4.20
传统制造业	6.03	7.19	10.10	8.82
软件产业	5.32	2.02	2.41	3.12
传播与文化娱乐	5.24	6.16	6.35	5.28
光电子与光机电一体化	4.89	4.62	3.49	3.78
其他制造业	4.67	5.30	4.83	4.98
IT 服务业	4.17	3.58	3.14	3.42
生物科技	4.17	2.27	2.80	4.80
环保工程	3.95	2.89	2.81	3.06
网络产业	3.74	1.90	2.05	2.82
其他行业	3.74	2.65	7.62	7.26
农林牧副渔	3.66	6.33	6.07	4.74
消费产品和服务	3.45	5.00	6.27	3.54
通讯设备	3.16	3.11	3.63	3.72
半导体	2.51	1.40	1.44	1.44
科技服务	1.94	1.02	1.64	2.58

① 有效样本数为 1392 份。

续表

行 业	2013 年		2012 年	
	投资金额	投资项目	投资金额	投资项目
社会服务	1.87	1.86	1.09	2.34
计算机硬件产业	1.22	0.68	1.10	1.50
建筑业	1.22	1.32	1.94	1.62
交通运输仓储和邮政业	1.15	2.57	0.35	0.24
其他 IT 产业	1.01	0.36	1.68	1.92
采掘业	0.57	0.51	1.30	0.48
批发和零售业	0.36	0.50	0.85	0.72
核应用技术	0.29	0.17	0.24	0.48
房地产业	0.29	0.21	1.24	0.54
水电煤气	0.29	0.25	0.29	0.42

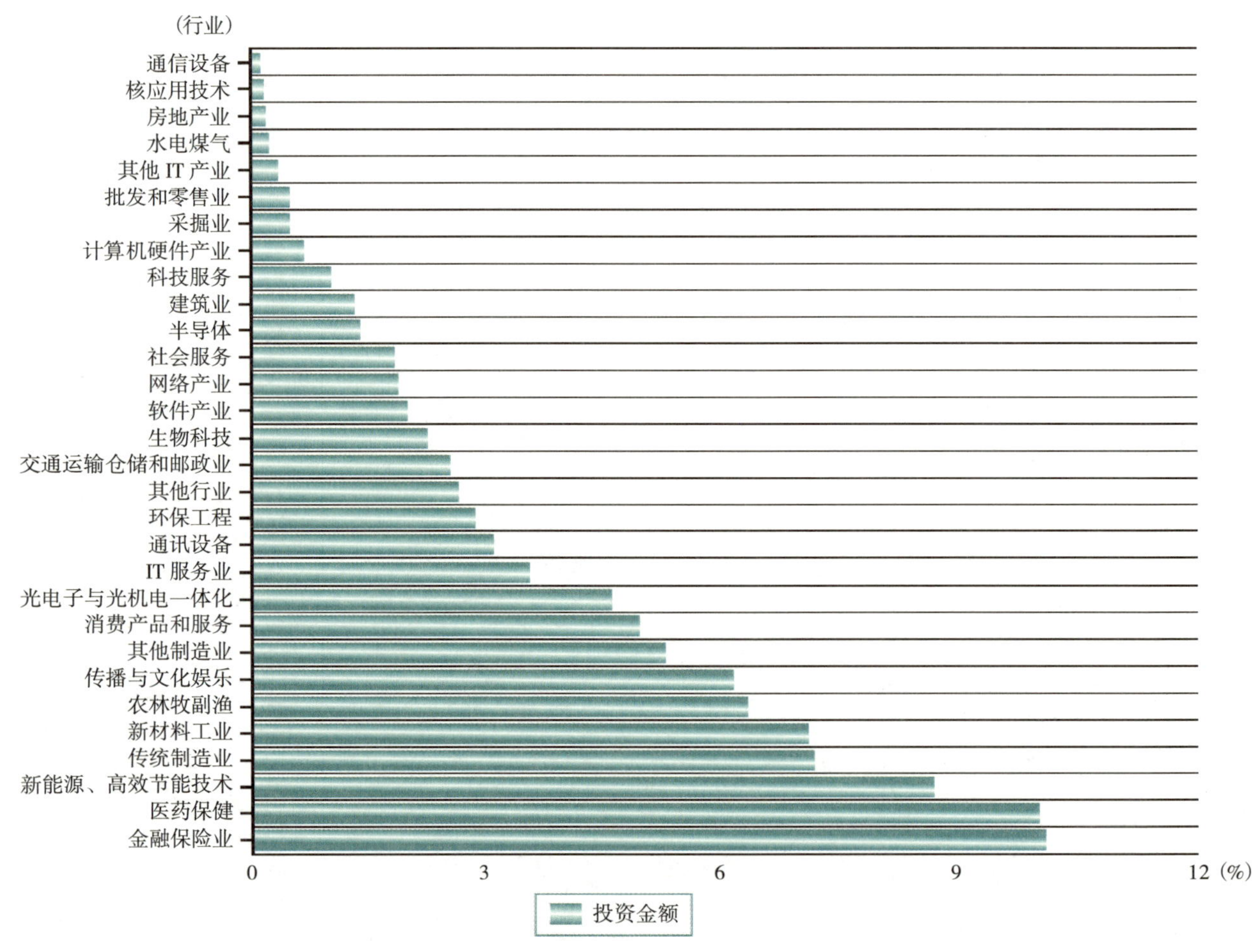

图 2-1 中国创业风险投资业投资项目的行业分布：按投资金额（2013）

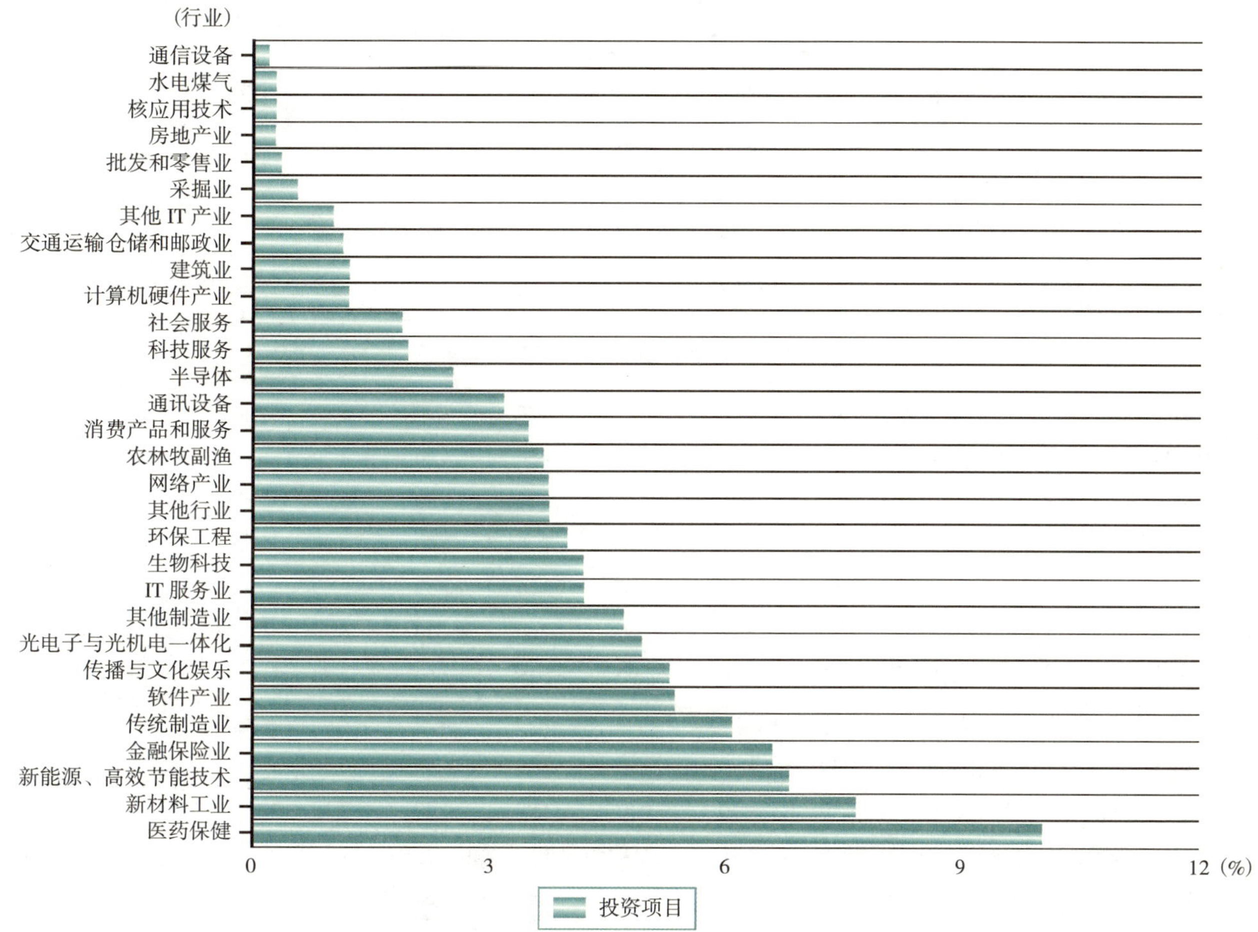

图 2-2　中国创业风险投资业投资项目的行业分布：按项目数（2013）

从近几年我国创业风险投资行业的变化趋势来看（见表 2-2、表 2-3），投资项目数和投资金额均表现为由主要投资制造业为主的传统产业向投资医药保健、金融保险业等新兴产业转变。新能源、高效节能技术以及新材料工业也吸引了大量创业风险投资。创业风险投资行业的变化趋势预示着我国经济结构转型初露端倪。

表 2-2 中国创业风险投资产业投资项目投资金额的行业分布（2004~2013） 单位：%

投资行业 \ 年份	2004	2005	2006	2007	2008	2009	2010	2011	2012	2013
软件产业	4.50	3.50	14.60	16.00	6.20	10.90	2.90	2.10	2.41	2.02
计算机硬件产业	0.70	0.90	0.40	0.60	3.40	0.10	1.10	0.70	1.10	0.68
网络产业	1.10	2.70	1.50	0.50	2.70	1.80	2.80	2.50	2.05	1.90
通讯设备	8.20	3.50	4.60	2.90	1.80	1.90	1.00	2.80	3.63	3.11
IT 服务业	10.00	7.10	3.10	1.00	4.60	1.50	3.20	2.80	3.14	3.58
半导体	4.60	16.50	2.10	1.30	2.90	2.30	1.20	1.30	1.44	1.40
其他 IT 产业	2.70	2.40	3.20	1.30	2.30	2.20	1.20	1.50	1.68	0.36
环保工程	1.00	3.10	1.30	1.50	1.30	1.80	3.30	2.60	2.81	2.89
生物科技	4.10	7.40	5.40	2.30	5.70	2.50	3.90	3.90	2.80	2.27
新材料工业	10.10	5.70	7.50	7.90	4.40	6.40	9.30	8.70	7.81	7.13
采掘业	2.30	4.50	3.70	1.90	3.60	1.50	2.50	0.60	1.30	0.51
光电子与光机电一体化	4.90	5.50	4.10	2.10	4.00	4.10	4.20	3.30	3.49	4.62
科技服务	1.50	2.10	1.20	4.90	2.10	2.00	2.30	1.60	1.64	1.02
新能源、高效节能技术	3.70	8.80	7.00	4.60	7.70	8.50	8.30	6.20	7.19	8.69
医药保健	8.30	4.30	2.70	2.00	2.50	4.90	5.30	3.80	4.85	10.04
消费产品和服务	2.40	1.70	4.10	1.40	3.90	4.30	7.10	9.40	6.27	5.00
传播与文化娱乐	6.00	3.20	1.10	2.20	1.80	2.50	2.10	2.20	6.35	6.16
传统制造业	3.80	8.90	11.30	12.60	15.60	11.90	10.10	7.70	10.10	7.19
农林牧副渔	9.10	0.50	9.40	1.20	2.60	3.50	4.10	4.10	6.07	6.33
金融保险业	5.70	3.40	3.80	22.10	8.20	15.20	7.80	2.40	5.42	10.12
批发和零售业	1.90	0.00	0.60	1.10	0.00	0.30	0.70	1.20	0.85	0.50
其他行业	3.50	4.00	7.60	8.30	12.70	10.00	15.70	11.20	7.62	2.65
核应用技术	0.00	0.30	0.00	0.00	0.00	0.10	0.00	0.40	0.24	0.17
房地产业	—	—	—	—	—	—	—	4.90	1.24	0.21
建筑业	—	—	—	—	—	—	—	1.60	1.94	1.32
交通运输仓储和邮政业	—	—	—	—	—	—	—	1.40	0.35	2.57
其他制造业	—	—	—	—	—	—	—	8.20	4.83	5.30
社会服务	—	—	—	—	—	—	—	0.70	1.09	1.86
水电煤气	—	—	—	—	—	—	—	0.10	0.29	0.25

表 2–3 中国创业风险投资业投资项目数的行业分布（2004~2013） 单位：%

投资行业 \ 年份	2004	2005	2006	2007	2008	2009	2010	2011	2012	2013
软件产业	7.20	10.00	12.50	17.10	9.70	13.90	7.00	3.50	3.12	5.32
计算机硬件产业	1.40	1.20	1.00	1.10	1.30	0.40	1.40	1.30	1.50	1.22
网络产业	2.00	2.40	2.60	2.40	2.00	3.10	4.80	3.20	2.82	3.74
通讯设备	7.90	6.00	4.10	2.70	3.90	3.00	2.50	3.20	3.72	3.16
IT 服务业	9.90	6.70	2.60	2.60	3.80	3.30	4.20	4.10	3.42	4.17
半导体	4.40	4.80	2.40	3.00	2.70	3.80	2.50	1.70	1.44	2.51
其他 IT 产业	3.40	2.10	3.80	2.60	3.20	3.70	2.30	2.40	1.92	1.01
环保工程	2.40	2.70	2.20	2.20	2.20	2.70	3.30	3.20	3.06	3.95
生物科技	5.50	8.20	7.90	5.60	6.10	5.50	5.60	3.30	4.80	4.17
新材料工业	9.60	7.60	10.30	9.60	6.60	7.20	10.10	9.50	8.76	7.61
采掘业	1.40	3.60	1.20	1.20	1.50	1.00	1.20	0.70	0.48	0.57
光电子与光机电一体化	7.20	10.00	5.00	4.50	5.90	5.10	6.00	4.60	3.78	4.89
科技服务	5.10	3.30	2.20	2.00	4.50	2.70	2.50	1.80	2.58	1.94
新能源、高效节能技术	2.00	4.50	5.00	5.70	5.10	6.30	7.80	6.00	7.20	6.75
医药保健	7.20	6.10	5.00	3.30	4.80	6.00	5.80	4.40	6.18	9.99
消费产品和服务	1.40	3.30	3.40	1.90	2.80	3.10	4.10	7.20	3.54	3.45
传播与文化娱乐	3.80	2.70	2.20	2.00	1.70	2.10	1.90	2.40	5.28	5.24
传统制造业	5.80	6.70	6.70	13.80	14.20	9.40	7.30	8.00	8.82	6.03
农林牧副渔	3.80	1.80	3.10	1.20	2.60	2.30	3.20	4.80	4.74	3.66
金融保险业	2.40	2.40	4.30	5.00	4.90	5.40	4.10	2.00	4.2	6.54
批发和零售业	1.40	0.00	1.90	1.20	0.20	0.30	0.70	1.20	0.72	0.36
其他行业	4.80	3.60	10.60	9.20	10.40	9.70	11.70	8.40	7.26	3.74
核应用技术	0.00	0.30	0.00	0.00	0.00	0.10	0.00	0.50	0.48	0.29
房地产业	—	—	—	—	—	—	—	0.30	0.54	0.29
建筑业	—	—	—	—	—	—	—	1.80	1.62	1.22
交通运输仓储和邮政业	—	—	—	—	—	—	—	0.80	0.24	1.15
其他制造业	—	—	—	—	—	—	—	8.30	4.98	4.67
社会服务	—	—	—	—	—	—	—	1.30	2.34	1.87
水电煤气	—	—	—	—	—	—	—	0.10	0.42	0.29

新能源和环保工业以及计算机、通信和其他电子设备制造业是创业风险投资的热点领域[①]。从近年来的发展趋势看，信息传输、软件和信息服务业以及医药生物业的投资项目数与投资金额快速增加，成为行业新宠（见表 2–4）。

① 2011 年，行业统计分类标准与国家统计局颁布的行业分类标准接轨，行业分类与 2011 年之前有所不同。

表 2–4 中国创业风险业投资项目的前十大行业分布（2012~2013） 单位：%

行业划分（代码）			2013		2012	
			投资金额	投资项目	投资金额	投资项目
C9	新能源和环保业	新能源、高效节能技术 新材料工业 环保工程 核应用技术	18.88	18.60	18.10	19.50
CA	传统制造业		7.19	6.03	10.10	8.80
C7	计算机、通信和其他电子设备制造业	通信设备 计算机硬件产业 半导体 光电子与光机电一体化	9.81	11.78	9.70	10.40
I	信息传输、软件和信息服务业	网络产业 IT 服务业 软件产业 其他 IT 产业	7.86	14.24	9.30	11.30
C8	医药生物业	医药保健 生物科技	12.31	14.16	7.70	11.00
O	其他行业		2.65	3.74	7.60	7.30
L	文化、体育和娱乐业（传播与文化娱乐业）		6.16	5.24	6.40	5.30
H	住宿和餐饮业（消费产品和服务业）		5.00	3.45	6.30	3.50
A	农林牧渔业		6.33	3.66	6.10	4.70
J6	金融保险业		10.12	6.54	5.40	4.20

按照国际行业代码（VEIC）分类标准对中国创业风险投资业投资项目的行业调整后与美国创业风险投资行业划分进行对比，可以发现，我国创业风险投资行业集中分布在新材料工业、新能源/高效节能技术和金融保险业，而美国创业风险投资中的资金集中分布在软件、生物技术、媒体娱乐业等行业。同美国相比我国的行业集中度较低；同 2012 年相比，我国的行业集中度也有所下降（见表 2–5）。

表 2–5 中国与美国创业风险投资业投资项目的行业分布：投资金额与投资项目① 单位：%

投资行业	中国		美国	
	投资金额	投资项目	投资金额	投资项目
软件	2.02	5.32	37.00	38.28
生物技术（生物科技）	2.27	4.17	15.00	11.73
工业/能源（新材料工业、新能源/高效节能技术）	8.69	6.75	5.00	5.94
医疗设备	—	—	7.00	7.70
IT 服务	3.58	4.17	7.00	8.51
媒体娱乐业（传播与文化娱乐）	6.16	5.24	10.00	11.26
消费产品与服务	5.00	3.45	4.00	4.23
半导体	1.40	2.51	2.00	2.28
通信（通信设备）	3.11	3.16	2.00	1.61
电子/仪器（光电子与光机电一体化）	4.62	4.89	1.00	1.04

① 此处行业中括号外为美国风险投资行业分类，括号内为我国风险投资行业分类，部分行业并无直接对等关系。

续表

投资行业	中国		美国	
	投资金额	投资项目	投资金额	投资项目
零售（批发和零售业）	0.50	0.36	1.00	1.21
金融服务（金融保险业）	10.12	6.54	2.00	1.53
网络与设备（网络产业）	1.90	3.74	2.00	0.62
电脑与外设（计算机硬件产业）	0.68	1.22	2.00	0.84
健康护理服务	—	—	1.00	1.04
商业产品与服务	—	—	0.40	1.63
其他	—	—	0.20	0.54

按照国民经济行业分类（GB/T 4754—2011）标准进行调整并与国内生产总值构成相比较，可以发现，创业风险投资更倾向于工业、金融业以及新兴领域的投资（见表2-6）。

表 2-6 中国国内生产总值构成与创业风险投资金额的行业分布（2013） 单位：%

行业	国内生产总值构成	创业风险投资金额
第一产业	10.01	6.33
第二产业	43.89	55.57
工业[①]	37.04	54.25
建筑业	6.86	1.32
第三产业	46.09	11.79
交通运输、仓储和邮政业	4.80	2.57
批发和零售业	9.79	0.50
住宿和餐饮业（消费品和服务业）	2.02	5.00
金融业	5.90	10.12
房地产业	5.85	0.21
其他[②]	17.74	19.55

2.1.2 中国创业风险投资对高新技术产业与传统产业的投资比较[③]

将被投资项目按照高新技术产业和传统产业划分，2013年，中国创业风险投资业对高新技术产业的投资项目和投资金额占比实现连续两年提高，但是仍然低于2011年之前的水平（见表2-7、图2-3、表2-8、图2-4）。

表 2-7 中国创业风险投资项目的年度行业分布：高新技术产业与传统产业（2003~2013） 单位：%

行业＼年份	2003	2004	2005	2006	2007	2008	2009	2010	2011	2012	2013
高新技术产业	73.1	76.7	78.3	67.9	65.5	63.2	67.7	67.0	53.4	55.3	61.3
传统产业	26.9	23.3	21.7	32.1	34.5	36.8	32.3	33.0	46.6	44.7	38.7

① 创业风险投资中工业包括：传统制造业、新材料工业、新能源/高效节能技术、医药保健、其他制造业、通信设备、光电子与光机电一体化、环保工程、生物科技、半导体、计算机硬件产业、采掘业、水电煤气和应用技术等。

② 创业风险投资中其他包括：传播与文化娱乐、IT服务业、软件产业、网络产业、其他IT产业、科技服务、社会服务和其他行业等。

③ 有效样本数：高新项目样本数为853份；传统项目样本数为536份。

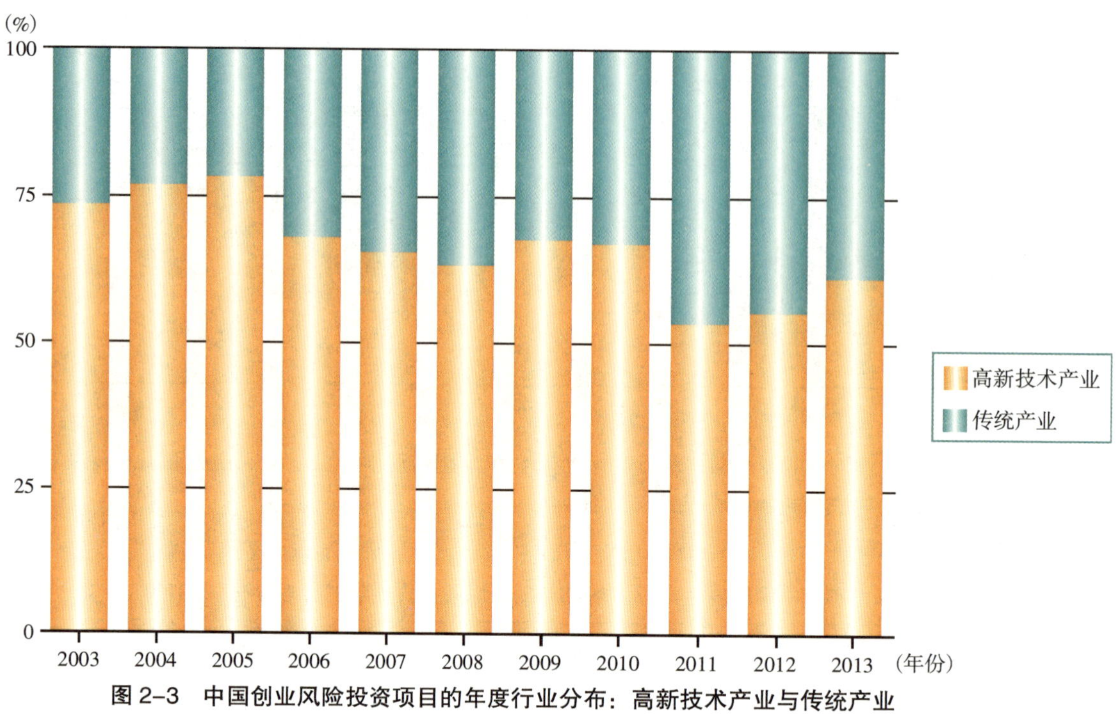

图 2-3 中国创业风险投资项目的年度行业分布：高新技术产业与传统产业

表 2-8 中国创业风险投资金额的年度行业分布：高新技术产业与传统产业（2003~2013） 单位：%

行业 \ 年份	2003	2004	2005	2006	2007	2008	2009	2010	2011	2012	2013
高新技术产业	79.8	67.7	79.5	62.2	51.1	55.2	52.3	52.4	44.9	47.6	50.4
传统产业	20.2	32.2	20.5	37.8	48.9	44.8	47.7	47.6	55.1	52.4	49.6

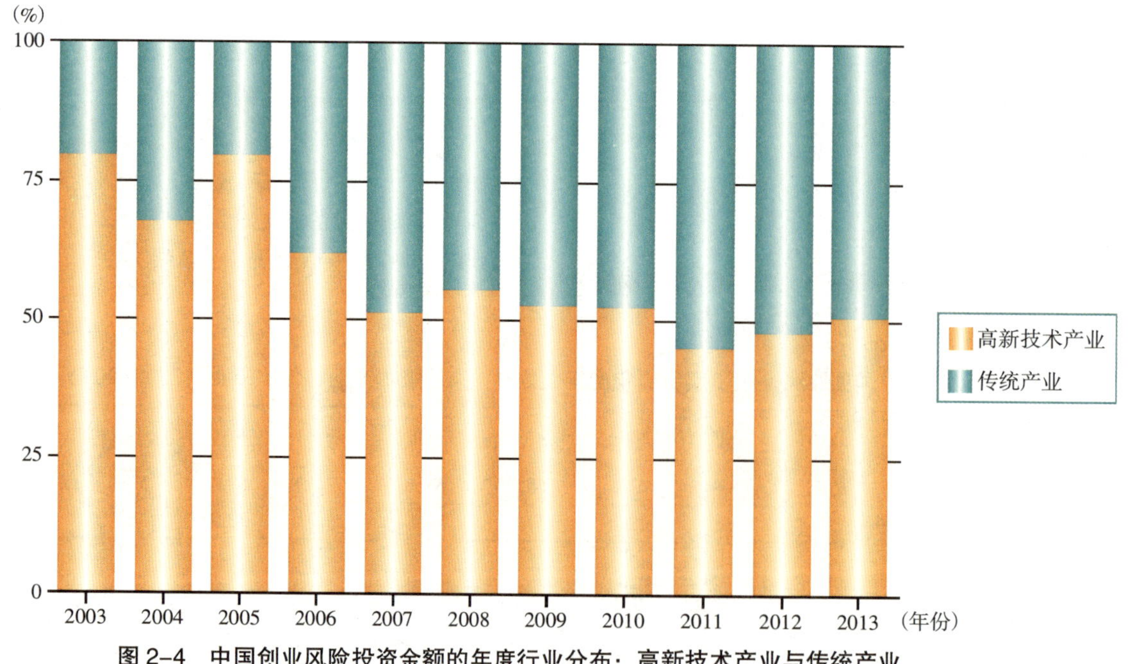

图 2-4 中国创业风险投资金额的年度行业分布：高新技术产业与传统产业

2.2 中国创业风险投资的投资阶段

2.2.1 中国创业风险投资所处阶段的总体分布①

2013年，中国创业风险投资机构的投资重心继续前移，对种子期的投资金额和投资项目分别增加至12.22%和18.36%，但仍低于2010年以前的投资水平；对起步期的投资金额和投资项目占比也有较大幅度上升。但投资机构对成长（扩张）期项目投资依然保持最多，投资金额和投资项目占比分别达到41.42%和38.21%；与2012年相比，对成熟（过渡）期的投资项目数略有下降，但投资金额有所上升（见表2-9、表2-10、图2-5、表2-11、图2-6）。

表2-9 中国创业风险投资项目所处阶段的总体分布：投资项目与投资金额（2013） 单位：%

成长阶段	投资金额	投资项目
种子期	12.22	18.36
起步期	22.38	32.46
成长（扩张）期	41.42	38.21
成熟（过渡）期	22.82	10.00
重建期	1.16	0.97

表2-10 中国创业风险投资项目所处阶段分布：投资项目（2003~2013） 单位：%

成长阶段 \ 年份	2003	2004	2005	2006	2007	2008	2009	2010	2011	2012	2013
种子期	13.0	15.8	15.4	37.4	26.6	19.3	32.2	19.9	9.7	12.3	18.4
起步期	19.3	20.6	30.1	21.3	18.9	30.2	20.3	27.0	22.7	28.7	32.5
成长（扩张）期	49.5	47.8	41.0	30.0	36.6	34.0	35.2	40.9	48.3	45.0	38.2
成熟（过渡）期	18.2	15.5	11.9	7.7	12.4	12.1	9.0	10.0	16.7	13.2	10.0
重建期	0.0	0.3	1.6	3.6	5.4	4.4	3.3	2.2	2.6	0.8	0.9

① 有效样本数为1310份。

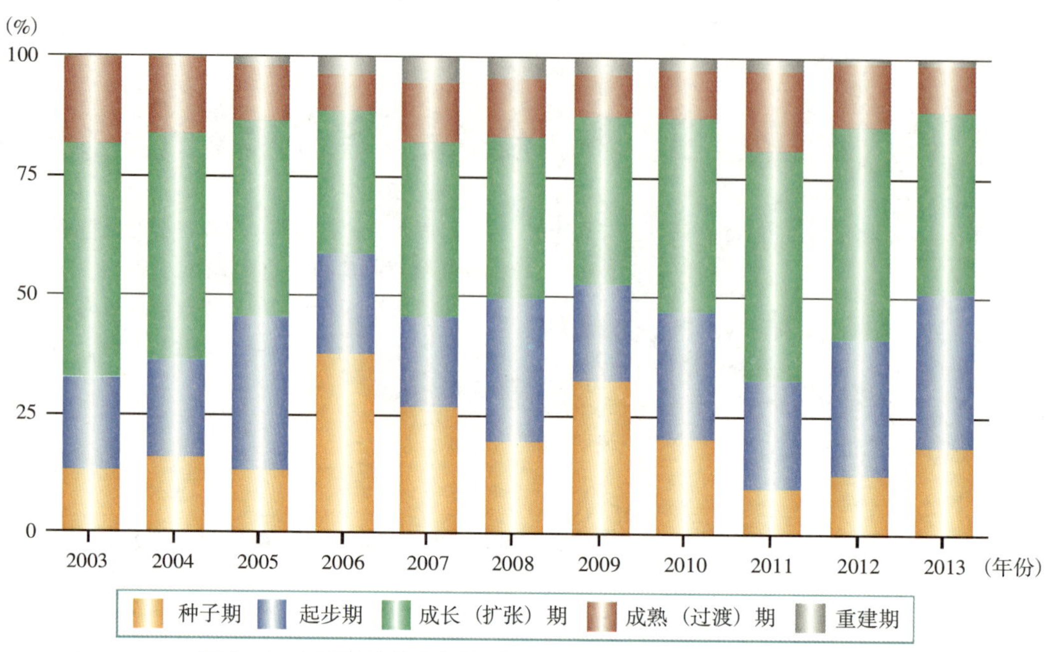

图 2-5 中国创业风险投资项目所处阶段分布（2003~2013）

表 2-11 中国创业风险投资项目所处阶段分布：投资金额（2003~2013）

单位：%

成长阶段＼年份	2003	2004	2005	2006	2007	2008	2009	2010	2011	2012	2013
种子期	5.3	4.5	5.2	30.2	12.7	9.4	19.9	10.2	4.3	6.5	12.2
起步期	16.8	12.3	20.0	11.5	8.9	19.0	12.8	17.4	14.8	19.3	22.4
成长（扩张）期	37.5	44.8	46.8	39.4	38.2	38.5	45.1	49.2	55.0	52.0	41.4
成熟（过渡）期	40.4	38.4	26.3	14.6	35.2	26.5	18.5	20.2	22.3	21.6	22.8
重建期	0.0	0.0	1.7	4.3	5.0	6.6	3.7	3.0	3.6	0.6	1.2

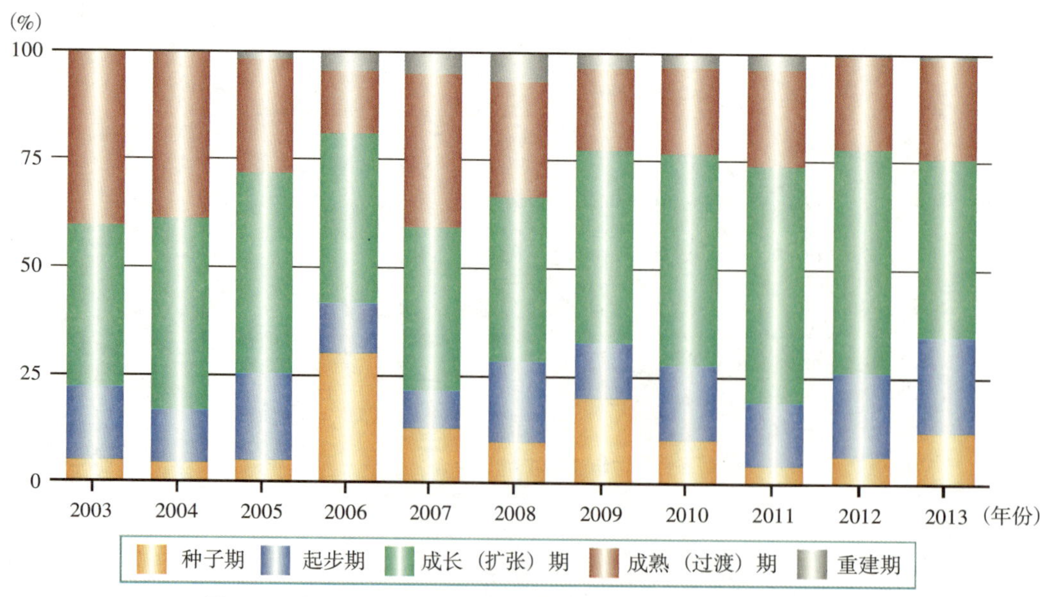

图 2-6 中国创业风险投资金额所处阶段分布（2003~2013）

2.2.2 中国创业风险投资在主要行业投资项目的阶段分布①

2013 年，中国创业风险投资主要投资行业的阶段分布特点表现为：采掘业、金融保险业、社会服务、网络产业的投资项目中种子期占比较高；金融保险业、社会服务、半导体、采掘业、其他行业以及网络服务的投资金额中种子期占比较高。这一投资偏好说明，创业风险投资机构认为这些产业具有早期投资价值，值得创业风险投资机构进行长期投资。计算机硬件产业、网络产业、房地产业、生物科技的起步期项目受到普遍关注，其他 IT 产业、批发和零售业、半导体、社会服务业在起步期投资金额较多。核应用技术、交通运输仓储和邮政业、光电子与光机电一体化、新材料工业在成长（扩张）期的投资项目较多，计算机硬件产业、核应用技术、新材料工业、环保工程在成长（扩张）期的投资金额较多（见表 2–12、表 2–13），符合资金密集型产业的要求。

表 2–12 中国创业风险投资项目主要行业的投资阶段分布：投资项目（2013）

单位：%

投资行业	种子期	起步期	成长（扩张）期	成熟（过渡）期	重建期
科技服务	25.00	33.33	41.67	0.00	0.00
交通运输仓储和邮政业	21.43	0.00	71.43	7.14	0.00
计算机硬件产业	18.75	50.00	31.25	0.00	0.00
网络产业	30.77	50.00	19.23	0.00	0.00
核应用技术	0.00	25.00	75.00	0.00	0.00
水电煤气	0.00	33.33	33.33	33.33	0.00
房地产业	0.00	50.00	25.00	25.00	0.00
社会服务	33.33	41.67	8.33	16.67	0.00
传播与文化娱乐	14.71	16.18	41.18	27.94	0.00
其他制造业	15.63	35.94	35.94	10.94	1.56
医药保健	23.48	31.06	35.61	8.33	1.52
半导体	17.65	47.06	32.35	2.94	0.00
新材料工业	11.49	25.29	52.87	9.20	1.15
其他 IT 产业	0.00	64.29	28.57	7.14	0.00
农林牧副渔	12.50	31.25	31.25	22.92	2.08
金融保险业	45.33	38.67	12.00	1.33	2.67
建筑业	12.50	0.00	43.75	43.75	0.00
环保工程	10.91	27.27	50.91	10.91	0.00
通讯设备	4.76	33.33	50.00	9.52	2.38
光电子与光机电一体化	10.77	23.08	53.85	12.31	0.00
生物科技	25.00	50.00	21.43	1.79	1.79
传统制造业	6.10	31.71	43.90	17.07	1.22
软件产业	12.50	44.44	38.89	4.17	0.00
采掘业	42.86	28.57	14.29	14.29	0.00
其他行业	29.41	31.37	37.25	1.96	0.00
新能源、高效节能技术	17.58	24.18	42.86	13.19	2.20
IT 服务业	18.18	34.55	43.64	1.82	1.82
消费产品和服务	6.38	27.66	51.06	14.89	0.00
批发和零售业	40.00	40.00	20.00	0.00	0.00

① 有效样本数为 1392 份。

表 2-13 中国创业风险投资项目主要行业的投资阶段分布：投资金额（2013） 单位：%

投资行业	种子期	起步期	成长（扩张）期	成熟（过渡）期	重建期
科技服务	23.60	28.01	48.39	—	—
交通运输仓储和邮政业	43.10	—	54.17	2.73	—
计算机硬件产业	2.49	12.74	84.76	—	—
网络产业	21.13	31.72	47.15	—	—
核应用技术	—	24.79	75.21	—	—
水电煤气	—	25.97	33.77	40.26	—
房地产业	—	24.24	35.35	40.40	—
医药保健	9.95	17.99	45.39	24.07	2.60
社会服务	49.60	40.46	6.52	3.41	—
传播与文化娱乐	9.42	8.27	50.39	31.92	—
其他制造业	6.92	38.09	23.95	28.30	2.74
新材料工业	3.45	15.08	60.61	20.24	0.62
半导体	22.32	46.17	28.97	2.53	—
其他 IT 产业	—	59.33	11.70	28.97	—
农林牧副渔	4.01	13.97	21.67	59.53	0.82
金融保险业	48.91	39.52	6.66	0.29	4.63
建筑业	4.84	—	39.30	55.85	—
环保工程	3.87	24.05	54.67	17.41	—
通讯设备	4.04	29.77	42.74	18.04	5.41
光电子与光机电一体化	4.78	18.94	52.37	23.91	—
生物科技	6.06	40.65	50.75	1.96	0.57
传统制造业	1.31	12.36	45.66	40.09	0.58
软件产业	9.51	34.62	50.69	5.18	—
新能源、高效节能技术	7.30	20.17	51.37	20.76	0.40
采掘业	24.72	24.09	33.12	18.07	—
其他行业	22.23	30.65	31.19	15.93	—
消费产品和服务	1.41	18.04	47.12	33.43	—
IT 服务业	5.77	17.68	56.60	19.83	0.12
批发和零售业	17.01	58.09	24.90	—	—

2.3 中国创业风险投资的投资强度

2.3.1 中国创业风险投资强度的变化趋势与行业差异[①]

2013 年，我国国民经济保持平稳增长，但受到 IPO 暂停等政策影响，中国创业风险投资强度持续下降，为 1282.12 万元/项，低于 2010 年的水平。按行业划分，批发和零售业、建筑业、金融保险业、消费产品和服务以及通讯设备等行业的项目平均投资强度较大（见表 2-14、图 2-7、表 2-15、图 2-8）。

① 有效样本数为 1425 份。

表 2-14 中国创业风险投资的投资强度（2004~2013） 单位：万元/项

年份	2004	2005	2006	2007	2008	2009	2010	2011	2012	2013
投资强度	972.10	901.10	802.51	973.37	1041.25	1059.77	1356.53	1550.53	1322.66	1282.12

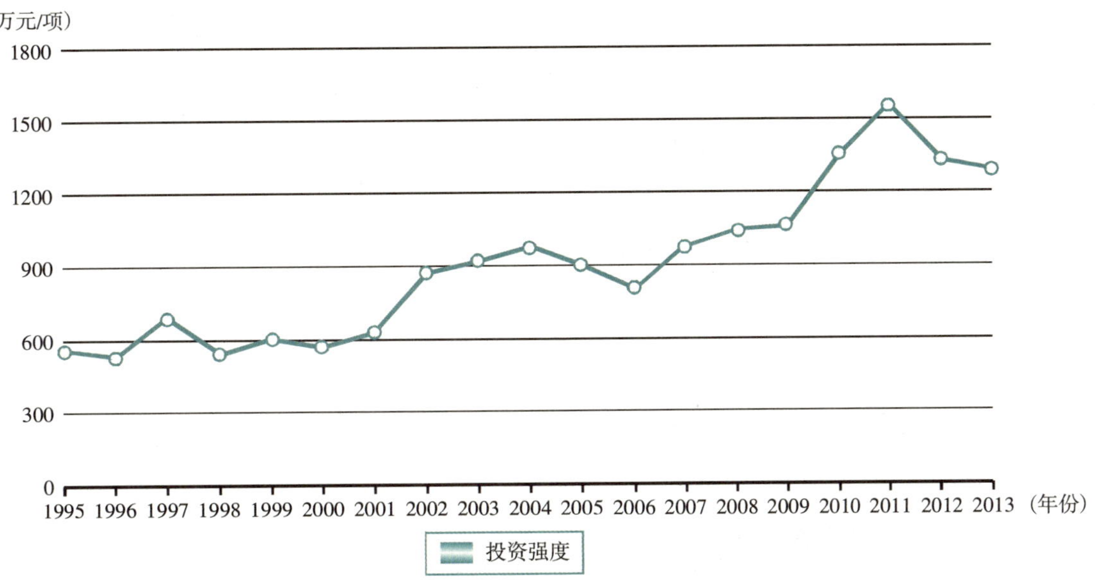

图 2-7 中国创业风险投资的投资强度（1995~2013）

表 2-15 中国创业风险投资的投资强度平均投资额（2004~2013） 单位：万元/项

行业 \ 年份	2004	2005	2006	2007	2008	2009	2010	2011	2012	2013
医药保健	976.5	635.7	541.7	884.0	678.8	1052.5	1409.3	1444.5	1144.5	1351.0
新能源、高效节能技术	2026.4	1649.4	915.1	1152.4	1447.4	1156.6	1302.8	1647.8	1373.0	1420.2
新材料工业	974.8	638.5	703.8	938.3	867.6	1212.9	1376.6	1639.7	1224.5	1444.0
消费产品和服务	277.9	533.9	1190.5	1010.6	1774.1	1435.8	2463.2	2102.0	2036.9	1712.8
网络产业	522.2	1077.4	559.3	309.0	1186.7	805.5	925.8	1487.4	1028.8	721.0
通讯设备	1011.9	486.8	1087.0	964.9	580.8	671.0	726.0	1791.6	1439.3	1704.3
生物科技	722.6	950.9	660.4	594.0	878.0	612.0	805.1	1369.0	904.5	960.5
软件产业	634.2	315.0	763.1	979.1	732.4	788.4	756.2	976.3	1029.8	677.8
其他行业	699.6	1124.0	701.7	1089.0	1155.6	1189.9	1542.2	1628.9	1110.4	1075.7
其他 IT 产业	769.0	972.9	800.3	696.5	942.3	827.4	980.7	1297.0	1171.2	616.4
批发和零售业	102.3	—	304.6	1273.1	30.0	1673.3	1988.2	1642.8	1810.3	2410.0
农林牧副渔	1921.1	380.0	913.6	1411.2	1327.8	1580.6	2054.7	1505.4	1836.0	1516.6
科技服务	293.5	531.8	529.7	456.4	600.8	785.9	1400.8	1391.7	842.4	944.0
金融保险业	2311.7	1178.1	843.5	1498.1	1537.0	1964.0	1326.1	977.6	1653.0	1885.6
计算机硬件产业	532.5	642.5	365.0	840.4	782.1	495.0	997.3	1117.0	799.6	581.5
环保工程	390.2	1095.8	567.8	982.2	760.8	893.7	1501.4	1368.9	1402.3	1268.6
核应用技术	—	700.0	—	—	—	1200.0	—	1517.3	757.4	1008.3

续表

行业 \ 年份	2004	2005	2006	2007	2008	2009	2010	2011	2012	2013
光电子与光机电一体化	619.4	466.1	788.8	670.3	898.9	879.1	1075.8	1420.0	1288.3	1294.2
传统制造业	668.2	1250.9	1316.0	1286.5	1320.7	1481.1	2057.8	1754.9	1390.3	1409.1
传播与文化娱乐	1313.8	1009.4	474.3	765.7	671.5	1437.6	1413.1	1458.1	1398.6	1441.9
采掘业	1615.5	1058.3	2979.2	1037.6	1850.5	1211.0	1633.2	1184.3	2130.4	1537.8
半导体	1011.9	3100.6	861.7	626.4	1407.6	688.7	895.4	1608.3	1312.6	963.9
IT 服务业	980.8	1002.2	506.0	607.3	791.0	609.1	1002.1	1208.5	1216.5	963.0
水电煤气	—	—	—	—	—	—	—	866.7	1050.0	1512.5
社会服务	—	—	—	—	—	—	—	1150.3	728.5	1370.1
其他制造业	—	—	—	—	—	—	—	1825.3	1483.5	959.4
交通运输仓储和邮政业	—	—	—	—	—	—	—	2163.9	2244.7	1432.4
建筑业	—	—	—	—	—	—	—	1466.7	1834.0	1989.3
房地产业	—	—	—	—	—	—	—	1492.2	1523.9	1237.5

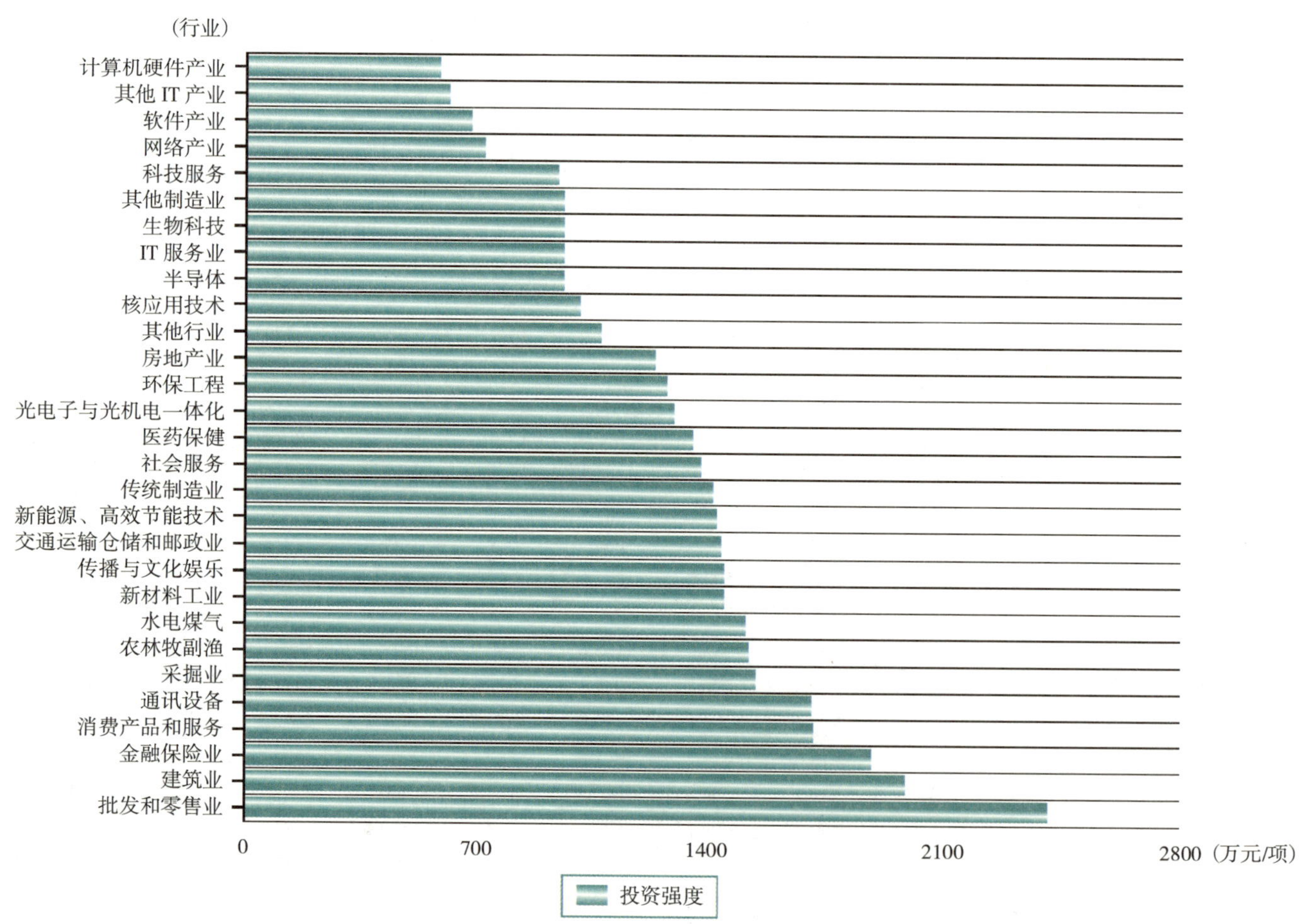

图 2-8 中国创业风险投资不同行业的投资强度（2013）

2.3.2 中国创业风险投资机构单项投资规模分布①

2013 年，中国创业风险投资机构单项投资金额整体出现下降，100 万元以下以及 500 万元以上的单项投资金额的百分比都有不同程度的下降。其中，1000 万~2000 万元的投资项目所占比例最大，达 20.1%；其次为 500 万~1000 万元和 2000 万元以上投资项目，单项投资在 3000 万元以下以及 300 万~500 万元的投资项目较 2012 年大幅度上升（见表 2-16、图 2-9）。

表 2-16 中国创业风险投资机构单项投资金额分布（2002~2013） 单位：%

年份 \ 金额（万元）	100 以下	100~300	300~500	500~1000	1000~2000	2000 以上
2002	16.4	28.0	19.4	17.4	10.6	8.2
2003	22.4	22.6	16.5	14.7	12.8	11.0
2004	25.5	14.6	15.8	18.5	12.2	13.4
2005	23.9	19.7	15.5	20.0	11.0	9.0
2006	24.1	25.1	9.0	19.3	12.0	10.5
2007	16.1	17.6	18.3	18.1	17.4	12.5
2008	17.1	22.0	11.7	15.0	18.9	15.2
2009	11.7	22.4	12.6	20.3	17.3	15.7
2010	13.4	15.5	8.9	17.5	21.5	23.2
2011	6.8	10.6	10.2	20.6	25.7	26.2
2012	10.2	13.1	11.3	21.2	24.7	19.5
2013	8.4	17.6	14.6	20.0	20.1	19.3

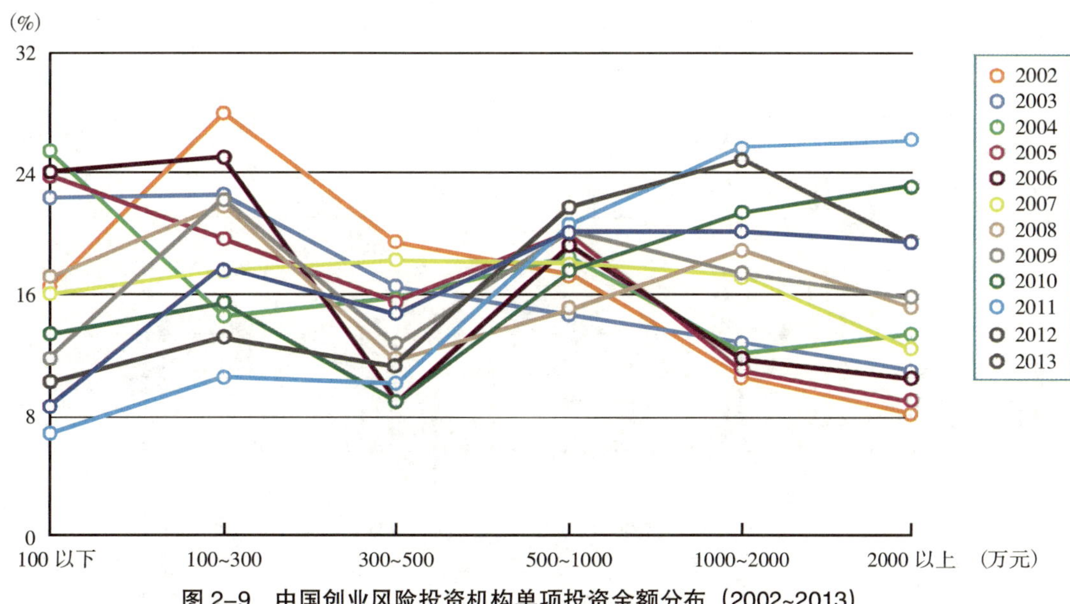

图 2-9 中国创业风险投资机构单项投资金额分布（2002~2013）

2.3.3 中国创业风险投资的投资策略（联合投资）

联合投资可有效分散创业风险投资公司风险，通过合作分享其他联合投资伙伴的专业知识和技能，实现资金使用效率的最大化，从而最终实现优化项目选择和提升整体投资组合价值的目标。2013 年，由创业风险投资机构和其

① 有效样本数为 1425 份。

他投资主体联合投资的项目占比持续降低。其中，100 万元以下和 1000 万元以上的项目中联合投资项目占比显著下降，100 万~1000 万元的联合投资项目所占比例上升。100 万~500 万元项目中，有 32%的项目为联合投资，是各投资规模项目中占比最高的（见表 2-17、图 2-10、表 2-18、图 2-11）。

表 2-17 中国创业风险投资联合投资的单项投资金额分布（2002~2013）[①] 单位：%

年份 \ 金额（万元）	100 以下	100~500	500~1000	1000~2000	2000 以上
2002	16.9	26.7	18.9	14.8	22.7
2003	15.9	27.1	17.1	12.9	27.0
2004	17.0	29.8	17.7	13.5	22.0
2005	16.5	24.1	19.5	15.0	24.9
2006	13.6	50.0	15.9	11.4	9.1
2007	9.1	39.4	9.1	30.3	12.1
2008	19.0	31.6	13.9	20.3	15.2
2009	13.0	28.0	21.0	19.0	19.0
2010	10.3	15.4	24.1	23.1	27.2
2011	6.1	22.0	18.3	25.6	28.0
2012	13.0	28.7	20.9	20.0	17.4
2013	12.0	32.0	28.0	12.0	16.0

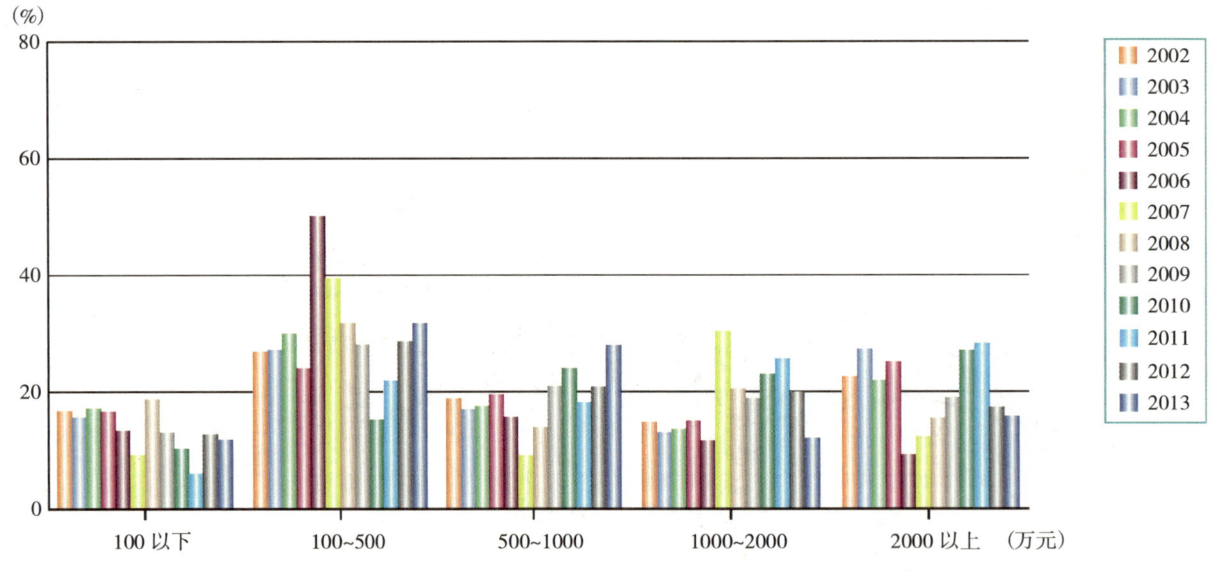

图 2-10 中国创业风险投资联合投资的单项投资金额分布（2002~2013）

表 2-18 中国创业风险投资机构与其他类型投资机构的联合投资（2013）[②] 单位：%

投资额分布 \ 金额（万元）	100 以下	100~300	300~500	500~1000	1000~2000	2000 以上
创业风险投资机构的投资额	0.38	3.14	5.37	12.79	25.69	52.63
其他类型投资机构的投资额	0.62	3.00	6.59	19.71	18.48	51.60

① 有效样本数为 50 份。
② 创业风险投资机构有效样本数为 1276 份；其他类型投资机构有效样本数为 50 份。

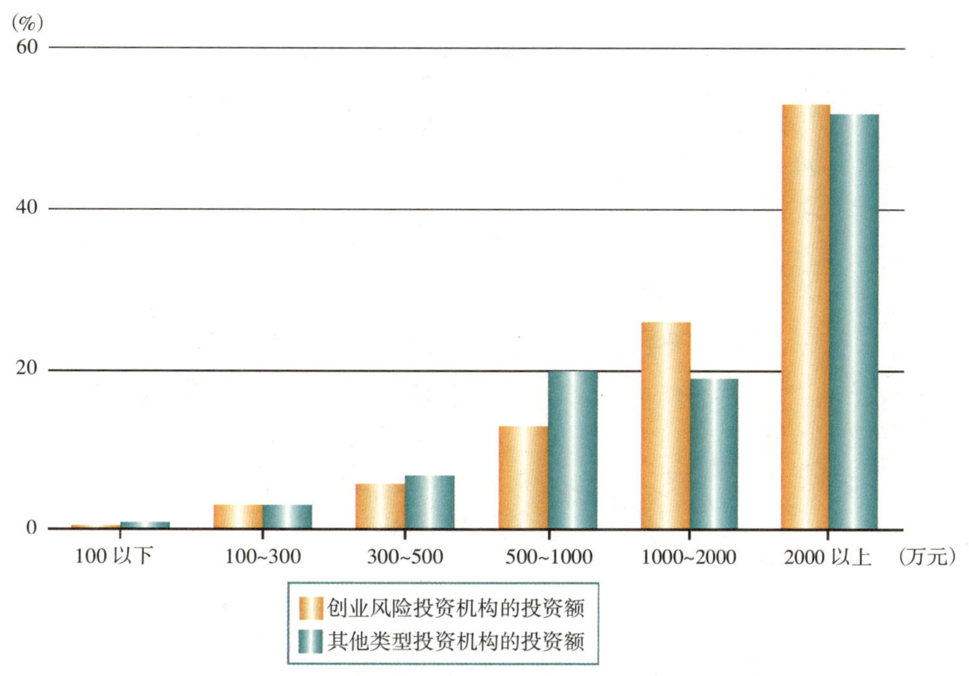

图 2-11 中国创业风险投资机构与其他类型投资机构的联合投资（2013）

2.4 中国创业风险投资的首轮投资与后续投资

2013 年，中国创业风险投资项目的首轮投资和后续投资分别占 77.5%和 22.5%，首轮投资仍然占主导地位，但后续投资的比例不断上升，基本延续了前几年投资轮次的格局（见表 2-19、图 2-12）。这与美国等发达国家创业风险投资的投资方式存在着巨大的差别。统计显示，美国 2013 年首轮投资金额占比仅为 17.28%，大多数为后续投资。

表 2-19 中国创业风险投资的首轮投资和后续投资（2002~2013）① 单位：%

项目＼年份	2002	2003	2004	2005	2006	2007	2008	2009	2010	2011	2012	2013
首轮投资	83.3	72.1	67.2	70.8	77.0	83.1	84.5	82.7	86.2	83.4	80.1	77.5
后续投资	16.7	27.9	32.8	29.2	23.0	16.9	15.5	17.3	13.8	16.6	19.9	22.5

① 有效样本数为 1068 份。

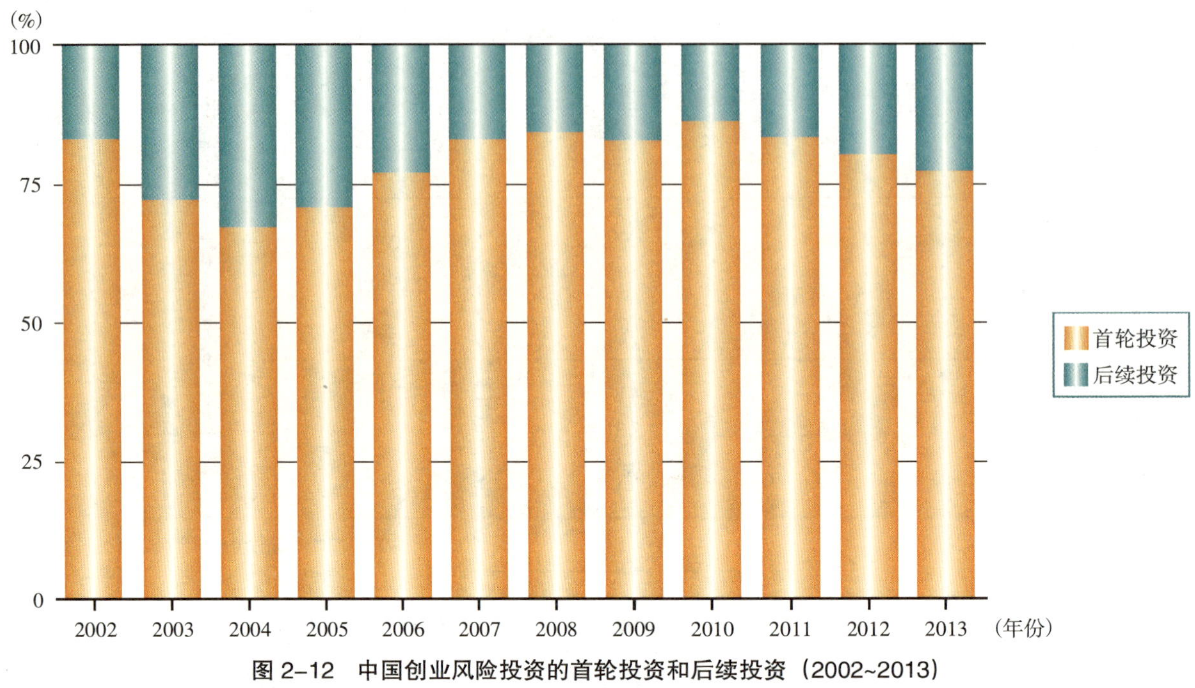

图 2-12 中国创业风险投资的首轮投资和后续投资（2002~2013）

2.5 中国创业风险投资机构持股结构

中国创业风险投资机构的股权结构仍然保持多元化趋势，其中参股和相对控股仍然是主要的投资方式。2013年，持股比例在10%~20%的项目所占比例较上一年有所上升（见表2-20、图2-13）。这一持股的趋势表明，不谋求控股的创业风险投资经营策略仍然占主导地位。与往年相比，尽管中国创业风险投资机构的投资额度总体呈上升趋势，其所占股权比例在10%~30%以及50%以上区间的比重有持续上升的趋势，但是其他股权比例所占的比重则在逐年下降。

表 2-20 中国创业风险投资机构持股结构分布（2003~2013）[①] 单位：%

年份＼股权比例	10%以下	10%~20%	20%~30%	30%~40%	40%~50%	50%以上
2003	23.20	20.00	20.00	12.00	12.00	12.80
2004	22.20	19.40	17.20	12.20	8.20	20.80
2005	16.70	26.40	14.50	20.30	6.90	15.20
2006	25.00	25.00	20.35	12.50	6.10	11.05
2007	43.33	20.32	14.44	8.41	4.92	8.57
2008	42.92	23.65	10.95	8.61	6.13	7.74
2009	44.60	22.77	13.64	5.98	5.14	7.87
2010	50.99	25.15	10.85	6.17	3.14	3.70
2011	61.04	20.46	7.08	4.38	2.24	4.80
2012	56.29	22.57	9.07	4.70	3.00	4.37
2013	50.32	25.60	11.60	4.40	2.88	5.20

① 有效样本数为1250份。

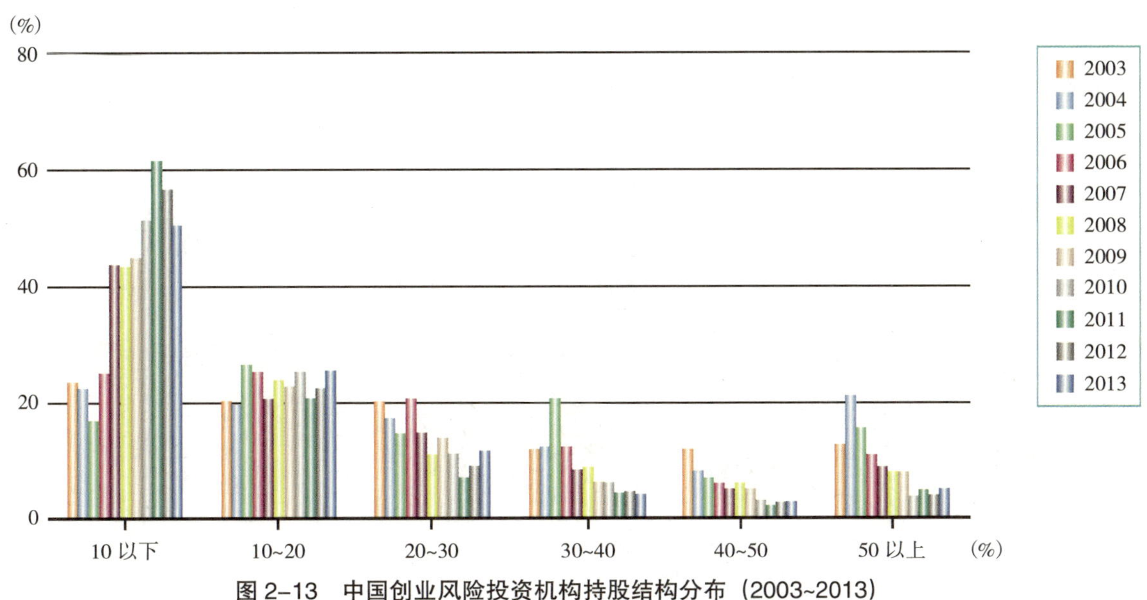

图 2-13 中国创业风险投资机构持股结构分布（2003~2013）

2.6 中国创业风险投资项目的特征

2.6.1 中国创业风险投资项目的资本规模

从被投资项目的实收资本而言，2013 年，规模在 5000 万元以上和 1000 万~3000 万元的项目是中国创业风险投资的重点对象。500 万元以下的中小投资项目的占比较 2012 年增加了 2.56 个百分点；5000 万元以上的投资项目占比与 2012 年相比下降了 2.25 个百分点。总体来看，中国创业风险投资项目规模分布的基本趋势表现为，对中小项目投资有所上升，对大型项目的投资略有下降，其他规模项目的比例大致稳定，这与投资阶段“前移”特征较为一致（见表 2-21、图 2-14）。

表 2-21 中国创业风险投资项目的实收资本规模分布（2002~2013）① 单位：%

年份 \ 成本规模	500 万元以下	500 万~1000 万元	1000 万~3000 万元	3000 万~5000 万元	5000 万元以上
2002	24.10	17.40	28.60	16.50	13.40
2003	25.80	15.90	27.00	12.30	19.00
2004	27.10	17.10	24.30	9.90	21.60
2005	34.40	12.80	26.10	8.90	17.80
2006	28.20	13.20	27.80	14.10	16.70
2007	26.82	12.83	20.41	13.12	26.82
2008	18.90	15.70	26.50	12.20	26.70
2009	21.60	13.90	23.50	15.40	25.60
2010	26.40	12.43	23.42	13.06	24.68
2011	15.23	11.50	24.23	13.56	35.48
2012	16.93	14.49	26.09	13.18	29.32
2013	19.49	15.25	23.74	14.44	27.07

① 有效样本数为 990 份。

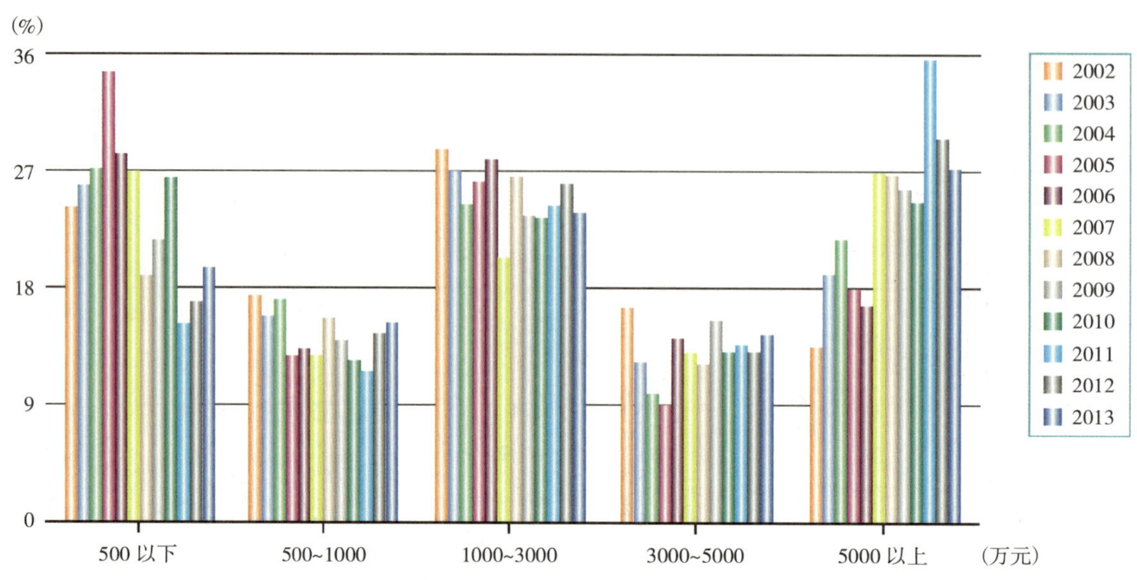

图 2-14 中国创业风险投资项目的实收资本规模分布（2002~2013）

2.6.2 中国创业风险投资项目的雇员规模

以项目雇员划分被投资项目的规模，2013 年，中国创业风险投资机构投资项目的规模与 2012 年相比发生了结构性变化。创业风险投资机构首选拥有雇员 10~50 人之间的项目，占比达到 30.38%；其次为雇员 200 人以上的项目，占比达 24.28%（见表 2-22、图 2-15）。

表 2-22 中国创业风险投资项目雇员规模分布（2002~2013）① 单位：%

年份＼雇员规模	10 人以下	10~50 人	50~100 人	100~150 人	150~200 人	200 人以上
2002	20.60	41.10	15.00	6.80	3.80	12.70
2003	19.80	41.10	13.20	3.50	3.90	18.50
2004	22.90	42.30	9.50	6.50	3.00	15.80
2005	17.70	37.10	13.70	7.40	7.40	16.70
2006	14.10	36.40	13.00	7.10	7.60	20.70
2007	14.70	26.10	12.90	8.50	7.00	30.10
2008	14.60	29.90	14.40	7.50	3.40	29.90
2009	21.80	36.70	9.80	6.20	4.80	19.90
2010	14.60	28.90	13.90	8.20	5.90	27.50
2011	11.30	24.30	13.30	8.90	6.90	34.10
2012	12.88	25.96	13.39	11.76	8.62	27.38
2013	13.75	30.38	13.97	10.20	7.43	24.28

① 有效样本数为 902 份。

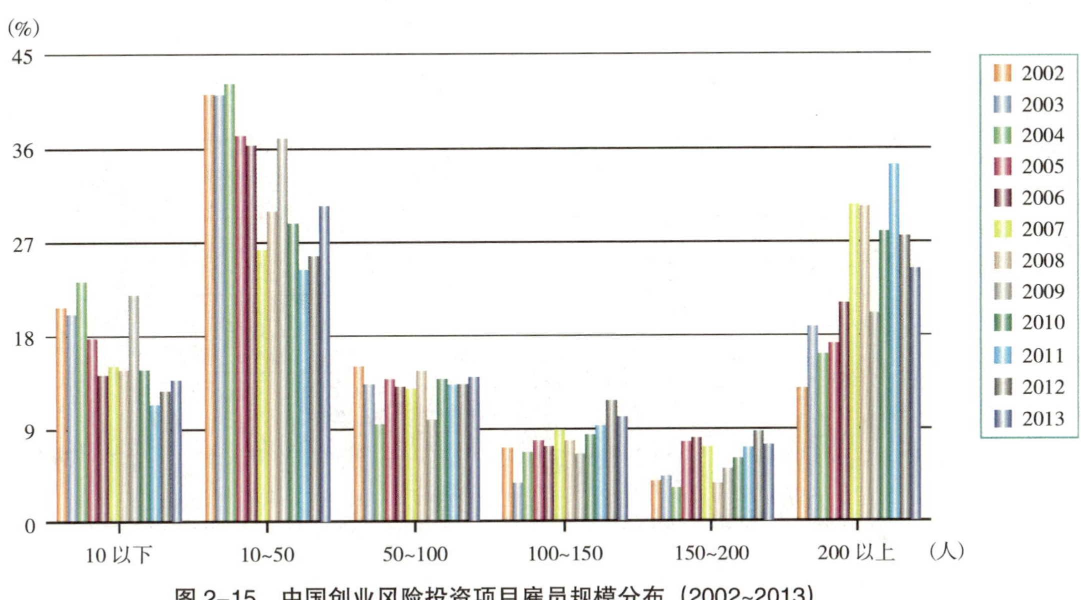

图 2-15 中国创业风险投资项目雇员规模分布（2002~2013）

2.6.3 中国创业风险投资项目的经营时间

从被投资项目的经营时间看，一方面，创业风险投资机构仍然偏好比较稳健的成熟项目，成立时间在 5 年以上的企业占比最高，达到 41.71%，但近两年来持续下降；另一方面，也有较多成立时间在 1~3 年的初创期企业获得投资机构青睐，占比为 21.54%，实现连续两年上升（见表 2-23、图 2-16）。结合投资项目的注册资本金额、雇员分布情况可以发现，这三组数据对 2013 年中国创业风险投资行为的描述基本一致。

表 2-23 中国创业风险投资项目经营时间分布（2002~2013）①　　单位：%

经营时间 / 年份	1 年以下	1~3 年	3~5 年	5 年以上
2002	17.20	47.60	22.30	12.90
2003	26.70	42.40	15.70	15.20
2004	27.70	36.40	20.10	15.80
2005	32.00	33.70	16.30	18.00
2006	18.80	32.10	16.50	32.60
2007	24.20	17.40	15.80	42.70
2008	17.30	24.30	19.00	39.40
2009	40.20	16.70	12.30	30.80
2010	13.60	28.80	13.60	43.90
2011	11.80	20.10	16.30	51.80
2012	14.25	20.51	15.19	50.05
2013	19.54	21.54	17.21	41.71

① 有效样本数为 765 份。

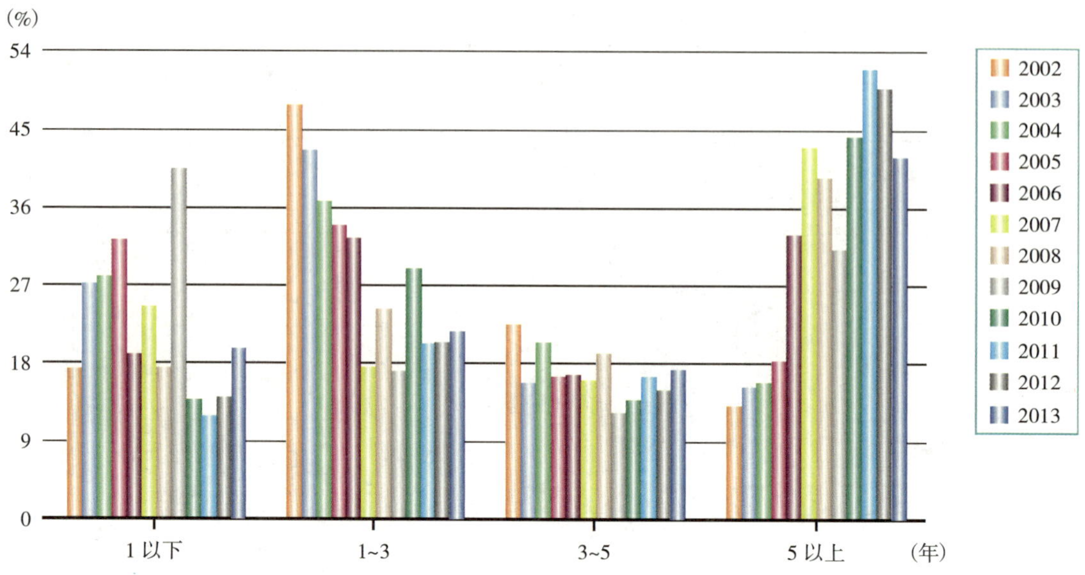

图 2-16 中国创业风险投资项目经营时间分布（2002~2013）

3 中国创业风险投资的退出

3.1 中国创业风险投资退出的基本情况[①]

在风险投资管理过程中，项目退出是实现风险资本增值的基本前提和盈利的主要手段。由于受到 2012 年底开始的 IPO 关闭的影响，2013 年我国的并购市场得到了充分的发展,客观上促进了多层次资本市场体系的建设与完善。

2013 年，中国创业风险投资项目退出收入规模总体上持续增加，收入规模在 1000 万~2000 万元的项目比例有显著的下降，收入规模在 2000 万元以上项目的比例与 2012 年基本持平，而收入在 1000 万元以下的项目均出现不同程度的增长（见表 3-1、图 3-1）。

表 3-1　中国创业风险投资项目退出的收入分布（2007~2013）　　单位：%

年份＼收入规模	100 万元以下	100 万~500 万元	500 万~1000 万元	1000 万~2000 万元	2000 万元以上
2007	37.2	27.9	9.3	11.6	14.0
2008	36.5	24.6	11.1	9.5	18.3
2009	26.8	27.5	15.7	12.4	17.6
2010	27.3	19.7	13.7	13.7	25.7
2011	22.9	24.1	11.0	10.6	31.4
2012	19.2	17.1	10.5	17.4	35.8
2013	21.8	19.8	10.6	11.8	35.9

① 有效样本数为 450 份。

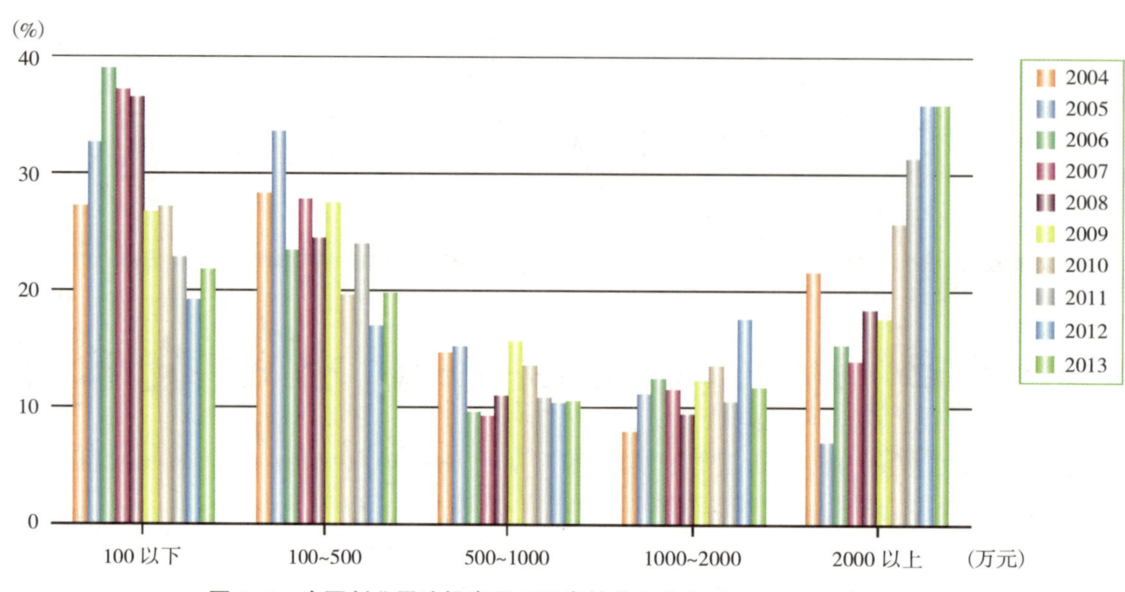

图 3-1 中国创业风险投资项目退出的收入分布(2004~2013)

3.2 中国创业风险投资的退出方式[①]

3.2.1 中国创业风险投资的主要退出方式

国际通行的风险投资退出方式主要有四种:企业首次公开发行(IPO)、企业并购(M&A)、股权回购、公司清算等。其中,IPO 是风险投资退出最理想的方式,收益率较高,有利于激励核心层考虑企业长远发展;并购的投资回收最迅速、操作便捷,并且可选择股票交换作为支付形式,能够减轻并购方的财务压力,此外,并购也是小企业不断成长壮大的重要手段;股权回购方式作为一种备用手段是风险投资能够收回的基本保障;清算则是在风险投资失败时减小并停止投资损失的有效方法。

2013 年,受国内资本市场 IPO 暂停、海外上市渠道狭窄等持续利空因素影响,中国企业在全球资本市场的活跃程度呈现持续下降态势。全年共有 66[②]家企业在境内外资本市场上市,远低于 2011 年的 356 家以及 2012 年的 154 家企业。尽管上市退出企业大幅度下降,但仍有 27 家具有 VC/PE 的背景。按照退出渠道划分,随着 IPO 退出绝对值有所下滑,上市退出比例占比也出现了 2008 年以来的首次下滑,这主要是受到了 2013 年 IPO 暂停的影响。与此同时,并购市场在 2013 年有了比较大的发展,可以看到在中国创业风险投资退出方式的分布中,2013 年通过并购方式退出的占比达到了 26.3%(见表 3-2、图 3-2)。

表 3-2 中国创业风险投资的退出方式分布(2003~2013) 单位:%

年份 \ 退出方式	上市	并购	回购	清算	其他
2003	5.4	40.4	36.3	14.9	3.0
2004	12.4	55.3	27.6	4.7	0.0
2005	11.9	44.4	33.3	10.4	0.0
2006	12.7	28.4	30.4	7.8	20.6
2007	24.2	29.0	27.4	5.6	13.7

① 有效样本数为 116 份。
② 清科研究中心.2013 年 66 家中企上市 A 股市场喜迎开闸[R]. 2014-01-02。

续表

年份＼退出方式	上市	并购	回购	清算	其他
2008	22.7	23.2	34.8	9.2	10.1
2009	25.3	33.0	35.3	6.3	0.0
2010	29.8	28.6	32.8	6.9	1.9
2011	29.4	30.0	32.3	3.2	5.1
2012	29.4	18.9	45.0	6.7	0.0
2013	24.3	26.3	44.8	4.6	0.0

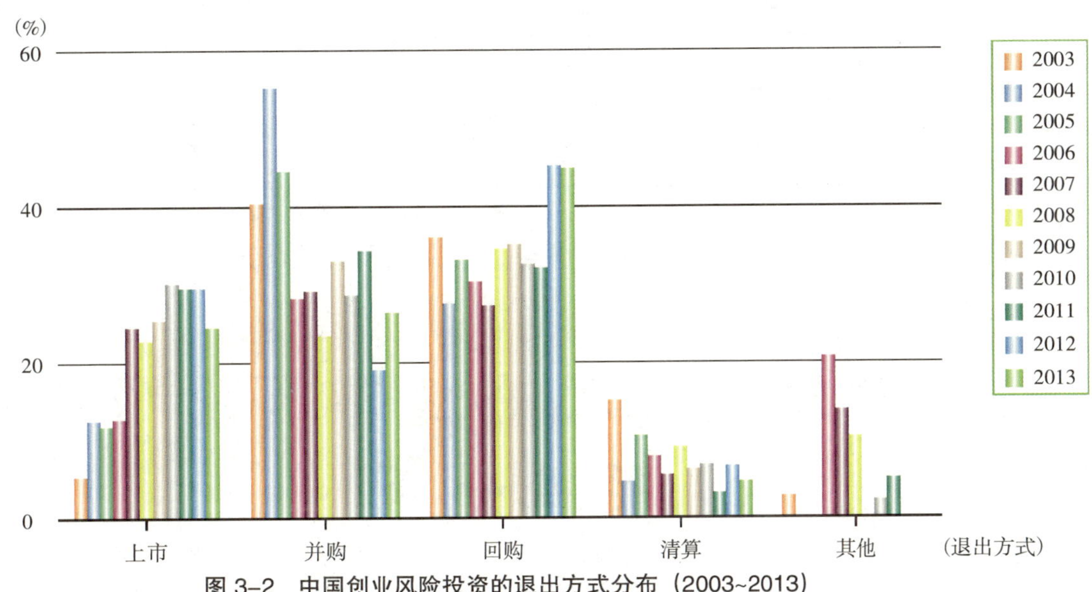

图 3-2 中国创业风险投资的退出方式分布（2003~2013）

3.2.2 中国创业风险投资的 IPO 退出渠道

目前，我国多层次资本市场已初步形成主板、中小板、创业板以及中小企业股份转让的构架。据统计显示，境内中小板及创业板仍然是创业风险投资机构企业退出的主要渠道。受国内外宏观环境影响，2013 年，21.26%的创业风险投资机构选择在境内主板上市，40.94%的创业风险投资机构选择在境内创业板上市退出；30.71%的企业通过境内中小板上市退出；仅有 7.09%通过境外上市方式退出，但是该比例已经比上一年增长 3.61%（见表 3-3、图 3-3）。

表 3-3 中国创业风险投资 IPO 分布（2010~2013）

单位：%

年份＼退出方式	境内主板上市	境内创业板上市	境内中小板上市	境外上市
2010	16.67	35.90	44.87	2.56
2011	14.71	30.39	49.02	5.88
2012	21.74	38.26	36.52	3.48
2013	21.26	40.94	30.71	7.09

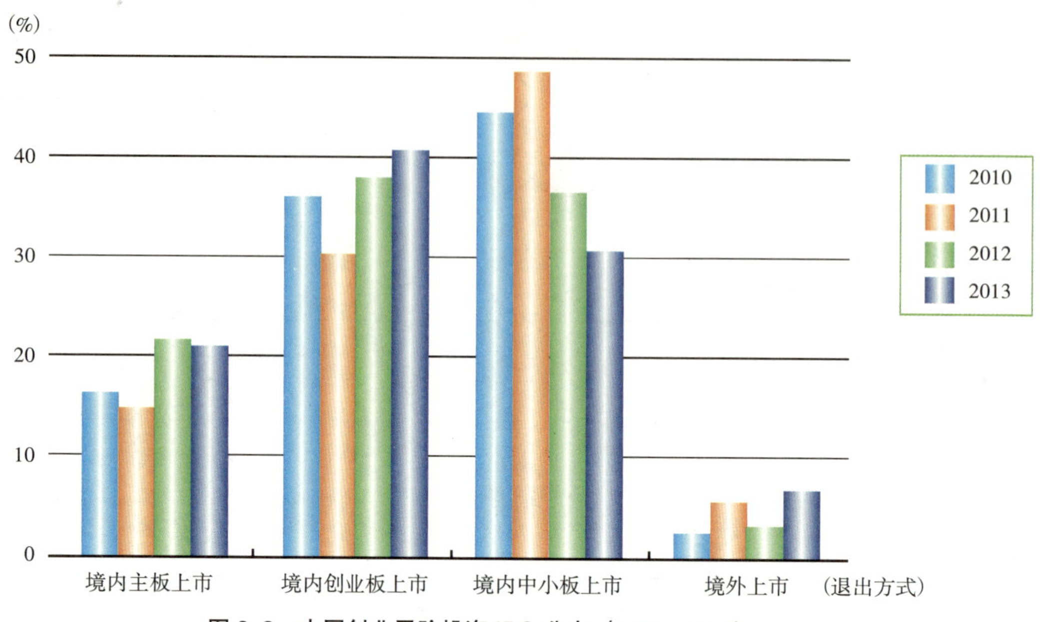

图 3-3 中国创业风险投资 IPO 分布（2010~2013）

3.3 中国创业风险投资退出项目的行业分布①

从二级行业划分的情况来看，2013 年，中国创业风险投资实现项目退出最多的 10 个行业分布为传统制造业（17.5%）、其他制造业（8.2%）、医药保健（7.6%）、新材料工业（6.9%）、光电子与光机电一体化（6.7%）、新能源/高效节能技术（6.7%）、生物科技（4.9%）、软件产业（4.1%）、其他行业（3.9%）和金融保险业（3.9%）。这 10 个行业中实现退出的项目占全部退出项目的 70.4%，集中度较 2012 年下降 2.6 个百分点（见图 3-4）。

① 有效样本数为 522 份。

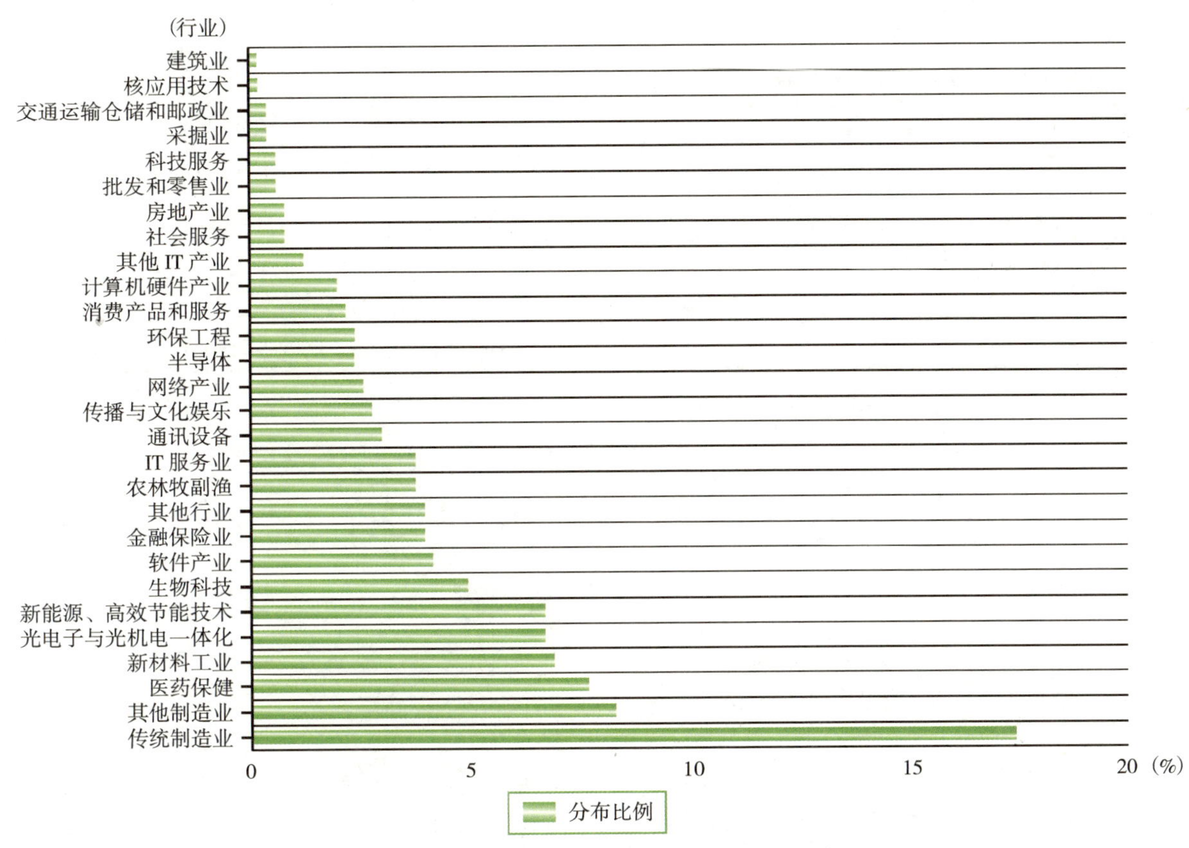

图 3–4 中国创业风险投资的退出项目的行业分布（2013）

从一级行业划分情况来看，2013 年，传统制造业、新能源和环保业、计算机、通信设备制造业以及医药生物业依然是行业投资较为集中的领域，其中，传统制造业和计算机、通信设备制造业都较上一年有显著增长。同时，与行业投资相对应，计算机、通信设备制造业是今年的退出新热点。

表 3–4 中国创业风险投资的退出项目的行业分布（2004~2013）① 单位：%

行业 \ 年份	2004	2005	2006	2007	2008	2009	2010	2011	2012	2013
新能源和环保业②	5.8	6.9	15.7	12.9	10.1	12.7	24.5	16.7	22.2	16.2
传统制造业	9.7	12.9	6.9	8.1	13.0	12.2	7.9	11.3	14.3	17.5
计算机、通信设备制造业③	13.6	13.8	18.6	8.8	16.0	18.1	14.2	14.4	10.6	14.0
医药生物业④	15.5	18.1	15.6	18.6	15.5	9.0	11.0	13.5	11.1	12.5
软件和信息服务业⑤	30.1	18.1	13.7	32.2	24.5	26.7	15.9	12.9	9.4	11.5
农林牧渔业	4.9	—	1.0	—	2.4	1.4	4.7	6.0	6.5	3.7
其他制造业	—	—	—	—	—	—	—	5.3	6.2	8.2

① 有效样本数为 510 份。
② 包括原有的新材料工业、新能源/高效节能技术、核应用技术、环保工程四个细分的二级行业。
③ 包括原有的通信设备、半导体、计算机硬件产业、光电子与光机电一体化四个细分的二级行业。
④ 包括原有的医药保健、生物科技两个细分的二级行业。
⑤ 包括原有的网络产业、IT 产业、软件产业、其他 IT 产业四个细分的二级行业。

续表

行业 \ 年份	2004	2005	2006	2007	2008	2009	2010	2011	2012	2013
其他行业	—	6.9	16.7	14.5	10.6	9.5	11.4	5.0	6.2	3.9
传播与文化娱乐	—	—	1.0	0.8	0.5	0.9	1.6	1.9	3.0	2.7
金融保险业	—	—	4.9	0.8	2.4	2.7	3.1	2.2	2.2	3.9
科技服务	3.9	—	2.9	1.6	3.4	2.7	1.6	0.6	2.2	0.6
社会服务	—	—	—	—	—	—	—	0.6	1.6	0.8

3.4 中国创业风险投资退出项目的地区分布①

2013 年，中国创业风险投资退出项目的地区分布总体上与创业风险投资机构分布情况较为一致，东部地区因创业风险投资发展相对成熟，江苏、浙江、广东等地区在项目退出方面长期处于领先地位，尤其是江苏仍然继续保持退出第一的地位，占比虽然比去年下跌近 1 个百分点，但仍然以 34.99%占据了首位。

从 2006~2013 年的总体趋势来看，每年前 10 名退出项目的地区所占比例之和依次为 80.9%、79.2%、86.0%、86.8%、85.7%、85.7%、89.0%以及 83.85%。说明“区域聚集”现象有所减弱（见表 3–5、图 3–5）。

表 3–5 中国创业风险投资退出项目的地区分布前 10 名（2006~2013） 单位：%

年份											
2006 年	地区	广东	江苏	浙江	上海	北京	黑龙江	深圳	陕西	安徽	四川
	比例	16.0	11.7	11.7	9.6	8.5	7.4	6.4	5.3	4.3	4.3
2007 年	地区	江苏	上海	广东	浙江	山东	湖北	安徽	云南	山西	辽宁
	比例	24.2	11.0	9.9	5.5	5.5	5.5	4.4	4.4	4.4	4.4
2008 年	地区	江苏	广东	上海	浙江	山东	安徽	湖南	北京	湖北	四川
	比例	15.9	14.0	13.4	10.8	6.4	6.4	5.7	5.1	4.5	3.8
2009 年	地区	江苏	广东	浙江	北京	陕西	安徽	上海	四川	湖北	天津
	比例	26.4	17.4	10.0	7.5	5.5	5.0	4.0	4.0	3.5	3.0
2010 年	地区	江苏	湖北	广东	浙江	上海	山东	北京	新疆	湖南	天津
	比例	26.6	16.7	12.4	9.0	6.4	3.4	3.0	3.0	2.6	2.6
2011 年	地区	江苏	上海	浙江	广东	天津	北京	河南	山东	湖北	福建
	比例	27.6	11.5	11.2	9.6	8.1	6.5	3.4	2.8	2.8	2.2
2012 年	地区	江苏	浙江	广东	湖北	北京	上海	河北	天津	安徽	湖南
	比例	35.6	9.8	8.4	7.6	7.3	5.4	3.8	3.8	3.8	3.5
2013 年	地区	江苏	浙江	上海	广东	北京	天津	安徽	山东	湖北	重庆
	比例	35.0	10.6	8.1	7.7	5.4	5.2	3.3	3.1	2.9	2.7

① 有效样本数为 483 份。

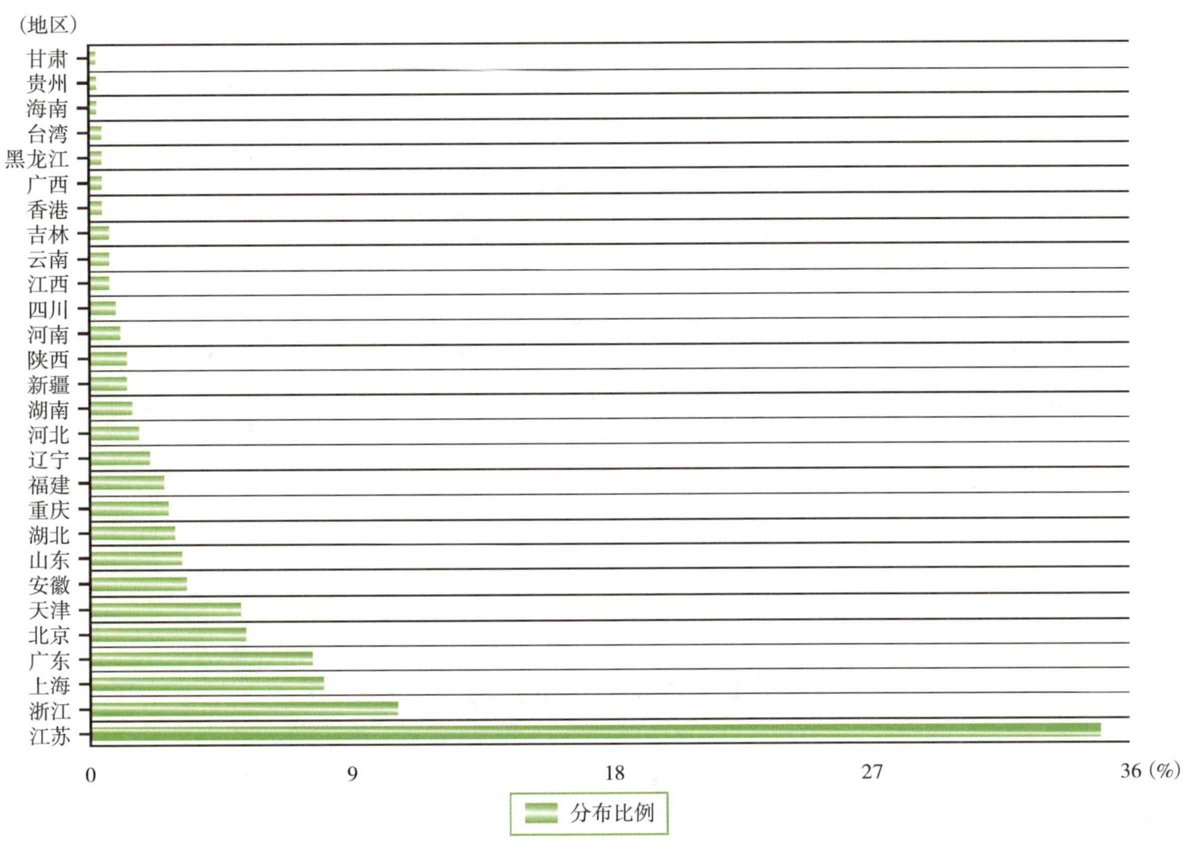

图 3–5　中国创业风险投资的退出项目的地区分布（2013）

3.5 中国创业风险投资项目的退出效果

3.5.1　中国创业风险投资退出的总体绩效表现

2013 年，国际金融市场与国内资本市场持续低迷，创业风险投资的退出绩效表现与 2012 年相比有较大下滑，全行业的项目退出收益率为 117.70%。同时，由于行业内的竞争加剧和 IPO 闭市的消息，客观上增加了项目持有的困难，因而大部分创业风险投资选择了并购等方式，使得整体项目退出时间缩短，全行业项目退出平均时间为 3.74 年，明显短于 2012 年的 4.3 年，整体行业平均收益率也因此暴跌至 13.85%（见表 3–6、图 3–6）。

表 3–6　中国创业风险投资退出的投资收益率（2005~2013）①　　单位：%

年份	2005	2006	2007	2008	2009	2010	2011	2012	2013
年度收益率	58.80	56.62	77.12	240.36	144.89	221.87	193.71	196.35	117.70
年度平均收益率	45.49	4.66	4.32	32.68	19.33	37.82	45.62	44.01	13.85

① 有效样本数为 1468 份。

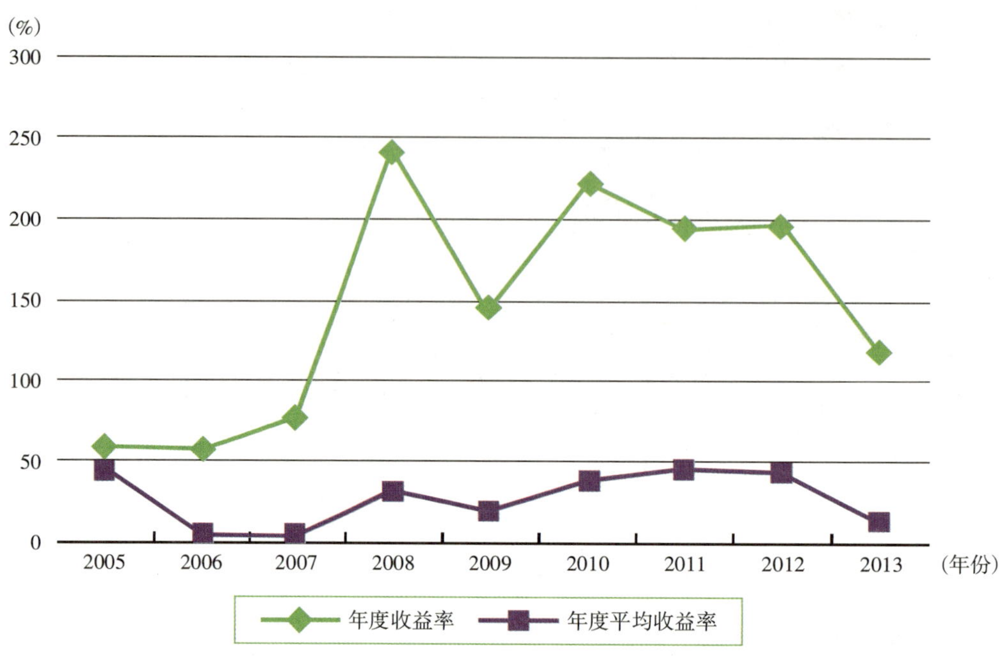

图 3-6 中国创业风险投资退出收益率（2005~2013）

根据退出项目的投资收益分布的趋势情况显示（见表3-7、图 3-7）：2013 年，中国创业风险投资退出项目中，亏损项目出现了大幅度反弹，为 67.1%，退出收益率在100%以上的为 16.9%，有明显下降。这在一定程度上表明，中国创业风险投资市场受到 IPO 闭市的严重影响，而外部宏观经济又在一定程度上恶化了这种态势。

表 3-7 中国创业风险投资退出收益率分布（2004~2013）① 单位：%

年份 \ 退出收益率（%）	亏损	0~15	15~20	20~50	50~100	100 以上
2004	58.1	2.3	3.5	16.3	8.1	11.6
2005	58.1	4.3	5.4	5.4	8.6	18.3
2006	73.8	6.0	0.0	3.6	2.4	14.2
2007	61.2	9.2	5.1	6.1	8.2	10.2
2008	65.1	3.4	1.4	4.1	8.9	17.1
2009	63.0	4.8	3.2	10.6	4.2	14.3
2010	63.2	8.0	1.9	4.7	4.2	17.9
2011	47.9	9.9	3.0	10.6	6.5	22.1
2012	47.0	8.6	3.5	10.5	4.5	25.9
2013	67.1	2.4	2.7	8.7	2.2	16.9

① 有效样本数为 450 份。

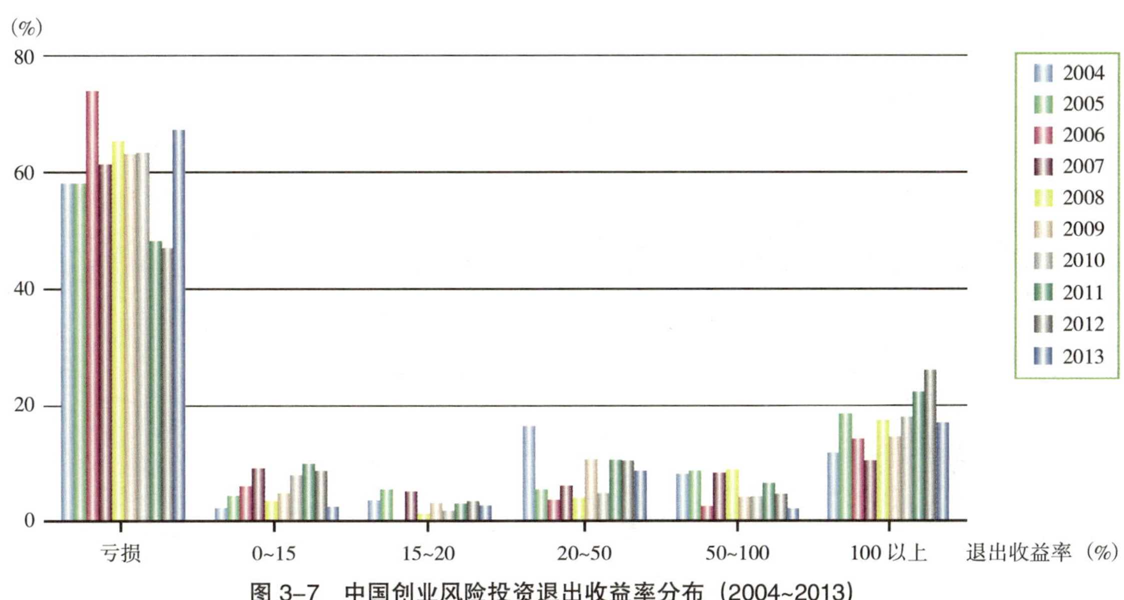

图 3-7 中国创业风险投资退出收益率分布（2004~2013）

3.5.2 中国创业风险投资不同退出方式的绩效表现

从历年不同退出渠道的绩效表现来看，一般而言，上市退出的收益最为可观，投资收益约为投资总额的 5 倍，最高实现收益高达 9 倍；并购退出收益其次，由于存在并购企业价值被低估的情况，部分年份并购退出未能获得收益；在大部分情况下，股份回购未能实现收益，投资收入存在部分损失；而清算退出则存在较大投资损失。因而，创业风险投资行业的投资收益主要由少数成功上市退出项目来弥补多数项目的损失（见表 3-8、图 3-8）。

2013 年，受 IPO 闭市的利空影响，上市退出收益持续了 2012 年的下滑态势，仅为 448.03%，即平均账目回报 4.48 倍；通过并购退出、回购及清算的收益率也均较 2012 年大幅下滑。

表 3-8 不同渠道的创业风险投资退出项目盈亏情况（2004~2013）①　　单位：%

退出渠道 / 年份	上市	并购	回购	清算
2004	159.81	9.23	-38.18	-41.03
2005	419.25	-20.56	20.53	-61.40
2006	491.45	27.35	-30.81	-53.63
2007	436.07	-15.37	-26.80	-42.63
2008	916.66	28.35	-41.98	-29.13
2009	327.75	4.74	-29.47	-42.66
2010	736.68	44.95	-21.19	-24.43
2011	799.38	44.16	-30.51	-65.37
2012	486.10	162.23	29.18	-15.34
2013	448.03	24.09	-34.28	-43.47

① 有效样本数为 1589 份。

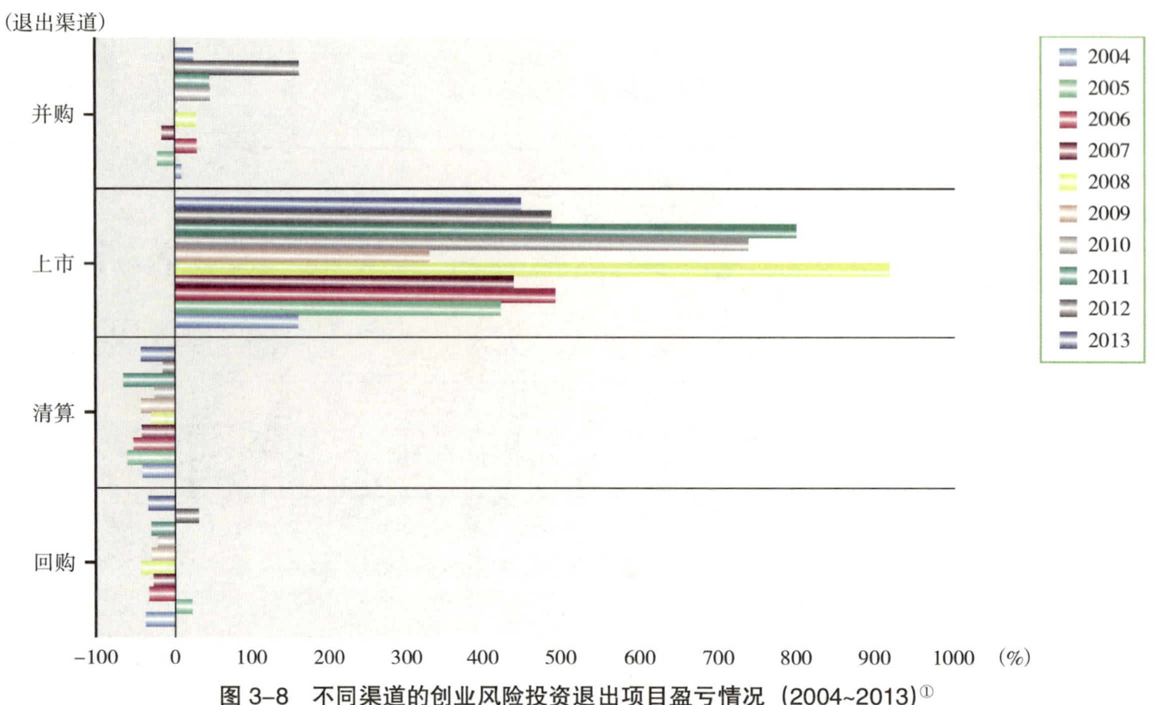

图 3-8 不同渠道的创业风险投资退出项目盈亏情况（2004~2013）[①]

3.5.3 中国创业风险投资不同行业退出的绩效表现

一般而言，创业风险投资行业的退出绩效呈现出“成三败七”的特点，往往需要用少数成功的投资项目来弥补多数的损失。但近年来，随着我国创业风险投资行业投资管理能力的逐步提升，项目的总体收率呈现上升趋势。

比较传统行业与高新技术行业的退出绩效可以看出，大部分情况下高新技术行业尽管面临着更高的投资风险，但投资盈利比例明显高于传统行业。但在 2013 年传统行业的投资盈利比例首次超过了高新技术行业（见表 3-9、图 3-9、表 3-10、图 3-10）。受 2013 年整体经济环境影响，无论是高新技术行业还是传统行业，盈利比例均较 2012 年大幅下滑。

表 3-9 高新技术行业创业风险投资退出项目盈亏状况（2007~2013）[①] 单位：%

行业 \ 年份	2007	2008	2009	2010	2011	2012	2013
盈利	41.43	37.86	39.06	38.97	52.87	55.62	32.13
亏损	58.57	62.14	60.94	61.03	47.13	44.38	67.87

① 有效样本数为 449 份。

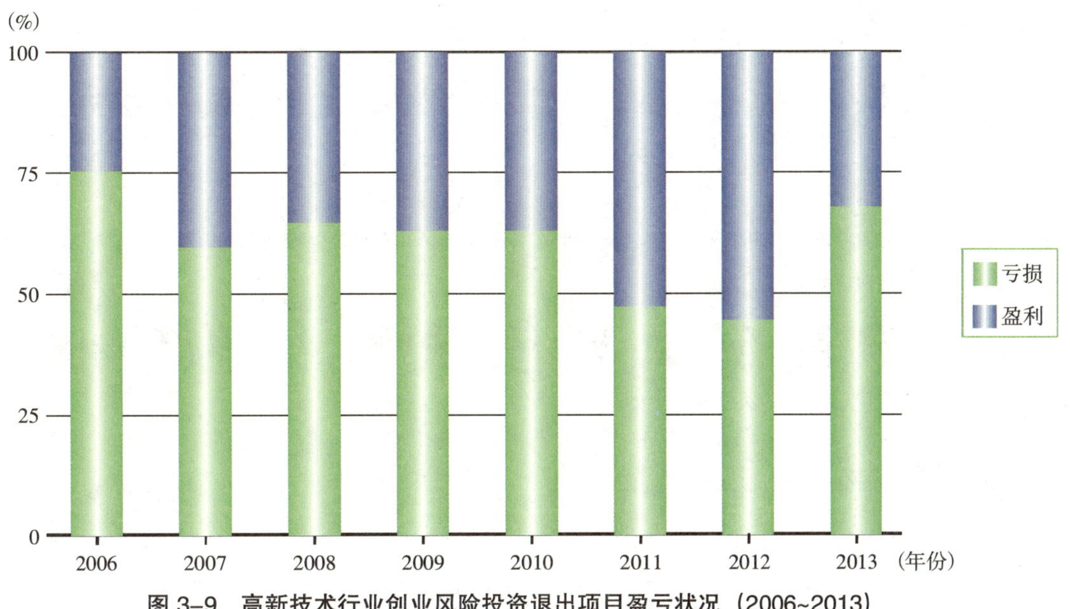

图 3-9 高新技术行业创业风险投资退出项目盈亏状况（2006~2013）

表 3-10 传统行业创业风险投资退出项目盈亏状况（2007~2013）①　　单位：%

年份 行业	2007	2008	2009	2010	2011	2012	2013
盈利	32.14	27.91	32.79	34.33	48.48	50.00	35.45
亏损	67.86	72.09	67.21	65.67	51.52	50.00	64.55

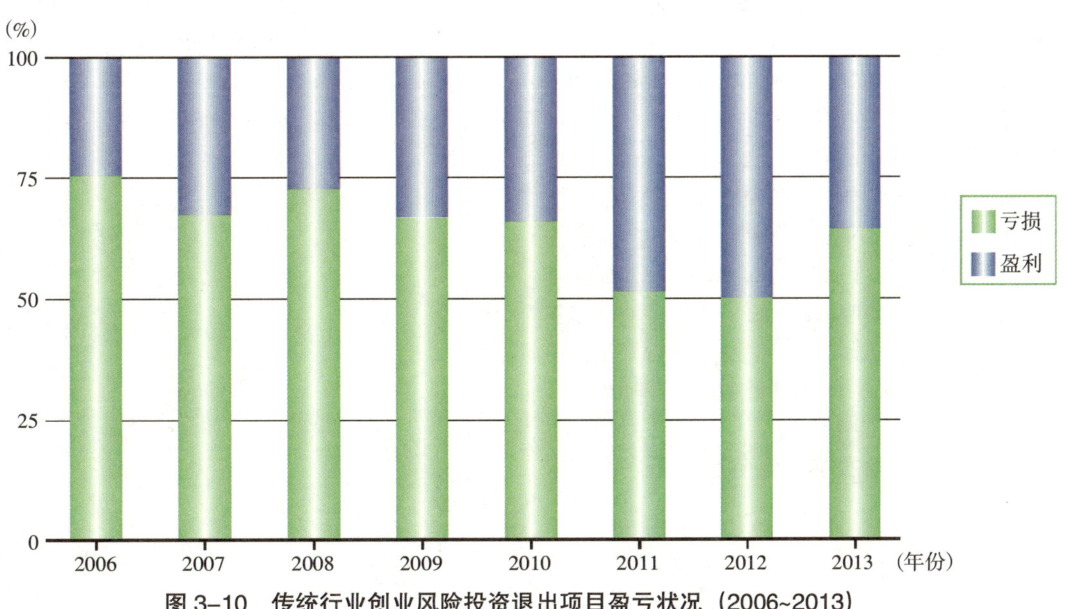

图 3-10 传统行业创业风险投资退出项目盈亏状况（2006~2013）

① 有效样本数为 189 份。

4 中国创业风险投资的绩效

4.1 中国创业风险投资机构的收入

4.1.1 中国创业风险投资机构的收入

2013 年，披露信息的 870 家创业风险投资机构的主营业务总收入达到 172.88 亿元，平均收入 1987.16 万元，较 2012 年上升 19.42%（见表 4–1）。

表 4–1 中国创业风险投资机构的收入状况（2009~2013）

年度	总收入（亿元）	披露信息机构数量（家）	平均收入（万元）
2009	61.05	321	1901.82
2010	173.58	569	3050.58
2011	106.89	581	1839.75
2012	120.97	727	1664.01
2013	172.88	870	1987.16

研究发现，所有制形式、机构类型、获得政府资助等方面不同的机构，收入表现出明显的差异。

首先，国有机构收入更高。按照创业风险投资机构的所有制形式划分，22 家外资机构企业的平均收入为 597.41 万元，255 家国有机构的平均收入为 2548.58 万元；其他 595 家非外资、非国有的机构平均收入为 1797.29 万元。

其次，公司制机构收入更高。按照创业风险投资机构的注册类型划分，16 家事业单位平均收入仅为 706.43 万元，170 家合伙制机构平均收入为 880.87 万元，630 家有限责任公司平均收入为 1845.95 万元，25 家股份有限公司平均收入为 13601.05 万元，29 家其他类型企业平均收入为 64799.94 万元。

最后，获得政府资金资助的机构收入更高。297 家得到政府资金支持的创业风险投资机构的平均主营业务收入为 1948.97 万元，527 家未得到政府资金资助的机构平均主营业务收入为 1978.81 万元，46 家未填写是否得到政府资金资助的创业风险投资机构的平均主营业务收入为 2329.34 万元，政府资金对于创业风险投资机构主营业务收入具有积极作用。

4.1.2 中国不同规模创业风险投资机构的收入特征[①]

2013 年，按机构管理资本规模从低到高，将创业风险投资机构划分为 5 组，统计不同规模创业风险投资机构的平均收入及不同规模机构收入占总收入的比重（见表 4–2）。

① 有效样本数为 1009 份。

表 4-2 中国创业风险投资机构收入的规模分布（2009~2013）

年份	机构规模（亿元）	≤0.5	0.5~1	1~2	2~5	≥5
2009	平均收入（万元）	9163.5	1090.1	17038.1	4774.5	5021.8
	占总收入比重（%）	26.8	3.5	44.7	13.6	11.4
2010	平均收入（万元）	1096.4	6361.3	4134.2	14877.4	6578.8
	占总收入比重（%）	3.1	25.1	10.9	40.8	20.1
2011	平均收入（万元）	694.4	486.7	983.9	2777.6	5577.4
	占总收入比重（%）	8.7	6.4	9.8	28.6	46.4
2012	平均收入（万元）	916.0	593.1	1224.9	1190.6	6794.9
	占总收入比重（%）	10.8	7.9	13.7	14.8	52.8
2013	平均收入（万元）①	443.4	945.4	1406.6	3150.7	7896.3
	占总收入比重（%）②	4.7	10.1	12.3	31.9	41.1

2013 年，中国创业风险投资机构收入分布具有如下特征：

首先，机构平均收入与机构规模正相关。管理资本 5000 万元以下的机构平均收入最低，为 443.4 万元，管理资本超过 5 亿元的机构平均收入最高，达到 7896.3 万元，是前者的十几倍。

其次，与 2012 年相比，大部分组的平均收入有所上升，其中增幅最大的是管理资本 2 亿~5 亿元的机构，增幅达到 164.63%，但是管理资本 5000 万元以下的机构平均收入出现大幅下降，降幅达到 51.59%。

最后，大型创业风险投资机构收入占比依然较高，2013 年，管理资本 2 亿元以上的机构收入占总收入的比重达到 73%，低于 2011 年，但仍然是各个组别中最高的；管理资本规模越小的创业风险投资机构组别，收入占总收入的比重就越低，其中管理资本 5000 万元以下的机构总收入占全国的比重仅为 4.7%。

4.1.3 中国创业风险投资机构的收入来源结构

2013 年，492 家③创业风险投资机构披露主营业务收入，其中，股权转让增值收入占全部收入的 51.1%，分红收入占 18.6%，管理费、咨询费收入占 16.0%，其他收入占 14.3%（见图 4-1）。与 2012 年相比，股权转让增值收入有所下降，其他三个渠道的收入均不同程度上升，其中分红收入占比上升了 13.1 个百分点，管理费和咨询费收入占比上升幅度较小。

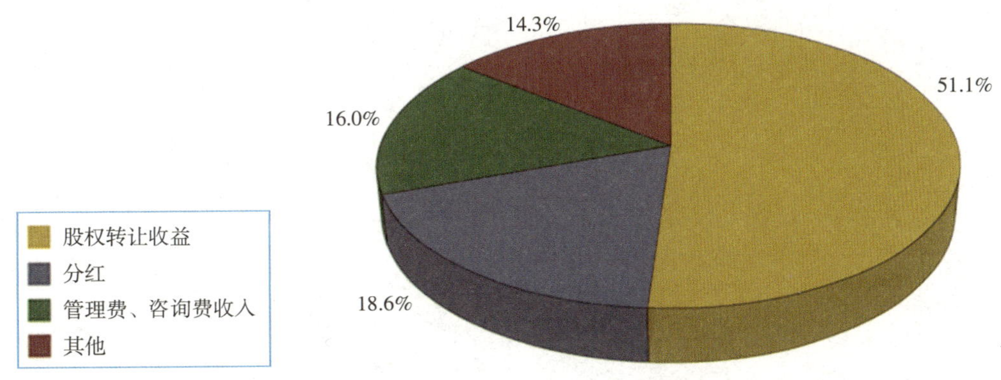

图 4-1 中国创业风险投资机构收入来源比例（2013）

① 有效样本数为 782 份。
② 有效样本数为 782 份。
③ 仅包括收入大于 0 且各项收入占比之和等于 100%的机构。

近年来，股权转让增值和分红收入对创业风险投资机构的贡献逐年增加，在一定程度上说明，随着资本市场的建设和完善，创业风险投资机构从长期的投资中获得的回报增长迅速。而 2013 年，股权转让增值收入占比下降从反面证明了退出渠道对创业风险投资机构收入结构的影响。2012 年 11 月 16 日，IPO 第八次暂停导致 2013 年全年被投资企业退出渠道出现断崖式收窄，从而股权转让增值收入占比从上一年的超过 70%下降为 50%。

4.1.4 中国创业风险投资机构当年收入的最大来源①

2013 年统计调查显示，中国创业风险投资机构最大收入来源分布与往年相比，未发生显著的结构变化。其中，以股权转让为最大收入来源的机构占 37.1%，较上年有所上升，恢复到接近 2011 年的水平；以分红为最大收入来源的创业风险投资机构占 15.0%，再次出现下降；以管理（顾问）费为最大收入来源的创业风险投资机构比例为 21.2%，较上年微弱下降；以咨询服务收入为最大收入来源的创业风险投资机构占比为 6.2%，连续两年均下降超过 1 个百分点；以其他收入为最大收入来源的创业风险投资机构占比为 20.5%（见图 4-2、表 4-3）。2013 年，创业投资机构的核心主营业务保持在较重要位置，连续三年有一半以上的创业风险投资机构的最大收入来源于股权收益和分红两个主要项目。

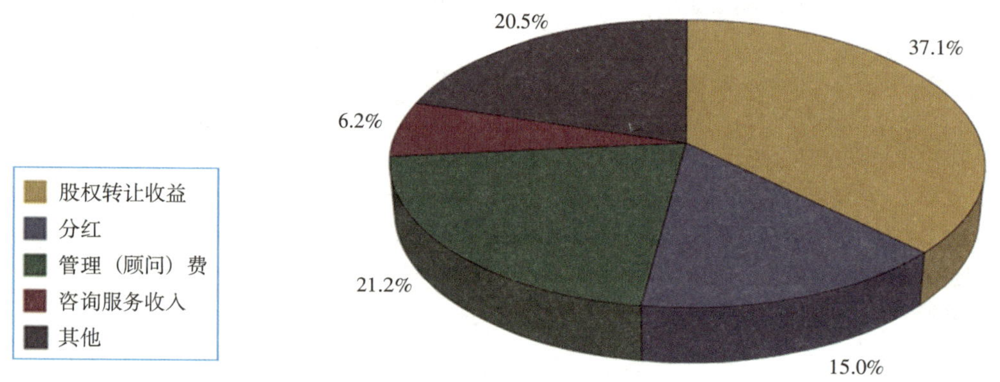

图 4-2 中国创业风险投资机构的最大收入来源（2013）

表 4-3 中国创业风险投资机构的最大收入来源（2009~2013） 单位：%

年份 \ 收入来源	股权转让	分红	管理（顾问）费	咨询服务费	其他
2009	33.8	17.4	20.7	9.1	19.0
2010	34.4	14.1	21.1	11.4	19.0
2011	36.8	15.5	21.6	8.7	17.3
2012	34.1	16.5	21.6	7.3	20.5
2013	37.1	15.0	21.2	6.2	20.5

近年来，中国创业风险投资机构的收入来源已经趋于稳定，越来越多的机构通过创业风险投资的核心业务，即股权收益和分红收益获得其最大的营收，这说明行业发展已经日趋成熟与稳定。

① 有效样本数为 1009 份。

4.2 中国创业风险投资项目的收益情况

4.2.1 中国创业风险投资项目的主营业务收入[①]

据统计，2013 年中国创业风险投资机构当年新增投资项目 1501 个，披露主营业务收入情况的项目 917 个，这些项目的主营业务收入具有以下特征（见表 4-4、图 4-3）：

（1）中国创业风险投资项目的主营业务收入表现为“W”形分布，其中，主营业务收入 100 万元以下和 5000 万元以上的项目占比较高，分别占到 29.9%和 38.6%，其他组别的项目分布相对平均，100 万~500 万元和 1000 万~3000 万元项目占比超过 10%，分别为 10.7%和 10.4%。

（2）从历年的变化趋势可以看出，主营业务收入大于 5000 万元的项目比例始终最高，2009 年以来连续上升，2011 年达到历史最高后经过连续两年下降到 38.6%；主营业务收入 500 万~1000 万元和 3000 万~5000 万元的项目比重始终是最低的两类，2013 年两类项目合计占比仅为 10.5%，其中 500 万~1000 万元的项目比重最低，仅为 4.6%；主营业务收入小于 100 万元的项目比重经过连续两年下滑后，2012 年、2013 年均出现较大幅度提高，上升到 29.9%，是各类项目中上升幅度最大的。

（3）2013 年，中国创业风险投资机构对大项目的偏好有所减弱，占比增长的主要是主营业务收入相对小的项目，如主营业务收入 100 万元以下、100 万~500 万元的项目占比分别增长了 9.6 个和 3 个百分点，而主营业务收入 3000 万~5000 万元和 5000 万元以上的项目占比分别下降了 0.8 个和 11.3 个百分点。

表 4-4 创业风险投资项目的主营业务收入分布（2009~2013） 单位：%

年份 \ 收入（万元）	<100	100~500	500~1000	1000~3000	3000~5000	>5000
2009	33.9	9.4	7.1	7.6	7.0	34.9
2010	29.1	6.8	5.0	12.3	4.8	41.9
2011	14.9	6.7	4.7	10.0	5.4	58.3
2012	20.3	7.7	5.5	9.8	6.7	49.9
2013	29.9	10.7	4.6	10.4	5.9	38.6

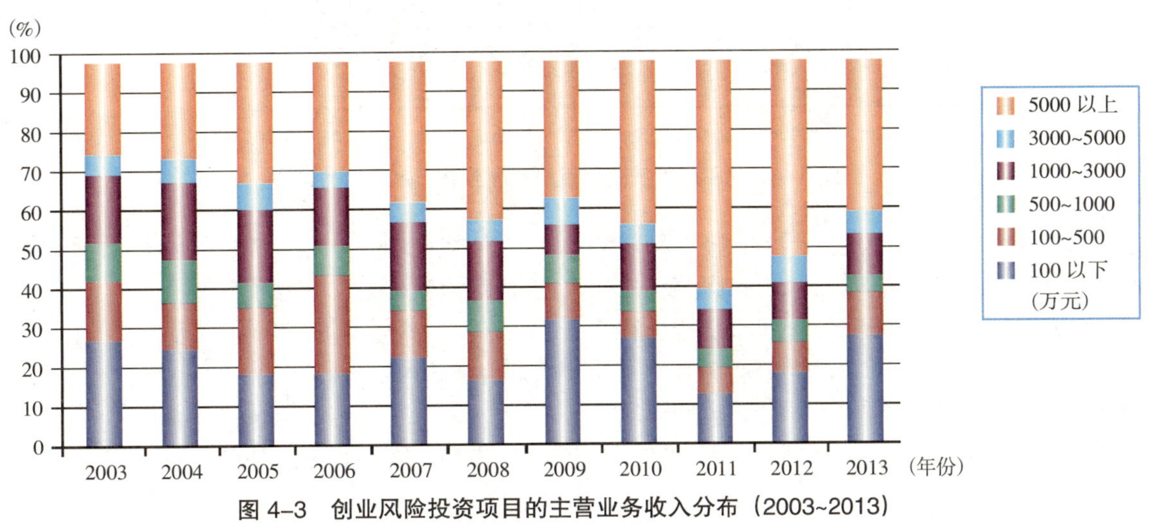

图 4-3 创业风险投资项目的主营业务收入分布（2003~2013）

① 有效样本数为 936 份。

4.2.2　中国创业风险投资项目的利润①

2013 年，中国创业风险投资项目的利润分布总体依然呈现为“U”形，利润超过 1000 万元以上和亏损的项目占比较高，分别为 32.1%和 39.1%，其他项目占比均未超过 10%（见表 4-5、图 4-4）。

其中，亏损项目比重连续两年大幅提高，较 2011 年上升了近 20 个百分点；利润不超过 100 万元的项目比重经过连续 7 年下降后，连续两年均提高了 0.8 个百分点，2013 年达 9.7%；利润在 100 万~300 万元和 300 万~500 万元的项目比重基本与 2012 年持平，均下降了 0.1 个百分点；利润 500 万~1000 万元的项目比重下降了 2 个百分点。

表 4-5　中国创业风险投资项目的利润分布（2009~2013）　　单位：%

利润（万元）/年份	亏损	0~100	100~300	300~500	500~1000	>1000
2009	38.6	13.3	5.9	2.8	4.8	34.6
2010	31.2	10.4	7.4	5.1	7.4	38.6
2011	19.6	8.1	7.3	4.2	7.6	53.2
2012	27.2	8.9	8.1	5.8	7.5	42.6
2013	39.1	9.7	8.0	5.7	5.5	32.1

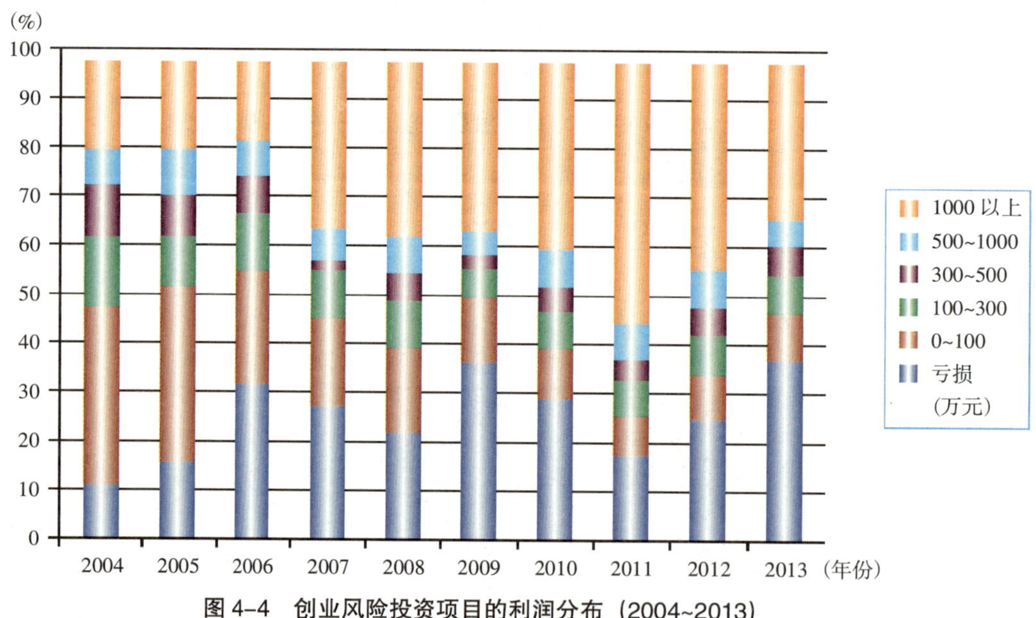

图 4-4　创业风险投资项目的利润分布（2004~2013）

金融危机的爆发使得创投机构对亏损及低利润项目投资比重增加，随着全球经济逐渐复苏，创投机构对亏损项目的投资比重有所下降，但是从 2012 年开始，中国的创投机构对亏损项目投资比重又出现持续增加。这与中国经济持续低迷关系密切，经济走低导致创投机构难以找到成长性较高的项目投资。此外，中国的创业环境不断完善，也为创投发现初创项目提供了良好的基础，这也会促使创投机构投资亏损和低利润项目增加。

4.2.3　中国创业风险投资项目主营业务收入与利润的关系

2013 年，中国创业风险投资机构投资项目②的平均利润率整体下降，主营业务收入 5000 万元以上的项目平均

① 有效样本数为 917 份。
② 有效样本数为 910 份。

利润率最高为 8.1%，但远低于上年；主营业务收入为 1000 万~3000 万元和 3000 万~5000 万元的项目平均利润率分别为 6.8%和 3.0%，也出现了大幅下降；但是，主营业务收入为 100 万~500 万元和 500 万~1000 万元的项目平均利润率较上年有所提高，分别为-39.1%和-6.2%。主营业务收入较小的项目通常都处于亏损状态（见图 4-5）。

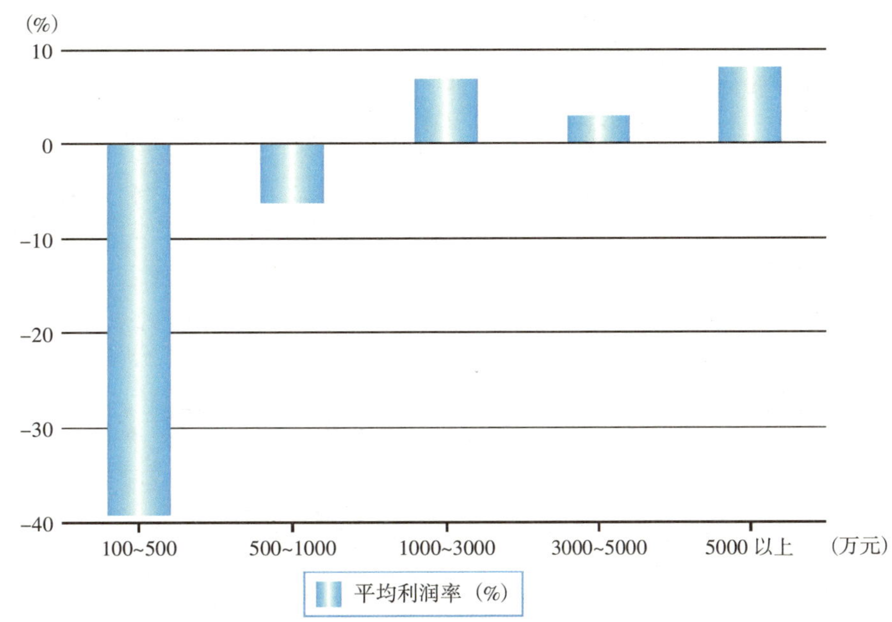

图 4-5 不同主营业务收入的创业风险投资项目平均利润率（2013）

根据项目主营业务收入不同来划分创业风险投资项目的规模发现，随着项目规模的增加，项目的利润率也在增加，但是当项目达到一定规模时，项目利润率反而可能下降。2013 年，主营业务收入 3000 万~5000 万元的项目平均利润率低于主营业务更小的组别，但当主营业务收入达到 5000 万元时，平均利润率又有所提高。

2009~2013 年，不同主营业务收入规模的创业风险投资项目的平均主营业务收入和平均利润关系具有如下特点（见表 4-6）：

（1）规模较小的项目出现亏损的可能性更大，其中，主营业务收入在 1000 万元以下的项目平均利润均为负，且项目规模越小，亏损越严重；主营业务收入 100 万~500 万元的项目已经连续五年为负平均利润，而主营业务收入在 500 万~1000 万元的项目平均利润也连续两年为负，1000 万元以上的项目平均利润继续保持正值。

（2）主营业务收入规模中等的项目与宏观经济环境的关系密切，金融危机对这部分项目的影响最大，这部分项目的平均利润总体上均随着金融危机爆发而出现下滑，在全球经济逐步复苏过程中有所提升，但近两年中国经济疲软又导致了这部分项目平均利润再次出现连续下滑。2013 年，主营业务收入 1000 万~3000 万元和 3000 万~5000 万元的项目平均利润均出现大幅下降，分别从 316 万元和 497 万元下降到 130 万元和 121 万元。

（3）2013 年，主营业务收入在 5000 万元以上的项目平均利润止跌回升，从上一年的 4192 万元增长到 5266 万元。

表 4–6 不同主营业务收入的创业风险投资项目的平均主营业务收入和平均利润（2009~2013） 单位：万元

主营业务收入（万元）		≤100	100~500	500~1000	1000~3000	3000~5000	>5000
2009 年	平均销售收入	10	270	785	1986	3975	51668
	平均利润	–45	–37	185	218	743	7007
2010 年	平均销售收入	11	249	751	1884	4200	51994
	平均利润	–39	–62	108	342	1109	7060
2011 年	平均主营业务收入	13	281	759	1971	3951	62777
	平均利润	–123	–15	114	270	593	5739
2012 年	平均主营业务收入	13	281	729	2170	4030	37292
	平均利润	58	–135	–52	316	497	4192
2013 年	平均主营业务收入①	13	253	776	1915	4040	64047
	平均利润②	–477	–99	–48	130	121	5266

4.3 中国创业风险投资项目的总体运行与趋势

4.3.1 中国创业风险投资项目总体运行情况

截至 2013 年底，中国创业风险投资机构③累计投资项目达到 12149 项，其中，65.9%继续运行，较上年有小幅下降；已上市和准备上市的项目分别占 6.6%和 10.6%，较 2012 年均有所下降；原股东（创业者）收购和管理层收购项目比重分别为 8.7%和 2.7%，均出现了不同程度的提高；被其他机构收购项目比重为 3.9%；清算的项目比重为 1.7%（见图 4–6）。

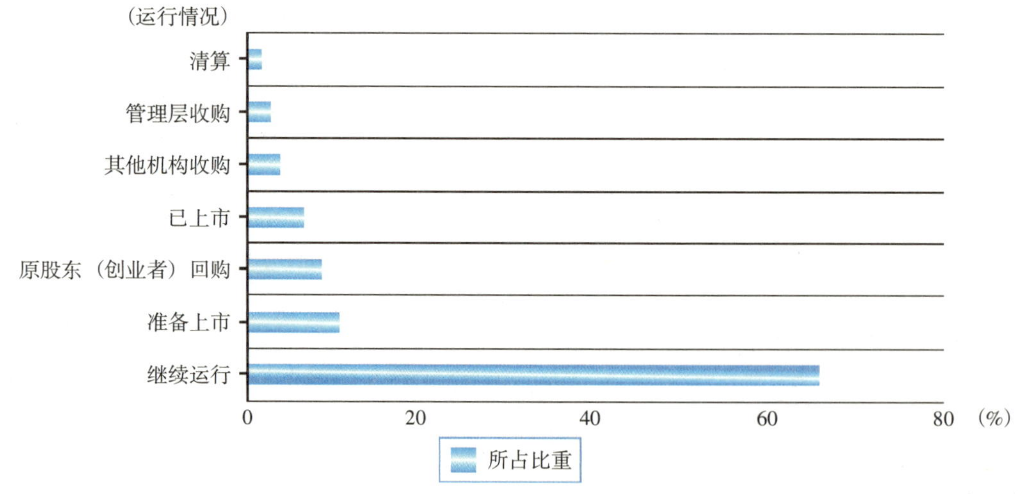

图 4–6 截至 2013 年年底累计被投资项目的总体运行状况（合项）

① 有效样本数为 936 份。
② 有效样本数为 968 份。
③ 有效样本数为 949 份。

4.3.2 中国创业风险投资项目总体运行趋势

2013 年，中国创业风险投资机构累计投资项目的运行趋势表现出如下特征（见表 4-7、图 4-7）：

（1）继续运行项目比重下降明显，较 2012 年略有下滑，下降 0.25 个百分点；准备上市项目占比连续两年下降，其中准备境内上市项目占比下降到 10.2%，准备境外上市的项目占比下降到 0.4%。

（2）成功上市的比例再次下降，其中境内上市项目占比下降到 5.7%，境外上市项目占比则仅为 0.9%，境内股票市场 IPO 暂停与国际资本市场中国概念股财务造假的负面消息严重影响了被投资项目的上市进程。

（3）五种不同类型的收购占比有明显上升，管理层收购项目占比上升了 1.7 个百分点，仅境外收购项目占比下降了 0.01 个百分点，这种下降趋势从国际金融危机以来始终未发生改变。

（4）被清算的项目占比经过连续四年下降后出现小幅回升，2013 年达到 1.66%。

表 4-7 截至年底累计被投资项目的总体运行状况（2009~2013） 单位：%

被投资项目运行情况 / 年份	已上市		准备上市		被收购			原股东收购	管理层收购	继续运行	清算
	境内	境外	境内	境外	境内上市公司	境内非上市公司或自然人	境外收购				
2009	4.61	1.76	9.94	0.49	0.54	4.00	0.35	13.24	1.01	60.78	3.28
2010	5.86	1.66	16.39	0.95	0.61	4.05	0.37	10.56	0.94	56.14	2.47
2011	6.74	1.53	15.70	0.43	0.32	3.34	0.22	7.96	1.42	60.62	1.72
2012	6.66	1.37	12.37	0.39	0.32	3.04	0.12	7.19	0.96	66.18	1.38
2013	5.71	0.88	10.19	0.38	0.55	3.20	0.11	8.66	2.73	65.93	1.66

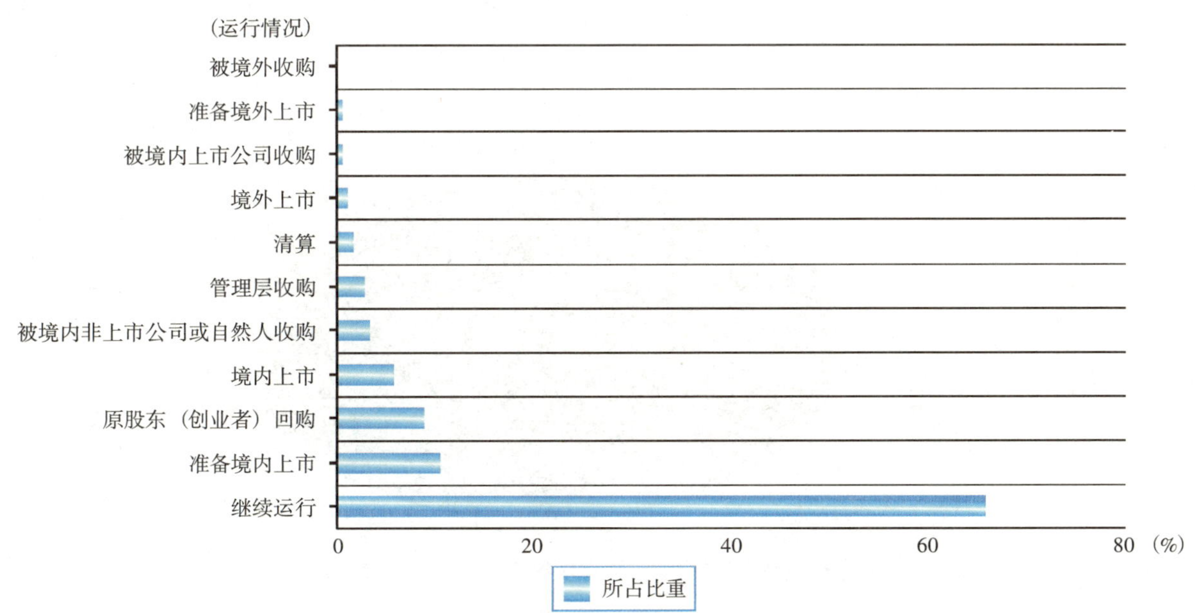

图 4-7 截至 2013 年年底累计被投资项目的总体运行状况（2009~2013）

近年来，当年实际上市项目占比与上一年准备上市项目占比之间的差距始终较大，2013 年虽然有所改善，但二者的差距依然超过 6%，也就是说大约一半准备上市的项目经过一年运营后未能实现上市。

4.4 中国创业风险投资机构的总体运行情况评价

4.4.1 中国创业风险投资机构对自身发展状况的评价①

2013 年的调查调整了问卷选项，细化了对自身发展、全行业发展、未来投资前景状况的评价，同时要求创业投资机构负责人填写有关选项，提高了调查结果的科学性。

1026 家创业风险投资机构对自身发展情况做出的评价较明显地服从正偏态分布，即对当年自身发展状况持乐观评价的机构占比明显高于悲观评价的机构。

据统计，2013 年有超过一半的创业风险投资机构认为自身发展较为乐观，其中包括 3.31%的机构认为自身发展状况非常好，11.79%的机构认为自身发展状况好，36.06%的机构认为自身发展状况较好，总体评价远高于 2012 年（见表 4–8、图 4–8）。

金融危机以来，创业风险投资机构对自身机构评价逐渐悲观，2010 年有所改善，但 2011 年和 2012 年持乐观态度的机构占比连续大幅下降。2013 年，受到国际国内资本市场回暖的影响，持乐观态度的机构数占比出现反弹。

表 4–8 创业风险投资机构对自身发展状况的评价（2013） 单位：%

评价	非常好	好	较好	一般	较差	差	非常差
占比	3.31	11.79	36.06	42.30	3.90	2.14	0.49

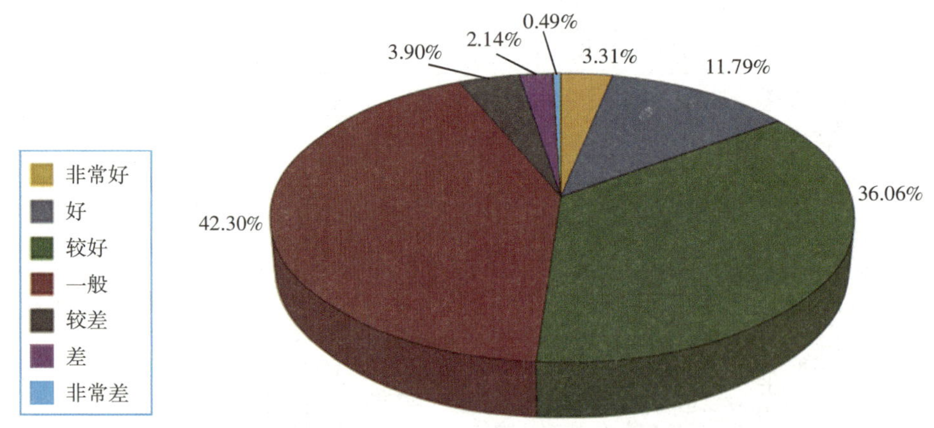

图 4–8 创业风险投资机构对自身发展状况的评价（2013）

① 有效样本数为 1026 份。

4.4.2 中国创业风险投资机构对全行业发展情况的评价[①]

1027 家创业风险投资机构对全行业发展情况做出的评价完全符合正态分布，认为一般的机构占比高达 48.10%，认为较好和较差的分别占 23.95%和 12.56%，认为好和差的分别占 5.45%和 7.40%；认为非常好和非常差的占比相当，均为 1.27%。

但是持乐观态度的机构占比仍然高于持悲观态度的机构，认为全行业整体发展非常好、好以及较好的机构占比达到 30.67%，认为全行业发展非常差、差和较差的机构占比为 21.23%（见表 4-9、图 4-9）。

与 2012 年相比，2013 年创业风险投资机构对全行业发展的判断有所改善，调查显示，一半以上的机构认为 2012 年全行业整体发展状况差，首次出现比例连续上升的情况。仅有 11.2%和 38.1%的机构认为全行业整体发展状况好和持平，均是历年来最低水平。机构对行业整体评价说明，当前总体经济状况欠佳对创业投资行业发展带来极为严重的负面影响，全行业发展处于困难时期。

表 4-9 中国创业风险投资机构对全行业的整体评价（2013） 单位：%

整体评价	非常好	好	较好	一般	较差	差	非常差
占比	1.27	5.45	23.95	48.10	12.56	7.40	1.27

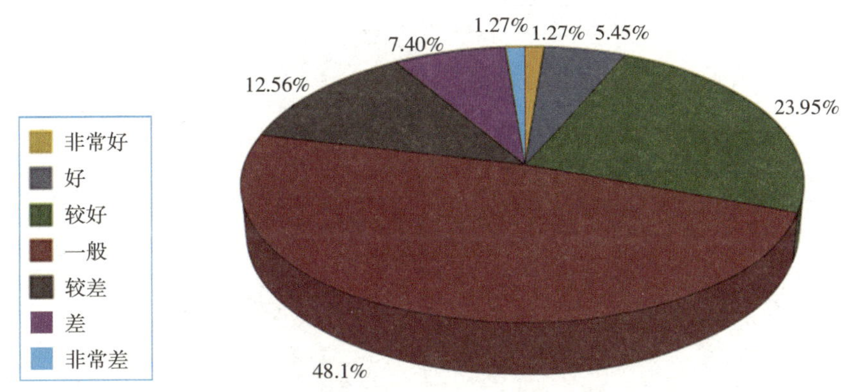

图 4-9 创业风险投资机构对全行业的整体评价（2013）

4.4.3 中国创业风险投资机构对 2014 年投资前景的预测[②]

对于 2014 年投资前景，中国创业风险投资机构给出了较为乐观的预测，超过一半的机构看好未来前景，其中 2.0%的机构认为前景非常好，11.3%的机构认为前景好，43.3%的机构认为前景较好。认为前景较为不好的机构仅占 3.3%，认为不好的机构仅为 1.9%（见表 4-10、图 4-10）。

国际金融危机以来，对下一年度创业风险投资前景持乐观预测的机构比例持续下降。经过几年调整，2012 年，创业风险投资机构对中国资本市场的预期下跌到低点，但是由于中国资本市场 IPO 再次重启以及全球市场的持续回暖，创业风险投资机构对 2014 年的预期明显向好。

① 有效样本数为 1027 份。
② 有效样本数为 1205 份。

表 4-10 创业风险投资机构对 2013 年投资前景的预测

单位：%

整体评价	非常好	好	较好	一般	较为不好	不好	非常不好
比重	2.0	11.3	43.3	37.9	3.3	1.9	0.3

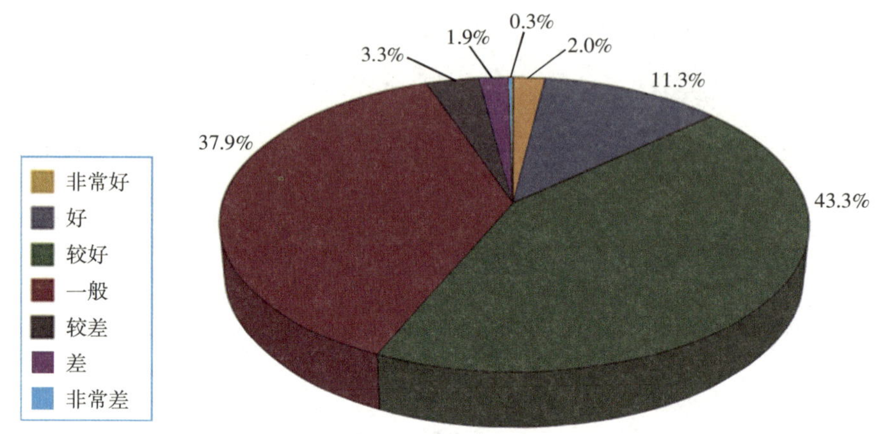

图 4-10 创业风险投资机构对 2014 年创业投资前景的评价

5 中国创业风险投资的经营管理

5.1 中国创业风险投资的项目来源

根据对 2013 年我国创业风险投资机构的调查显示①，与 2011 年和 2012 年相比，项目来源总体上并没有发生实质性的变化，但呈现出了一些新的特点（见表 5-1、图 5-1）。

（1）创业风险投资项目的前三大信息来源依然是“政府部门推荐”、“朋友介绍”以及“项目中介介绍”，三者占比合计 64.5%，较 2011 年、2012 年的 62.6%和 63%有所上升。其中，“政府部门推荐”仍然是创投行业首要的项目来源，但是所占比重有所下降，而“朋友介绍”和“项目中介介绍”所占比重却有所上升，尤其是“朋友介绍”增长至 19.9%。

（2）来源于“股东推荐”项目与 2012 年相比持平，而来源于“项目业主”的项目略有下降，其所占的比重从 2012 年的 11.5%跌至 10.1%。表明项目来源于股东和客户两方面的作用趋于稳定。

（3）来源于“银行介绍”的项目所占比重持续了之前的下降趋势，说明银行对于我国创业风险投资的关注和综合作用正在稳步下降。而“媒体宣传”所占比重则出现了明显反弹。这与众筹等项目媒体的兴起有很大联系。

（4）来源于“其他”的项目比重出现明显上升，相比 2011 年的 2.1%、2012 年的 3.2%上升到了 3.6%。这说明创业风险投资的项目来源渠道正在变得多样化。

表 5-1 创业风险投资机构获取项目信息来源渠道（2008~2013） 单位：%

年份 \ 信息渠道	政府部门推荐	朋友介绍	项目中介机构	股东推荐	项目业主	银行介绍	其他	媒体宣传
2008	25.7	17.7	16.1	13.6	15.5	5.6	2.8	2.9
2009	25.9	19.1	16.1	13.4	13.0	6.6	2.9	3.0
2010	26.2	17.9	18.5	13.2	11.3	7.2	2.7	2.9
2011	25.4	18.7	18.5	13.3	11.7	7.4	2.1	2.8
2012	25.2	19.2	18.6	13.2	11.5	6.9	3.2	2.2
2013	25.5	19.9	19.1	13.2	10.1	6.0	3.6	2.6

① 有效样本数为 1062 份。

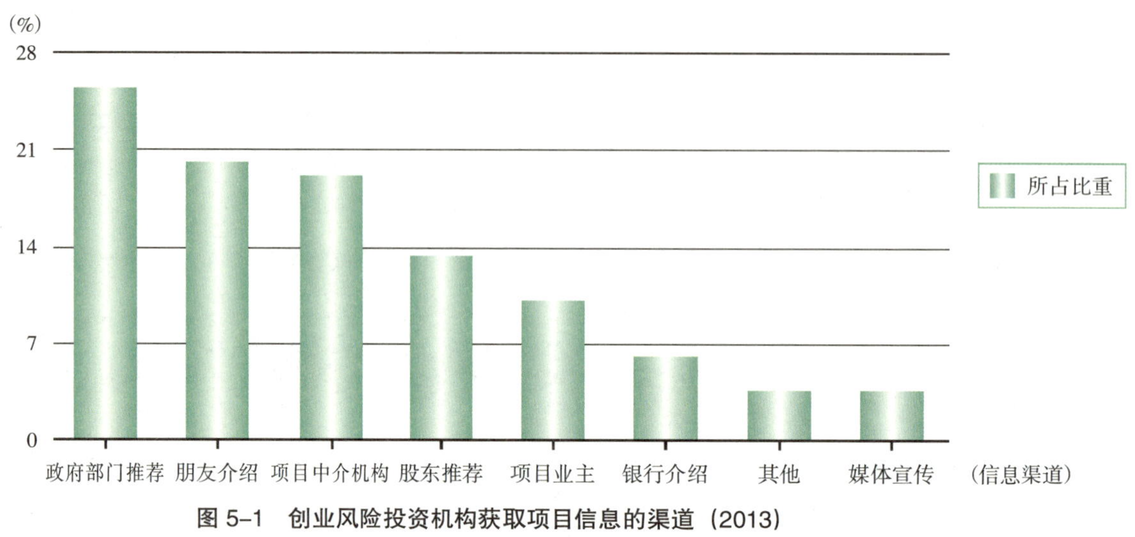

图 5-1 创业风险投资机构获取项目信息的渠道（2013）

5.2 中国创业风险投资的决策要素

调查结果显示①（见图 5-2），2013 年各要素影响创投机构投资决策的重要程度排序比 2012 年略有变化。其中，“市场前景”仍然是创业风险投资机构投资所考虑的首要因素，且较 2012 年略微下降，降至 24.1%。这表明创业风险投资机构投资对于被投项目的市场前景非常看重。对于“管理团队”因素，仍然和上年一样位居第二位，其所占比重仍保持在 22.5%。“技术因素”占比 12.7%，居于影响中国创投决策要素的第三位。而“盈利模式”仍然排位第四，但是保持了持续的下降趋势，降至 12.4%。“财务状况”、“股权价格”、“公司治理结构”以及“资信状况”和 2012 年相比排序没有发生变化，但“财务状况”、“资信状况”所占比例有所上升，分别升至 9.9%、3.2%。而“股权价格”和“公司治理结构”却出现了一定的下降，分别为 5.1%和 4.5%。这说明创业风险投资机构在 2013 年更为务实，重新开始加大对于“财务状况”和“资信状况”的关注。

此外，“竞争对手情况”和“投资地点”等因素相对 2012 年稳中有升，所占比重分别为 2.9%、2.1%。“中介服务机构”和“其他”对于投资决策而言，作用尽管仍然很小，但都有所上升，所占比重为 0.6%和 0.3%。

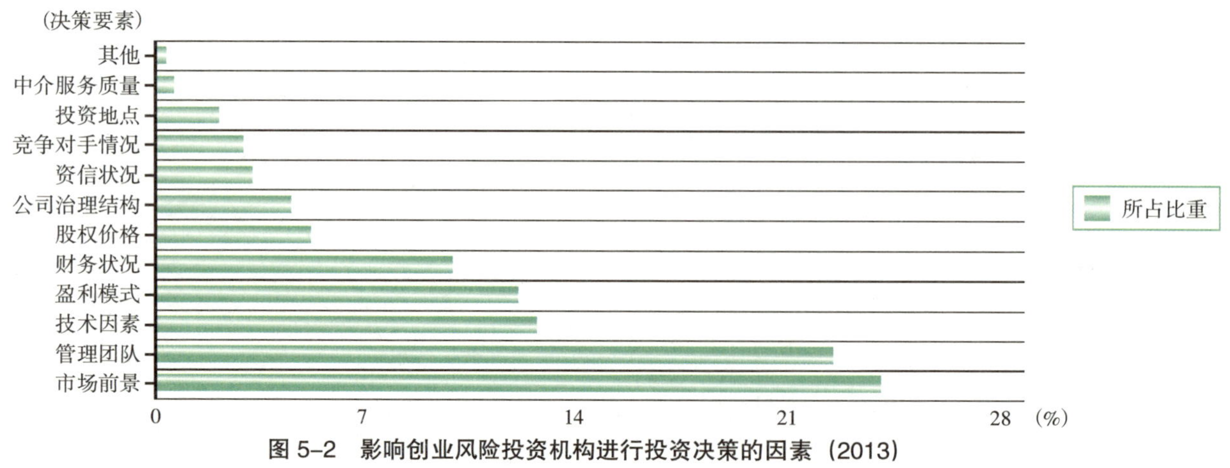

图 5-2 影响创业风险投资机构进行投资决策的因素（2013）

① 有效样本数为 1062 份。

5.3 中国创业风险投资对被投资项目的监管方式

调查显示[①]（见图 5-3），2013 年创业风险投资行业对被投项目的监管方式没有出现明显的变化。“提供管理咨询”仍然是创业风险投资机构监管投资项目的首要选择，但是相对 2012 年仍略有下降，降至 33.2%；通过获得“董事会席位”直接对被投资企业进行监管的占比依然位于第二位，与 2012 年大致持平；以“财务咨询”的监管方式相对 2012 年有所上升，升至 25.6%；“只限监管”与 2012 年大致持平，在 10.1%；选择通过“其他”监管方式的创业风险投资机构依然很少，所占比重为 2.2%，相比 2011 年和 2012 年都有所下降。综合来看，采用“董事会席位”监管方式的占比呈一直下降趋势，说明我国创业风险投资机构直接介入被投资项目经营的情况有弱化趋势，而采用其他间接监管方式的趋势在增强。

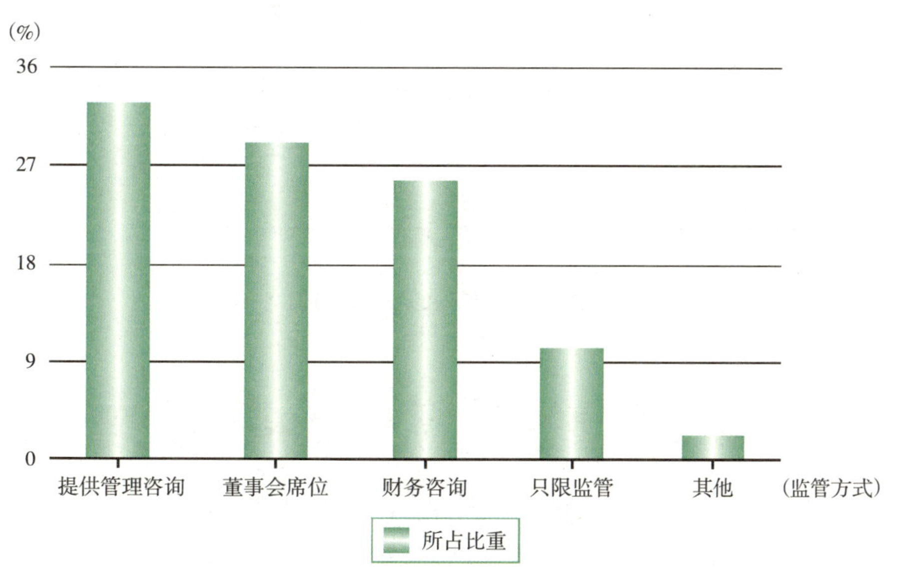

图 5-3 创业风险投资机构对被投资企业的监管方式（2013）

调查显示[②]（见表 5-2、图 5-4），2013 年创业风险投资机构对被投资项目的参股程度呈现以下特点：“一般参股”方式依然是大多数创投机构选择的方式，但与 2012 年大致持平，没有出现下跌趋势；与此同时，以“绝对控股”方式所占比重出现了这几年来最大的反弹，升至 5.20%；而以“相对控股”方式参股所占比重有所下降。这表明我国创业风险投资机构在股权控制上依旧是以非绝对控股为主。

① 有效样本数为 1055 份。
② 有效样本数为 1250 份。

表 5-2 创业风险投资机构股权参与程度（2008~2013） 单位：%

年份 \ 股权参与程度	绝对控股	相对控股	一般参股	其他
2008	3.90	15.70	80.00	0.40
2009	7.70	16.10	76.30	0.00
2010	3.70	12.10	84.20	0.00
2011	4.90	8.60	86.50	0.00
2012	4.37	11.02	84.61	0.00
2013	5.20	10.16	84.64	0.00

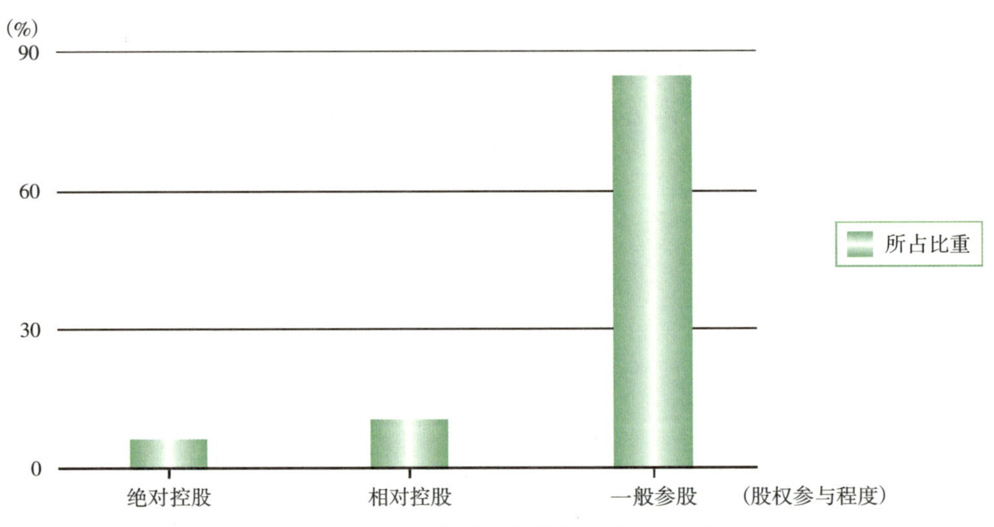

图 5-4 创业风险投资机构的股权参与程度（2013）

5.4 与创业风险投资经营管理有关的人力资源因素

调查显示①（见图 5-5），2013 年创业风险投资机构认为，从业人员缺乏的各项背景和能力的排序与 2012 年相比没有发生大幅度的结构性变化：

（1）“资本运作能力”依然被视为合格从业人员应具备的首要素质，但其所占比重有小幅度下降，相比 2011 年的 20.5%、2012 年的 21.2%，2013 年为 20.2%。此外，“技术背景”也较上年下降，降至 11.6%，打破了延续三年的上升趋势。

（2）“商务谈判能力”与“财务管理能力”两种因素所占比重与 2012 年相比有所提升，分别为 16.5%、16.1%。

（3）“判断力和洞察力”与“人际关系网络和协调能力”的因素，与 2012 年相比均有所下降，所占比重分别为 18.3%、15.2%。

综上所述，创业风险投资机构对合格从业人员所应具备素质的要求发生的变化是对 2013 年宏观经济环境和行业状况的反应。总的来看，由于 2013 年我国整体经济状况以及创业风险投资行业内部盘整，因而创业风险投资机构对合格人员所具备的素质提出了更高的要求。

① 有效样本数为 1057 份。

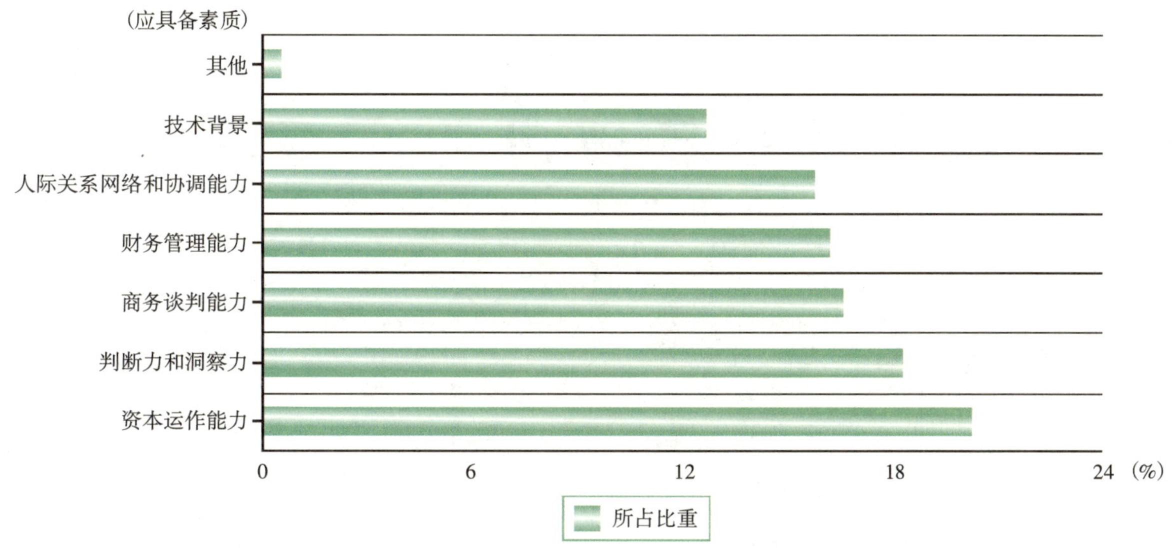

图 5-5 合格的创业风险投资人员应该具备的素质(2013)

调查显示[①](见图 5-6),2013 年创业风险投资机构认为从业人员缺乏的各项背景和能力的排序与 2012 年相比有较大差异。

(1)认为从业人员缺乏"技术评估"能力的机构占比相对 2012 年大幅度上升,增至 18.4%,且超过"资本运作"。与 2012 年相比,2013 年创业风险投资行业出现了新的技术浪潮,因而对于从业人员的"技术评估"能力要求骤升。

(2)认为从业人员缺乏"项目识别"、"企业管理"及"商务谈判能力"这三方面背景和能力的创业投资机构占比相比 2012 年均有所下降,分别下降至 15.1%、15.0%以及 6.1%。

(3)与 2012 年相比,认为"技术背景"、"法律知识"及"财务管理能力"这三方面缺乏的机构比重分别为 12.8%、9.2%和 7.2%。

由此可知,随着每年外界环境和行业的变化,创业风险投资机构对从业人员应该具备的素质和人员实际具备的素质都会发生变化,且两者之间存在着一定的差距。这表明,从业人员应及时根据环境变化调整自身的知识储备。

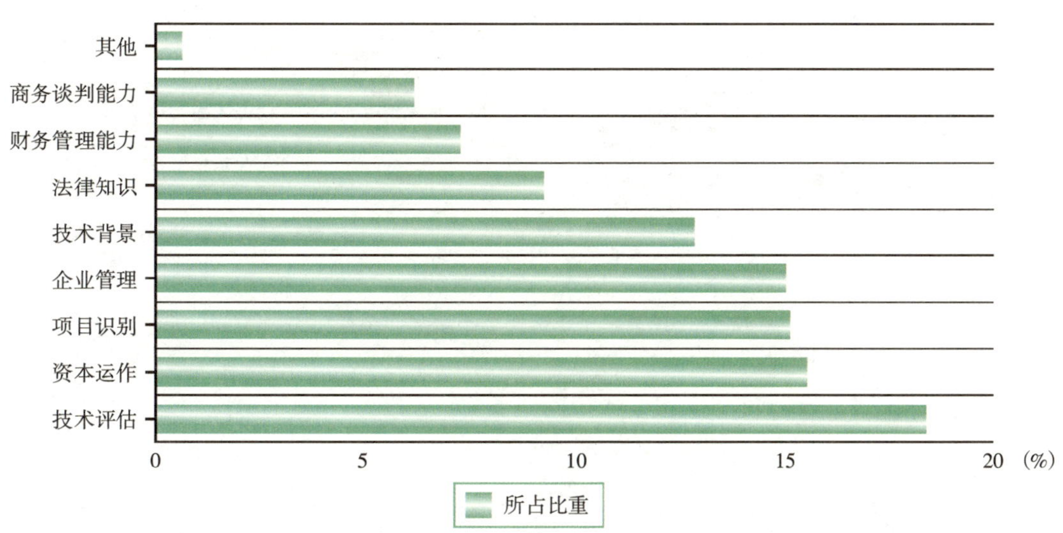

图 5-6 创业风险投资人员缺乏的专业知识(2013)

① 有效样本数为 1044 份。

5.5 投资效果不理想的主要原因

调查显示[①]（见图 5-7），2013 年投资效果不理想的主要原因发生了一些变化，其主要表现为：

（1）“政策环境变化”依然是导致投资效果不理想的首要因素，且其所占比重呈现出持续上升的趋势，从 2011 年的 17.4%、2012 年的 18.9%持续上升至 2013 年的 26.7%；“市场竞争”因素所占比重也较 2012 年的 17.4%上升了 0.5 个百分点。这表明 2013 年创业风险投资行业市场竞争程度日趋加剧，政策环境影响始终存在。

（2）“退出渠道不畅”这一因素由 2012 年的排名第四位跃至 2013 年的排名第二位影响创业风险投资机构投资效果的因素，并且占比高达 26.6%。而“内部管理水平有限”及“技术不成熟”作为导致投资效果不理想的因素相比 2012 年有所下降，占比分别降至 8.2%和 6.8%。说明自 2012 年 10 月起的 IPO 关闭对于创业风险投资产业的整体影响比较显著。“内部管理水平”和“技术不成熟”的占比分别为 8.2%和 6.8%，相比 2012 年分别下降了 8.4%和 5.6%。这说明我国创业风险投资市场正在日趋成熟，对于“内部管理水平”和“技术不成熟”导致的投资影响可以进行较为有效的管控。

（3）2013 年，造成投资不理想的主要原因中，“其他”因素所占比重略有上升，增至 4.6%，超过了“缺乏诚信”因素。而“缺乏诚信”因素所占比重出现了大幅度的下滑，从 2011 年的 10%、2012 年的 8.4%下滑至 2013 年的 3.1%。说明我国投资行业所面临的诚信状况正在日益改善。

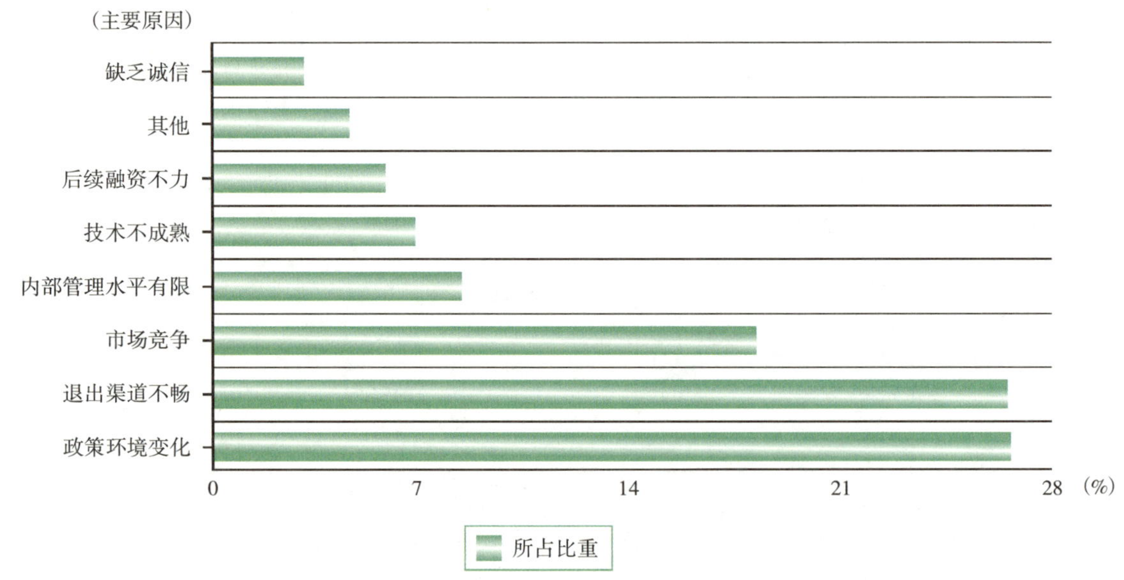

图 5-7 创业风险投资机构投资效果不理想的主要原因（2013）

① 有效样本数 989 份。

5.6 中国创业风险投资机构的预期持股时间

调查显示[①]（见图 5-8），尽管 2013 年创业风险投资行业总体仍然呈现出比较严峻的态势，对于退出的预期时间仍然延续了上一年度的消极态势，但是整体形势相比 2012 年有所起色，预期持股时间有所缩短。与 2012 年相比，预期持股时间在 3~5 年、5 年以上所占比重均出现了下降趋势，分别为 64.1%、14.9%，尤其预期持股在 3~5 年的跌幅达到了 4.1%。

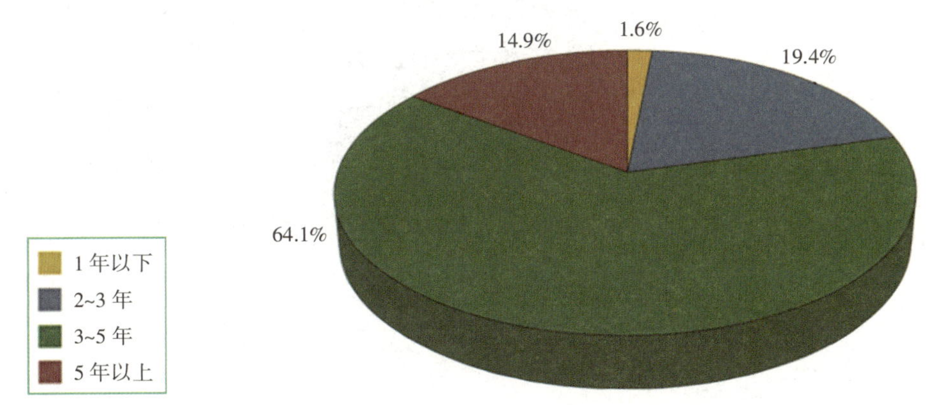

图 5-8 创业风险投资机构对被投资企业的预期持股时间（2013）

5.7 影响中国创业风险投资经营的外部因素

调查显示[②]（见图 5-9），2013 年影响中国创业风险投资经营的外部因素与 2012 年相比基本一致，"其他"、"政策不明朗"以及"缺乏好项目"因素开始成为制约创投行业发展的前三大外部因素，这与 2011 年、2012 年的情况相比发生了显著变化。

（1）由于 2013 年世界经济状况从总体上来看相比 2012 年有显著改善，尽管我国资本市场保持了上一年度的走低态势，但是并购市场的新兴使得资本市场的完善度得以有效提升，因而"多层次资本市场不完善"所占比重从 2011 年的 30.8%、2012 年的 32.9%锐减到 2013 年的 0.9%。这表明从 2013 年开始，我国多层次市场建设有了有效进展。

（2）2013 年"政策不明朗"与 2012 年相比所占比重有所上升，从 17.0%上升到 19.7%，并位居所有外部因素的首位，成为制约我国创业风险投资行业发展最重要的瓶颈。2013 年中国创业风险投资机构认为"缺乏好项目"对投资经营的影响有所增强，占比从 15%上升至 17.3%，成为第二位制约我国创业风险投资行业发展的瓶颈。这表明

① 有效样本数为 1023 份。
② 有效样本数为 1011 份。

2013 年我国宏观经济增速持续放缓和创业投资机构持续扩张的趋势，持续地加剧了行业内的竞争态势，从而使得优质的投资项目相对匮乏。而与此同时，制约中国创业风险投资经营的外部因素也呈现出多样化的趋势。

总体而言，中国创业投资行业的整体外部环境完善度和行业内的专业水平在稳步提升。2013 年“缺乏创业风险投资行业法律法规”的重要性下降明显，由此前的 13.5% 锐减到了 5.3%。这说明我国有关创业风险投资行业发展的法律法规在不断完善，对创业风险投资行业经营的直接影响越来越低。“企业管理水平”、“创业风险投资人员的素质低”这两种因素的作用也有大幅度下降，其中“企业管理水平”所占比重下降至 3.7%；“创业风险投资人员的素质低”的占比由 2012 年的 9%下降至 1.7%。

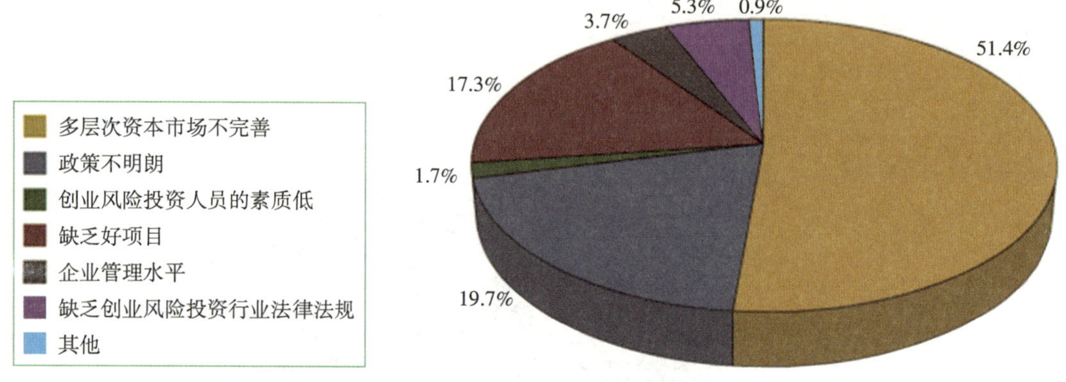

图 5–9 影响创业风险投资发展的主要困难（2013）

6 中国创业风险投资区域运行情况

6.1 创业风险投资机构数量和管理资本的地区分布

从全国地域分布看，2013 年中国创业风险投资公司分布在全国 30 个省、直辖市和自治区行政区划内，相比 2012 年的 29 个地区，越来越多的地区开始重视创业风险投资在发展地区经济和促进技术创新过程中的重要作用，通过设立创业风险投资来推动地区经济增长和科技成果转化和产业化（见表 6-1、图 6-1）。

整体上看，2013 年我国创业风险投资在全国的分布具有以下几个特点：

（1）创业风险投资管理机构仍旧主要集中在经济发达地区，其中以江苏、浙江等地居多。西部地区创业风险投资机构数量仍相对较少，部分地区机构数量在个位数以下。

全国创业风险投资机构呈现“两超多强”的局面，江浙一带仍然是我国创业风险投资最多的地区。江苏省创业风险投资发展迅速，继 2011 年、2012 年之后，2013 年江苏省依旧是全国创业风险投资机构数量最多的地区，创投机构数量有 510 家，是全国机构总数的 1/3，占比达 34.55%，比 2012 年增加了 172 家，增速为 50.89%，其中投资基金（公司）有 403 家，比 2012 年增长了 40.01%。浙江省内的创业风险投资机构有 224 家，占全国总数的比例是 15.18%。两省合计占全国的比重约 50%。

（2）上海和广东的创业风险投资机构数量依旧在全国排名前列。2013 年，上海市创业风险投资机构数量有 70 家，比 2012 年增加了 6 家，排名也跃居全国第三位；广东省创业风险投资机构数量共有机构 62 家，全国排名第五位，比 2012 年减少了 10 家。

（3）安徽、湖北、湖南、重庆等中西部地区创投发展迅速。安徽省 2013 年的创业风险投资机构数量达到了 65 家，比 2012 年增加了 23 家，排名跃居全国第四位，其中投资基金（公司）数量达到了 55 家，比 2012 年增加了 19 家。重庆市创业风险投资机构数量达到了 47 家，比上年度增加了 12 家。

表 6-1 中国各地区创业风险投资机构数量（2013） 单位：家

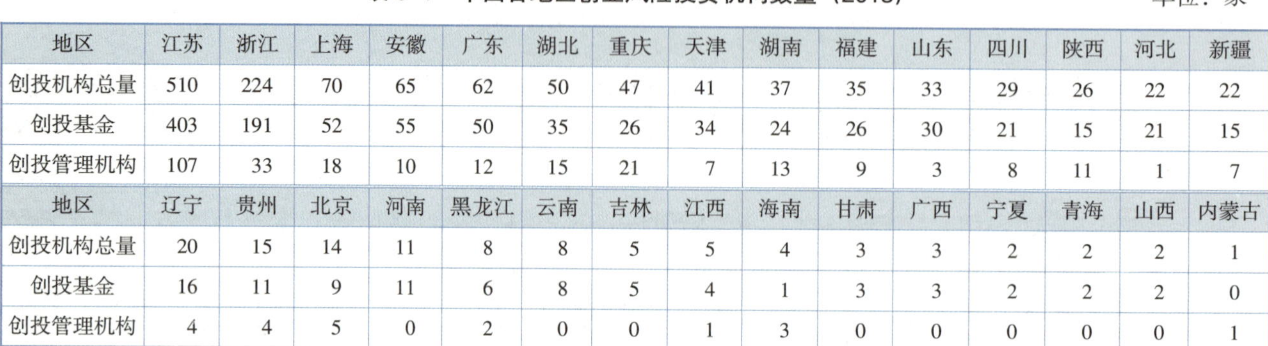

地区	江苏	浙江	上海	安徽	广东	湖北	重庆	天津	湖南	福建	山东	四川	陕西	河北	新疆
创投机构总量	510	224	70	65	62	50	47	41	37	35	33	29	26	22	22
创投基金	403	191	52	55	50	35	26	34	24	26	30	21	15	21	15
创投管理机构	107	33	18	10	12	15	21	7	13	9	3	8	11	1	7
地区	辽宁	贵州	北京	河南	黑龙江	云南	吉林	江西	海南	甘肃	广西	宁夏	青海	山西	内蒙古
创投机构总量	20	15	14	11	8	8	5	5	4	3	3	2	2	2	1
创投基金	16	11	9	11	6	8	5	4	1	3	3	2	2	2	0
创投管理机构	4	4	5	0	2	0	0	1	3	0	0	0	0	0	1

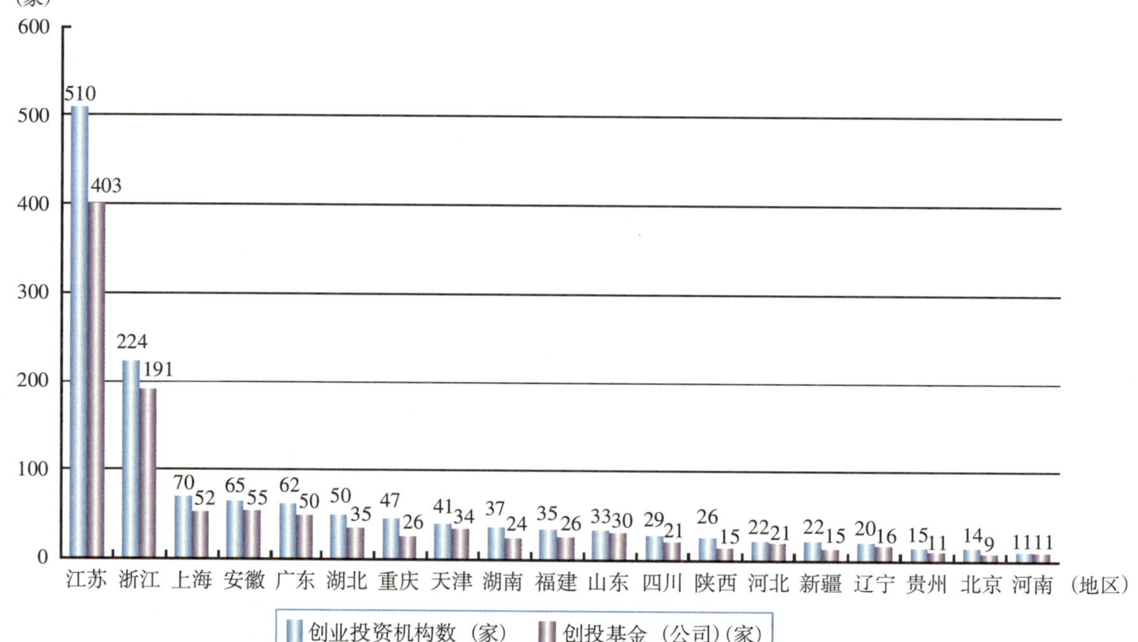

图 6-1 部分地区创业风险投资机构数量分布（2013）

表 6-2 和图 6-2 显示了 2013 年我国不同地区创业风险投资的管理资本规模。

与 2012 年比较，2013 年全国创业风险投资管理资本的地区分布有如下特点：

（1）全国创业风险投资管理资本的地区差异性较大。东部发达地区仍然是我国创业风险投资资本集中和聚集的地区，最高的地区在 1000 亿元以上，而西部地区的创业风险投资的资本规模都相对偏小，大部分地区的管理资本规模在 10 亿元以下，部分地区只有 1 亿~5 亿元，最低的只有 1 亿多元。

（2）江苏省持续成为我国创业风险投资管理资本最多的地区。江苏省不但创业风险投资机构数量连续排名全国第一，而且管理资本总量也连续多年稳居国内榜首。2013 年，江苏省创业风险投资机构管理资本仍位居榜首，管理资金达到了 1407.52 亿元，占全国总数的 39.38%，比 2012 年增加 466 亿元，增速达 49.47%

（3）广东、浙江和上海仍然是全国创业风险投资管理资本较多的地区。2013 年，广东、浙江和上海创业风险投资机构的管理资本在全国的排名与 2012 年一样，其中，广东省创业风险投资机构数量虽然位居第五位，但是管理资本持续排名全国第二位，管理资金达到了612.74亿元，浙江省创业风险投资机构在全国排名第二位，但是机构相对较小，因此资金管理规模在广东省之后，排名第三位，管理资本规模达到了312.60亿元。

（4）福建、安徽、四川、湖北等地区的创业风险投资发展势头强劲。2013年，福建省创业风险投资管理资本增长迅速，2013年管理资本达到120.41亿元，比2012年增加了近30亿元，全国排名跃居第五位。安徽省创业风险投资管理资金规模达到了117.08亿元，排名第六位。另外，四川、湖北等地创业风险投资管理资金规模也都接近100亿元。

表6–2 部分地区创业风险投资的管理资本分布（2013）

地区	创投基金（公司）（家）	管理资本总量（亿元）
江苏	403	1407.52
浙江	191	312.60
上海	52	224.83
安徽	55	117.08
广东	50	612.74
湖北	35	80.10
重庆	26	44.75
天津	34	51.81
湖南	24	57.36
福建	26	120.41
山东	30	52.05
四川	21	93.67

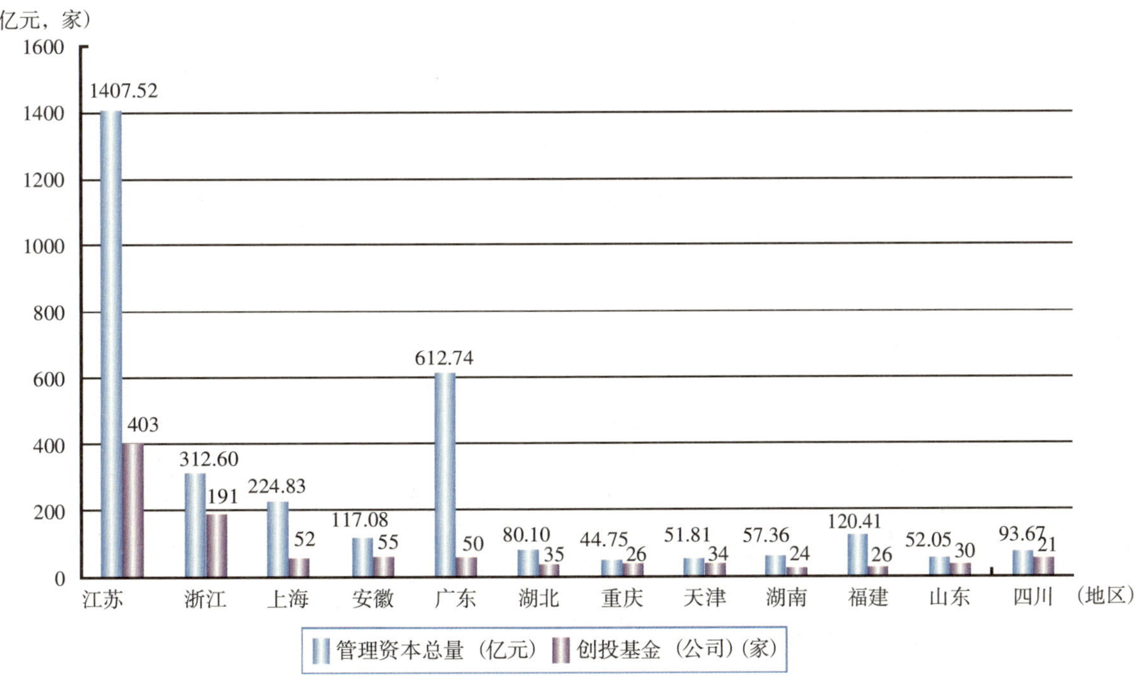

图6–2 部分地区创业风险投资的管理资本分布（2013）

6.2 各地区创业风险投资机构的规模分布

表 6-3 和图 6-3 显示了 2013 年我国不同地区创业风险投资管理资本的规模分布。整体上看，2013 年全国大部分地区创业风险投资机构的规模,以管理资本在 5000 万元以下、1 亿~2 亿元和 2 亿~5 亿元的居多。与 2012 年类似，经济发达地区的创业风险投资发展迅速，不同规模的创业风险投资机构都有，而一些经济欠发达地区的创业风险投资规模则相对集中。如内蒙古的都在 5000 万~1 亿元资本之间，青海省的则在 5000 万~1 亿元和 1 亿~2 亿元之间，宁夏均匀分布在 5000 万~1 亿元和 5 亿元以上。值得注意是，广东省的创业风险投资机构以规模大的机构为主，管理资本在 5 亿元以上的机构占比达 40.68%。另外上海、四川等地管理资本在 5 亿元以上的创投机构也较多。

表 6-3 各地区不同规模创业风险投资机构的数量分布（2013） 单位：%

地区	5000 万元以下	5000 万~1 亿元	1 亿~2 亿元	2 亿~5 亿元	5 亿元以上
河南	12.50	0.00	50.00	37.50	0.00
陕西	21.43	14.29	28.57	21.43	14.29
广东	15.25	11.86	15.25	16.95	40.68
湖北	28.57	21.43	14.29	28.57	7.14
山西	50.00	0.00	0.00	0.00	50.00
福建	29.17	20.83	16.67	25.00	8.33
山东	35.00	25.00	25.00	10.00	5.00
四川	21.43	10.71	21.43	25.00	21.43
重庆	23.81	7.14	21.43	38.10	9.52
广西	66.67	0.00	33.33	0.00	0.00
甘肃	33.33	0.00	33.33	33.33	0.00
江苏	17.25	18.56	31.22	23.58	9.39
浙江	14.62	19.81	33.49	24.06	8.02
江西	25.00	0.00	50.00	25.00	0.00
上海	27.27	0.00	21.21	33.33	18.18
河北	53.33	6.67	20.00	13.33	6.67
天津	25.00	21.88	25.00	12.50	15.63
辽宁	20.00	20.00	26.67	20.00	13.33
湖南	9.52	14.29	38.10	19.05	19.05
安徽	8.00	12.00	34.00	34.00	12.00
新疆	18.18	27.27	36.36	9.09	9.09
贵州	42.86	14.29	14.29	28.57	—
北京	11.11	33.33	22.22	22.22	11.11
宁夏	0.00	50.00	0.00	0.00	50.00

续表

地区	5000 万元以下	5000 万~1 亿元	1 亿~2 亿元	2 亿~5 亿元	5 亿元以上
黑龙江	0.00	12.50	25.00	25.00	37.50
青海	0.00	50.00	50.00	0.00	0.00
吉林	0.00	25.00	0.00	75.00	0.00
云南	0.00	40.00	20.00	20.00	20.00
海南	0.00	25.00	50.00	25.00	0.00
内蒙古	0.00	100.00	0.00	0.00	0.00

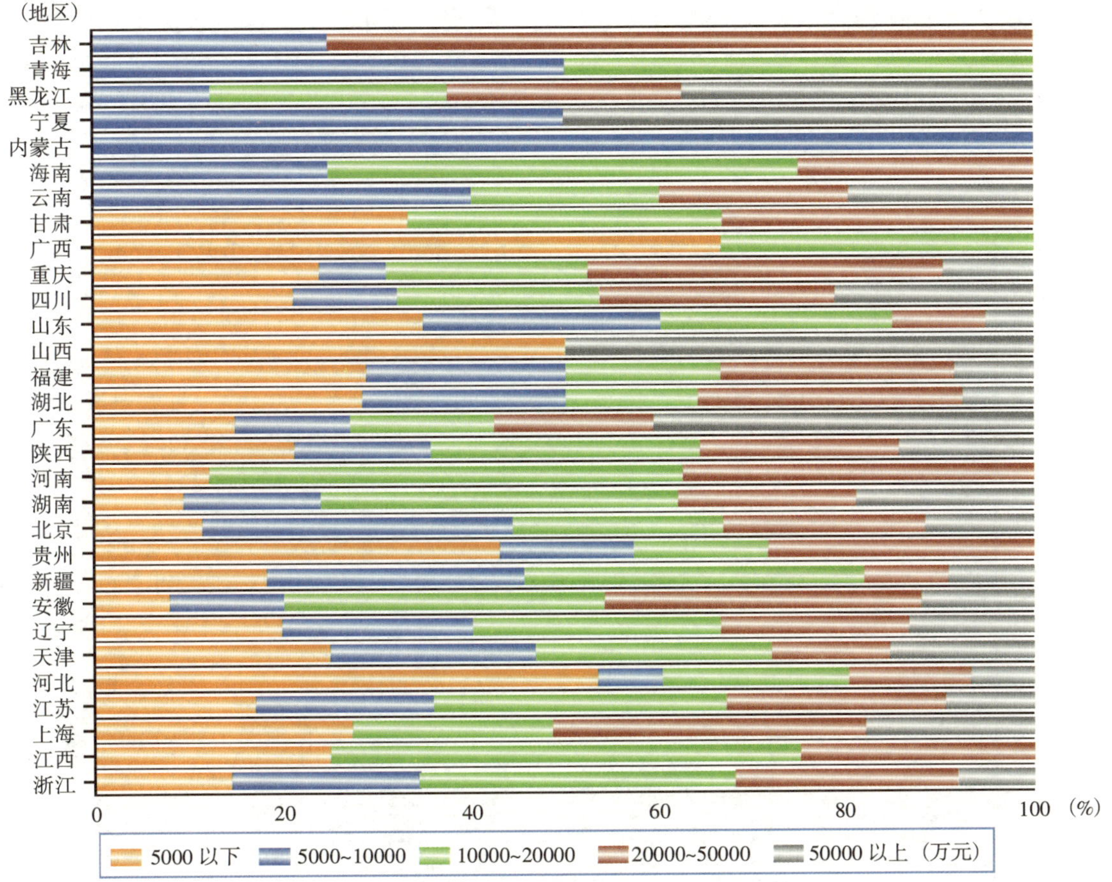

图 6-3 各地区不同规模创业风险投资机构的数量分布

6.3 各地区创业风险投资机构的资本来源

2013 年全国各地区创业风险投资机构的资本来源见图 6-4，基本保持了 2012 年的特点，以政府财政资金、国有独立投资机构、企业出资和个人为主要来源。

(1) 政府财政资金仍然是国内各地区创业风险投资

机构的主要资金来源。政府直接出资和由国有独资投资机构出资的资金比例之和超过50%的地区有河北、海南、云南、黑龙江、湖南、吉林、内蒙古、宁夏、山西、上海、青海 11 个地区。其中，内蒙古和山西与 2011 年和 2012 年情况相同，仍然完全是由政府出资，宁夏地区的政府出资在 90%以上。

（2） 企业资金成为国内很多地区创业风险投资机构的主要来源。2013 年，北京、福建、广西、山东、天津、浙江 6 个地区的创业风险投资机构来源于企业的资金占比都超过了 50%，其中最高的是福建，比例达 84.6%，其次是广西，比例达 71.3%。另外，浙江省内创业风险投资机构来源于企业的资金占比达到了 61.2%。安徽、湖北、江苏、云南、广东、贵州、四川、江西等地企业的资金占比都超过了 40%。

（3） 部分地区内个人资金出资设立创业风险投资机构的比例增高。2013 年，广东、海南、江西、陕西、辽宁、浙江、湖北、湖南、河南、山东、重庆等地的个人资本占全部创业投资机构管理资本的比例都在 10%以上，其中新疆最高，占比达 59.4%。广东省的个人出资占比是 27.6%，浙江省是 23.4%，虽然不是最高，但由于浙江全省创业投资管理资本量大，因此参与浙江创业风险投资的民间资本总量较大。

（4） 境外资金成为部分地区创业风险投资机构的重要来源。2013 年，黑龙江、青海地区的创业风险投资机构中，境外资金的比例较高，分别达 8.8%和 31.6%。

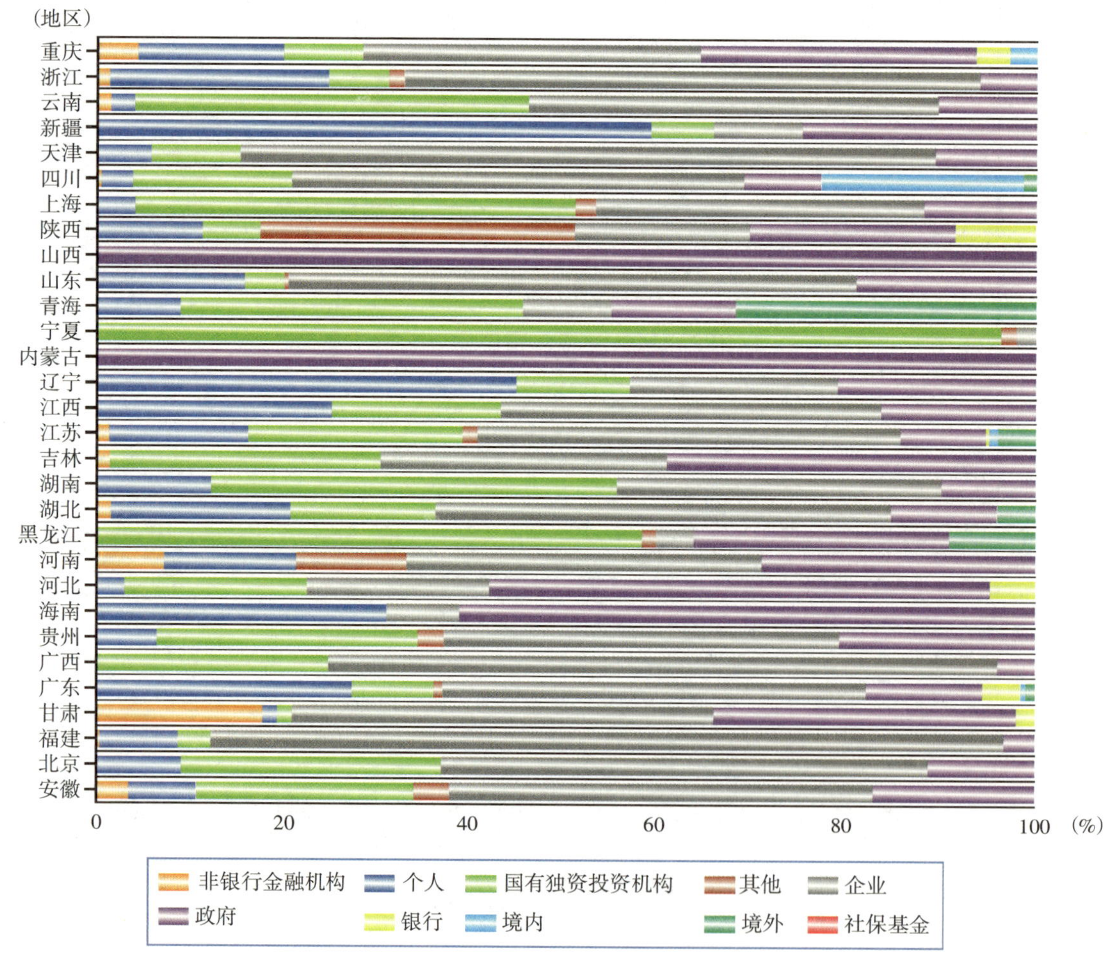

图 6-4 各地区创业风险投资资本来源（2013）

6.4 各地区创业风险投资的投资特征

6.4.1 创业风险投资项目的地区分布

表 6-4 显示了 2013 年我国不同地区创业风险投资机构所投资项目的情况。

2013 年，在调查统计的地区内，全国 28 个地区的创业风险投资机构进行了投资，总共投资了 1493 个项目，江苏、广东和浙江投资项目占比依然位列三甲，而且排列顺序未变。其中，江苏省内的创投机构投资项目最多，项目数量超过全国的 1/3，占比达 37%，其次是广东省，投资项目占比是 14.5%，浙江是 9.6%。与 2012 年比较，江苏省内创业投资机构所投资的项目占比提高了四个多百分点，广东和浙江有很小幅度的下降。另外，投资项目相对较多的地区还有上海、安徽、重庆、湖南、湖北、天津和四川等地区。

表 6-4 2013 年我国创业风险投资机构所投资项目的地区分布 单位：%

地 区	项目占比
江 苏	37.0
广 东	14.5
浙 江	9.6
上 海	4.6
安 徽	4.6
重 庆	4.0
湖 南	2.9
湖 北	2.7
天 津	2.5
四 川	2.1
辽 宁	1.9
福 建	1.8
河 南	1.6
山 东	1.5
北 京	1.2
陕 西	1.1
贵 州	1.1
新 疆	1.1
黑龙江	0.8
河 北	0.7
广 西	0.6
宁 夏	0.6
甘 肃	0.3
云 南	0.3
吉 林	0.3
山 西	0.2
江 西	0.1
海 南	0.1

6.4.2 各地区创业风险投资的投资强度

2013 年，全国 28 个地区的创业风险投资机构都进行了投资，各地区创业风险投资所投资项目的投资强度见表 6-5 和图 6-5。

表 6-5 2013 年各地区创业风险投资的投资强度 单位：万元/项

地 区	投资强度
海 南	10000.00
天 津	3621.15
湖 南	2719.31
广 东	2548.43
陕 西	2379.62
辽 宁	2338.64
云 南	2260.00
江 西	2165.00
上 海	2076.64
四 川	1755.20
湖 北	1739.23
安 徽	1515.07
浙 江	1492.21
重 庆	1446.76
新 疆	1436.02
江 苏	1412.41
山 东	1360.78
北 京	1184.78
吉 林	1056.00
福 建	904.85
河 南	785.62
宁 夏	710.00
广 西	588.89
贵 州	565.63
河 北	453.00
甘 肃	437.50
黑龙江	138.33
山 西	86.67

2013 年，全国各地创业风险投资项目投资强度上限和下限都超出了 2012 年的范围，最高的仍然是海南省，投资强度达 1 亿元/项，远高于 2012 年的 3958.6 万元/项，最低的是山西省，投资强度达 86.67 万元/项，远低于 2012 年甘肃省的 250 万元/项。

整体上看，2013 年我国创业风险投资的项目投资强度大于 2012 年，大部分地区的项目投资金额在 1000 万~4000 万元之间，有 18 个地区的创业投资项目的平均投资金额在这个范围之内，超过 2012 年的 16 个地区。

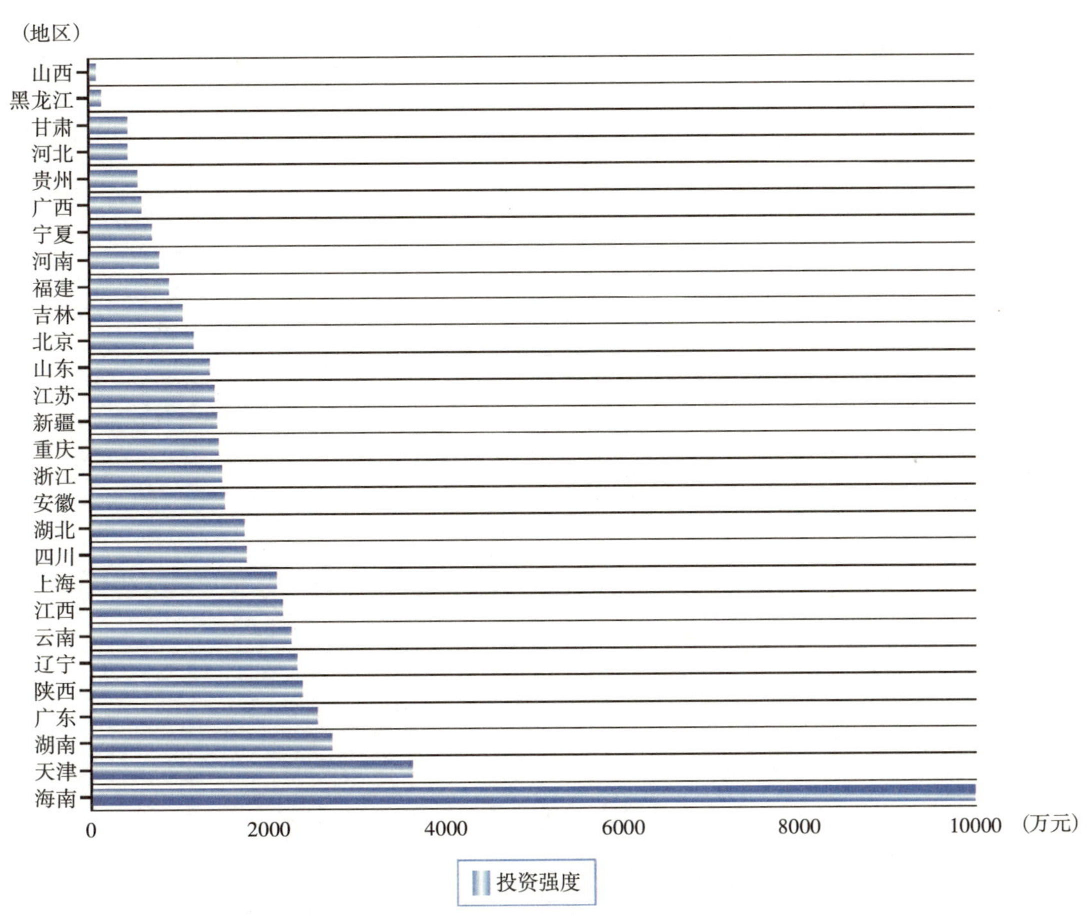

图 6-5 各地区创业风险投资的投资强度（2013）

6.4.3 各地区创业风险投资机构的项目持股结构

2013 年，追求绝对控股的创业风险投资的地区数量在减少，项目持股比例≥50%的地区数量比 2012 年减少了 4 个，只有 15 个地区，有 13 个地区的项目持股比例全部是在 50%以下的。从各地区持股比例≥50%项目占比来看，2013 年全国各地区的创业风险投资也在追求多元化投资，持股比例≥50%项目占比远远低于 2012 年的数值，其中，持股比例≥50%项目占比最高的辽宁，占比只有 36%，低于 2012 年的 62.5%（见表 6–6、图 6–6）。

表 6–6 2013 年中国创业风险投资机构所投资项目持股结构的地区分布

单位：%

省 份	持股比例≥50%	持股比例<50%
辽 宁	36.00	64.00
河 南	29.17	70.83
福 建	18.52	81.48
陕 西	17.65	82.35
山 东	13.04	86.96
安 徽	7.46	92.54
上 海	7.25	92.75
贵 州	6.25	93.75
重 庆	5.45	94.55
湖 北	5.13	94.87
湖 南	5.13	94.87
江 苏	4.06	95.94
天 津	3.70	96.30
浙 江	2.96	97.04
广 东	2.65	97.35
河 北	0.00	100.00
江 西	0.00	100.00
四 川	0.00	100.00
广 西	0.00	100.00
吉 林	0.00	100.00
宁 夏	0.00	100.00
新 疆	0.00	100.00
云 南	0.00	100.00
山 西	0.00	100.00
黑龙江	0.00	100.00
海 南	0.00	100.00
北 京	0.00	100.00
甘 肃	0.00	100.00

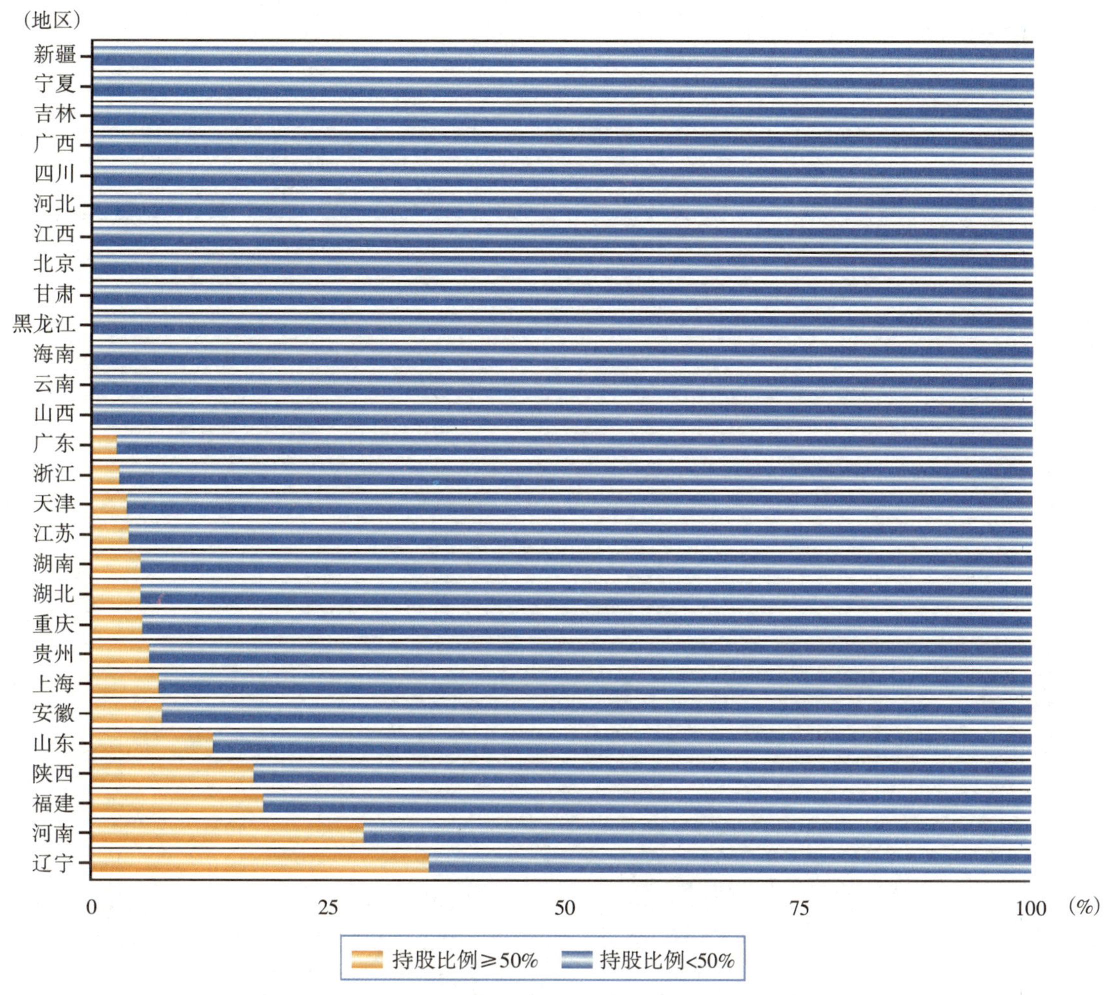

图 6-6 各地区创业风险投资机构的持股结构（2013）

6.4.4 各地区创业风险投资项目的所处阶段

表 6-7 和图 6-7 显示了 2013 年度我国各地创业风险投资机构所投资项目的所处阶段。

表 6-7 2013 年各地区创业风险投资项目的所处阶段

单位：%

地 区	种子期	起步期	成长（扩张）期	成熟（过渡）期	重建期
北 京	5.6	44.4	27.8	22.2	0.0
天 津	2.8	25.0	44.4	27.8	0.0
河 北	14.3	71.4	0.0	14.3	0.0
山 西	33.3	66.7	0.0	0.0	0.0
辽 宁	20.0	0.0	60.0	20.0	0.0
吉 林	40.0	20.0	40.0	0.0	0.0
黑龙江	33.3	66.7	0.0	0.0	0.0
上 海	10.1	37.7	31.9	14.5	5.8
江 苏	20.6	30.2	39.2	8.8	1.2
浙 江	14.9	31.9	46.8	6.4	0.0
安 徽	15.0	28.3	48.3	8.3	0.0
福 建	25.9	51.9	18.5	3.7	0.0
江 西	0.0	100.0	0.0	0.0	0.0
山 东	21.7	30.4	43.5	4.3	0.0
河 南	45.8	29.2	20.8	4.2	0.0
湖 北	17.1	31.7	46.3	4.9	0.0
湖 南	8.1	45.9	35.1	10.8	0.0
广 东	17.0	27.5	41.0	14.0	0.5
广 西	0.0	0.0	50.0	50.0	0.0
海 南	0.0	0.0	100.0	0.0	0.0
四 川	23.1	34.6	38.5	3.8	0.0
贵 州	43.8	25.0	25.0	6.3	0.0
云 南	75.0	25.0	0.0	0.0	0.0
重 庆	21.6	35.3	41.2	2.0	0.0
陕 西	0.0	50.0	6.3	31.3	12.5
甘 肃	25.0	50.0	0.0	25.0	0.0
宁 夏	14.3	14.3	42.9	28.6	0.0
新 疆	9.1	72.7	9.1	9.1	0.0

2013 年，我国各地创业风险投资的项目投资所处阶段具有以下特点：

（1）与 2012 年类似，成长（扩展）期阶段的项目仍然是 2013 年我国大部分地区创业风险投资机构投资最多的项目，大部分地区投资在这个阶段的项目占比超过 1/3，其中，最高的是海南，占比 100%，辽宁排名第二，占比 60%，广西第三，占比达 50%。

（2）起步期阶段的项目受到国内很多地区创业风险投资机构的大力关注。2013 年，有 8 个地区创业风险投资机构所投资起步期阶段的项目比例超过了 50%，分别是河北、山西、黑龙江、福建、江西、陕西、甘肃和新疆，比 2012 年多出 2 个地区，其中，最高的是江西，比例是 100%，新疆也比较高，达到 72.7%；值得注意的是，上述地区大部分属于经济不发达地区，这充分说明，国内经济欠发达地区已经充分认识到了创业风险投资在促进初创期企业发展的重要作用，开始利用创业风险投资来培育和促进本地区内早期企业的成长。

（3）越来越多地区的创业风险投资重视种子期阶段的项目。2013 年，有 13 个地区的创业风险投资，投资于种子期阶段的项目比例超过 20%，分别是山西、辽宁、吉林、黑龙江、江苏、福建、山东、河南、四川、贵州、云南、重庆和甘肃；其中最高的云南省达到了 75%。

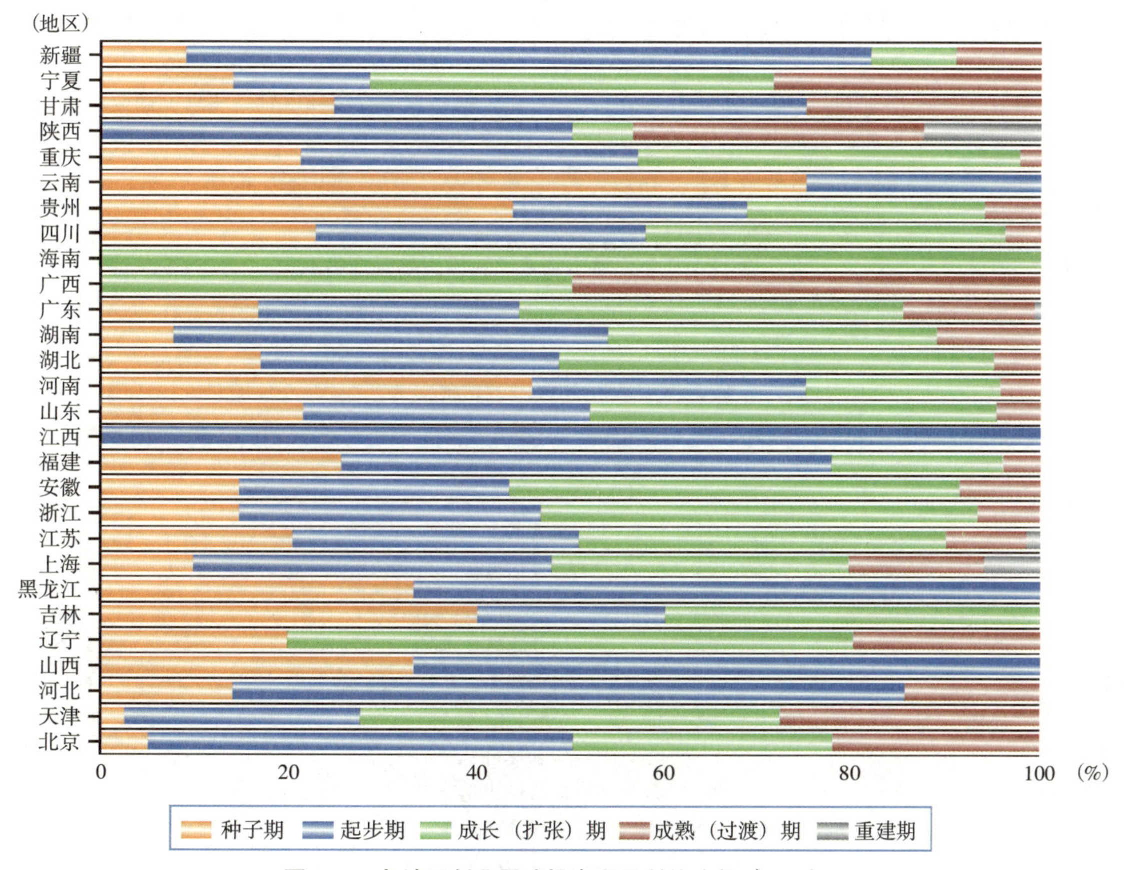

图 6–7 各地区创业风险投资项目所处阶段（2013）

6.4.5 部分地区创业风险投资对不同行业的投资

根据 2013 年全国创业风险投资调查统计，本章选取了 2013 年我国创业风险投资较为活跃地区进行单独分析，以便掌握和了解这些地区投资项目的行业分布和资金情况（见表 6–8 至表 6–16）。

表 6–8　2013 年北京市创业风险投资的行业特点

项目数		投资强度	
行业	百分比（%）	行业	行业投资强度（万元/项）
新材料工业	16.7	传统制造业	2698.4
医药保健	16.7	网络产业	1678.0
光电子与光机电一体化	11.1	新材料工业	1300.0
网络产业	11.1	光电子与光机电一体化	1090.0
传统制造业	11.1	生物科技	1000.0
传播与文化娱乐	11.1	其他制造业	1000.0
生物科技	5.6	医药保健	944.8
其他制造业	5.6	IT 服务业	500.0
新能源、高效节能技术	5.6	新能源、高效节能技术	472.0
IT 服务业	5.6	传播与文化娱乐	343.4

2013 年，北京市的创业风险投资项目分布在 10 个行业，比上年度减少了 10 个行业，大部分属于国家重点发展和鼓励的行业，其中比较多的是新材料工业、医药保健。从行业的投资强度看，北京市创业风险投资平均投资最多的是传统制造业，2600 多万元/项，最低的是传播与文化娱乐，只有 300 多万元/项。

表 6–9　2013 年天津市创业风险投资的行业特点

项目数		投资强度	
行业	百分比（%）	行业	行业投资强度（万元/项）
软件产业	16.2	农林牧副渔	25520.0
新能源、高效节能技术	13.5	其他制造业	21450.0
其他行业	8.1	金融保险业	3900.0
新材料工业	8.1	环保工程	3100.0
农林牧副渔	8.1	社会服务	2000.0
消费产品和服务	5.4	通讯设备	2000.0
生物科技	5.4	医药保健	1991.4
环保工程	5.4	生物科技	1500.0
房地产业	2.7	新能源、高效节能技术	1414.6
光电子与光机电一体化	2.7	科技服务	1000.0
其他 IT 产业	2.7	新材料工业	966.7
通讯设备	2.7	软件产业	931.7
半导体	2.7	IT 服务业	700.0
其他制造业	2.7	房地产业	500.0
社会服务	2.7	光电子与光机电一体化	500.0
医药保健	2.7	其他 IT 产业	450.0
IT 服务业	2.7	消费产品和服务	425.0
金融保险业	2.7	其他行业	254.3
科技服务	2.7	半导体	76.6

2013 年，天津市创业风险投资的投资领域更广泛，项目分布在 19 个行业，行业数量比 2012 年多出 6 个，主要集中在软件产业、新能源/高效节能技术，另外新材料工业、农林牧副渔、其他行业的投资也相对较多。与 2012 年比较，软件产业替代金融保险业成为天津市创业风险投资最关注的行业，占比达 16.2%，新能源/高效节能技术则重新成为创业风险投资机构比较关注的领域，投资占比达 13.5%。

至于行业的投资强度，2013 年，天津市创业风险投资的行业项目平均投资资金差距很大，最高的农林牧副渔有 25520 万元/项，最低的半导体只有 76.6 万元/项。与 2012 年比较，天津市创业风险投资的行业项目平均投资资金明显增加，投资强度在 1000 万元/项以上的有 10 个行业，远多于 2012 年的 5 个，投资强度在前 2 位的农林牧副渔、其他制造业都在 2 亿元以上，远高于上一年度投资强度最高的软件产业的 1750 万元/项。

表 6–10　2013 年上海市创业风险投资的行业特点

项目数		投资强度	
行业	百分比（%）	行业	行业投资强度（万元/项）
金融保险业	11.6	传统制造业	8500.0
软件产业	7.2	金融保险业	4712.5
环保工程	7.2	建筑业	4643.5
半导体	7.2	传播与文化娱乐	3679.4
新材料工业	7.2	交通运输仓储和邮政业	2000.0
光电子与光机电一体化	7.2	农林牧副渔	2000.0
IT 服务业	5.8	IT 服务业	1805.0
其他 IT 产业	5.8	其他行业	1649.5
传播与文化娱乐	5.8	医药保健	1640.0
网络产业	4.3	新材料工业	1560.4
新能源、高效节能技术	4.3	网络产业	1500.0
生物科技	2.9	通信设备	1500.0
建筑业	2.9	新能源、高效节能技术	1400.1
其他行业	2.9	光电子与光机电一体化	1324.0
医药保健	2.9	环保工程	1235.6
传统制造业	2.9	半导体	1144.0
农林牧副渔	1.4	其他制造业	1000.0
其他制造业	1.4	计算机硬件产业	1000.0
交通运输仓储和邮政业	1.4	通讯设备	1000.0
科技服务	1.4	软件产业	762.1
计算机硬件产业	1.4	其他 IT 产业	650.0
通讯设备	1.4	生物科技	400.0
通信设备	1.4	核应用技术	33.3
核应用技术	1.4	科技服务	20.0

2013 年，上海市创业风险投资所投资的领域更广泛，项目分布在 24 个行业，比 2012 年多出 1 个行业；项目投资较多的金融保险业、软件产业、环保工程、半导体、新材料工业、光电子与光机电一体化。与 2012 年明显不同的是，金融保险业一跃成为上海市创业风险投资机构最关注的行业，项目占比达 11.6%，这也符合上海市国内金融中心的地位；2012 年投资项目占比较高的农林牧副渔、通讯设备、医药保健等行业则相对较低。

从投资强度上看，2013 年上海市创业风险投资的行业平均投资资金差距较大，最高的是传统制造业，高达 8500 万元/项，最低的是科技服务业，平均只有 20 万元/项。整体上看，上海市创业风险投资的行业投资强度超过了 2012 年，投资强度在 1000 万元/项以上的有 19 个行业，远远超过 2012 年的 13 个；而且最高的传统制造业也远远高于 2012 年投资强度最高的金融保险业的 5194.3 万元/项。但软件产业等的投资强度下降幅度较大。

表 6–11　2013 年广东省创业风险投资的行业特点

项目数		投资强度	
行业	百分比（%）	行业	行业投资强度（万元/项）
金融保险业	14.7	其他制造业	4810.8
医药保健	9.0	传统制造业	4004.7
消费产品和服务	7.6	传播与文化娱乐	3908.9
网络产业	7.1	光电子与光机电一体化	3720.1
通讯设备	6.6	医药保健	3278.5
传统制造业	6.2	新材料工业	3171.7
生物科技	6.2	批发和零售业	3000.0
传播与文化娱乐	5.7	新能源、高效节能技术	2985.2
新能源、高效节能技术	5.2	农林牧副渔	2914.3
光电子与光机电一体化	4.7	金融保险业	2857.1
新材料工业	4.3	消费产品和服务	2841.6
IT 服务业	3.8	IT 服务业	2387.6
农林牧副渔	3.3	计算机硬件产业	2299.7
计算机硬件产业	2.8	通讯设备	1818.2
其他制造业	1.9	半导体	1667.0
社会服务	1.9	软件产业	1537.8
软件产业	1.9	环保工程	1416.7
其他行业	1.4	生物科技	1372.6
环保工程	1.4	水电煤气	1300.0
半导体	0.9	建筑业	1000.0
交通运输仓储和邮政业	0.9	社会服务	914.5
水电煤气	0.5	其他 IT 产业	870.0
建筑业	0.5	其他行业	706.0
科技服务	0.5	网络产业	585.0
其他 IT 产业	0.5	科技服务	300.0
批发和零售业	0.5	交通运输仓储和邮政业	167.0

2013 年，广东省创业风险投资所投资行业很广泛，投资行业数有 26 个，与 2011 年和 2012 年持平；投资较多的行业有金融保险业、医药保健行业；另外，消费产品和服务、网络产业、通讯设备、传统制造业、生物科技、传播与文化娱乐、新能源/高效节能技术的投资也相对较多。

与 2012 年比较，广东省创业风险投资机构投资重点关注的行业基本没变化。金融保险业仍旧是广东省创业风险投资机构投资最多的行业，比 2012 年还高出了近 3 个百分点，达 14.7%；消费产品和服务、传统制造业和新能源/高效节能技术一直是广东省创业风险投资重点投资的领域。

从投资强度来看，2013 年广东省创业风险投资的行业投资强度整体有所下降，平均投资规模在 1000 万元/项的行业有 20 个，低于 2012 年的 23 个。其中，其他制造业最高，只有 4810.8 万元/项，低于 2012 年最高的 9000 多万元/项，最低的是交通运输仓储和邮政业，只有 167 万元/项，远低于 2012 年的最低值 879.1 万元/项。

表 6–12　2013 年江苏省创业风险投资项目的行业特点

项目数		投资强度	
行业	百分比（%）	行业	行业投资强度（万元/项）
医药保健	14.9	批发和零售业	5000.0
新材料工业	12.0	消费产品和服务	3649.9
传统制造业	7.0	交通运输仓储和邮政业	2918.4
新能源、高效节能技术	6.8	采掘业	2125.0
传播与文化娱乐	6.4	其他制造业	1991.0
其他制造业	5.8	传统制造业	1936.7
软件产业	5.4	房地产业	1875.0
环保工程	5.2	IT 服务业	1733.6
生物科技	4.4	传播与文化娱乐	1626.8
IT 服务业	4.2	通讯设备	1605.7
半导体	3.6	新材料工业	1580.7
其他行业	3.4	核应用技术	1500.0
网络产业	3.4	环保工程	1226.4
消费产品和服务	3.2	光电子与光机电一体化	1213.3
光电子与光机电一体化	3.0	医药保健	1168.9
通讯设备	2.2	网络产业	1071.9
金融保险业	2.0	金融保险业	1016.4
交通运输仓储和邮政业	1.4	其他行业	978.3
科技服务	1.4	科技服务	957.0
计算机硬件产业	1.0	新能源、高效节能技术	893.2
农林牧副渔	1.0	半导体	772.5
其他 IT 产业	0.8	生物科技	755.6
房地产业	0.4	农林牧副渔	622.0
核应用技术	0.4	建筑业	600.0
建筑业	0.4	软件产业	524.0
采掘业	0.4	其他 IT 产业	325.0
批发和零售业	0.2	计算机硬件产业	190.8

2013 年，江苏省创业风险投资所投资的行业有 27 个，总数与 2012 年持平，其中投资行业较多的是医药保健和新材料工业；另外，传统制造业、新能源/高效节能技术、传播与文化娱乐、其他制造业、软件产业、环保工程领域内的项目也相对较多。

与 2012 年比较，2013 年江苏省创业风险投资机构重点投资的行业基本保持了连续性。新材料工业、医药保健、传统制造业、新能源/高效节能技术、传播与文化娱乐一直是江苏省创业风险投资重点关注的领域，只是在项目占比上有所变化，如新材料工业跃居首位，成为 2013 年江苏省创业风险投资机构投资最多的行业。

至于行业投资强度，2013 年江苏省创业风险投资的行业投资强度相差比 2012 年大，平均投资最高的是批发和零售业，达 5000 万元/项，远高于 2012 年最高的消费产品和服务 2541.3 万元/项，最低的是计算机硬件产业，只有 190.8 万元/项，远低于 2012 年最小的科技服务的 517 万元/项。整体上看，2013 年江苏省创业风险投资的行业投资强度比 2012 年有所下降，投资强度在 1000 万元/项以上的行业只有 17 个，比 2012 年少 3 个，有 13 个行业的投资强度在 1000 万~2000 万元/项内。

表 6–13　2013 年浙江省创业风险投资项目的行业特点

项目数		投资强度	
行业	百分比（%）	行业	行业投资强度（万元/项）
IT 服务业	7.8	医药保健	3263.1
软件产业	7.8	社会服务	3198.1
光电子与光机电一体化	7.1	传统制造业	2625.3
社会服务	7.1	传播与文化娱乐	2023.9
医药保健	6.4	批发和零售业	2000.0
传播与文化娱乐	6.4	建筑业	1921.2
农林牧副渔	6.4	其他行业	1822.7
网络产业	6.4	交通运输仓储和邮政业	1612.0
新能源、高效节能技术	5.7	IT 服务业	1472.0
半导体	5.0	新能源、高效节能技术	1452.6
建筑业	4.3	环保工程	1432.0
环保工程	3.5	半导体	1357.1
其他制造业	3.5	其他制造业	1321.2
金融保险业	2.8	科技服务	1318.8
科技服务	2.8	农林牧副渔	1298.8
生物科技	2.8	通讯设备	1241.7
传统制造业	2.8	新材料工业	1214.8
其他行业	2.1	消费产品和服务	1000.0
通讯设备	2.1	网络产业	878.9
新材料工业	2.1	光电子与光机电一体化	845.4
批发和零售业	1.4	其他 IT 产业	500.0
采掘业	0.7	金融保险业	423.3
交通运输仓储和邮政业	0.7	生物科技	330.0
消费产品和服务	0.7	采掘业	300.0
计算机硬件产业	0.7	软件产业	269.4
其他 IT 产业	0.7	计算机硬件产业	120.0

2013 年，浙江省创业风险投资所涉及的领域更广泛，投资的行业有 26 个，比 2012 年增加 3 个；浙江省创业风险投资的关注领域相对分散，不像上述其他地区一样，某个行业在全省内的投资占比比较凸显，投资占比最高的 IT 服务业和软件产业也只有 7.8%，远低于 2012 年最高的制造业；另外，投资占比较多的还有光电子与光机电一体化、社会服务、医药保健、传播与文化娱乐、农林牧副渔、网络产业、新能源/高效节能技术、半导体，投资占比在 5%~7%之间。与 2012 年比较，IT 服务业、农林牧副渔、传播与文化娱乐一直是浙江省创业风险投资重点关注的领域。

2013 年，浙江省创业风险投资在各个行业之间的投资强度差别比 2012 年有所增加，最高的医药保健有 3263.1 万元/项，高于 2012 年最高的其他 IT 产业的 2666.7 万元/项，最低的是计算机硬件产业，有 120 万元/项，低于 2012 年最低的网络产业的 622.5 万元/项。26 个行业中，有 18 个行业的平均投资金额在 1000 万元/项以上，占比比 2012 年有所降低。

表 6–14　2013 年湖北省创业风险投资项目的行业特点

项目数		投资强度	
行业	百分比（%）	行业	行业投资强度（万元/项）
光电子与光机电一体化	24.3	通讯设备	3477.0
医药保健	18.9	光电子与光机电一体化	2333.3
新能源、高效节能技术	13.5	医药保健	2254.8
农林牧副渔	8.1	消费产品和服务	2000.0
传播与文化娱乐	5.4	金融保险业	1950.0
金融保险业	5.4	农林牧副渔	1883.3
传统制造业	5.4	传播与文化娱乐	1069.0
消费产品和服务	5.4	新能源、高效节能技术	1062.0
通讯设备	2.7	水电煤气	1000.0
科技服务	2.7	传统制造业	600.0
环保工程	2.7	科技服务	500.0
水电煤气	2.7	建筑业	500.0
建筑业	2.7	环保工程	200.0

2013 年，湖北省创业风险投资项目的行业分布在 13 个行业，只有 2012 年所投资行业的一半，主要分布在光电子与光机电一体化、医药保健、新能源/高效节能技术、农林牧副渔等行业。与 2012 年一样，光电子与光机电一体化仍然是湖北省创业风险投资项目最多的行业，项目占比是 24.3%，这也符合武汉市作为全国知名的“光谷”的称号，医药保健成为 2013 年投资较多的行业，占比升到了 18.9%，另外新能源/高效节能技术的项目比例也提高较多。

从行业投资强度看，2013 年湖北省创业风险投资的行业投资强度最高的是通讯设备，高达 3477 万元/项，最低的是环保工程，只有 200 万元/项。与 2012 年比较，光电子与光机电一体化的平均投资强度增幅较大，从 2012 年的 1533.2 万元/项提高到 2333.3 万元/项，医药保健行业的平均投资金额与 2012 年基本持平，而新能源/高效节能技术的投资强度则有所下降。

表 6–15 2013 年湖南省创业风险投资项目的行业特点

项目数		投资强度	
行业	百分比（%）	行业	行业投资强度（万元/项）
医药保健	12.2	新能源、高效节能技术	18981.0
其他行业	9.8	建筑业	5001.0
新能源、高效节能技术	9.8	农林牧副渔	1976.7
其他制造业	9.8	环保工程	1900.0
新材料工业	9.8	生物科技	1600.0
传播与文化娱乐	7.3	通信设备	1575.0
农林牧副渔	7.3	其他 IT 产业	1350.0
环保工程	7.3	传播与文化娱乐	866.7
生物科技	4.9	其他行业	593.8
其他 IT 产业	4.9	医药保健	488.2
光电子与光机电一体化	4.9	其他制造业	445.0
通信设备	2.4	新材料工业	351.1
软件产业	2.4	交通运输仓储和邮政业	350.0
交通运输仓储和邮政业	2.4	光电子与光机电一体化	325.0
建筑业	2.4	金融保险业	200.0
金融保险业	2.4	软件产业	120.0

2013 年，湖南省创业风险投资项目主要分布在 16 个行业，比 2012 年减少 1 个行业，主要集中在医药保健、其他行业、新能源/高效节能技术、其他制造业、新材料工业等行业。其中最多的是医药保健，占比达 12.2%。与 2012 年相比，新能源/高效节能技术、新材料工业是湖南省创业风险投资比较关注的领域。

从行业投资强度看，2013 年湖南省创业风险投资的行业投资强度差距很大，最高的新能源/高效节能技术达到了 18981 万元/项，建筑业排名第二，高达 5001 万元/项，其他行业的平均投资金额都在 2000 万元/项以下，其中，最低的软件产业则只有 120 万元/项。

表 6-16　2013 年安徽省创业风险投资项目的行业特点

项目数		投资强度	
行业	百分比（%）	行业	行业投资强度（万元/项）
光电子与光机电一体化	10.3	交通运输仓储和邮政业	9277.5
新能源、高效节能技术	8.8	新材料工业	2603.3
新材料工业	8.8	生物科技	2450.0
传播与文化娱乐	8.8	新能源、高效节能技术	2244.7
传统制造业	8.8	消费产品和服务	2100.0
IT 服务业	7.4	科技服务	1666.7
农林牧副渔	7.4	其他制造业	1230.7
其他制造业	5.9	建筑业	1218.8
环保工程	4.4	传播与文化娱乐	1200.0
医药保健	4.4	医药保健	1200.0
科技服务	4.4	金融保险业	1100.0
其他行业	2.9	农林牧副渔	1090.1
交通运输仓储和邮政业	2.9	采掘业	1000.0
社会服务	2.9	核应用技术	1000.0
生物科技	2.9	光电子与光机电一体化	850.0
建筑业	1.5	传统制造业	833.3
消费产品和服务	1.5	环保工程	766.7
批发和零售业	1.5	其他行业	600.0
采掘业	1.5	IT 服务业	508.0
核应用技术	1.5	社会服务	425.0
金融保险业	1.5	批发和零售业	50.0

2013 年安徽省创业风险投资项目分布在 21 个行业，投资较多的行业包括光电子与光机电一体化、新能源/高效节能技术、新材料工业、传播与文化娱乐、传统制造业、IT 服务业、农林牧副渔，其中投资最多的是光电子与光机电一体化，占比达 10.3%。

从行业投资强度来看，2103 年安徽省创业风险投资的行业投资强度差距较大，最高的是交通运输仓储和邮政业，超过 9000 万元/项，最低的是批发和零售业，只有 50 万元/项；投资金额超过 1000 万元/项的有 14 个行业。

6.5 各经济区域创业投资活动情况

本节将从经济区域角度来比较、分析我国 2013 年创业风险投资的运行状况，通过比较经济发达、有特色的地区与经济相对不发达、创投活动不活跃地区之间的差异，为我国创业风险投资今后的发展起到一个指南针作用。

本节的区域划分，是根据经济发展的联系紧密程度以及发展特色，并参照国家现有的经济区域划分，本着研究的连续性来划分的。当前我国最为关注的几个经济区域增长带是珠三角、长三角以及围绕北京、天津这样的大型城市、具有知识高密度的地区京津冀等地区，同时还有正在重新振兴的东北三省老工业基地。因此本节划分的区域有：

（1）京津冀地区；

（2）长三角地区（包括浙江、上海、江苏）；

（3）珠三角地区：广东（深圳）；

（4）东三省地区：辽宁、吉林、黑龙江；

（5）其他区域（福建省放在这个部分统计）。

本章选取这五个区域，出发点之一是前三个区域是中国目前经济发展最快，也是最有活力的区域，充分代表了当前我国创业投资的前沿面；东三省地区是我国的老工业基地，国有企业比重大，现在正面临经济转型，而且国家也提出了振兴东北的政策，而创业投资的发展，可以鼓励民营和科技经济发展，有效提升产业转型和升级，因此把东三省地区单独列出来。由于本次调查的原因，把其他的地区归并到一起，用以比较这些地区与上述其他地区的不同。

6.5.1 2013 年我国不同区域创业风险投资的投资强度

表 6-17、图 6-8 显示了 2013 年中国各经济区域内创业风险投资的投资强度。2013 年，投资强度最高的仍然是珠三角地区，比 2012 年平均增加了近 180 万元/项，京津冀地区的投资强度跃升到第二位，达 2476.7 万元/项，比 2012 年增加了超过 1500 万元/项。长三角和东北三省地区的创业风险投资的投资强度与 2012 年基本持平，其他地区的创业风险投资的投资强度稍有增加。其中，东北三省地区的创业风险投资的投资强度是最低的。

表 6-17 2013 年中国创业风险投资强度的区域分布 单位：万元/项

区域	珠三角	长三角	其他	东北三省	京津冀
投资强度	2548.4	1487.2	1549.5	1069.4	2476.7

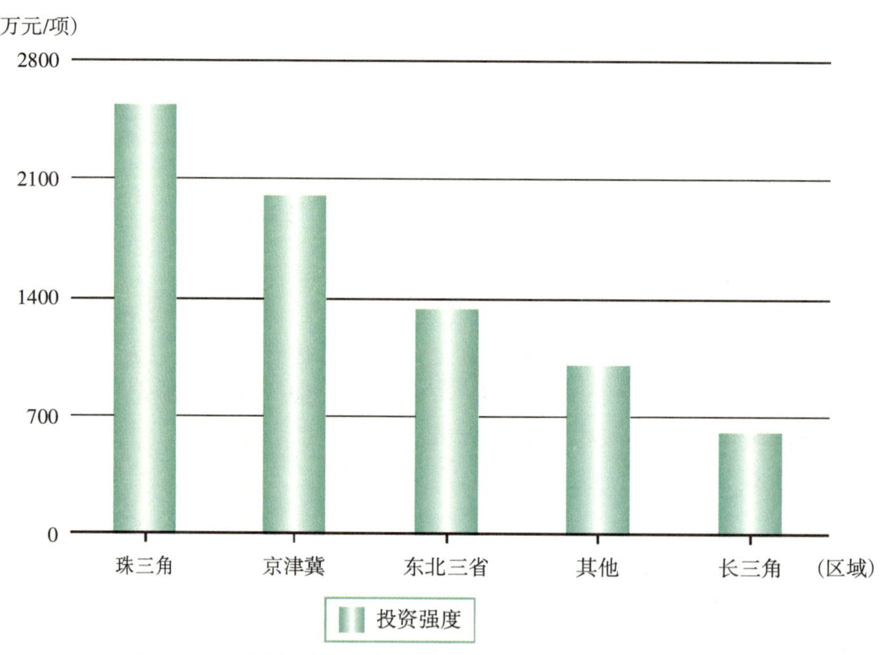

图 6-8 中国创业风险投资强度的区域分布（2013）

6.5.2 不同区域创业风险投资的持股结构

2013 年，全国各经济区域的创业风险投资机构在投资项目时仍然以持股比例<50%的项目为主，尤其是经济发达地区的创业风险投资机构基本以联合投资、非绝对控股的为主。与 2012 年比较，东北三省地区的创业风险投资机构追求绝对控股的项目比例仍然是最高的，而且项目占比大幅提高，比 2012 年增加了约 12 个百分点，达 21.4%；京津冀地区的创业风险投资机构持股超过 50%的项目比例下降较大，从 2012 年的 9.2%下降为 1.8%，成为超过 50%的项目比例占比最少的地区。另外，长三角地区的超过 50%的项目占比有所增加，而珠三角地区则有所下降。值得注意的是，其他地区的创业风险投资机构的超过 50%的项目比例基本与 2012 年持平（见表6-18、图 6-19）。

表 6-18 2013 年各经济区域创业风险投资的持股结构 单位：%

区域	东北三省	京津冀	其他	珠三角	长三角
持股比例≥50%	21.4	1.8	8.2	2.6	4.2
持股比例<50%	78.6	98.2	91.8	97.4	95.8

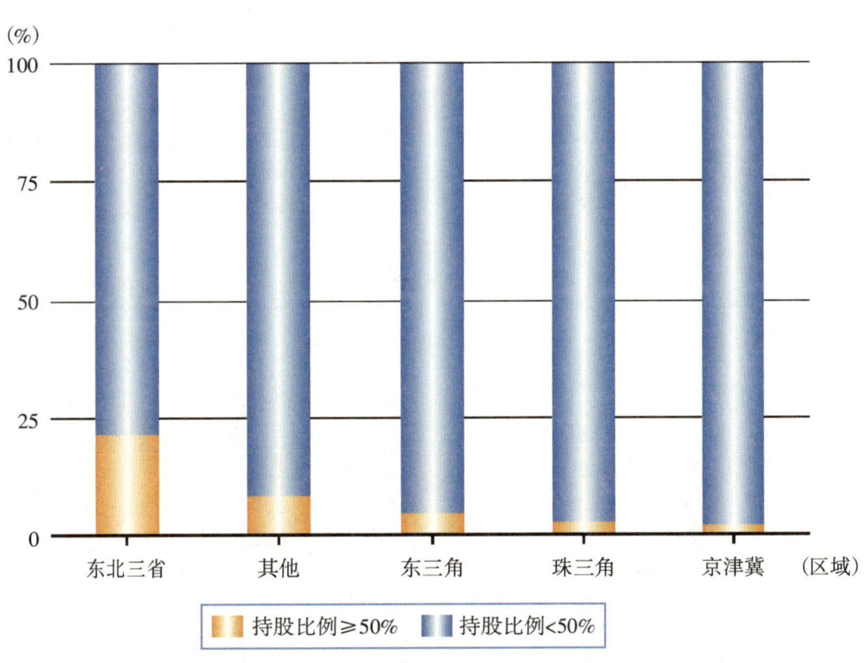

图 6-9 各经济区域创业风险投资的持股结构（2013）

6.5.3 不同经济区域创业风险投资项目所处阶段

表 6-19 和图 6-10 显示了 2013 年我国各个经济区域创业风险投资项目的阶段分布。整体上看，2013 年各区域创业风险投资机构投资最多的成长（扩张）期的项目，其次是起步期的项目，再次是种子期的项目，成熟（过渡）期和重建期的项目相对较少。与 2012 年相比，各地区创业风险投资越来越关注早期阶段的项目，起步期阶段的项目占比明显提高，东北三省、其他地区和京津冀地区创业风险投资在起步期的项目占比最高，其中东北三省是 40.9%，京津冀地区是 36.1%，其他地区是 36.4%。另外，投资于种子期阶段的项目占比也明显提高，东北三省投资于种子期阶段的项目占比是 31.8%，比 2012 年略有下降；长三角地区投资于种子期阶段的项目占比是 18.4%，珠三角地区投资于种子期阶段的项目占比是 17%，其他地区投资于种子期阶段的项目占比是 20.4%，都比 2012 年多出 7 个百分点。

与 2012 年类似，各地区创业风险投资在重建期阶段的项目占比都很少，占比最高的长三角地区也只有 1.4%。至于成熟期的项目，2013 年京津冀地区创业风险投资在这个阶段的项目占比最高，达 24.6%，超出 2012 年 20 个百分点；珠三角地区和其他地区与去年基本持平，长三角地区则大幅下降，由 2012 年的 17.4%下降为 2013 年的8.9%。

表 6-19 2013 年各区域创业风险投资项目所处阶段　　单位：%

区域 \ 所处阶段	种子期	起步期	成长（扩张）期	成熟（过渡）期	重建期
珠三角	17.0	27.5	41.0	14.0	0.5
东北三省	31.8	40.9	22.7	4.5	—
其他	20.4	36.4	34.7	7.8	0.6
长三角	18.4	31.3	40.0	8.9	1.4
京津冀	4.9	36.1	34.4	24.6	—

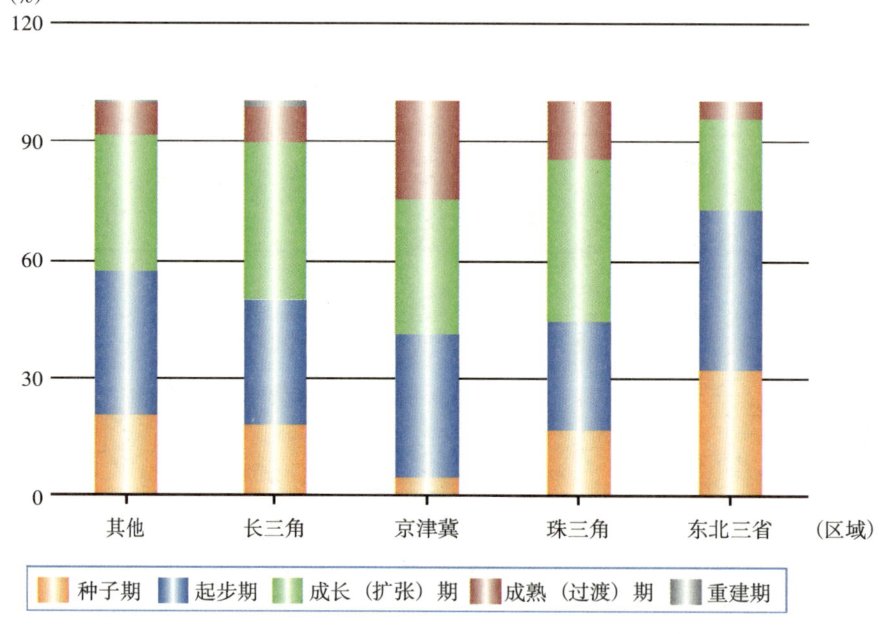

图 6-10 各经济区域创业风险投资项目的阶段分析（2013）

6.5.4 各经济区域创业风险投资项目的行业分布

图 6-11 至 图 6-15 分别显示了 2013 年我国不同经济区域创业风险投资的行业分布。

图 6-11 显示：2013 年长三角地区的创业风险投资分布在 29 行业，行业总数比 2012 年多 1 个；与 2012 年比较，2013 年长三角地区的创业风险机构投资重点关注的行业变化不大，投资比例较多的行业有医药保健、新材料工业、新能源/高效节能技术、传播与文化娱乐、软件产业、传统制造业、IT 服务业和环保工程，占比合计是 56.3%，其中最高的医药保健有 12.1%，比 2012 年明显增多。

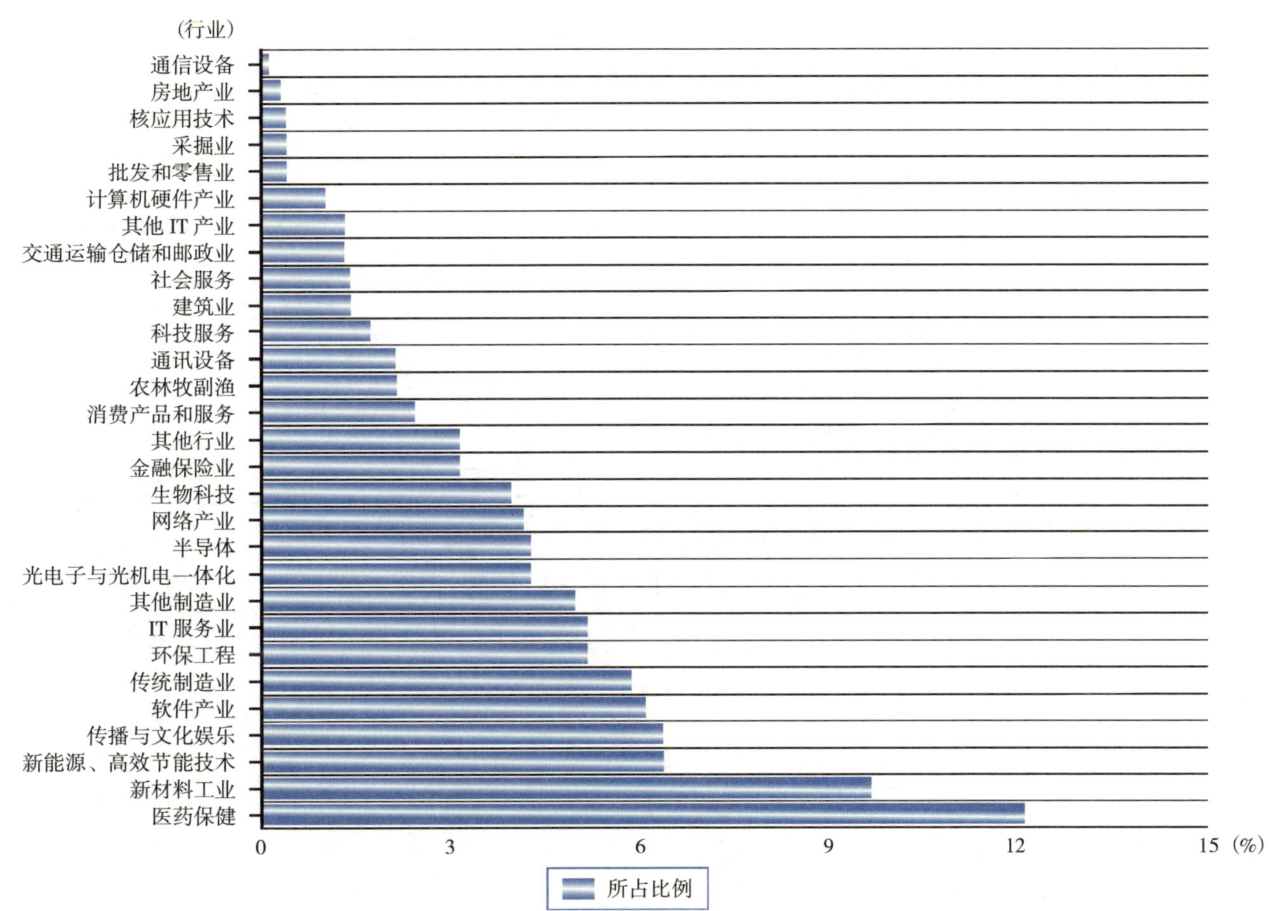

图 6-11 长三角地区创业风险投资项目的行业分布（2013）

图 6-12 显示了 2013 年京津冀地区创业风险投资的行业分布。2013 年，京津冀地区的创业风险投资分布在 23 个行业，行业总数与 2012 年持平；投资较多的行业有软件产业、新能源/高效节能技术、新材料工业、生物科技、医药保健和传统制造业，上述行业比例合计达 52.4%，其中最多的是软件产业和新能源/高效节能技术，占比都是 10.8%。

与 2012 年比较，软件产业项目成为 2013 年京津冀地区创业风险投资热点;新能源/高效节能技术、新材料工业、传统制造业和医药保健一直是京津冀地区创业风险投资机构比较关注的行业，投资比例较高；而 IT 服务业、网络产业的项目占比则有所下降。

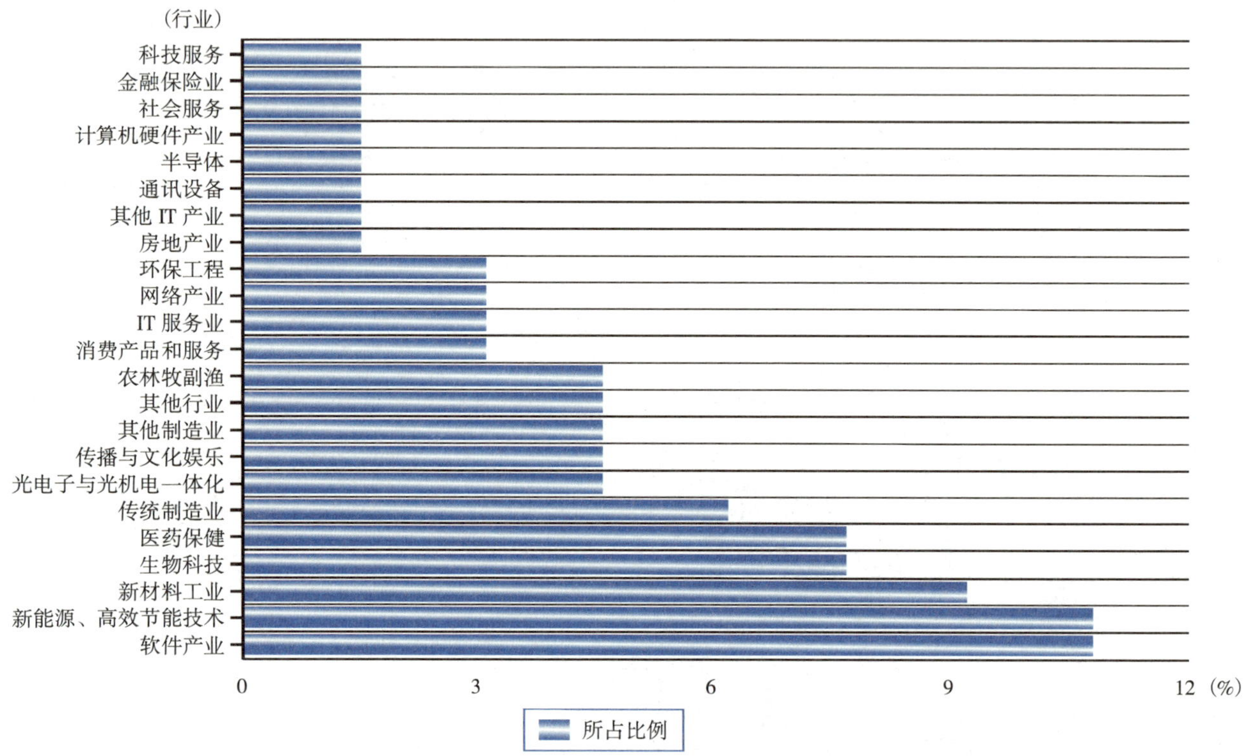

图 6-12 京津冀地区创业风险投资项目的行业分布（2013）

图 6-13 显示：2013 年珠三角地区创业风险投资的行业分布在 26 个行业，与 2012 年持平；投资较多的行业有：金融保险业、医药保健、消费产品和服务、网络产业、通讯设备、传统制造业、生物科技、传播与文化娱乐、新能源/高效节能技术，上述行业比例合计达 68.3%，其中最多的是金融保险业，比例达 14.7%。

与 2012 年比较，金融保险业、消费产品和服务、新能源/高效节能技术、传统制造业、传播与文化娱乐一直是珠三角地区创业风险投资青睐的行业，生物科技、网络产业、通讯设备也成为 2013 年珠三角地区创业风险投资机构新的投资热点，而新材料工业的项目占比则有所下降。

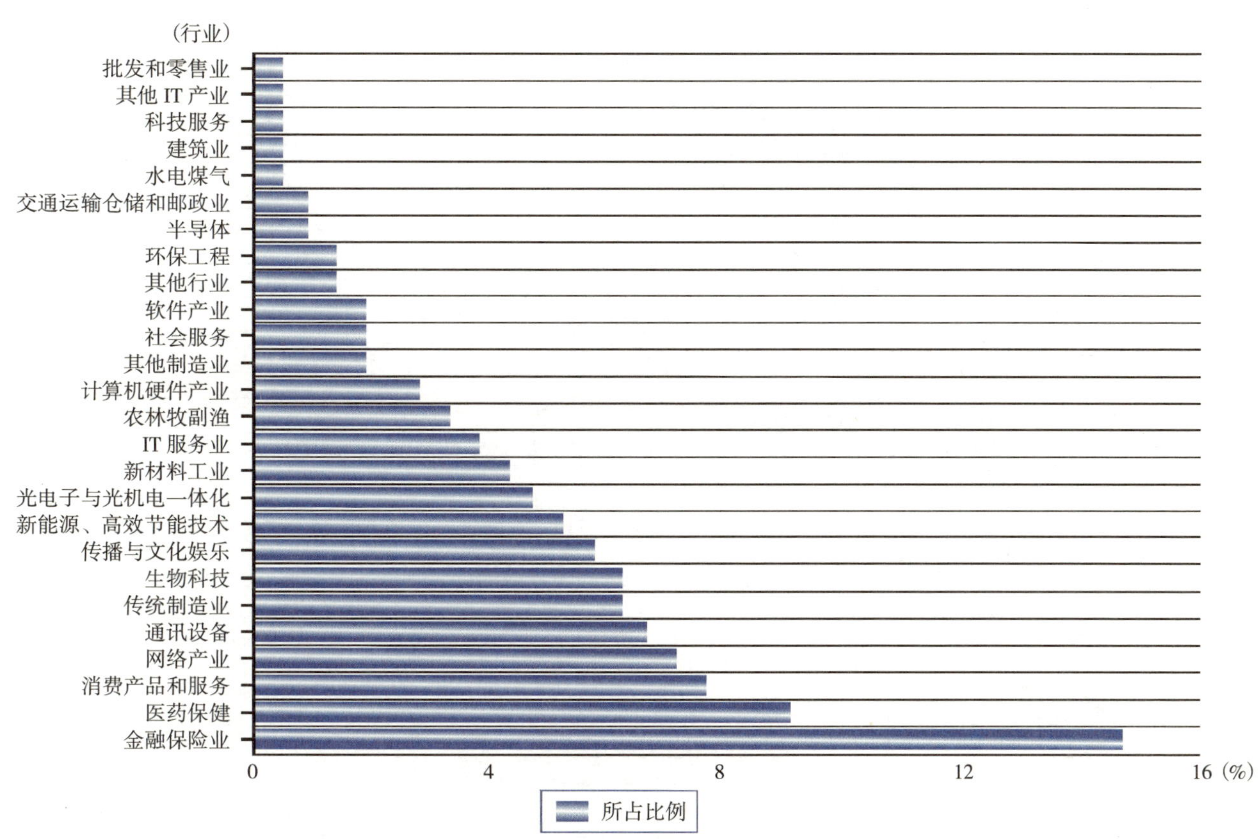

图 6-13 珠三角地区创业风险投资项目的行业分布（2013）

从图 6–14 看出，2013 年东北三省地区的创业风险投资分布在 16 个行业，比 2012 年增加了 1 个行业。其中，投资最多的是通讯设备，占比达 12.5%，另外，其他制造业、科技服务、新材料工业、金融保险业、软件产业、计算机硬件产业也是投资相对较多的行业；上述行业比例合计达 62.3%。与 2012 年比较，通讯设备成为 2013 年东三省地区的创业风险投资的投资重点关注领域。

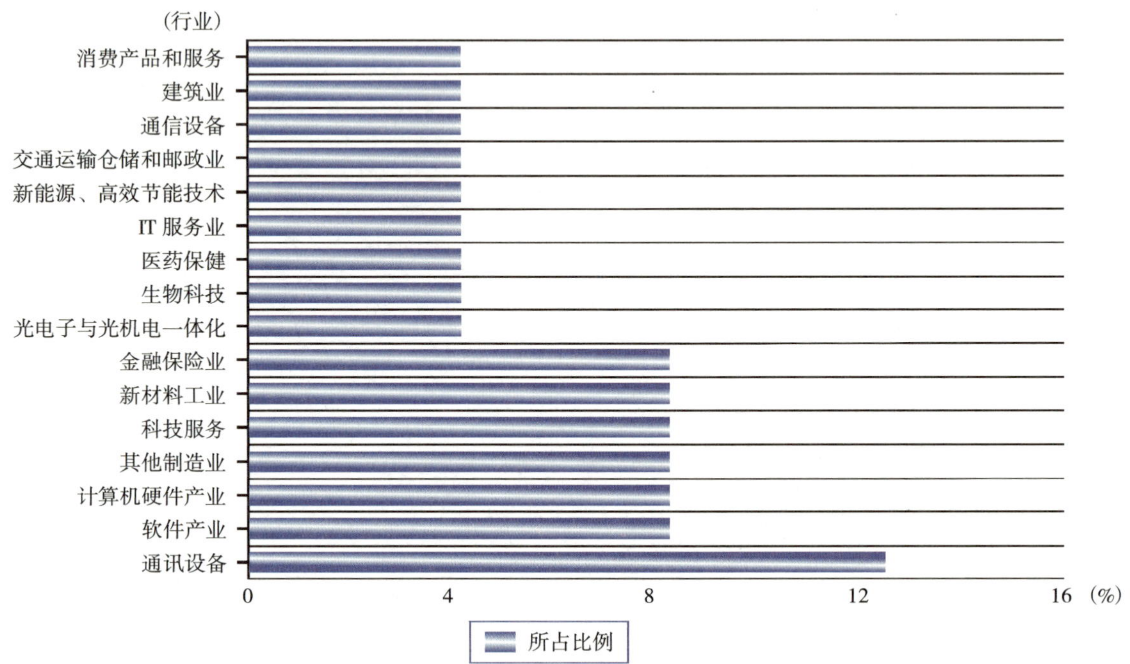

图 6–14 东北三省地区创业风险投资项目的行业分布（2013）

从图 6–15 可以看出，2013 年其他区域的创业风险投资分布在 30 个行业，比 2012 年多 1 个行业；主要集中在金融保险业、新能源/高效节能技术、医药保健、农林牧副渔、传统制造业、光电子与光机电一体化、新材料工业、其他制造业等行业，合计占比达 61.7%。与 2012 年比较，2013 年其他区域的创业风险投资较多的行业基本没有变化，只是个别行业的项目占比有所改变，如金融保险业跃居成为创业风险投资最多的行业，占比提高了 3 个百分点，达 9.2%。

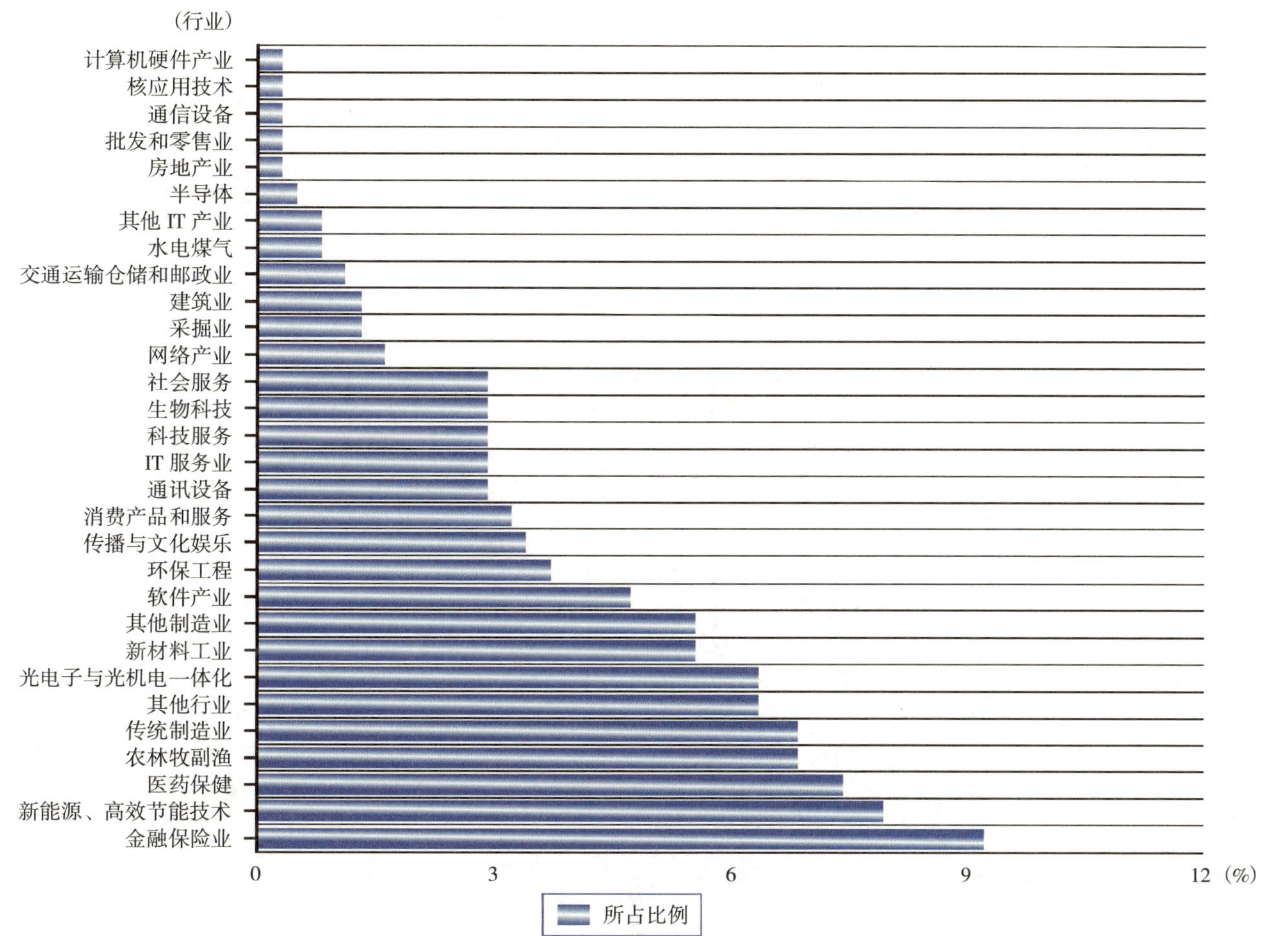

图 6–15 其他地区创业风险投资项目的行业分布（2013）

7 外资创业风险投资机构的运作

外资创业风险投资机构包括境内外资和境外外资两部分。境内外资是指通过外商独资（含港、澳、台）和合资合作方式而获得的创业资本；境外外资是指境外机构通过在中国大陆设立办事机构等方式投资于中国大陆的创业资本。本章统计分析对象为参与 2013 年全国创业风险投资调查的 44 家外资创业风险投资机构，以中外合资合作机构为主。限于样本的局限性，可能很难全面反映外资风险投资机构的真实状况，但是通过历史数据以及内资创业风险投资机构的相关情况对比，可以发现外资创业风险投资机构现存的一些主要特征。

7.1 外资创业风险投资项目的行业分布

调查显示[①]（见表 7-1、图 7-1、图 7-2），2013 年外资创业风险投资机构投资的项目主要分布在 24 个领域，其中，按投资金额划分排名前五位的是："消费产品和服务"、"传播与文化娱乐"、"光电子与光机电一体化"、"新材料工业"和"金融保险业"，所占比例合计为 60.35%，低于 2012 年的 65.3%；从投资项目来看，"传播与文化娱乐"、"金融保险业"、"消费产品和服务"、"新材料工业"和"光电子与光机电一体化"等行业居前五位，所占比重合计为 54.47%，比 2012 年所占比重高出 2.97 个百分点。

从具体行业分析来看，"消费产品和服务"行业增长显著，成为外资创业风险投资机构投资最集中的行业，投资金额所占比重从 2012 年的 9.15%上升至 16.61%，"传播与文化娱乐"从投资金额来看位居第二位，所占比重从 2012 年的 29.15%下跌至 13.97%，投资项目数也从 21.01%下降到 15.18%，这表明 2013 年外资创业风险投资机构的投资热点发生了显著转移。"光电子与光机电一体化"、"新材料工业"和"金融保险业"无论在投资金额上还是在投资项目上都比 2012 年比重有所增加，这表明外资创业风险投资机构对中国的传统制造业和高新技术产业重视程度加强；"医药保健"投资金额比重较 2012 年有所下降，但投资项目比重却有所上升。

表 7-1 外资创业风险投资项目行业分布：投资金额与投资项目（2013） 单位：%

投资行业	投资金额所占比例	投资项目所占比例
消费产品和服务	16.61	11.61
传播与文化娱乐	13.97	15.18
光电子与光机电一体化	11.45	7.14
新材料工业	10.01	8.93
金融保险业	8.31	11.61
医药保健	5.43	7.14
其他制造业	4.49	0.89
其他行业	4.13	1.79
计算机硬件产业	3.83	2.68

① 有效样本数 112 份。

续表

投资行业	投资金额所占比例	投资项目所占比例
通讯设备	3.44	4.46
生物科技	3.17	4.46
传统制造业	3.06	1.79
交通运输仓储和邮政业	2.98	2.68
新能源、高效节能技术	2.81	5.36
半导体	1.46	1.79
环保工程	1.29	2.68
批发和零售业	0.92	0.89
网络产业	0.83	4.46
软件产业	0.66	1.79
房地产业	0.54	0.89
IT 服务业	0.31	0.89
采掘业	0.31	0.89

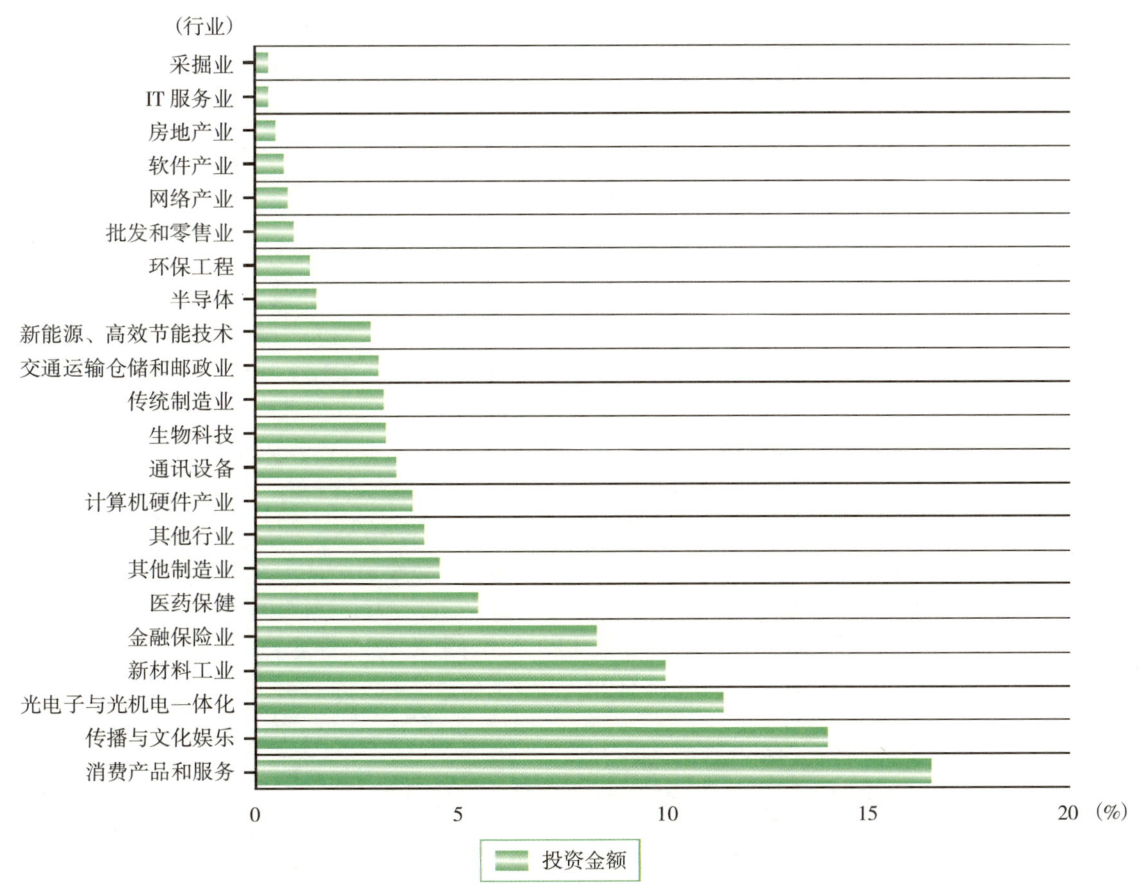

图 7-1 外资创业投资项目的行业分布：按投资金额（2013）

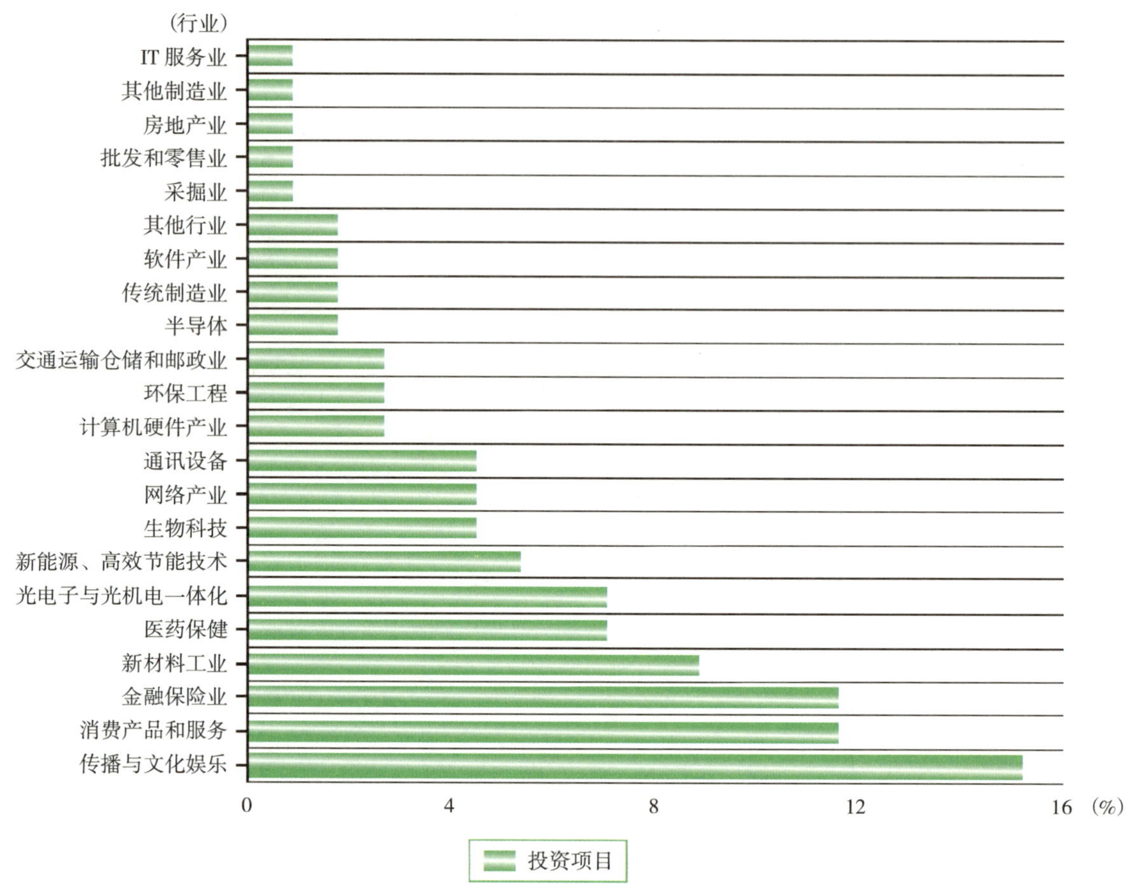

图 7-2 外资创业投资项目的行业分布：按投资项目（2013）

与 2013 年内资情况相比、外资创业风险投资项目的十大行业分布情况①(见表 7-2)，可以得出以下结论：

第一，内资创业风险投资机构投资的行业相对分散，外资创业风险投资机构投资行业的集中度较高。无论是从投资金额还是投资项目数量上，外资所投行业的集中度均高于内资，从投资金额来看，内资创业风险投资机构投资前十大行业分布所占比重合计为 70.6%，而外资所占比重合计为 81.5%；从投资项目数数量来看，内资创业风险投资机构前十大行业所占比重合计为 59.7%，而外资所占比重合计为 71.4%。但是和 2012 年相比，行业集中度有明显下降趋势。

第二，内资、外资创业风险投资机构所关注的领域差异较大。从投资金额来看，内资最关注的领域是“医药保健”，而外资创业风险投资机构最为关注的投资领域是“消费产品和服务”；内资创业风险投资机构所投资的十大行业中排名前五的为“医药保健”、“金融保险业”、“新能源、高效节能技术”、“传统制造业”和“农林牧副渔”，投资金额占比达 45.9%，而外资创业风险投资机构投资金额最高的五个行业是“消费产品和服务”、“传播与文化娱乐”、“光电子与光机电一体化”、“新材料工业”和“金融保险业”。从投资项目数量来看，内资投资机构 2013 年投资项目数量最多的行业为“医药保健”，外资投资机构 2013 年投资项目数量最多的行业为“传播与文化娱乐”，占比分别为 10.2%和 15.2%；内资创业风险投资机构投资项目数量排名前五的行业依次为“医药保健”、“新材料工业”、“新能源、高效节能技术”、“传统制造业”和“金融保险业”，而“传播与文化娱乐”、“消费产品和服务”、“金融保险业”、“新材料工业”、“光电子与光机电一体化”和“医药保健”是外资机构投资项目数量最多的行业。

① 有效样本数：内资为 1280 份，外资为 112 份。

表 7-2　内资、外资创业风险投资项目的十大行业分布：投资金额与投资项目（2013）　单位：%

内资			外资		
投资行业	投资金额	投资项目	投资行业	投资金额	投资项目
医药保健	10.8	10.2	消费产品和服务	16.6	11.6
金融保险业	10.4	6.1	传播与文化娱乐	14.0	15.2
新能源、高效节能技术	9.6	6.9	光电子与光机电一体化	11.4	7.1
传统制造业	7.8	6.4	新材料工业	10.0	8.9
农林牧副渔	7.3	4.0	金融保险业	8.3	11.6
新材料工业	6.7	7.5	医药保健	5.4	7.1
其他制造业	5.4	5.0	其他制造业	4.5	0.9
传播与文化娱乐	4.9	4.4	其他行业	4.1	1.8
IT 服务业	4.1	4.5	计算机硬件产业	3.8	2.7
光电子与光机电一体化	3.6	4.7	通讯设备	3.4	4.5

注：以“投资金额”占比排序。

7.2 外资创业风险投资项目所处阶段

通过对 2013 年的调查结果[①]分析（见图 7-3）显示，外资对于处于“成长（扩张）期”、“成熟（过渡）期”阶段的项目有显著的投资偏好，与 2012 年相比，外资创业风险投资机构的投资阶段有所后移。和 2012 年相比，2013 年外资机构主要投资于“成长（扩张）期”、“成熟（过渡）期”两阶段，两者所占比重均有所上升。从投资金额来看，两者合计所占比重从 2012 年的 70.9%上升至 81.6%；从投资项目数来看，两者所占比重合计为 68.2%，上升了 12.7 个百分点。投资于“种子期”和“起步期”等前期项目的投资金额和投资项目相比 2012 年均有显著下降，尤其是投资于“起步期”阶段的投资金额和投资项目，分别由 2012 年的 21.1%、36.5%下降至 14.8%和 23.6%。这一方面可能是由于上一种子期、起步期项目的后续投资，另一方面也说明“短平快”项目仍是外资创业风险投资行业的优先选择。

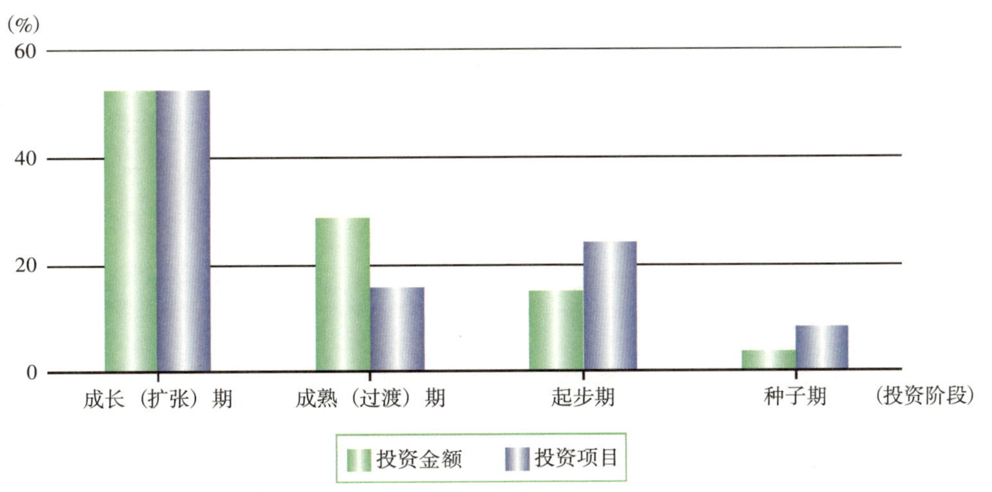

图 7-3　外资创业风险投资项目所处阶段（2013）

① 有效样本数：内资为 1230 份，外资为 110 份。

对于 2013 年内资、外资创业风险投资项目的阶段（见表 7-3），可以看出，内资、外资机构均以“成长（扩张）期”和“成熟（过渡）期”为重点投资阶段，内资、外资机构对这两个投资阶段的投资金额占比分别为 61.3% 和 81.6%，对这两个阶段的投资项目占比分别为 46.4%和 68.2%。但外资机构相对内资机构更加倾向于“成长（扩张）期”的项目投资，从项目金额占比来看，外资机构投资“成长（扩张）期”项目占比为 52.8%，比内资机构高出 13.3 个百分点；从投资项目来看，外资机构投资“成长（扩张）期”项目占比比内资机构高出了 15.8 个百分点。

表 7-3　内资、外资创业风险投资项目所处阶段（2013）　单位：%

投资阶段	项目金额占比		项目数量占比	
	内资	外资	内资	外资
种子期	13.7	3.6	19.3	8.2
起步期	23.7	14.8	33.3	23.6
成长（扩张）期	39.5	52.8	36.9	52.7
成熟（过渡）期	21.8	28.8	9.5	15.5
重建期	1.4	0.0	1.1	0.0

7.3 外资创业风险投资的投资强度

调查结果[①]显示（见表 7-4、图 7-4），2013 年外资机构单项投资金额的规模分布仍然以 2000 万元以上的大项目为主，但其所占比重有小幅度上升，由 2012 年的 63.7%上升至 78.2%。单项投资金额 2000 万元以下的项目所占比重相比 2012 年有所下降，其中，投资于 500 万~1000 万元和 1000 万~2000 万元的项目比重相比 2012 年有大幅度下降，但仍然比 2011 年有所上升。这说明外资创业风险投资机构投资阶段前移并未成气候，成熟大型项目仍是其投资首选，但这种前移的趋势是存在的。

表 7-4　外资创业风险投资单项投资金额的规模分布（2011~2013）　单位：%

投资额分布 / 年份	100 万元以下	100 万~300 万元	300 万~500 万元	500 万~1000 万元	1000 万~2000 万元	2000 万元以上
2011	0.0	0.2	0.3	3.3	13.9	82.3
2012	0.4	0.4	1.4	9.7	24.5	63.7
2013	0.0	0.1	1.3	4.2	16.1	78.2

① 有效样本数为 121 份。

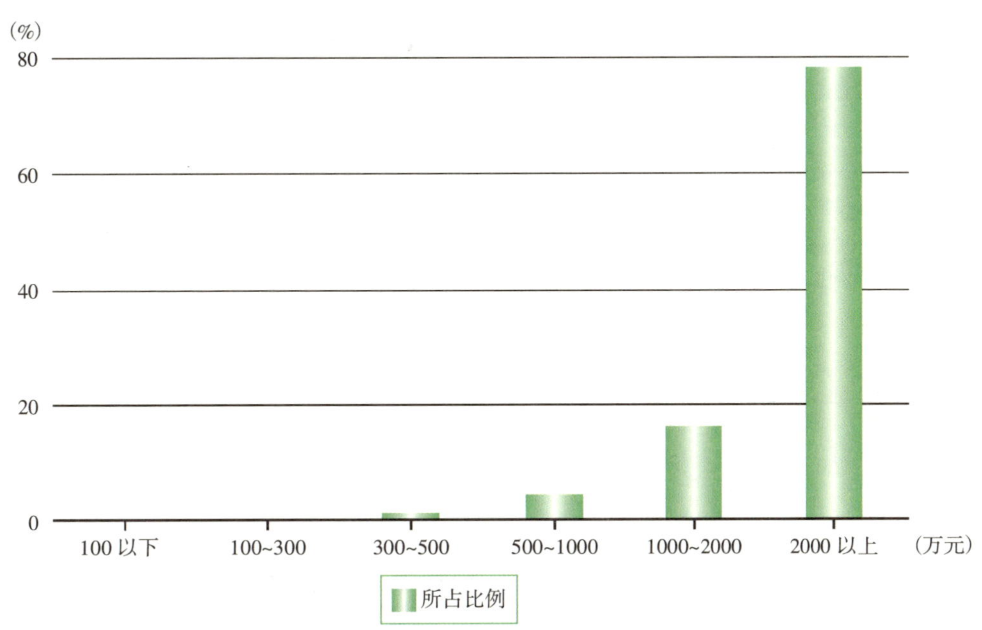

图 7–4 外资创业风险投资单项投资金额分布（2013）

通过对比发现[①](见表 7–5、图 7–5)，内资、外资创业风险投资机构投资主要集中在单项规模 1000 万~2000 万元和 2000 万元以上的大中型项目上，尤其是外资创业风险投资机构对大项目的投资集中度更高，内资、外资机构投资两类项目合计占比分别为 78.2%、64.1%。但与 2012 年对比，内资、外资创业风险投资机构投资项目集中度却有集中趋势，2000 万元以上项目占比有所上升。相比外资投资机构，内资投资机构在 1000 万元以下的中小型项目上的投资相对更多。

表 7–5 内资和外资创业风险投资单项投资金额的规模分布（2013） 单位：%

投资金额	100 万元以下	100 万~300 万元	300 万~500 万元	500 万~1000 万元	1000 万~2000 万元	2000 万元以上
外资	0.0	0.1	1.3	4.2	16.1	78.2
内资	0.3	2.5	4.1	10.0	18.8	64.1

① 有效样本数：内资为 1493 份，外资为 121 份。

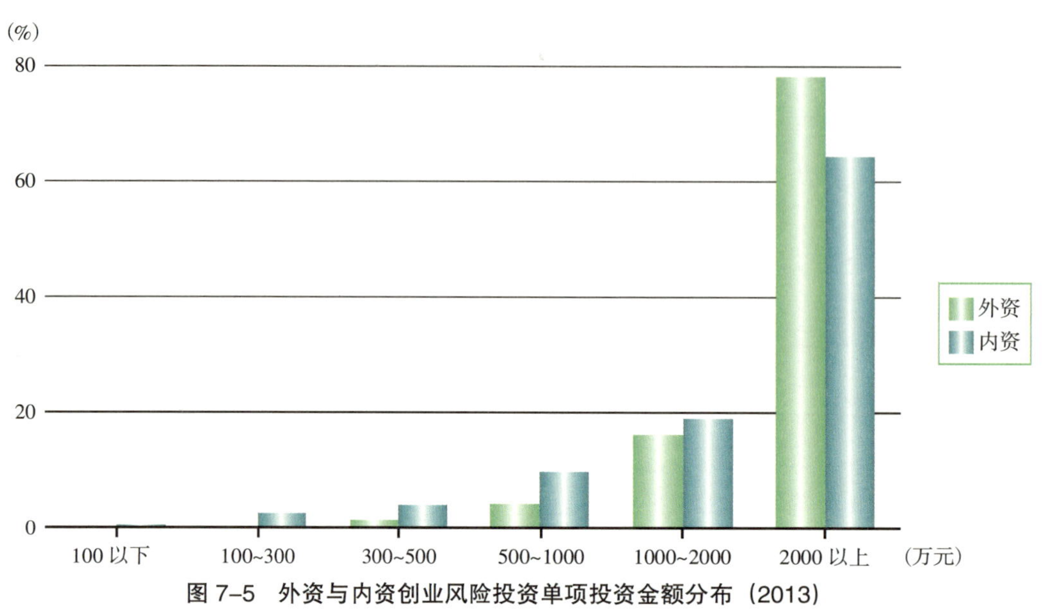

图 7-5 外资与内资创业风险投资单项投资金额分布（2013）

7.4 外资创业风险投资项目状况分析

7.4.1 创业风险投资项目的实收资本情况

调查结果[①]显示（见表 7-6、图 7-6），2013 年外资创业风险投资机构项目的实收资本规模总体上有显著上升，实收资本规模在 3000 万~5000 万元和 5000 万元以上项目所占比重有显著上升，分别由 2012 年的 11.0%、34.0%上升至 2013 年的 17.5%和 52.6%；而实收资本在 3000 万元以下的项目所占比重均有较大幅度的下降。这说明外资创业风险投资机构的投资偏好近几年来有比较大的浮动，投资项目的规模呈现出多元化态势。

表 7-6 外资创业风险投资项目实收资本的规模分布（2011~2013） 单位：%

实收资本／年份	500 万元以下	500 万~1000 万元	1000 万~3000 万元	3000 万~5000 万元	5000 万元以上
2011	9.3	5.9	27.1	16.9	40.7
2012	11.0	15.0	29.0	11.0	34.0
2013	5.3	8.8	15.8	17.5	52.6

① 有效样本数为 57 份。

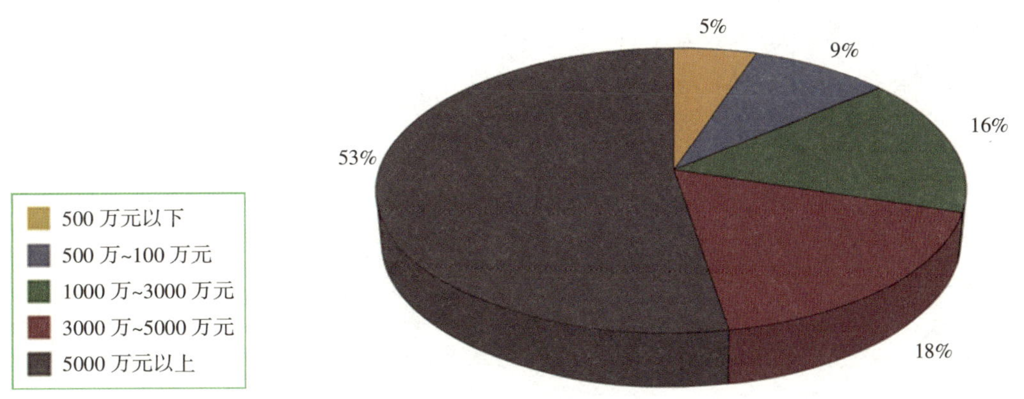

图 7-6　外资创业风险投资项目实收资本的规模分布（2013）

2013 年，内资、外资机构依然主要投资于实收资本 1000 万~3000 万元和 5000 万元以上的项目，其中实收资本 5000 万元以上项目占比分别为 25.5%和 52.6%，实收资本 1000 万~3000 万元的项目比分别为 24.2%和 15.8%。总体上，外资机构投资项目的实收资本规模要高于内资投资机构，外资机构投资于实收资本 1000 万元以上的项目比重为 85.9%，较内资机构高出 21.9 个百分点，差距较 2012 年有进一步扩大。此外，内资机构对不同规模项目的投资较外资机构更为均衡，外资机构投资实收资本为 1000 万元以下的项目比重为 8.8%和 5.3%，明显低于其他规模项目所占比重（见表 7-7、图 7-7）。

表 7-7　外资和内资创业风险投资项目实收资本的规模分布（2013）　单位：%

分布比例	500 万元以下	500 万~1000 万元	1000 万~3000 万元	3000 万~5000 万元	5000 万元以上
外资	5.3	8.8	15.8	17.5	52.6
内资	20.4	15.6	24.2	14.3	25.5

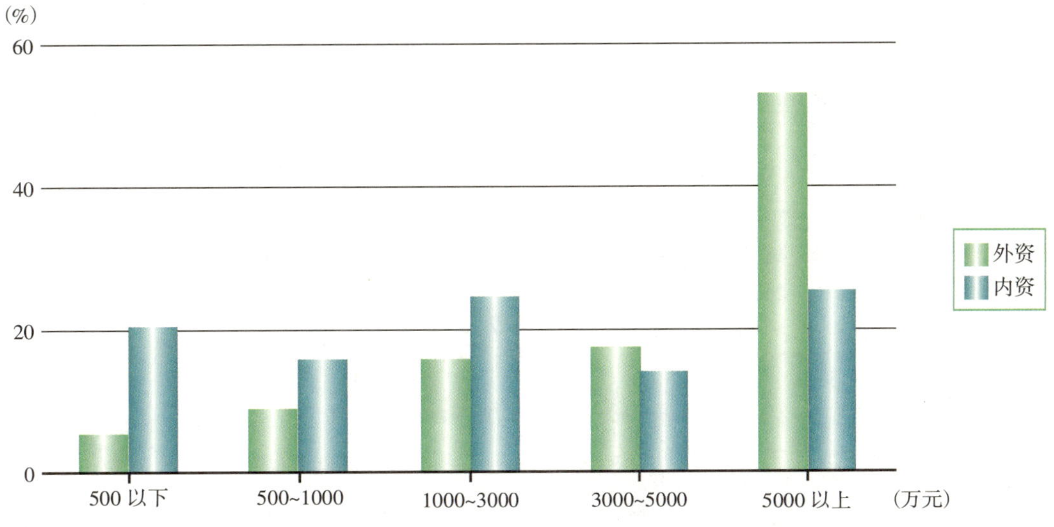

图 7-7　外资与内资创业风险投资项目实收资本的规模分布（2013）

7.4.2 创业风险投资项目的雇员情况

调查显示①（见表 7-8、图 7-8），2013 年外资创业风险投资项目雇员人数规模分布基本保持稳定。但雇员人数 10~50 人、100~150 人以及 150~200 人的投资项目比均低于 2011 年和 2012 年，而人数在 10 人以下和 200 人以上的投资项目数都有显著增长，增幅分别为 5 个百分点和 7.9 个百分点。

表 7-8 外资创业风险投资项目雇员人数分布（2011~2013） 单位：%

年份 \ 分布比例（人）	10 以下	10~50	50~100	100~150	150~200	200 以上
2011	3.6	13.4	8.9	14.3	13.4	46.4
2012	8.3	17.9	9.5	21.4	10.7	32.1
2013	13.3	13.3	16.7	10.0	6.7	40.0

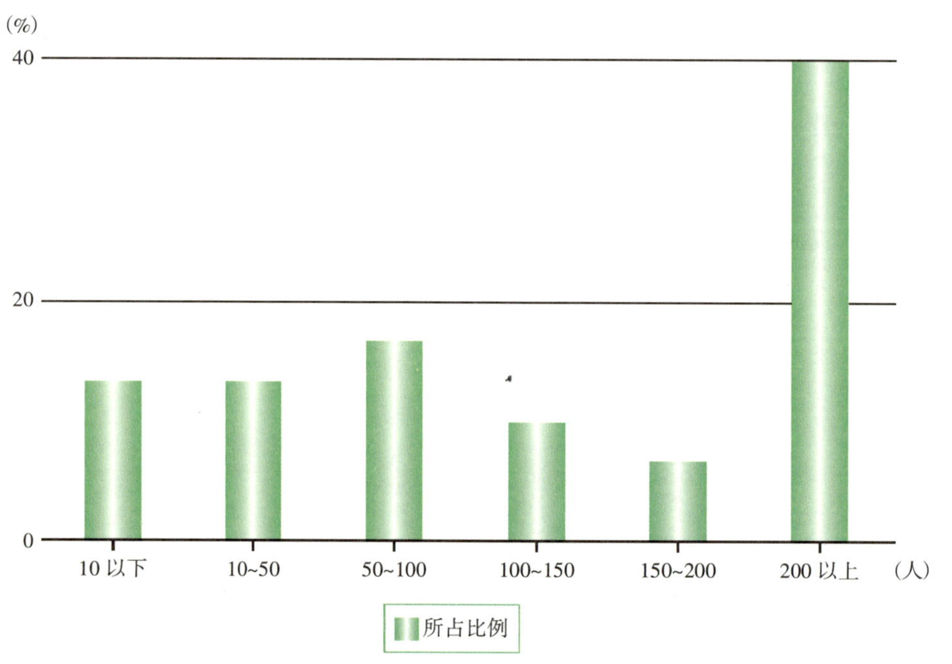

图 7-8 外资创业风险投资项目雇员人数分布（2013）

① 有效样本数为 60 份。

对比内资、外资机构投资项目的雇员人数分布情况①（见表 7-9、图 7-9），外资机构相对内资机构更偏好雇员人数为中等规模和较大规模的项目，外资机构投资于雇员人数在 50~100 人以及 200 人的项目所占比重都显著高于内资机构，其中投资于 200 人以上项目外资占比高于内资占比 16.8 个百分点，表现出了外资机构对于这一类大型项目的显著偏好。

表 7-9 外资与内资创业风险投资项目雇员人数分布（2013） 单位：%

分布比例（人）	10 以下	10~50	50~100	100~150	150~200	200 以上
外资	13.3	13.3	16.7	10.0	6.7	40.0
内资	13.8	31.6	13.8	10.2	7.5	23.2

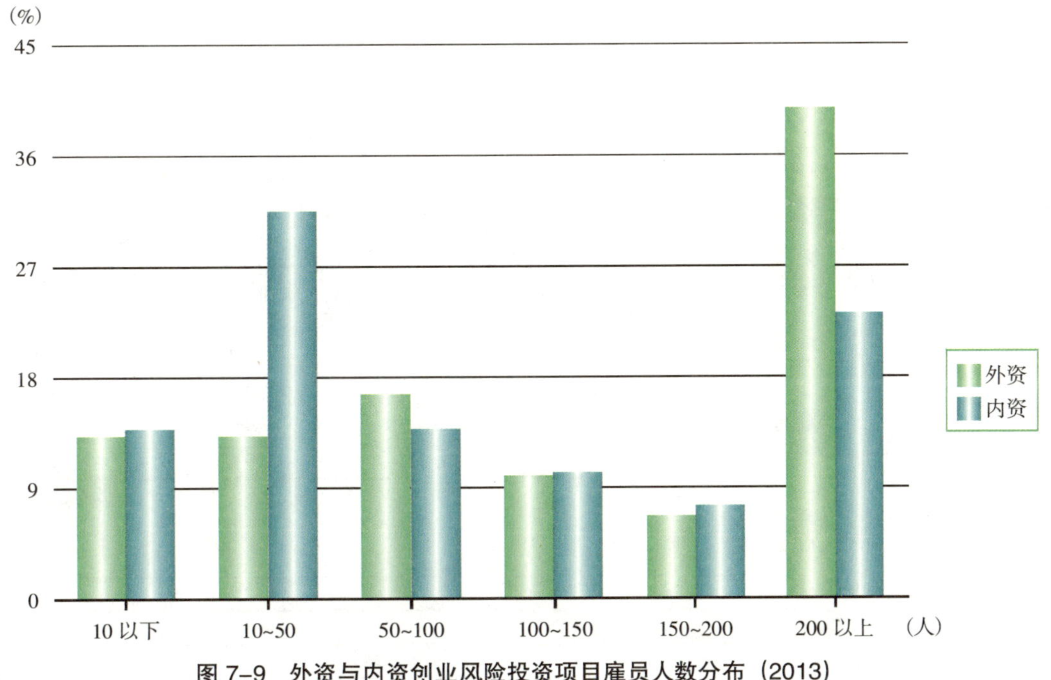

图 7-9 外资与内资创业风险投资项目雇员人数分布（2013）

① 有效样本数：内资为 842 份，外资为 60 份。

7.5 外资创业风险投资项目的总体运作情况

调查显示①（见表 7-10、图 7-10），2013 年外资创业风险投资机构投资项目运行情况有以下三个特点：

（1）继续运行的项目占比由 2012 年的峰值 68.8%下降至 52.0%，但仍然超过 2011 年的 49.1%；相应准备上市的占比仍然维持在 7%，比 2012 年上升 0.8 个百分点，但是和 2011 年的 46.7%相比仍然处于低位。

（2）大幅度下降的准备上市项目通过各种渠道退出，其中已在境内外上市的占比仍占据了比较大的比重，比 2011 年的 1.9%上升了近 9 个百分点，这可能与 2011 年准备上市公司比重高达 46.7%有较高相关性；除境外收购，被其他机构收购的百分比都有大幅度下降。原股东（创业者）回购和管理层收购所占比重分别比 2012 年上升了 3.5 个和 13.3 个百分点。

（3）清算项目的占比与上一年度持平。尽管 2013 年该类项目的占比有所回升，但仍低于往年，由此可见，尽管受到 IPO 暂定的利空影响，外资机构投资项目的运营质量仍然处于较高水平。

表 7-10 截至 2012 年、2013 年底外资创业风险投资项目运行情况 单位：%

投资项目运作情况	已上市		准备上市		被其他机构收购			原股东（创业者）回购	管理层收购	继续运行	清算
	境内上市	境外上市	境内上市	境外上市	境内上市公司收购	境内非上市公司或自然人收购	境外收购				
2012 年	10.7		6.2		6.0			6.5	0.7	68.8	1.1
	7.6	3.1	5.1	1.1	1.1	4.9	0.0	6.5	0.7	68.8	1.1
2013 年	10.8		7.0		5.1			10.0	14.0	52.0	1.1
	7.4	3.4	6.5	0.5	0.8	4.1	0.2	10.0	14.0	52.0	1.1

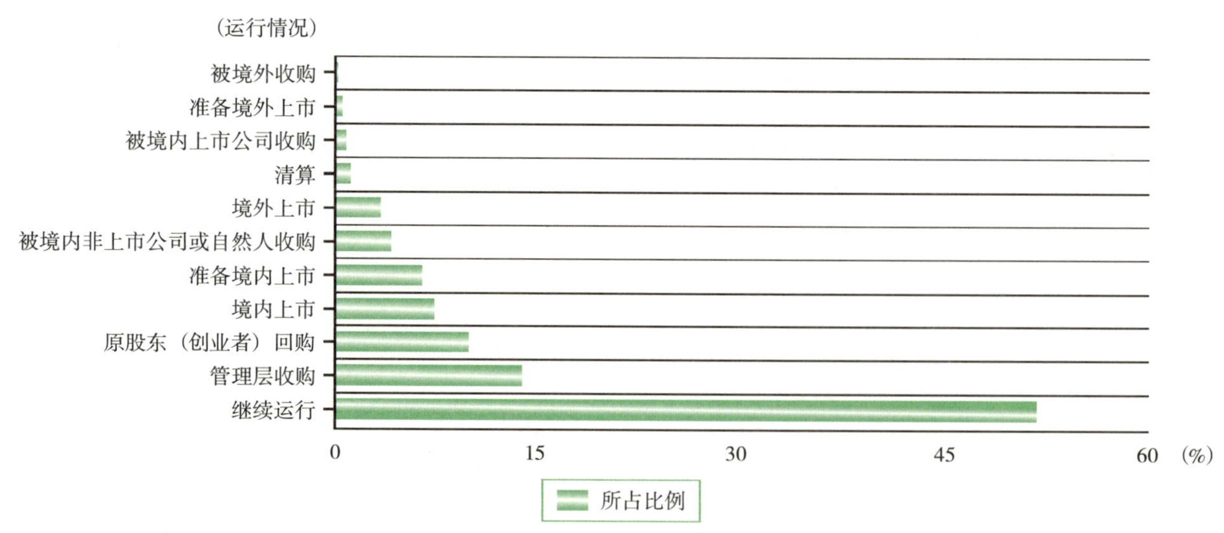

图 7-10 截至 2013 年底外资创业风险投资项目的运作情况

① 有效样本数为 48 份。

对比2013年内、外资创业风险投资项目运行情况[①]（见表7-11、图7-11），内资、外资机构投资项目主要是"继续运行"，项目占比较为接近，所占比重分别为52.0%、67.9%；内资、外资投资项目运行选择"准备上市"所占比重分别为7.0%、11.1%，内资高出外资4.1个百分点；上市不再是内、外资机构投资项目的主要退出方式，外资机构以管理层收购方式退出的项目占比为最高，而内资主要以原股东（创业者）回购的方式退出占比最高；上市在内资、外资退出方式中均占比第二，而且外资高出内资4.8个百分点。

表7-11 截至2013年底外资与内资创业风险投资项目运作情况 单位：%

运作情况	继续运行	管理层收购	已上市	原股东（创业者）回购	准备上市	其他机构收购	清算
外资	52.0	14.0	10.8	10.0	7.0	5.1	1.1
内资	67.9	1.1	6.0	8.5	11.1	3.7	1.7

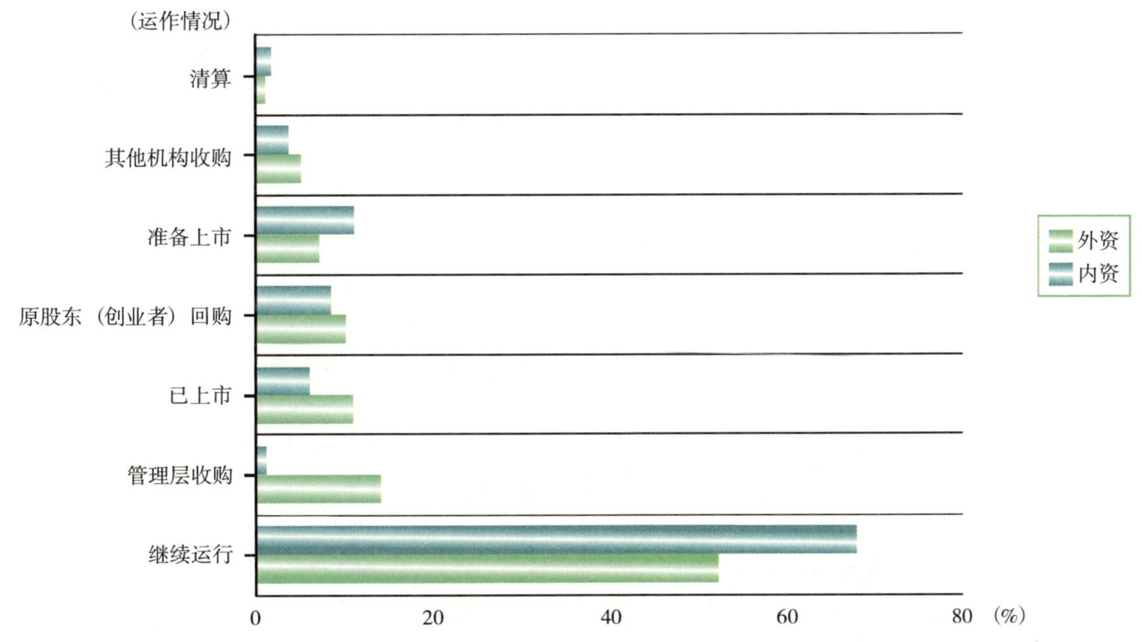

图7-11 截至2013年底外资与内资创业风险投资项目的运作情况

① 有效样本数：内资为842份，外资为60份。

7.6 影响外资创业风险投资机构投资决策的因素

调查显示①（见图 7-12），影响外资创业风险投资机构投资决策的各因素重要性排序略有变化，“管理团队”和“市场前景”依然是 2013 年影响外资创业风险投资机构投资的前两大因素，两者占比均为 19.2%。与 2012 年相比，“盈利模式”超过“技术因素”成为影响外资创投机构投资决策的第三大因素，所占比重为 15.7%；而“公司治理结构”超过“股权价格”，排序比 2012 年上升一位至 2013 年的第六位，占比重为 7.6%；此外，“资信状况”上升两位，“其他”因素上升一位，相应地，“竞争对手情况”、“投资地点”、“中介服务质量”均下降一位。

比较 2013 年影响内资、外资机构投资决策的各项因素发现，“管理团队”、“市场前景”、“盈利模式”、“技术因素”、“财务状况”等因素为影响内、外资创业风险投资的最主要的五大因素，所占比例合计为 79.9%和 81.4%，但各影响因素的重要性有所差别。“管理团队”和“市场前景”是影响内资、外资创业风险投资机构投资决策的两大因素，但内资机构更看重“市场前景”，而外资机构兼顾两者。外资机构较内资机构更重视“公司治理结构”的重要性，认为该因素重要的外资机构占比较内资机构高出 3.3 个百分点。影响外资机构投资决策的因素重要程度在“盈利模式”、“技术因素”、“财务状况”、“公司治理结构”、“股权价格”、“资信状况”、“竞争对手情况”和“投资地点”等因素上的分布相对内资更为均衡，表明外资创业风险投资机构依然更加注重对投资项目进行多种因素的综合考察。

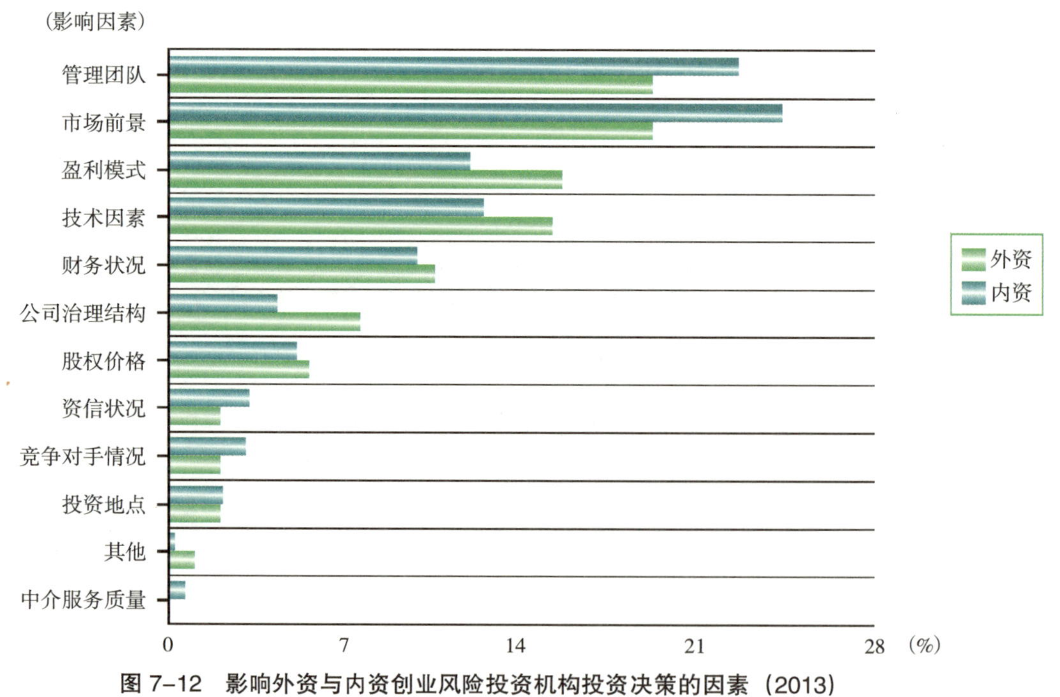

图 7-12 影响外资与内资创业风险投资机构投资决策的因素（2013）

① 有效样本数：内资为 1015 份，外资为 47 份。

7.7 外资创业风险投资机构获取信息的主要渠道

调查显示[①]（见图 7-13），2013 年外资创业风险投资机构获取信息的主要渠道与 2012 年相比发生较大变化，具体表现为：

首先，“项目中介机构”成为外资机构最重要的信息渠道，占比排名由第三位上升至第一位，为 20.6%。

其次，“朋友介绍”渠道仍然保持了 2012 年的排名，占据第二位，为 18.7%。

最后，“政府部门推荐”由 2012 年占比排名第一位下降至第三位，占比由 21.4%下降至 18.1%。此外，“银行介绍”也相比 2012 年下降，由 2012 年的排名第六位下降至 2013 年的排名第七位。其他信息渠道排名结构并没有显著变化。

2013 年，内资、外资机构获取信息的渠道基本一致，“项目中介机构”、“朋友介绍”和“政府部门推荐”等渠道为内、外资机构的前三大渠道。其中，内资机构中通过“政府部门推荐”获取信息的机构占比明显高于外资机构，内资机构依靠“股东推荐”的结构多于“项目业主”，外资机构则恰恰相反。

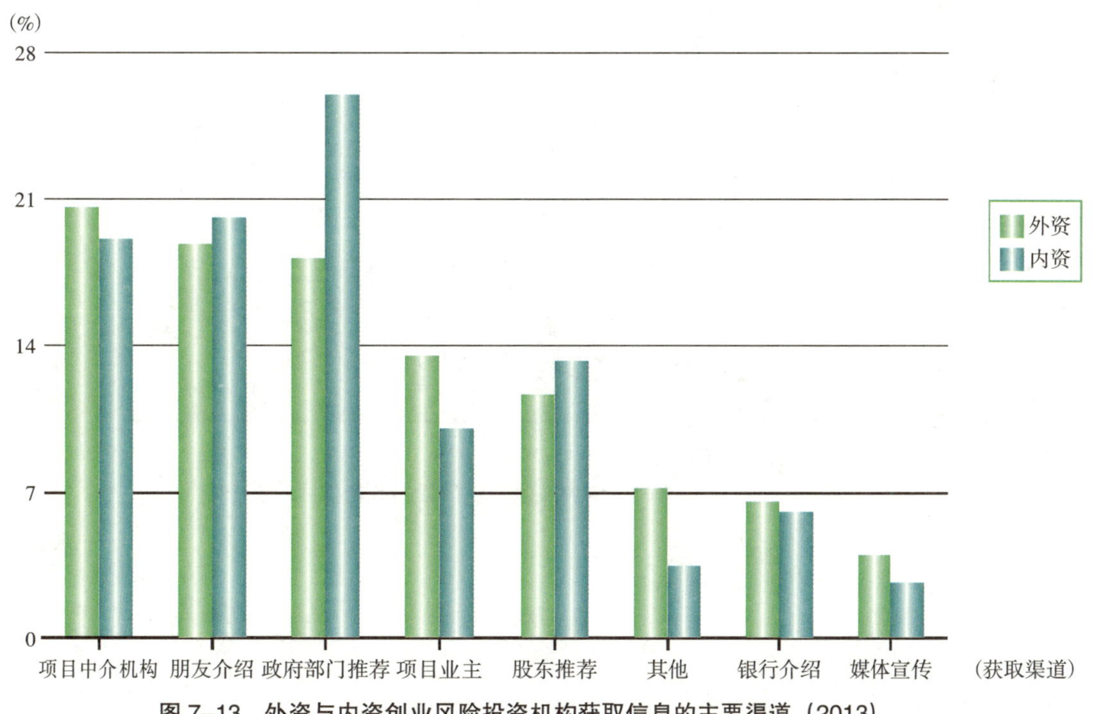

图 7-13　外资与内资创业风险投资机构获取信息的主要渠道（2013）

① 有效样本数：内资为 842 份，外资为 60 份。

7.8 外资创业风险投资项目的监管模式

调查显示①(见图 7-14)，2013 年外资创业风险投资项目的监管模式与 2012 年相比发生了显著变化，“董事会席位”、“提供管理咨询”、“财务咨询”尽管仍然是最主要的三种监管方式，三者所占比重合计为 88.0%，但“董事会席位”由 2012 年的第三位跃至第一位。对比内资、外资风险投资项目的监管方式可以发现，“提供管理咨询”仍然是内资、外资机构最主要的监管方式，占比分别为 33.2%、32.3%；外资机构采用“董事会席位”和“财务咨询”的占比为 33.1%和 22.6%，内资机构采用“董事会席位”和“财务咨询”的机构占比多了 3.1 个百分比。此外，内资机构采用“只限监管”方式的比重也高于外资机构。

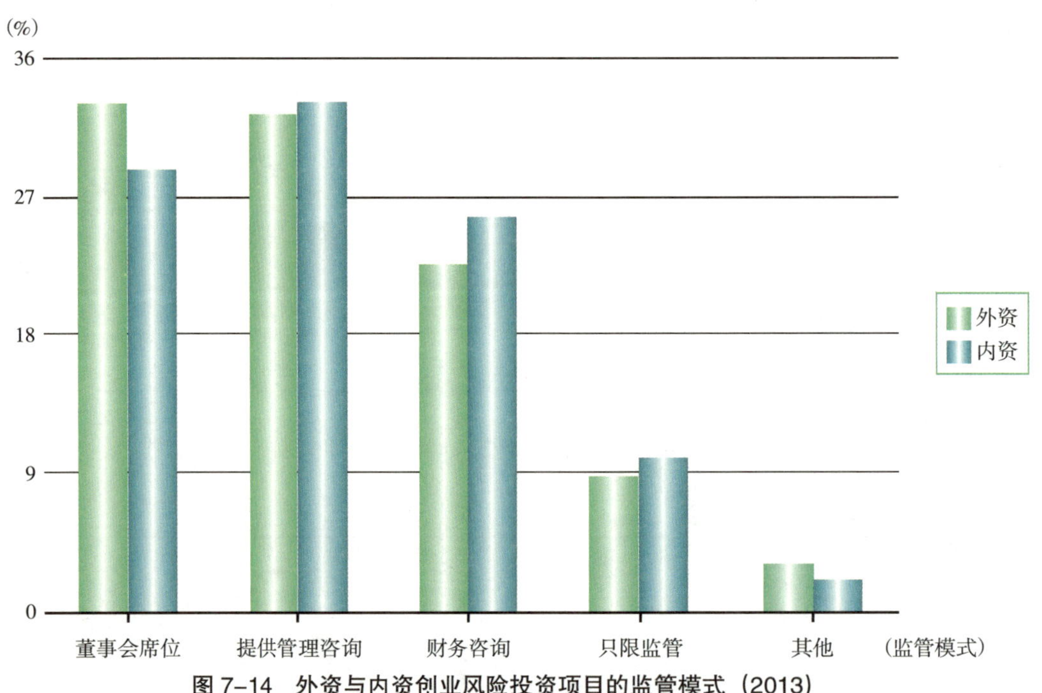

图 7-14 外资与内资创业风险投资项目的监管模式（2013）

① 有效样本数：内资为 1008 份，外资为 47 份。

7.9 与外资创业风险投资机构经营有关的人力资源因素

调查显示[①]（见图 7-15），外资创业风险投资机构认为“人际关系网络和协调能力”是合格创业投资人员最应该具备的素质，“财务管理能力”次之，二者所占比重合计为 35.8%，低于 2012 年前两个因素占比合计的 40.6%。此外，外资创业风险投资机构认为，合格的创业风险投资人员也应该具备“资本运作能力”和“技术背景”等，所占比重分别为 16.1%和 15.5%。与 2012 年相比，各个因素被重视程度更加离散，2012 年外资机构认为“判断力和洞察力”、“资本运作能力”和“人际关系网络和协调能力”三项因素重要的比例均超过 18%，而 2013 年仅有“人际关系网络和协调能力”一项因素的比例为 18.7%，除“其他”因素以外的其他 5 项因素均分布在 17.1%~14.5%。

对比内资、外资创业风险投资机构在合格创业投资人员应具备素质方面的认识，“判断力和洞察力”和“财务管理能力”是内资、外资创业风险投资机构认为合格创业风险投资人员素质应该具备的两个重要因素，但外资机构认为“人际关系网络和协调能力”和“技术背景”更为重要，而内资机构则认为“资本运作能力”、“商务谈判能力”等因素更值得关注。

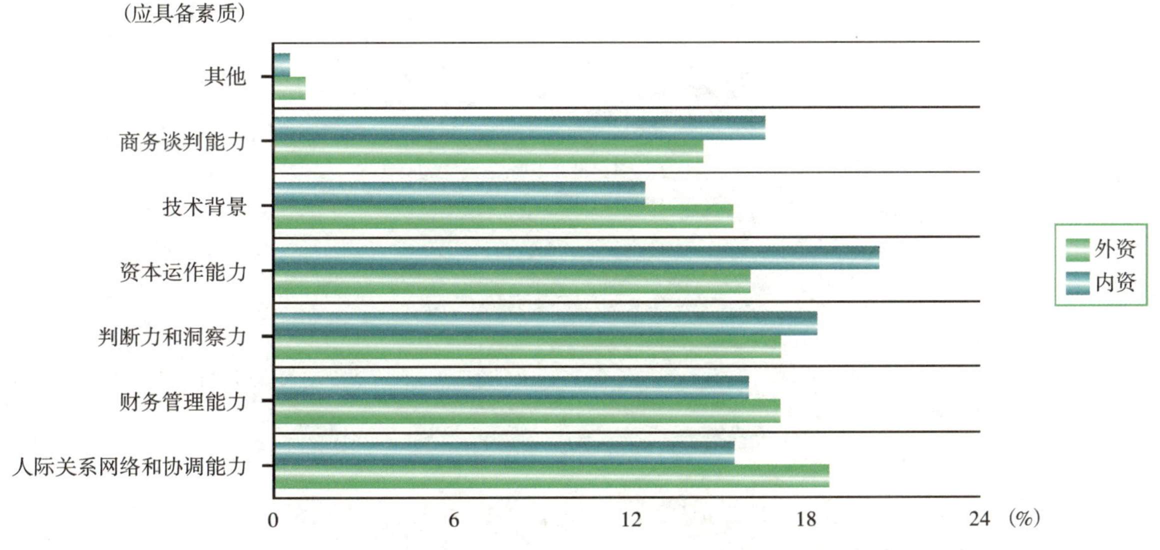

图 7-15　外资与内资创业风险投资机构对合格创业风险投资人员素质的要求（2013）

① 有效样本数：内资为 1001 份，外资为 43 份。

调查显示[①]（见图 7–16），2013 年外资创业风险投资机构认为“技术评估”和“技术背景”是从业人员最缺乏的两种专业知识，选择这两项的外资机构占比分别为 16.8% 和 15.9%，认为从业人员最缺乏“企业管理”的机构占比为 14.2%。认为从业人员缺乏“项目识别”、“资本运作”和“法律知识”的外资机构占比依次下降。与 2012 年相比，选择“企业管理”和“资本运作”的外资机构比重下降明显，分别由第一、二位下降至第三、五位；上升位次最大的是“技术评估”，从第五位上升至首位；总的来看，2013 年涉及技术和项目因素的被重视程度有显著提升。

对比内资、外资机构，内资机构把“技术评估”、“资本运作”视为创业风险投资机构从业人员最缺乏的知识，“项目识别”、“企业管理”分列其后，其他依次为“技术背景”、“法律知识”、“财务管理能力”和“商务谈判能力”等方面的知识。其中，最值得关注的是，内资、外资创业风险投资机构对从业人员缺乏“技术评估”和“技术背景”两方面知识的关注程度有很大不同。内资更为关注的是“技术评估”，该因素所占比重比外资高出 1.7 个百分点，但是对于“技术背景”的关注占比则低于外资 3.2 个百分点。这表明了内外资创业风险投资的从业人员不同的技术特征，即外资从业人员对于技术方面的知识掌握上比内资的从业人员更加全面，而内资则要求懂得如何评估特定技术的能力而并不特别注重于技术背景的要求。

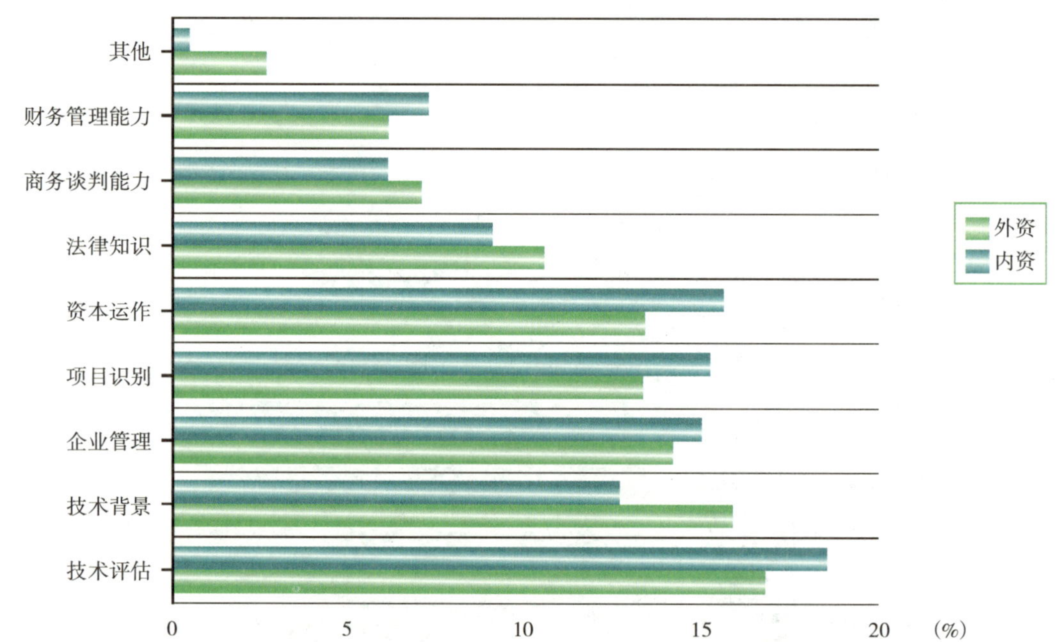

图 7–16 外资与内资创业风险投资机构认为我国创业风险投资从业人员缺乏的专业知识（2013）

① 有效样本数：内资为 1005 份，外资为 46 份。

7.10 外资创业风险投资机构对总体发展环境的评价

调查显示①（见图 7-17），外资创业风险投资机构投资效果不理想的原因与 2012 年相比大体保持一致，“退出渠道不畅”和“政策环境变化”仍被认为是两大主要因素。具体表现为：

（1）2013 年由于受到 2012 年下半年开始的第 8 次 IPO 暂停的持续利空消息，导致了“退出渠道不畅”成为影响投资效果的首要原因，占比为 28.2%。

（2）2013 年，尽管美国经济开始呈现出复苏，但是国内政策调整的不确定因素仍然存在，因而“政策环境变化”被外资机构认为是导致其创业风险投资机构投资效果不理想的第二大因素，仅次于“退出渠道不畅”。

认为“其他”因素导致创业风险投资机构投资效果不佳的外资机构占比由 2012 年的 4.6%上升至 17.9%；认为“市场竞争”导致投资效果比价的外资机构数占比有大幅度下降；“技术不成熟”、“后续融资不力”和“缺乏诚信”因素的作用均呈现出下降趋势，其中“缺乏诚信”因素的作用出现了显著的下降，说明我国的外部信用环境有所改善。

对比内、外资机构对行业总体发展环境的评价（见图 7-17），外资认为“退出渠道不畅”是导致投资效果欠佳的最主要原因，而内资认为“政策环境变化”才是导致投资效果欠佳的主要原因。此外，内资机构认为行业内“市场竞争”是导致投资效果欠佳的第三大因素，而“内部管理水平有限”对于投资效果产生的负面作用也很显著，远高于外资机构的占比。另外，认为“其他”、“技术不成熟”和“缺乏诚信”导致投资效果欠佳的内资企业占比显著低于外资机构，而认为“后续融资不力”的内资机构略高于外资机构。这说明外资机构在后续融资能力上高于内资机构。

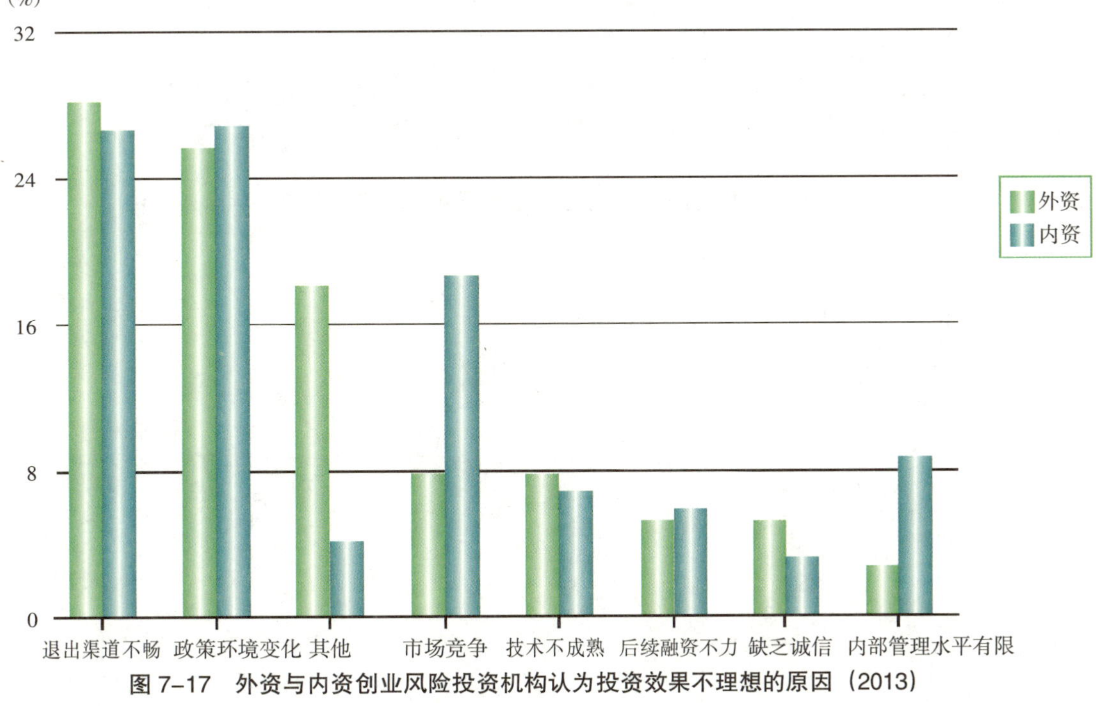

图 7-17 外资与内资创业风险投资机构认为投资效果不理想的原因（2013）

① 有效样本数：内资为 950 份，外资为 39 份。

2013 年对创业风险投资行业发展环境的调查显示①（见图 7-18），外资创业风险投资机构认为"多层次资本市场不完善"和"缺乏好项目"是创业风险投资行业发展的两大主要障碍，两者占比合计达 75.0%，"政策不明朗"次之。可以看到 2013 年中国创业风险投资行业发展环境的问题集中度非常高，占比最高的三项合计占总数的 93.2%。这说明在 2013 年，我国宏观经济形式和资本市场局势整体的不明朗、优质项目匮乏，使得这几个问题成为外资机构在国内发展所面临的最大问题。而与此同时，可以看到和 2012 年相比行业环境有了很好的改善，认为"缺乏行业法规"的外资机构比重有大幅度下降，仅占 2.3%。

比较内资、外资创业风险投资机构认为行业发展所面临的困难（见图 7-18），内资机构对于"政策不明朗"的感受比"缺乏好项目"更加强烈，其他因素对于内资、外资机构而言，影响程度相当。

此外，内资、外资机构所面临的发展障碍分布较为集中，"多层次资本市场不完善"、"缺乏好项目"和"政策不明朗"与其他几个因素相比差异很显著，其中，"多层次资本市场不完善"所占比重，外资比内资高出 0.9%，而"缺乏好项目"所占比重外资比内资高出 5.6%，"政策不明朗"所占比重内资则比外资高出 1.6%。综上所述，说明内资机构相对更依赖于政策性因素的支持，而外资判断未来创业风险投资行业的发展则更看重投资项目本身。

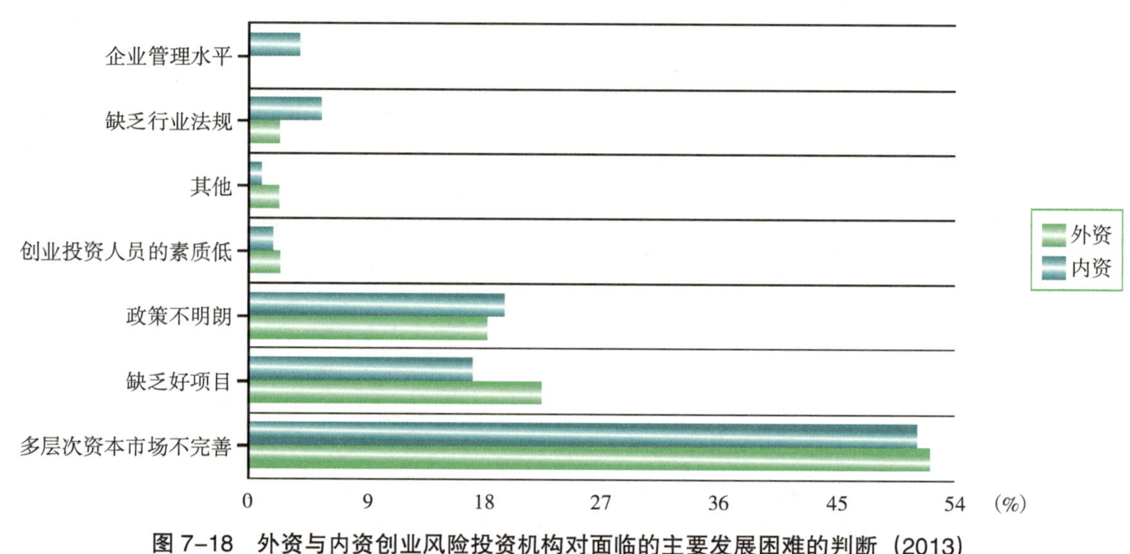

图 7-18 外资与内资创业风险投资机构对面临的主要发展困难的判断（2013）

① 有效样本数：内资为 967 份，外资为 44 份。

8 中国创业风险投资发展环境

8.1 中国创业风险投资机构的政策环境

根据调研样本数据，本节将主要分析中国创业风险投资机构当前所处的政策环境，梳理中国创业风险投资机构最希望出台的有关政策等信息。

8.1.1 中国创业风险投资机构可以享受到的政府扶持政策

近年来，中央及地方都出台了一系列相关政策措施支持我国创业风险投资发展。2013 年调查显示，约有 22.0%的创业风险投资机构享受到政府资金支持，比例低于 2012 年的 28.9%；25.0%的创业风险投资机构享受到所得税减免政策优惠，低于 2012 年的 29.2%；28.2%的创业风险投资机构在信息交流方面得到了政府支持；12.2%的创业风险投资机构在人员培训方面得到了政府帮助（见图 8-1），可以看出，政府对创投机构在财税方面的直接支持在减少，但给予的间接服务支持比例在增加。

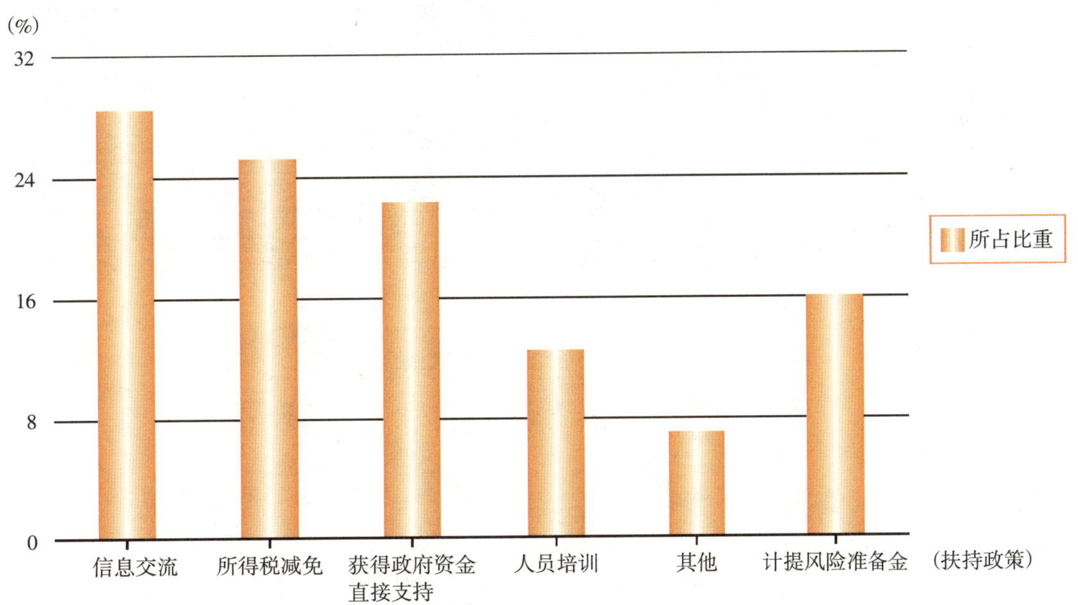

图 8-1　创业风险投资机构可以享受到的政府扶持政策（2013）

2013 年调查显示[①]，各地实施了多项政府扶持政策措施支持创业风险投资机构发展，北京、江苏等地区都有20%以上的创业投资机构获得政府资金支持，较往年有所下降，天津约有 43.2%的创业投资机构获得政府资金支持。所得税减免依然是政府直接支持创业投资机构的主要措施，约 25%的创业风险投资机构获得所得税减免，广东、浙江、上海等地超过 30%的创业风险投资机构获得所得税减免；河北、甘肃等许多地区的创业风险投资机构可以计提风险准备金，降低了投资风险和成本；同时，各地普遍为创业风险投资机构提供了信息交流服务（见图 8-2），较往年有了较大比例的增长。各项扶持政策的受惠面进一步扩大，为创业风险投资机构发展营造了良好环境。

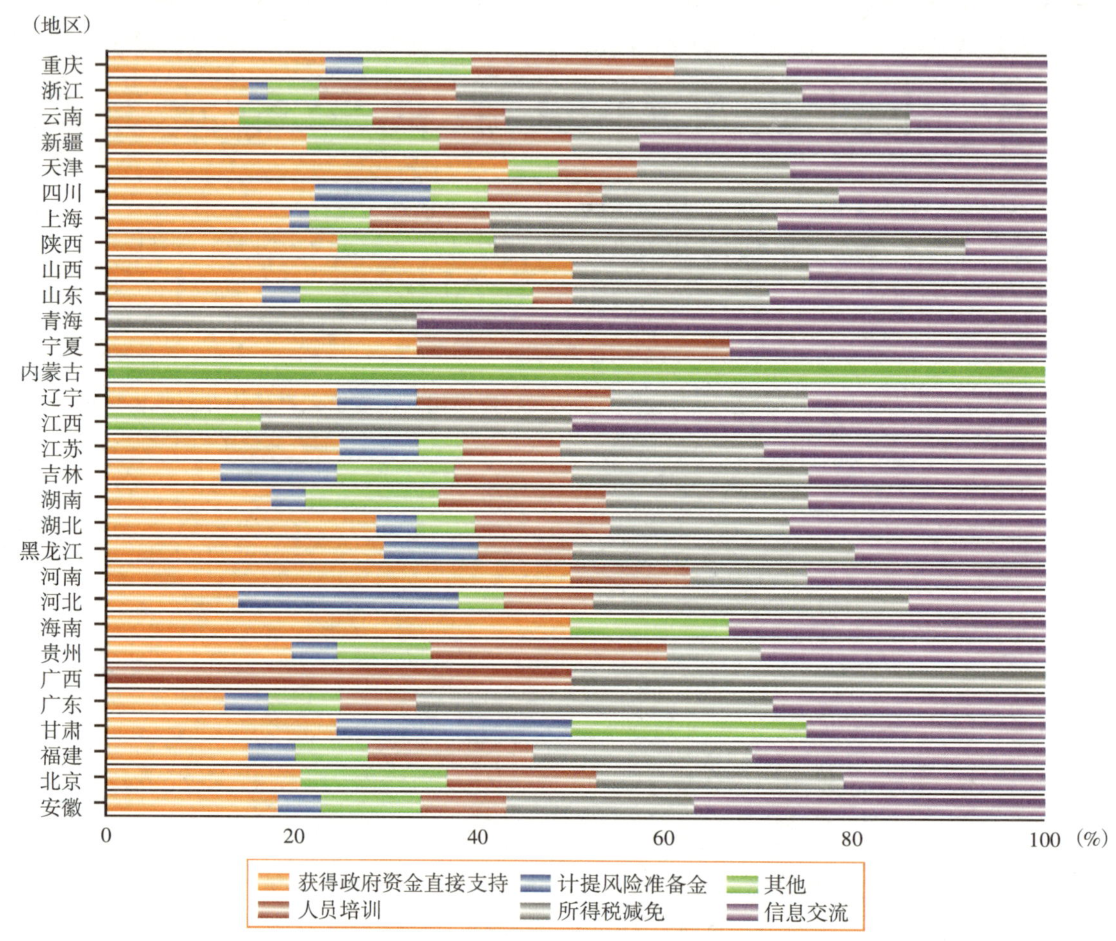

图 8-2 创业风险投资机构可以享受到的政府扶持政策（2013）

8.1.2 中国创业风险投资机构税收负担情况

2007 年财政部、国家税务总局出台了《关于促进创业投资企业发展有关税收政策的通知》（财税〔2007〕31 号），对创业风险投资机构实行税收优惠政策。根据 2013 年调查显示，53.5%的创业风险投资机构税收负担在 10%以下，21.5%的创业风险投资机构税收负担在 10%~20%，16.7%的创业风险投资机构税收负担在 20%~30%，仅 8.3%的创业风险投资机构承担着 30%以上的高税收负担（见图 8-3）。与近几年相比，2013 年我国创业风险投资行业整体税收负担有所减少，高税收负担的创业风险投资机构占比略有下降。尽管绝大部分创业风险投资机构税收占比分布于 30%以下，但仍有一些地区税收优惠政策并未有效落实，在一定程度上影响创业风险投资行业发展。

① 有效样本数为 890 份。

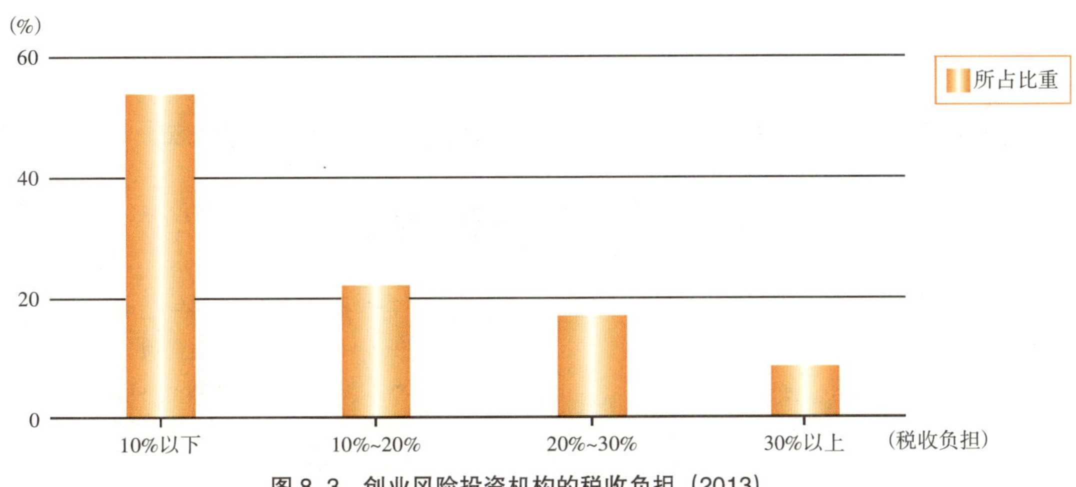

图 8-3 创业风险投资机构的税收负担(2013)

8.1.3 中国创业风险投资机构希望的政府激励政策

2013 年调查样本显示，中国创业风险投资机构最希望出台的政府激励政策主要有以下几类（见图 8-4）：

(1) 税收减免。根据调查，中国创业风险投资机构最希望出台的政府激励政策是税收减免类，占 25.4%，比 2012 年有所降低，这与近年来税收优惠政策进一步落实有关。

(2) 设立政策类引导基金。根据调查，22.5%的调查对象希望设立政策性引导基金，并通过参股或融资担保等方式支持创业风险投资发展。

(3) 完善多层次资本市场。根据调查，19.1%的调查对象希望进一步完善多层次资本市场建设。2013 年 IPO 暂停对于创业投资机构退出影响较大，但新三板的扩容为创业风险投资机构通过多层次资本市场退出带来了希望。

(4) 政府奖励。根据调查，12.3%的创业风险投资机构希望能够出台相关政府奖励政策，鼓励创业风险投资发展，支持科技成果转化和科技型中小企业发展。

(5) 扩大资金来源。4.5%的创业风险投资机构希望允许保险等机构投资者进入创业风险投资，但目前，由于受到《商业银行法》、《保险法》等限制，我国数十万亿元的社会保险、银行、保险等机构资金还无法大规模进入创业风险投资领域。

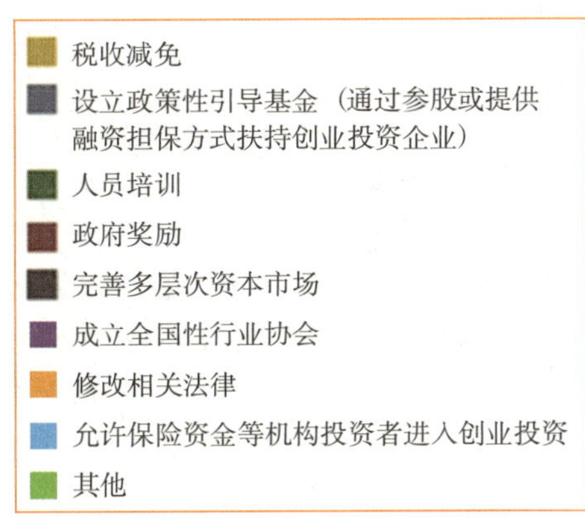

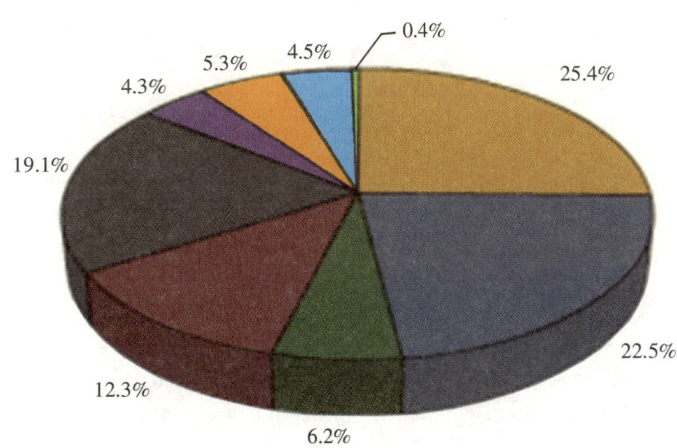

图 8-4 创业风险投资机构希望的政府激励政策(2013)

8.2 国家科技计划支持创业风险投资发展

8.2.1 国家科技计划对创业风险投资项目的支持情况

2013 年调查样本显示①，中国创业风险投资项目中，约有 10.2%的项目获得了国家科技计划的支持，低于 2012 年的 10.4%；其中，3.08%创业风险投资项目获得了科技型中小企业技术创新基金支持，低于 2012 年的 3.2%；有 1.88%和 1.14%创业风险投资项目分别受到“火炬计划”和“863 计划”的支持，约有 3.82%受到了其他国家级计划支持（见图 8-5），较 2012 年增长了 0.82%，创业风险投资项目中获得国家科技计划项目的占比略微减少。

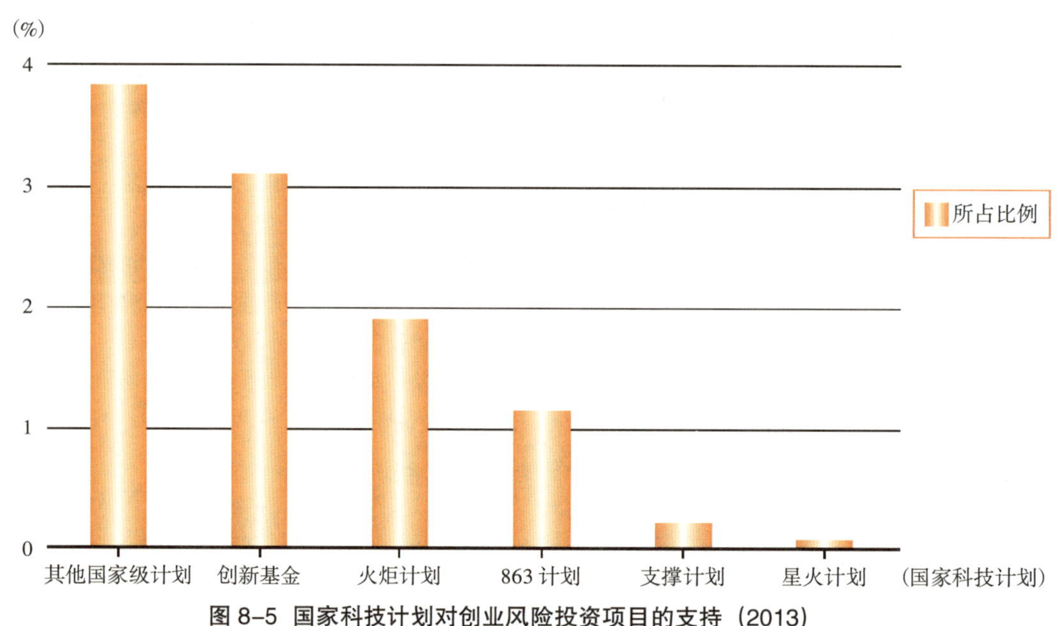

图 8-5 国家科技计划对创业风险投资项目的支持（2013）

8.2.2 国家科技计划与创业风险投资项目对接的关键因素

2013 年调查显示，33.6%的创业风险投资机构认为加大基础、应用和开发投入能够促进国家科技计划和创业风险投资项目的对接，比例大幅高于 2012 年的 23.7%；22.6%的创业风险投资机构认为需要尽快设立科技型中小企业上市的绿色通道，较 2012 年略有增长；16.1%的创业风险投资机构认为应鼓励、资助创业风险投资与“孵化器”之间的合作；20.0%的创业风险投资机构认为应对创业风险投资项目给予直接资助（见图 8-6），高于 2012 年的 18.1%；仅 4.8%的创投机构要求加大科技项目信息的公开度，远低于 2012 年的 13.0%，这与近年来政府深化科技体制改革，加强政府信息透明度相关。

① 有效样本数为 1493 份。

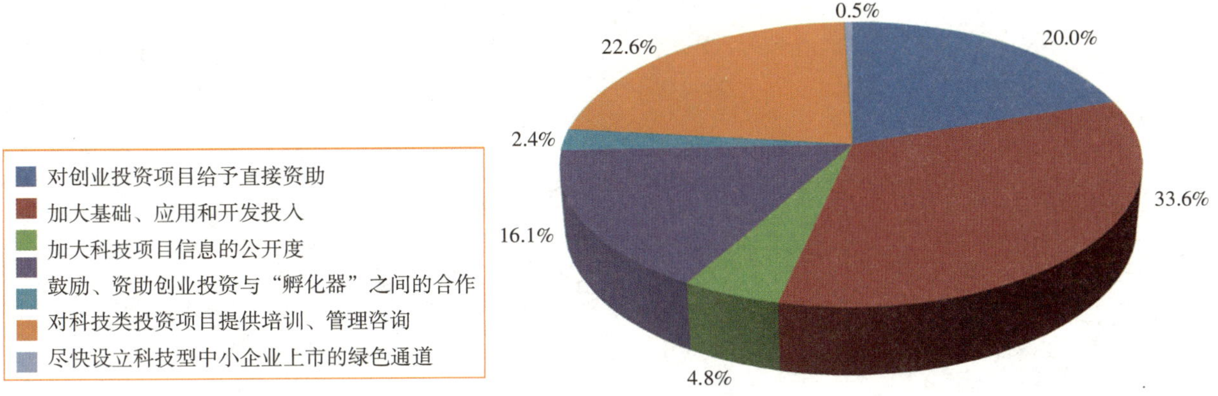

图 8-6 国家科技计划与创业风险投资良好对接的关键字（2013）

8.3 中国促进创业风险投资发展的主要政策

本节对中国促进创业风险投资发展出台的国家层面政策文件进行了梳理（见表 8-1），自 1999 年国务院办公厅转发科技部等七部门联合出台的《关于建立风险投资机制的若干意见》开始，我国各有关部门相继出台了支持创业风险投资发展的相关政策，涉及外商投资创业风险投资机构、管理监管、税收优惠、专项引导基金等多个方面，有效推动了我国创业风险投资事业的快速健康发展。

表 8-1 中国促进创业风险投资发展的主要政策文件

文件名称	出台时间	出台组织及部门等	主要精神
《关于建立风险投资机制的若干意见》	1999 年	科技部、国家计委、国家经贸委、财政部、人民银行、税务总局、证监会	明确发展创业风险投资重要意义，并提出指导、规范我国创业风险投资发展的基本原则
《中华人民共和国信托法》	2001 年	第九届全国人民代表大会常务委员会第二十一次会议通过	明确了委托人和受托人之间的法律关系，为创业风险投资发展提供依据
《中华人民共和国中小企业促进法》	2002 年	第九届全国人民代表大会常务委员会第二十八次会议通过	提出通过税收政策鼓励各类依法设立的创业风险投资机构增加对中小企业的投资
《外商投资创业投资企业管理规定》	2003 年	外经贸部、科技部、国家工商总局、国家税务总局、国家外汇管理局	为鼓励、规范外国公司、企业和其他经济组织或个人从事创业风险投资提供管理依据
《关于外商投资创业投资公司缴纳企业所得税有关税收问题的通知》	2003 年	国家税务总局	为外商投资创业风险投资企业组建为法人及非法人的创业风险投资企业明确了有关税收问题

续表

文件名称	出台时间	出台组织及部门等	主要精神
《关于外商投资举办投资性公司的规定》	2004 年	商务部	对外商投资举办投资性公司的注册资本、组织形式、投资行为等提出了管理规定
《创业投资企业管理暂行办法》	2005 年	发改委、科技部、财政部、商务部、人民银行、税务总局、工商总局、银监会、证监会、国家外汇管理局	对创业风险投资企业实行备案管理，并对其经营范围、投资行为等进行了规定
《关于促进创业投资企业发展有关税收政策的通知》	2007 年	财政部、国家税务总局	对投资支持中小高新技术企业的创业风险投资企业给予税收优惠
《科技型中小企业创业投资引导基金管理暂行办法》	2007 年	财政部、科技部	开展设立科技型中小企业创业风险投资引导基金，支持引导创业风险投资机构向初创期科技型中小企业投资
《关于创业投资引导基金规范设立与运作的指导意见》	2008 年	发改委、财政部、商务部	对规范设立创业风险投资引导基金提出要求
《关于外商投资创业投资企业创业投资管理企业审批有关事项的通知》	2009 年	商务部	对总投资在 1 亿美元以下的外商投资创业风险投资企业、创业风险投资管理企业的审批权限等进行了下放
《关于加强创业投资企业备案管理严格规范创业投资企业募资行为的通知》	2009 年	发改委	明确创业风险投资企业备案条件，严控“募集有限合伙基金”和“从事代理业务”等名义的非法集资活动
《关于实施创业投资企业所得税优惠问题的通知》	2009 年	国家税务总局	对合伙企业、外商投资创业风险投资企业等有关问题明确了税收优惠政策
《关于实施新兴产业创投计划、开展产业技术研究与开发资金参股设立创业投资基金试点工作的通知》	2009 年	发改委、财政部	扩大产业技术研发资金创业风险投资试点，推动利用国家产业技术研发资金，参股设立创业风险投资基金（即创业投资企业）试点工作
《首次公开发行股票并在创业板上市管理办法》	2009 年	证监会	创业板的推出为我国创业风险投资发展提供了良好的退出渠道，将进一步促进创业风险投资事业健康、快速发展
《关于豁免国有创业投资机构和国有创业投资引导基金国有股转持义务有关问题的通知》	2010 年	财政部	规避相关政策影响，提高了国有创业风险投资机构的积极性，鼓励和引导国有创业风险投资机构加大对中早期项目的投资
《科技型中小企业创业投资引导基金股权投资收入收缴暂行办法》	2010 年	财政部	明确了科技型中小企业创业投资引导基金收入的上缴办法及相关管理权责等事宜
《国家科技成果转化引导基金管理暂行办法》	2011 年	财政部、科技部	明确提出以政府创业风险投资引导基金模式运作支持科技成果转化的相关事宜
《新兴产业创投计划参股创业投资基金管理暂行办法》	2011 年	财政部、国家发改委	提出政府公共资金以直接投资或参股投资等方式支持战略性新兴产业发展的事宜
《关于促进科技和金融结合加快实施自主创新战略的若干意见》	2011 年	科技部、财政部、中国人民银行、国务院国资委、国家税务总局、中国银监会、中国证监会、中国保监会	八部委联合文件指导全国开展科技和金融结合工作，对于各级政府开展创业风险投资提出了指导建议

续表

文件名称	出台时间	出台组织及部门等	主要精神
《关于促进股权投资企业规范发展的通知》	2011 年	发改委	对于股权投资企业的设立、募资、投资，以及风险控制、基本职责、信息披露等提出了要求
《非上市公众公司监督管理办法》	2012 年	证监会	将非上市公众公司纳入合法监管，有利于中小企业融资，对促进创业风险投资投资中小企业有积极意义
《全国中小企业股份转让系统有限责任公司管理暂行办法》	2013 年	证监会	进一步完善多层次资本市场建设，有利于创业风险投资机构股权退出
《国务院关于全国中小企业股份转让系统有关问题的决定》	2013 年	国务院	对全国股份转让系统的定位、市场体系建设、行政许可制度改革、投资者管理、投资者权益保护及监管协作六个方面作了规定

2013 年 2 月，中国证监会发布第 89 号令《全国中小企业股份转让系统有限责任公司管理暂行办法》（以下简称《办法》），主要明确了三方面内容：一是确立全国中小企业股份转让系统、全国中小企业股份转让系统有限责任公司及挂牌公司的法律地位；二是明确全国股份转让系统公司的职能，对其组织结构提出特殊要求，对其履行自律监管职责提出明确要求；三是建立全国股份转让系统的基本监管框架，在明确和突出全国股份转让系统公司自律监管职责的同时，规定中国证监会依法实行统一监管。该《办法》在公众公司人数、交易制度、监管方式等方面都有所突破，进一步大规模“扩容”也为创业风险投资机构通过全国中小企业股份转让系统实现投资退出提供了巨大空间，将进一步推动我国创业风险投资行业发展。

按照党的十八大、十八届三中全会关于发展多层次资本市场的精神和国务院常务会议有关要求，国务院 2013 年 12 月 23 日发布《关于全国中小企业股份转让系统有关问题的决定》（以下简称《决定》）。《决定》的出台，对于更好发挥金融对经济结构调整和转型升级的支持作用，进一步拓展民间投资渠道，充分发挥全国股份转让系统的功能和缓解中小微企业融资难都具有重要意义，标志着多层次资本市场建设取得实质性进展。《决定》对全国股份转让系统的定位、市场体系建设、行政许可制度改革、投资者管理、投资者权益保护及监管协作等六个方面作了规定。

9 中国创业风险投资引导基金发展情况

9.1 中国创业风险投资引导基金发展现状[①]

调查样本显示，截至 2013 年底，获得政府创业风险投资引导基金参股支持的创业风险投资机构数量累计达到 252 家，政府创业风险投资引导基金累计出资 326.91 亿元，引导带动的创业风险投资管理资金规模超过 1600 亿元。

2013 年调查样本显示：引导基金支持的创业风险投资机构平均管理资本规模达 51418.1 万元，高于非引导基金支持的创业风险投资机构的 30744.6 万元，但低于 2012 年的 56547.8 万元（见图 9-1）。

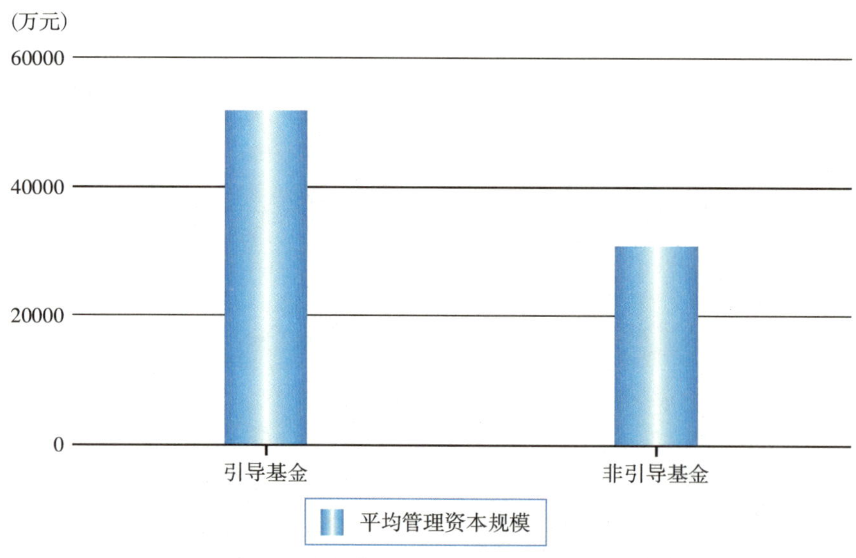

图 9-1 创业风险投资机构平均管理资本规模（2013）

① 有效样本数为 1007 份。

从资本构成结构来看，有引导基金支持的创业风险投资机构资本构成中，14.8%来自于政府部门，22.4%来自于国有独资投资机构，36.6%来自非上市企业，与2012年相比，非上市公司出资占比有所提升，政府部门占比继续下降。而非引导基金支持的创业风险投资机构资本更多地来自于非上市企业、国有独资投资机构和个人，三者合计占到总资本的80.1%（见图9-2），较2012年进一步增加。

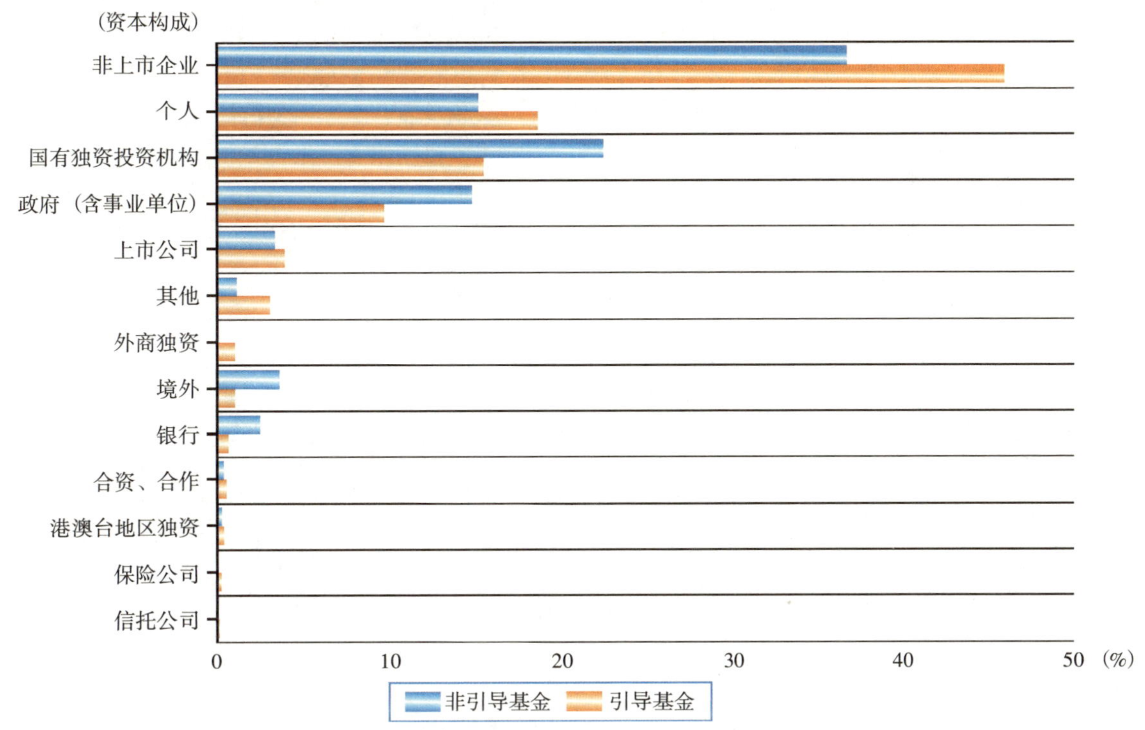

图 9-2 创业风险投资机构的资本构成（2013）

从国家层面来看，截至2013年底，由财政部、科技部设立的“科技型中小企业创业投资引导基金”采取风险补助、投资保障、阶段参股等方式，共投入财政资金30.59亿元。其中，出资20.09亿元以阶段参股方式参股了71家重点投资于科技型中小企业的创业投资企业，累计注册资本约150亿元；通过风险补助和投资保障方式共立项1411项，累计安排补助资金10.5亿元（见表9-1）。

表 9-1 科技部科技型中小企业创业投资引导基金运行情况（2007~2013）

分类 年份	风险补助		投资保障（前、后）		共计	
	数量（项）	资金（万元）	数量（项）	资金（万元）	数量（项）	资金（万元）
2007	50	7115	52	2885	102	10000
2008	77	6590	75	3410	152	10000
2009	55	4670	131	10330	186	15000
2010	66	4540	180	10460	246	15000
2011	56	4110	125	10890	181	15000
2012	87	7033	199	12967	286	20000
2013	96	9655	162	10345	258	20000
共计	487	43713	924	61287	1411	105000

资料来源：科技部创新基金管理中心。

9.2 中国创业风险投资引导基金投资项目的行业分布[①]

从投资金额分布看，2013 年引导基金支持的创业风险投资机构有 3.8%的资金投向传统制造业，较 2012 年的 7.4%进一步下降；11.6%的资金投向新材料工业，较 2012 年大幅增加；此外，医药保健、传播与文化娱乐、交通运输仓储和邮政业的投资金额占比也较往年有了大幅增长。从投资项目数看，10.1%的资金投向新材料工业，较 2012 年大幅增加；投向医药保健、新能源/高效节能技术产业、消费产品和服务行业、网络产业的项目数量，均较 2012 年明显增加。综合来看，2013 年有引导基金支持创业风险投资机构的投资领域更加分散，投向了许多热点新兴产业领域（见表 9–2）。

表 9–2 引导基金支持创业风险投资机构投资项目行业分布（2012~2013）[②] 单位：%

投资行业	投资金额		投资项目	
	2012 年	2013 年	2012 年	2013 年
新材料工业	6.4	11.6	7.2	10.1
传统制造业	7.4	3.8	8.7	5.9
其他制造业	6.8	4.9	7.1	4.8
其他行业	18.9	2.1	13.2	2.4
消费产品和服务	3.5	6.6	2.6	5.2
新能源、高效节能技术	5.1	6.8	6.9	7.2
生物科技	2.4	2.3	3.9	4.4
光电子与光机电一体化	3.3	6.3	4.3	5.0
农林牧副渔	9.3	4.6	6.5	4.1
医药保健	5.0	12.3	6.1	10.0
网络产业	3.3	2.8	3.5	5.5
通讯设备	3.8	0.2	3.7	0.2
金融保险业	3.5	4.0	1.7	1.7
科技服务	2.2	1.4	3.3	2.4
半导体	1.4	2.5	1.5	3.3
软件产业	2.0	1.4	2.6	4.2
环保工程	2.8	2.4	2.4	3.1
IT 服务业	2.4	3.4	4.3	4.2
传播与文化娱乐	2.5	5.9	2.6	5.0
建筑业	1.2	1.4	0.7	1.1
批发和零售业	0.4	0.8	0.6	0.6
其他 IT 产业	2.3	0.4	1.9	0.7
社会服务	1.1	0.9	2.0	1.1
计算机硬件产业	0.5	1.6	1.1	1.5
交通运输仓储和邮政业	0.2	5.0	0.2	1.5
核应用技术	0.4	0.1	0.7	0.2
水电煤气	0.4	0.3	0.4	0.4
采掘业	1.5	0.4	0.4	0.6

① 有效样本：获引导基金支持创投 542 份、非引导基金支持创投 850 份。
② 2013 年有效样本 542 份，2012 年有效样本 539 份。

引导基金支持创业风险投资机构投资项目行业分布与非引导基金支持创业风险投资机构有一定差异（见图 9-3）。2013 年，有引导基金支持的创业风险投资机构倾向于投资消费产品和服务、网络产业、新材料工业等领域；非引导基金支持的创业风险投资机构更加倾向于投资金融保险业、环保工程、软件产业、社会服务业等领域。

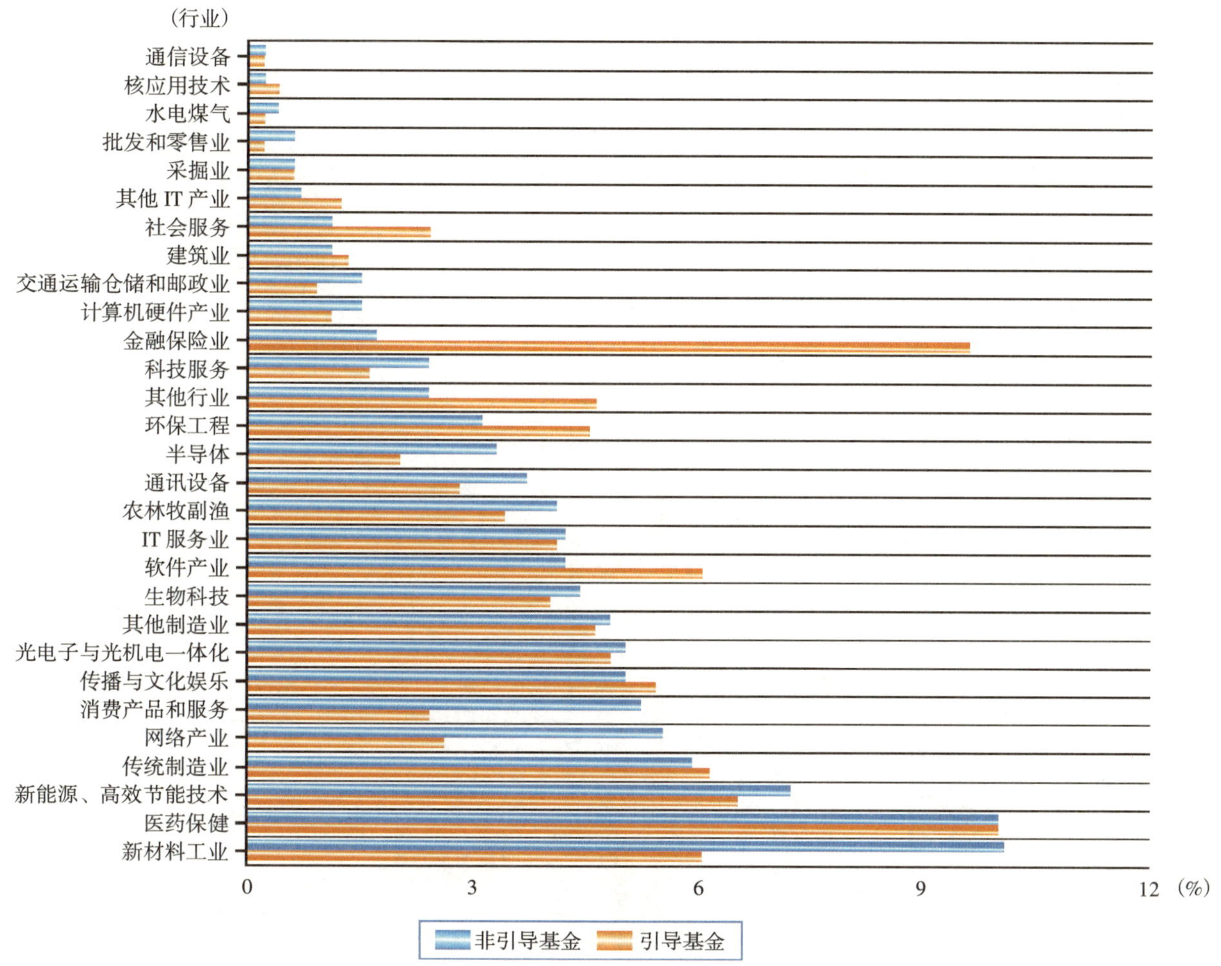

图 9-3 创业风险投资机构投资项目的行业分布（2013）

9.3 中国创业风险投资引导基金投资项目所处阶段[①]

2013 年，政府引导基金支持的创业风险投资机构主要投资处于种子期、起步期和成长期的项目，投资金额分别占 11.4%、25.8%、47.3%，其中投资种子期的金额占比较上年增长 8.4 个百分点；投资项目数分别占 18.7%、32.7%、39.2%，与 2012 年相比，投资种子期、成长期等项目数量占比大幅上涨。从投资金额与投资项目的占比可以看出，2013 年有引导基金支持的创业风险投资机构投资行为有所转变，投资种子期和成长期的比例大幅增长（见图 9–4），符合政府引导基金政策目标。

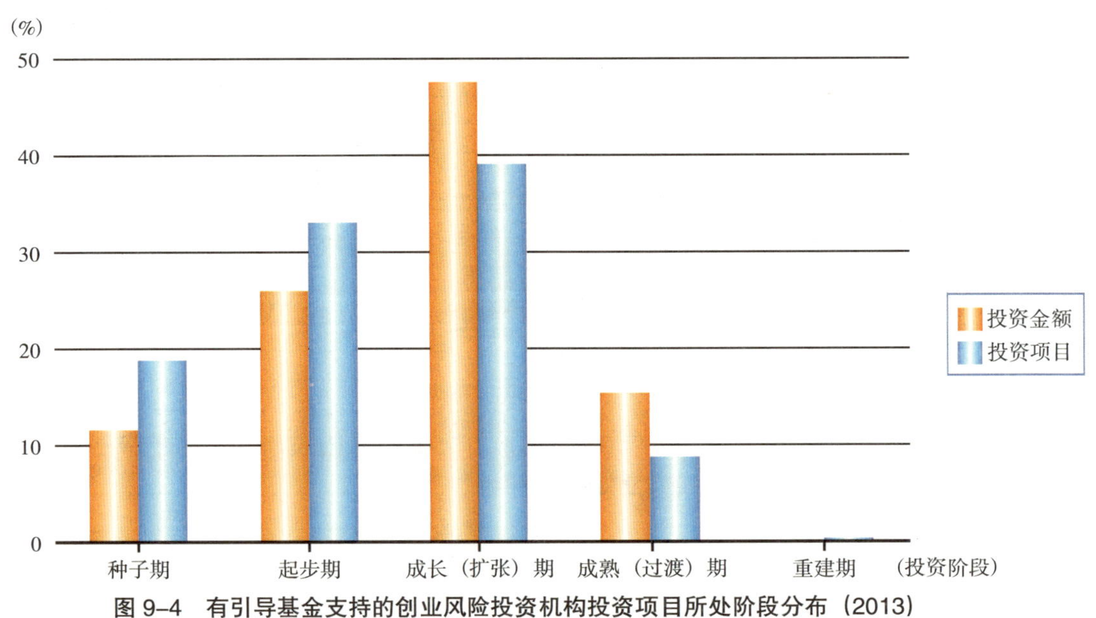

图 9–4 有引导基金支持的创业风险投资机构投资项目所处阶段分布（2013）

与非引导基金支持创业风险投资机构相比，2013 年，引导基金支持创业风险投资机构更加倾向于投资早前期企业，投资于早前期的企业资金占比明显高于非引导基金支持创业风险投资机构（投资种子期的占比明显低于非引导基金支持的机构）（见图 9–5）。

① 有效样本：获引导基金支持创投 513 份、非引导基金支持创投 827 份。

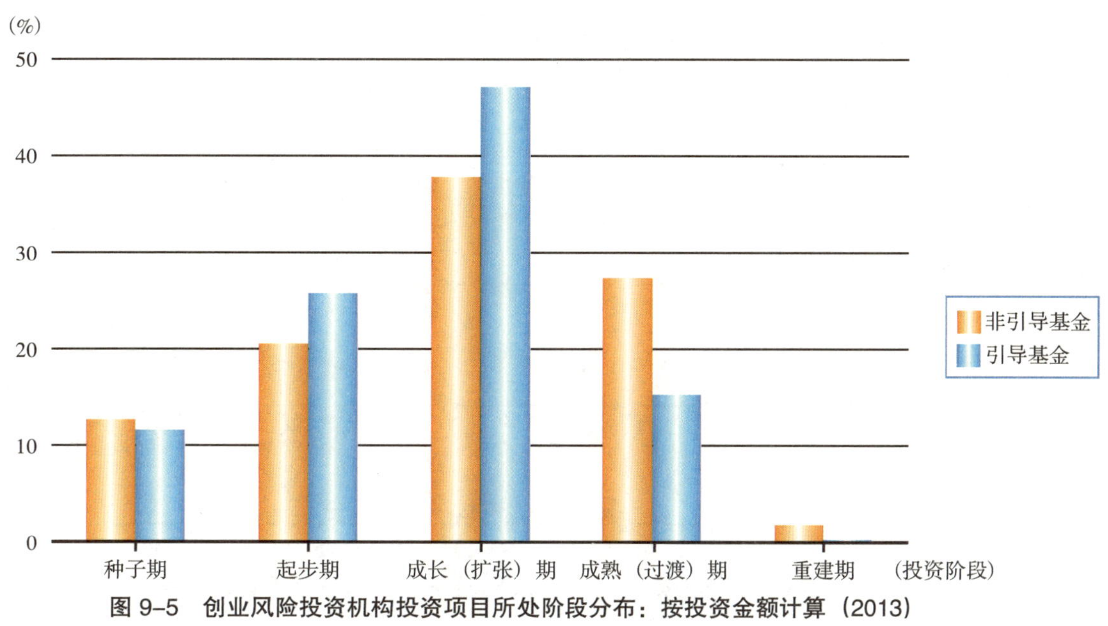

图 9–5 创业风险投资机构投资项目所处阶段分布：按投资金额计算（2013）

9.4 中国创业风险投资引导基金投资项目运作状况①

2013 年调查样本显示，有引导基金支持的创业风险投资机构与非引导基金支持的创业风险投资机构的投资强度没有明显差异，单笔投资金额在 1000 万元以上的占比超过 80%，单笔投资低于 500 万元的占比不足 6%，较非引导基金支持的创业风险投资机构低 1.5 个百分点，略高于 2012 年。与 2012 年相比，投资超过 2000 万元的占比有了大幅增加（见表 9–3、图 9–6）。

表 9–3 创业风险投资机构的项目投资金额占比（2013）

分布比例（万元）	100 以下	100~300	300~500	500~1000	1000~2000	2000 以上
引导基金支持的 VC	0.2	2.1	3.3	10.7	20.4	63.3
非引导基金支持的 VC	0.4	2.4	4.3	8.5	17.8	66.6

① 有效样本数：获引导基金支持创投 554 份，非引导基金支持创投 827 份。

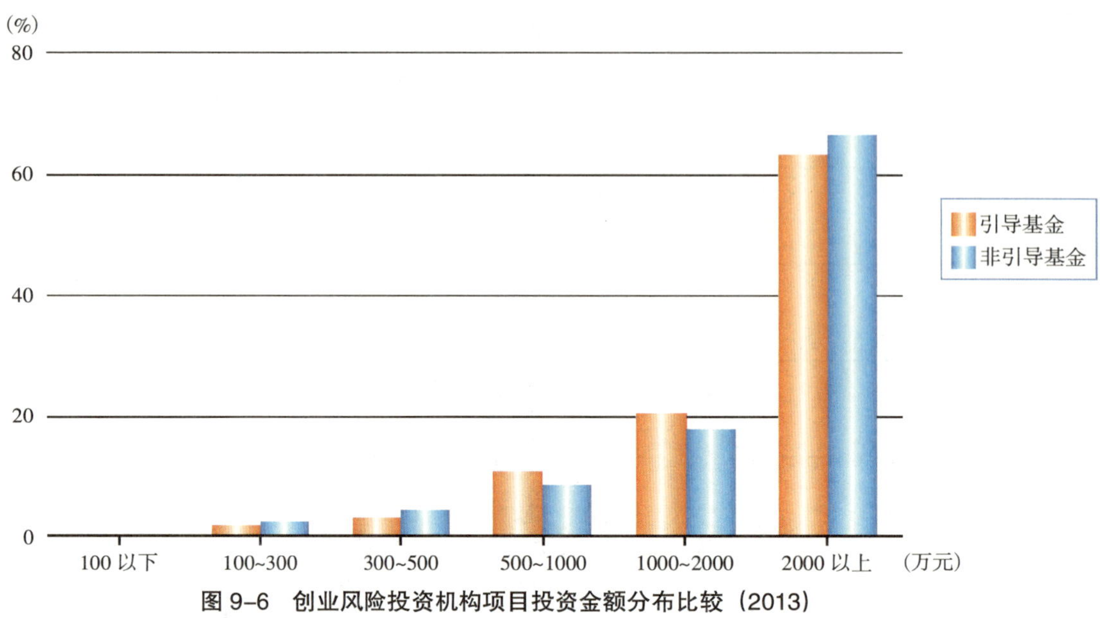

图 9-6　创业风险投资机构项目投资金额分布比较（2013）

2013 年调查样本显示，获引导基金支持的创业风险投资机构共计投资了 209 家高新技术企业，占总投资项目数的 37.7%；非引导基金支持的创业风险投资机构共计投资了 273 家高新技术企业，占总投资项目数的 29.1%；与 2012 年相比，获引导基金支持的创业风险投资机构投资高新技术企业的项目数比重略有下降，但平均投资金额较 2012 年有所增加（见表 9-4）。

表 9-4　创业风险投资机构投资项目中投资高新技术企业的情况（2013）①

企业分类	投资高企数（个）	投资高企项目数占比（%）	平均投资金额（万元）
非引导基金支持的 VC	273	29.1	1884.4
引导基金支持的 VC	209	37.7	1923.4

注：投资项目中存在非引导基金和引导基金支持创投同时投资情况。

2013 年调查样本显示，获引导基金支持的创业风险投资机构投资项目中管理层回购等比例相对较高，而非引导基金支持的创业风险投资机构投资项目中准备境内上市、清算的比例较高，两类样本均有超过 60%的投资项目仍处于运行阶段。与 2012 年相比，由于 IPO 退出渠道不畅，大部分创业投资机构投资项目保持继续运行状态，准备上市项目比例较 2012 年有明显下降（见表 9-5、图 9-7）。

表 9-5　创业风险投资机构投资项目运作状况（2013）②　　单位：%

运作情况	继续运行	准备境内上市	已境内上市	原股东（创业者）回购	被境内非上市公司或自然人收购	已境外上市	清算	管理层收购	被境内上市公司收购	准备境外上市	被境外收购
引导基金支持的 VC	63.4	9.8	5.9	8.2	3.4	1.5	0.9	5.7	0.7	0.3	0.1
非引导基金支持的 VC	67.3	10.4	5.6	8.9	3.1	0.5	2.1	1.1	0.4	0.4	0.1

① 有效样本数：获引导基金支持创投 209 份，非引导基金支持创投 273 份。
② 有效样本数：获引导基金支持创投 244 份，非引导基金支持创投 779 份。

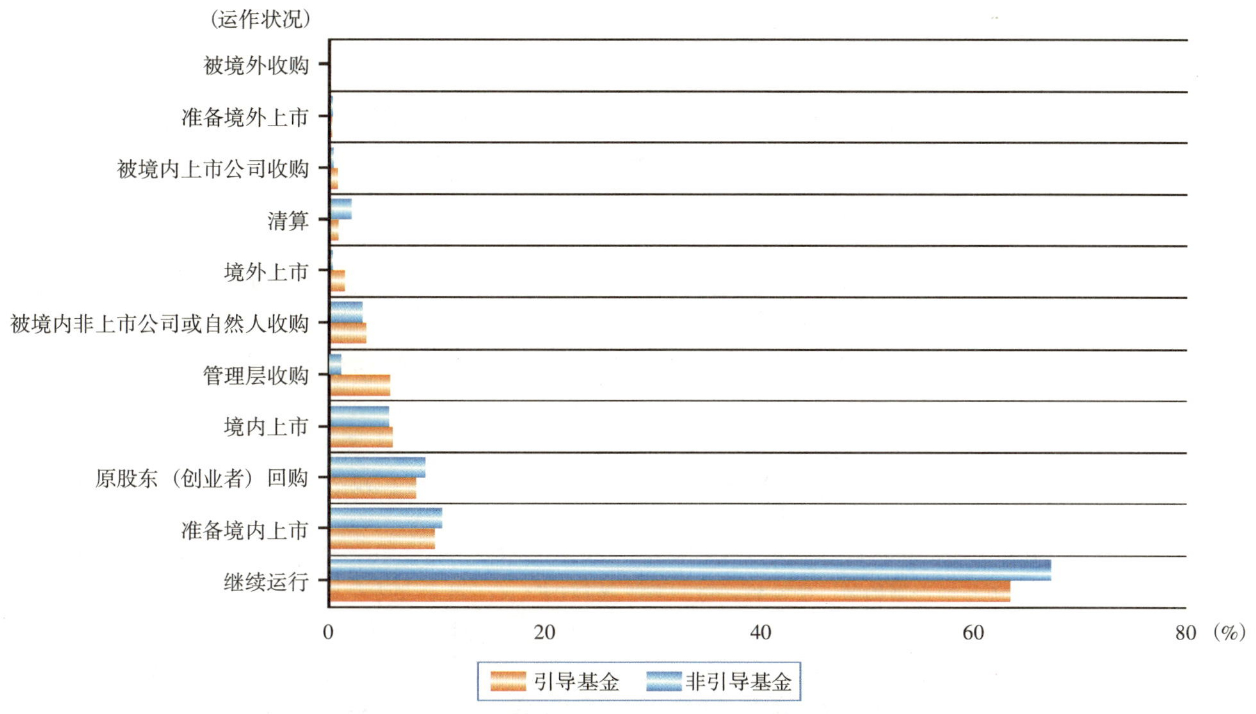

图 9-7 创业风险投资机构投资项目运作状况（2013）

附录 1 2013 年美国创业风险投资回顾

一、总体概况

2013 年，尽管对 IPO 市场复苏的期望值很高，美国的风险投资业持续了之前三年的发展趋势。资本管理量如预期地延续了下降的趋势，但是下降的程度有所缓和。创业投资主要集中于种子期和早期阶段的投资。与此同时，很多长期处于在投状态的新企业最终实现了上市，其中领头的是一批生物技术公司，在 2013 年上半年首先实现了 IPO。尽管第四季度生物技术公司的第一批基金投资的收益令人鼓舞，但是针对早期生命科学企业的投资延续了下降趋势。

对于大部分创业投资企业来说，募集资金仍然是巨大的挑战。这主要是因为 2012 年缺乏顺畅的退出渠道，使得未变现收益要被均摊到最近这几年的基金投资，从而影响到基金的整体收益率。除了 2012 年上市的 Facebook（在 2012 年总募集额 215 亿万美元中占了 160 亿万元美元），2013 年共有 81 家有风险投资支持的新企业上市，相对 2012 年来说有了明显改善。值得注意的是，超过半数的上市企业是生物技术企业。2014 年的早期迹象表明，这一 IPO 上市趋势将至少延续到今年的第一季度。

一个健康的创业投资生态系统要求其衡量标准是平衡的。尽管新的商业机会质量，也就是交易量仍然非常高，并且好的项目机会也能够得到资助，但是行业的整体压力仍然存在。

《全美风险投资——2014》提供了美国创业投资的投资总体概况，包括从投资、投资组合、普通合伙人管理资本、有限合伙人的募集、获得过创业投资的企业估值及其上市、退出及并购。本报告的统计土要来源于普华永道和美国风险投资协会提供的 MoneyTreeTM 报告，基于汤森路透（Thomson）的数据，对 Thomson ONE（原 VentureXpert）数据库进行分析。汤森路透已通过美国风险投资协会的认证，作为官方的行业活动数据库。总体情况见表 1。

表 1 美国创业风险投资（VC）总体情况统计

指标 \ 年份	1993	2003	2013
现存 VC 企业数量（家）	370	951	874
现存 VC 基金数量（家）	613	1788	1331
从事 VC 行业的专业人员（人）	5217	14777	5891
首次设立的 VC 基金数量（家）	25	34	53
当年获得融资的 VC 基金数量（家）	93	160	187
VC 当年募集资本额（十亿美元）	4.5	9.1	16.8
运营中的 VC 管理资本额（十亿美元）	29.3	263.9	192.9
平均每家 VC 企业管理资本额（百万美元）	79.2	277.5	220.7

续表

指标＼年份	1993	2003	2013
截至目前的 VC 基金平均规模（百万美元）	40.2	94.4	110.3
当年新增 VC 基金平均规模（百万美元）	48.3	102.9	89.7
截止目前最大规模 VC 基金募集（百万美元）	1775.0	6300.0	6300.0

二、行业资源

2013 年，美国风险投资行业的活动水平大致相当于 2000 年高峰时期的一半。2000 年，共有 1050 家创业投资企业，每家当年投资平均超过 500 万美元，而 2013 年投资超过 500 万美元的企业仅有 548 家 。

截至 2013 年底，创业风险投资企业平均管理资本减少至 1929 亿美元。然而，从数据背后可以看出，该行业自 2006 年管理资本高达 2889 亿美元以来，之后一直持续地收缩。2000 年管理资本的高峰是由于当年科技股泡沫，新的公募基金募集导致的统计异常造成的。2013 年，美国创业风险投资企业数量和管理资本均略有下降。

与 6 年前平均每家创业投资企业管理 8.7 位投资经理相比，2013 年每家管理的投资经理缩水到 6.7 位。投资经理数量相应下降到 6000 人，比 2007 年的减少了近 1/3。这意味着，每个投资经理管理的资本平均数都有普遍增加。每家企业的投资经理人数增加而管理的企业数量减少的趋势可能会持续。这是由于大量新募资金是由较大的、专业的创业投资企业募集的。这里，我们定义的投资经理是需要去参加被投资的新企业董事会的人员，即包括这笔交易的合作伙伴在内，而不包括企业的 CFO。

大规模风险投资企业的地理位置也很集中。行业中 49%管理资本的企业都在加利福尼亚州注册，尽管这些企业积极投资于其他州和国家。这个集中度持续了很多年，并可能会因为东海岸基金向西的移动而保持一贯的增长。综上所述，五大州（加利福尼亚州、马萨诸塞州、纽约州、康涅狄格州和伊利诺伊州）与往年一样持有全美风险资本总额的 81.1%。

只有 43 家企业管理资本超过了 10 亿美元。相比之下，277 家企业管理的资本低于 2500 万美元（见表 2、图 1）。

表 2 美国创业风险投资基金与企业情况（1985~2013）

年份	累计基金数（只）	累计企业数（家）	累计管理资本（百万美元）	现存基金数（只）	现存企业数（最近八年）（家）	管理资本（十亿美元）	平均基金规模（百万美元）	平均企业规模（百万美元）
1985	631	323	20.0	532	294	17.6	33.1	59.9
1986	707	353	23.4	590	324	20.7	35.1	63.9
1987	810	388	27.4	670	353	23.7	35.4	67.1
1988	888	406	30.9	701	365	24.9	35.5	68.2
1989	980	435	35.9	728	380	27.8	38.2	73.2
1990	1037	451	38.2	716	383	28.2	39.4	73.6
1991	1075	458	40.4	639	360	26.8	41.9	74.4
1992	1147	478	44.1	601	352	27.2	45.3	77.3
1993	1244	509	49.3	613	370	29.3	47.8	79.2
1994	1342	542	56.7	635	385	33.2	52.3	86.2
1995	1498	608	66.2	688	425	38.9	56.5	91.5
1996	1648	670	78.8	760	471	47.9	63.0	101.7

续表

年份	累计基金数（只）	累计企业数（家）	累计管理资本（百万美元）	现存基金数（只）	现存企业数（最近八年）（家）	管理资本（十亿美元）	平均基金规模（百万美元）	平均企业规模（百万美元）
1997	1862	764	98.1	882	545	62.2	70.5	114.1
1998	2099	843	129.3	1062	616	91.1	85.8	147.9
1999	2435	969	184.1	1360	736	143.7	105.7	195.2
2000	2851	1111	268.9	1704	866	224.8	131.9	256.9
2001	3096	1194	311.3	1852	923	262.0	141.5	283.9
2002	3178	1211	319.0	1836	921	262.3	142.9	284.8
2003	3286	1264	330.1	1788	951	263.9	147.6	277.5
2004	3451	1332	349.9	1803	985	271.1	150.4	275.2
2005	3626	1402	376.3	1764	1009	278.2	157.7	275.7
2006	3815	1481	418.2	1716	1022	288.9	168.4	282.7
2007	4034	1567	448.4	1599	1016	264.3	165.3	260.1
2008	4221	1631	475.2	1370	886	206.3	150.6	232.8
2009	4327	1672	491.0	1231	823	179.7	146.0	218.3
2010	4456	1736	503.7	1278	853	184.7	144.5	216.5
2011	4621	1801	529.4	1335	881	199.3	149.3	226.2
2012	4785	1868	550.0	1334	883	200.2	150.1	226.7
2013	4957	1938	569.2	1331	874	192.9	144.9	220.7

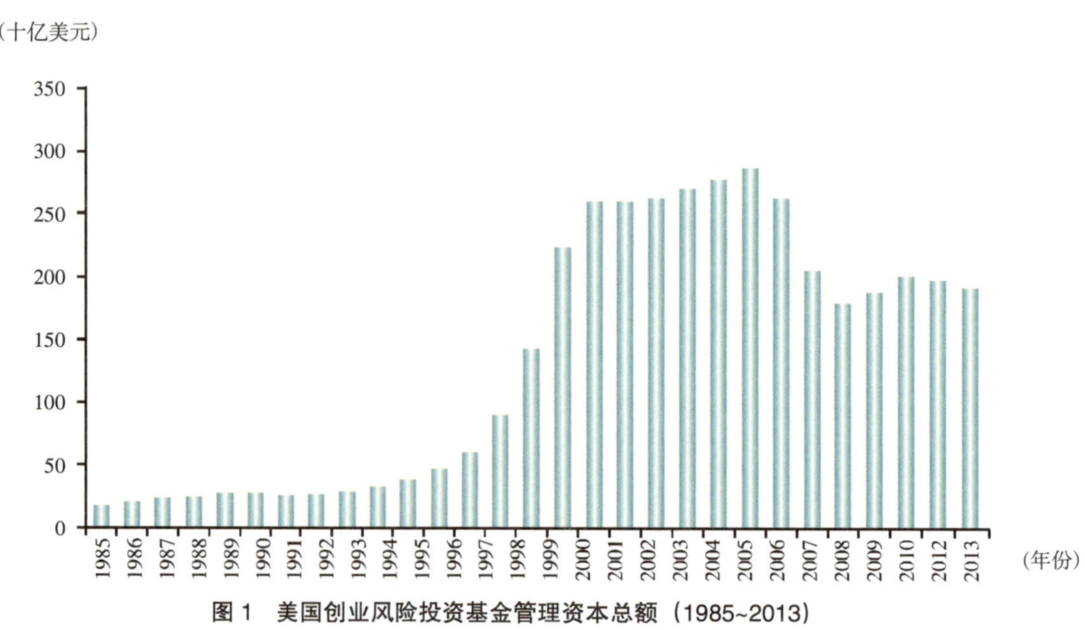

图 1 美国创业风险投资基金管理资本总额（1985~2013）

三、新募资金

2013 年，对于美国大部分的创业投资企业而言，募资仍然是非常具有挑战性的。这主要是由于最近紧缩的退出市场所导致的，与 10 年前相比，最近 10 年许多创业投资基金的回报都乏善可陈，并且对于另类资产投资来说最大的挑战是由于规模限制，要在这一资产类别投资中把资金投在许多规模较小的基金中。2013 年 187 只基金只筹集到 168 亿美元。比 2012 年筹集到的 196 亿美元和 2011 年筹集到的 190 亿美元减少很多。由创业投资基金新募集的资金要少于投资于公司的金额（见图 2）。

2013 年，马萨诸塞州筹款最高，为 55 亿美元，而典型的区域领袖加利福尼亚州则募集了 53 亿美元，纽约州募集的资金为加利福尼亚州的一半左右，排名第三。华盛顿州和弗吉尼亚州位居前五名。总体而言，马萨诸塞州和加利福尼亚州募集资金占总额的 64%。如果加上纽约州，前三个州募集量逾总量的 3/4（达到 77%）。

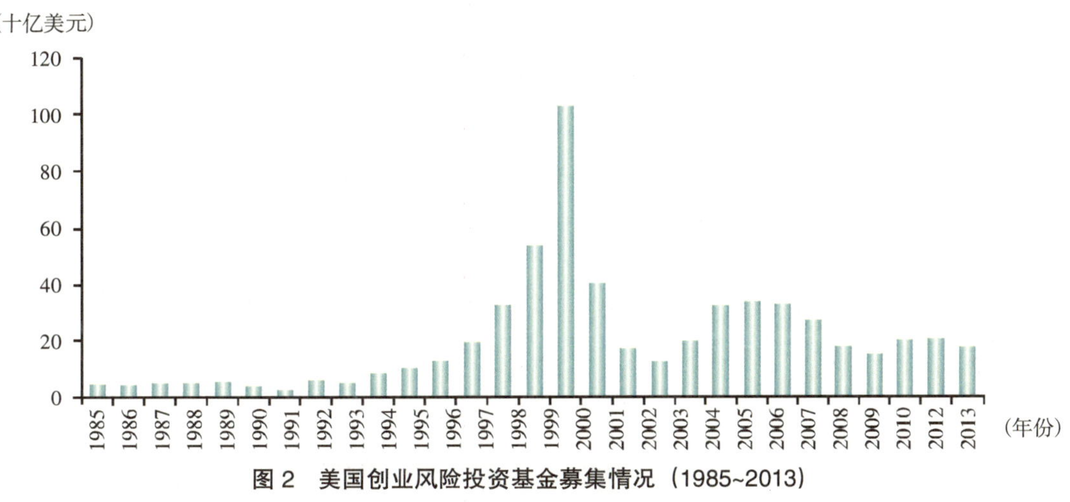

图 2 美国创业风险投资基金募集情况（1985~2013）

四、投资活动

通过投资总量来看，创业风险投资业自 2002 年以来年投资总额持续保持在 200 亿~300 亿美元（见图 3）。2013 年，共有 295 亿美元通过 4041 笔交易投资到 3382 家新企业中。交易总额比 2012 年高了 4%，与 2011 年基本持平。首次融资的企业数量由之前的 1275 增加到 2013 年的 1334 家。进一步的分析数据表明，投资金额的 50%都被投资于加利福尼亚州的企业，与 2012 年的 53%相比有所下降，但和前三年保持一致。

2013 年，美国风险投资创纪录地实现了 72%的资金投资于种子期和早期，相比之下，更典型的情况是仅有 1/3 的交易处于这两个阶段。主要是生命科学领域的投资具有该特征。

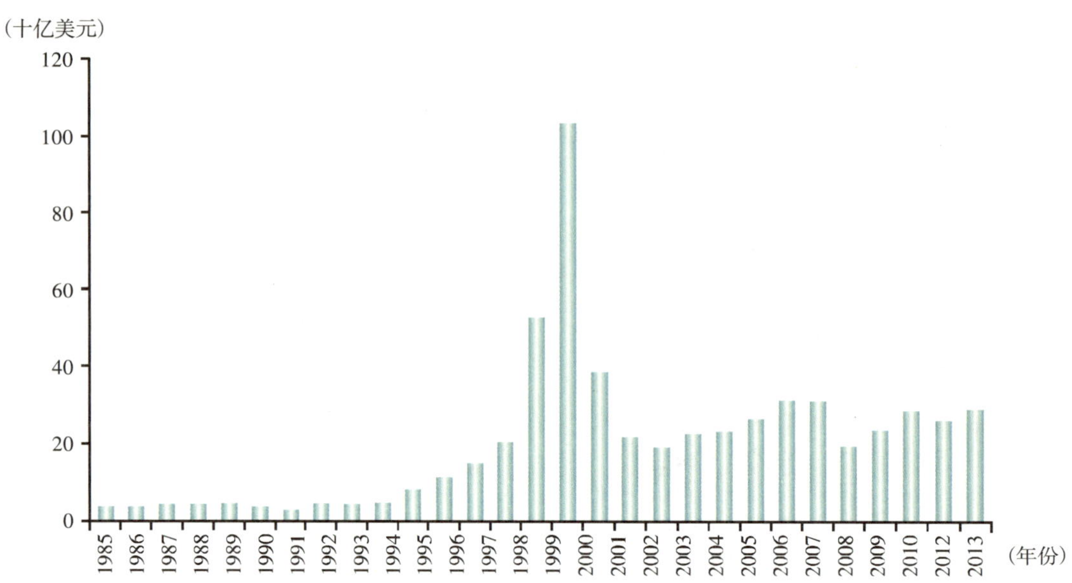

图 3 投资资金总额（1985~2013）

（一）投资行业

按照行业划分（见表 3、图 4），信息技术行业是 2013 年的主导产业，接受了 37.3%的投资金额；位居第二大行业是生物技术，仅占总投资额的 15.4%；传媒和娱乐业，即社交网络涉及的产业目录，获得了 9.9%的投资，而医疗仪器和设备行业获得了 7.2%的投资。

生命科学获得创业投资资本总量在 2013 年达到了自 2001 年以来的最低值，为投资总额的 23.6%（生命科学包括三个生命科学目录，有些目录还包括健康医疗），此数值是由 2009 年峰值 32.7%下降到该水平（1992 年的 36.3%为所有年份中的峰值）。

表 3 按行业分类统计的投资情况（2013）

行业分类	全部投资			首轮投资		
	企业数（家）	交易数（起）	投资数量（十亿美元）	企业数（家）	交易数（起）	投资数量（十亿美元）
信息技术	2360	2784	20.0	1009	1009	3.5
医学/健康学/生命科学	649	816	6.9	167	167	1.2
非高科技类	373	441	2.7	158	158	0.4
总数	3382	4041	29.6	1334	1444	5.1

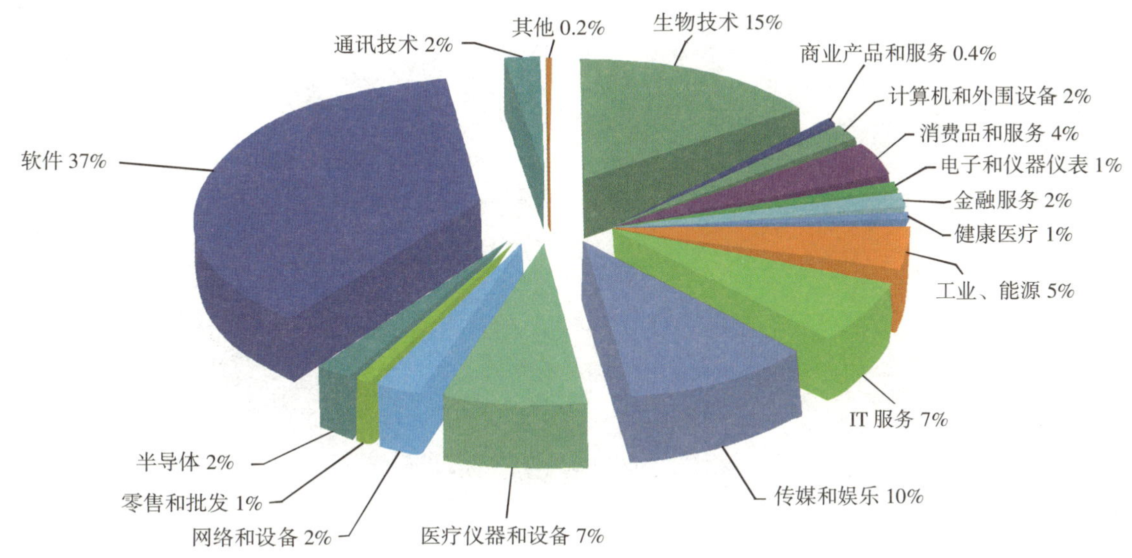

图 4 按行业部门统计的创业资本投资（2013）

（二）投资阶段

产业中的投资活动出现了两个趋势，一方面大量的后期企业希望在2013年底登陆公募市场，而另一方面也有很大一部分新企业获得投资。与此同时，很多被投资企业、IPO和并购占据了头条并获得了知名度。2013年，种子期和早期阶段的交易金额达到了总交易的72%，这超过了2012年的52.6%。这毫无疑问地挑战了创业投资产业注意力仅聚焦于后期企业投资的观点。尽管2013年一系列IPO活动以及在2014年年初的并购，还有创纪录数量的后期企业在投资组合中，但在大多数其他情况下处于这种商业周期的企业已经上市或被收购（见图5、图6）。

从经验来看，健康的创业投资业每年会投资1000~1300家新企业，2013年该数据达1334家。不出预料的话，这次首轮投资中有83%的资金将用于种子期和早期的项目投资。

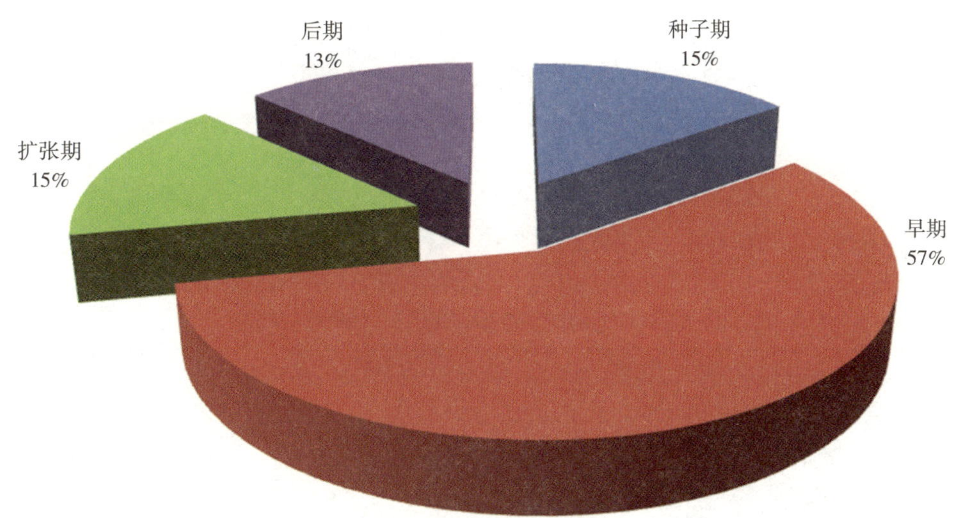

图 5 创业投资基金的投资阶段（按资金占比）(2013)

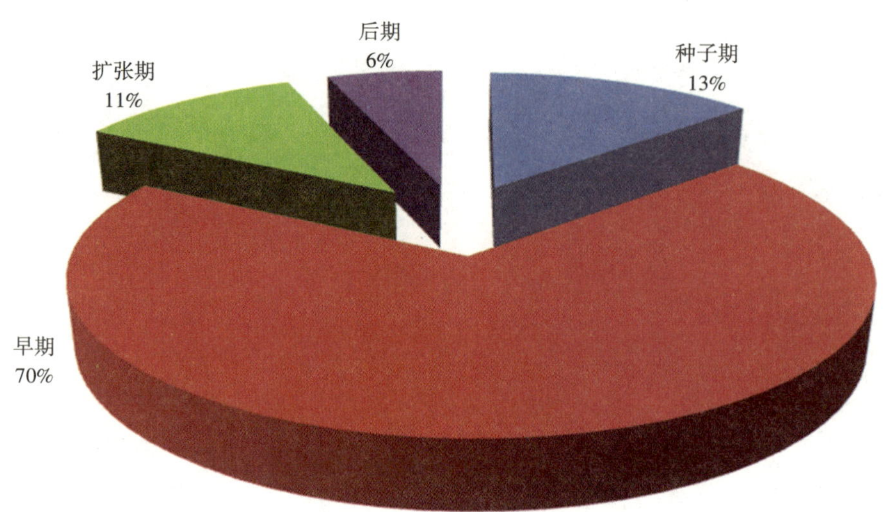

图 6 创业投资基金的投资阶段（按项目占比）(2013)

（三）投资地区

按投资地区划分，2013 年，美国加利福尼亚州的创业投资企业投资了全美 38 个州。投资于加州的资金中有大约 48%是来自加利福尼亚州的创业投资企业。与此同时，据统计，48 个州实现了新创业投资基金的募集，这与 2012 年的历史记录有很大的关系。排名前五的地区（加利福尼亚州、马萨诸塞州、纽约州、华盛顿州和得克萨斯州）投资资金占总投资的 78%（见表 4）。与 2011 年相比，投资地区的集中度有所下降。

表 4 按地区划分的风险资本投资（2013）

地区	企业数量（家）	占总数的比例（%）	投资额（百万美元）	占总数的比例（%）
加利福尼亚州	1362	60	14.8	67
马萨诸塞州	387	15	3.1	16
纽约州	344	14	2.9	9
得克萨斯州	134	5	1.3	4
华盛顿州	107	6	0.9	4
合　计	2334	100	23.0	100

（四）投资轮次

从投资轮次分布来看，2013 年，美国创业投资中首轮投资金额仅占 13%，87%的金额用于后续投资（见表 5、图 7）。

表 5 创业风险投资的首轮投资与后续投资（1985~2013） 单位：百万美元

年份	首轮	后续	总数
1985	727.3	2051.7	2779.0
1986	905.3	2226.9	3132.3
1987	1008.4	2352.9	3361.3
1988	1098.4	2312.9	3411.3
1989	907.4	2425.6	3333.0

续表

年份	首轮	后续	总数
1990	847.2	1985.9	2833.1
1991	551.7	1707.9	2259.7
1992	1302.5	2291.7	3594.2
1993	1274.8	2388.4	3663.2
1994	1644.6	2485.5	4130.1
1995	3976.7	4038.0	8014.8
1996	4198.9	7142.7	11341.6
1997	4869.1	10135.5	15004.6
1998	7154.7	14318.3	21473.0
1999	16333.3	38513.4	54846.7
2000	28542.8	76561.8	105104.6
2001	7300.7	33651.4	40952.1
2002	4343.6	17833.5	22177.1
2003	3692.1	15327.9	19620.0
2004	5402.7	17806.1	23208.8
2005	5885.4	17639.1	23524.5
2006	6266.8	21247.7	27514.5
2007	7721.4	24221.5	31942.9
2008	6515.5	23433.3	29948.9
2009	3506.0	16780.2	20286.2
2010	4294.3	19074.3	23368.6
2011	5498.2	24231.8	29730.0
2012	4440.6	22911.7	27352.3
2013	5104.7	24220.5	29545.2

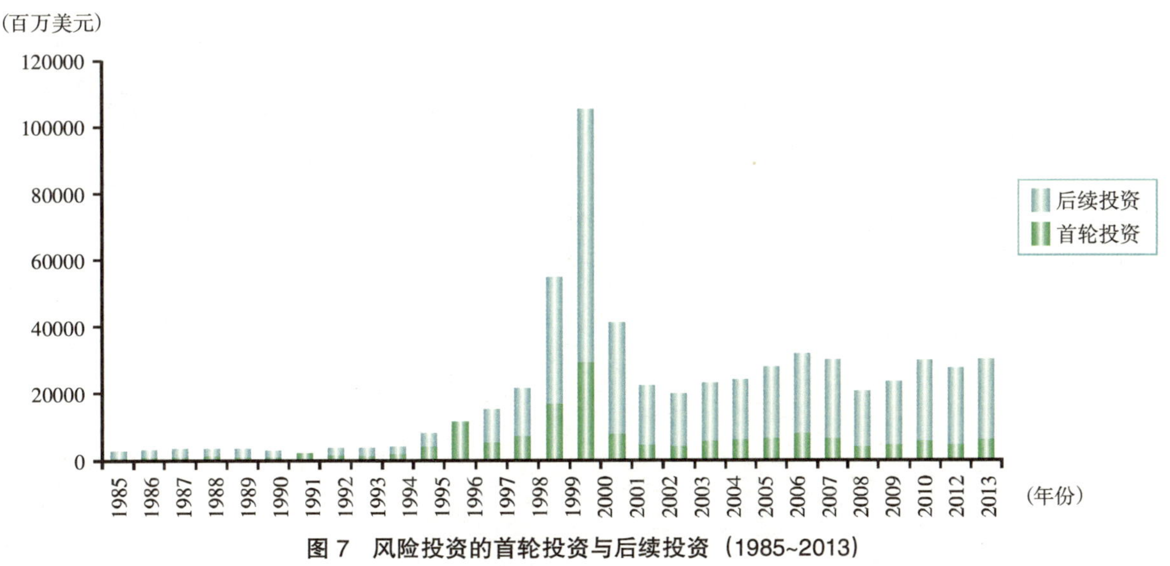

图 7　风险投资的首轮投资与后续投资（1985~2013）

五、获得投资的企业价值估值

从表 6 的数据可以发现，2013 年创业风险投资机构的投资情况与 2012 年相比发生了很大变化。对均值而言，企业价值估值出现了自 2008 年以来的首次下降，并且下降幅度显著，相比 2012 年价值估值下降超过了 2/3；但从中值来说，情况却有所不同，2013 年价值估值的中值下降并不明显。之所以会出现这种情况，是因为 2012 年的价值估值出现了特大型的 IPO 项目，这种异常值从企业价值估值的最大值数据序列中也可以看出，2013 年的最大值为 144 亿美元，远远小于 2012 年的 812 亿美元。

表 6 被投资企业（项目）IPO 时的价值估值（1995~2013） 单位：百万美元

年份	平均估值	最大值	上四分位数	中位数	下四分位数	最小值
1995	152.0	2128.6	144.8	104.2	61.4	10.4
1996	239.6	9989.8	183.4	111.6	65.2	9.5
1997	148.1	1106.3	161.1	99.3	57.2	6.6
1998	324.4	4623.9	288.0	163.9	106.9	7.1
1999	531.9	10203.2	537.0	303.7	186.7	5.9
2000	494.5	4227.7	550.7	325.4	185.0	1.7
2001	534.2	3464.1	617.7	326.6	158.6	46.6
2002	346.7	822.4	537.8	266.2	175.6	36.8
2003	285.1	821.9	353.2	251.9	171.2	41.9
2004	613.0	23053.7	389.2	254.1	152.3	21.6
2005	672.9	22422.9	392.2	201.9	136.6	4.6
2006	1077.6	39248.4	529.2	283.2	179.9	70.9
2007	749.5	14035.4	762.8	364.7	274.1	50.0
2008	520.7	1443.1	713.2	278.5	210.7	75.8
2009	707.1	1622.0	852.5	547.9	313.0	212.9
2010	1642.6	23725.8	1419.9	428.1	222.7	23.4
2011	1856.0	16465.6	1496.6	606.3	336.2	94.8
2012	2493.2	81247.2	704.0	371.0	247.3	75.2
2013	783.8	14435.1	587.8	354.1	212.7	42.9

六、投资退出

美国创业风险投资机构主要采取 IPO 和并购这两种退出方式。2013 年，81 家有创业投资支持的企业在美国上市，是自 2007 年以来上市企业数最多的一年。值得注意的是，IPO 中一半以上是生物技术企业，其中很多是中等规模。而在 2012 年，通过 IPO 募集的总量高于 215 亿美元，其中有 160 亿美元是来自 Facebook 一家企业，余下的 55 亿美元是由其他 48 家上市公司募集的。而在 2013 年，这是完全不同的，81 家企业募集了 111 亿美元。从退出时间的平均数和中位数来看，许多的 IPO 企业是成熟企业，其中不少是在生命科学领域的，这些企业为了获取 IPO 需要等待几个月甚至几年（见图 8）。

根据 2012 年的 JOBs 法案，较小规模的 IPO 和生物技术 IPO 的增长很是鼓舞人心。

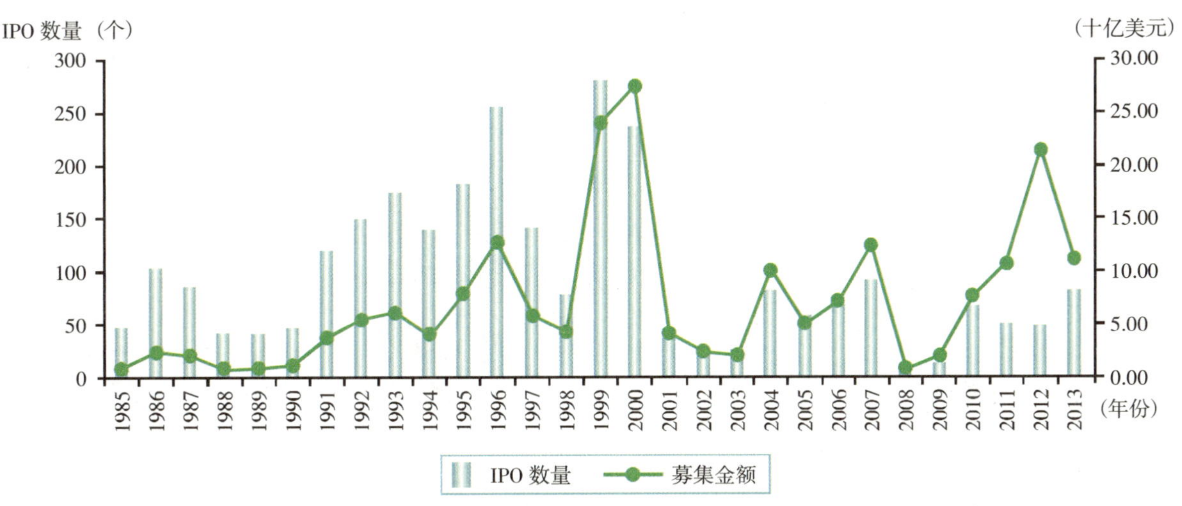

图 8　获得创业风险投资企业的 IPO 数量（1985~2013）

2013 年并购领域持续疲软，交易总数自上年度的 473 笔下降到 376 笔，收益下降了 27%。需要注意的是，376 笔中仅 94 笔收购披露了交易价值。从历史来看，未披露的交易销售价格是相当小的，而且在许多情况下，都是折价出售。然而，越来越多的交易条款清单都对各方提出了保密限制。展望未来，除了最大的和最明显的收购，其他的交易都可能难以衡量。

资料来源：数据由美国风险投资协会 National Venture Capital Association 提供。

附录 2 2013 年欧洲创业风险投资回顾

一、总体概况

2013 年，受全球经济复苏影响，欧洲创业风险投资行业总体状况有所回升，募资与投资均较前一年有大幅度上升。投资的主要行业集中在生命科学、计算机和消费电子、通讯业和能源环境等领域，初创项目投资占主导，全年仅有 4 家风险投资资助的企业通过 IPO 实现退出。

二、资金募集

2013 年总共募集资金达 536 亿欧元，是 2012 年总量的 2 倍。这主要由并购基金驱动。有 12 只并购基金募集了超过 10 亿欧元，占据了总募集量的 66%。

募集基金的数量由 2012 年的 266 只下降到 253 只。养老保险基金提供几乎 40%的资金来源。基金捐款占 16%，另外，主权财富基金占 11%和保险公司占 11%。大约一半的金额（262 亿欧元）是来自欧洲以外的机构投资者。

创业投资占据了总募集量中的 8%，总额达 40 亿欧元，相比 2012 年上涨 4%。

相比 2012 年，2013 年整个欧洲股权投资市场募集资金上升了 118%，升至 53.6 亿欧元。这种增加主要来自大中型基金的增加，全年有 32 只募集超过 2.5 亿欧元的基金，远高于 2012 年的 13 只。其中风险投资资本占整个资金募集的 7.4%，达到 40 亿欧元，高于 2012 年的募集量。与 2012 年全年募集的 1102 只各类股权类基金相比，2013年新募集了 253 只各类股权类基金（见表 1、图 1）。风险投资获得了 40 亿欧元占总筹款额的 8%，与 2012 年相比增长了 4%。其中政府机构的贡献仍然稳定在 38%，家族企业和个人贡献了 23%，基金贡献了 12%的资金。并购资金从 2013 年的 167 亿欧元增长到了 449 亿欧元，占据了募集资金的 84%。成长基金募集金额超过 1 倍，达到 12 亿欧元。

表 1 欧洲股权投资市场募集资金主要特征（2013）

2013 年	所有股权类基金	风险投资	并购	成长资本	其他
新募集基金额（十亿欧元）	53.6	4.0	44.9	1.2	3.4
新募集基金数（只）	253	105	77	22	49

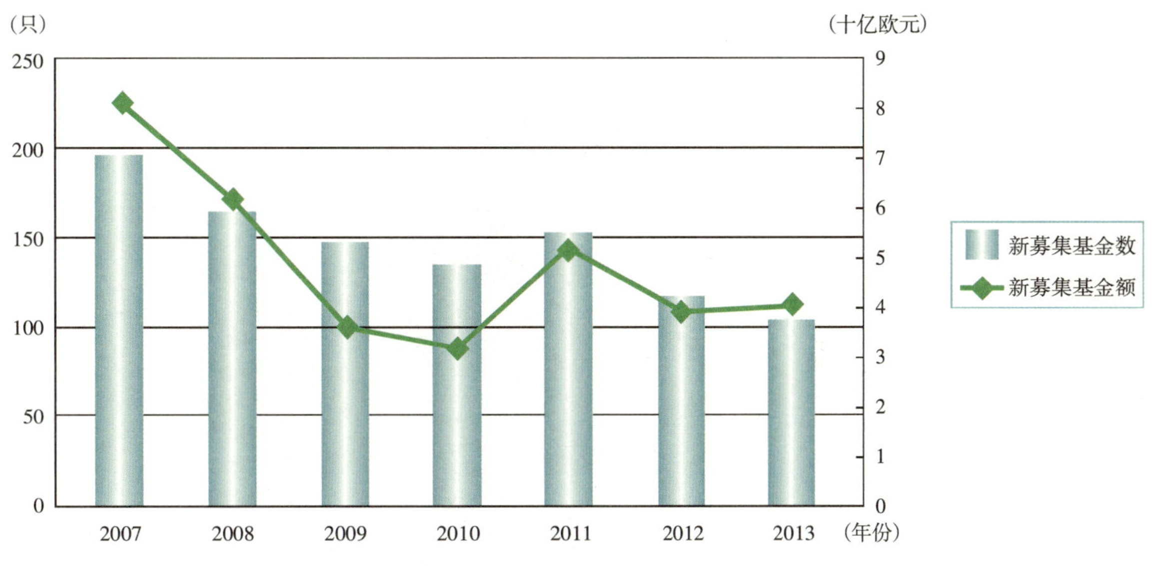

图1　欧洲创业风险投资基金募集情况（2007~2013）

按资金来源划分，在整个欧洲股权投资市场中，养老基金和母基金是最主要的资金来源。但对于创业风险投资资金募集而言，政府出资的资金占主导，约占40%（见图2、图3）。

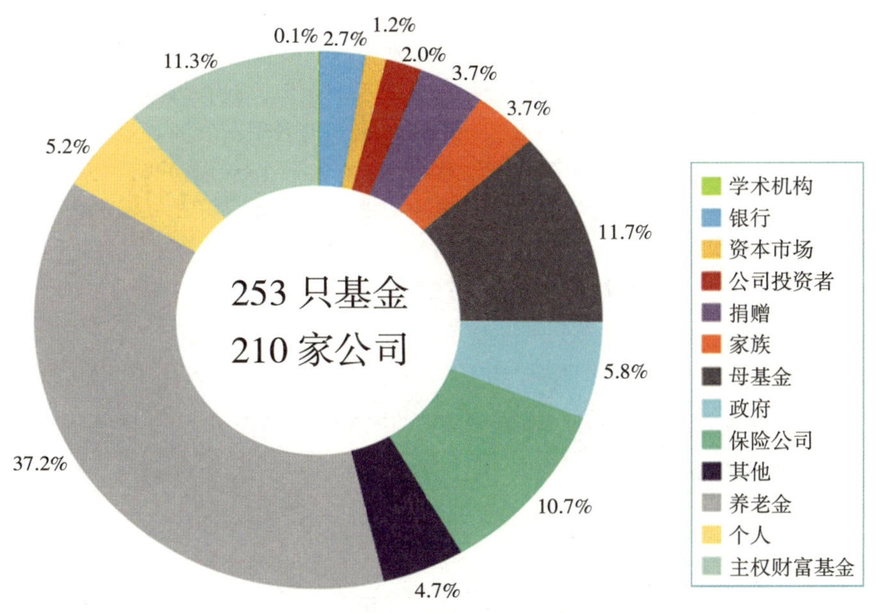

图2　欧洲股权投资市场募集基金来源（2013）

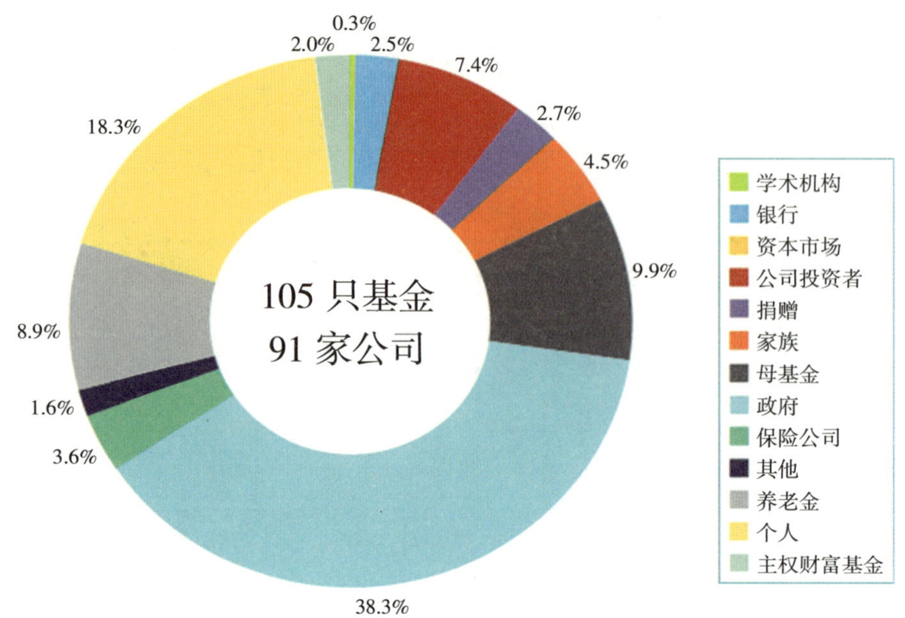

图 3 欧洲创业风险投资募集基金来源（2013）

三、投资活动

2013 年，整个欧洲股权投资市场保持了稳定。其中欧洲创业风险投资市场共投资 357 亿欧元，与 2012 年相比上升了 11.6%。2013 年有超过 5000 家企业获得了投资，与前一年基本持平（见表 2）。整体的股权投资下滑了 3 个百分点，投资总额为 357 亿欧元。2013 年有超过 40%的企业是第一次获得股权投资资助。总体来看，风险资本投资的总金额增加了 5%达 34 亿欧元，有超过 3000 家公司有风险投资背景。大部分的风险投资活动（55%）和风险投资所投的企业（59%）处于启动阶段。有超过 800 家企业进行了并购。相关的股权投资金额总量和 2012 年相比减少了 2%，公司数减少了 9%。超过 1000 家企业吸引了成长资本。企业数量增长了 6%而股权投资总数下降了 10%。

表 2 欧洲股权投资市场投资活动的主要特征（2013）

2013 年	所有股权类基金	风险投资	并购	成长资本	其他
投资金额（十亿欧元）	35.7	3.4	27.7	3.6	1.0
投资项目数（家）	5089	3034	812	1131	112
涉及的企业数（家）	1073	641	420	334	—
涉及的基金数（只）	1654	994	552	500	—

从 2000 年至今，整个欧洲股权投资市场投资金额占 GDP 的比重为 0.2%~0.6%。2013 年，欧洲股权投资市场投资金额占 GDP 的比重为 0.27%，其中，风险投资的投资金额 GDP 的比重为 0.024%（见图 4、图 5）。

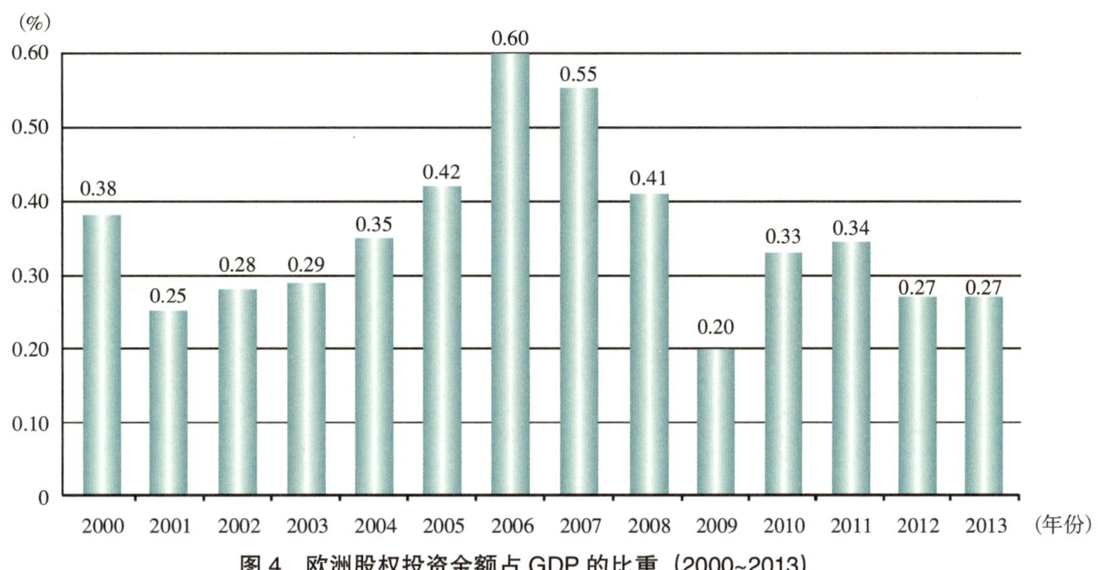

图 4　欧洲股权投资金额占 GDP 的比重（2000~2013）

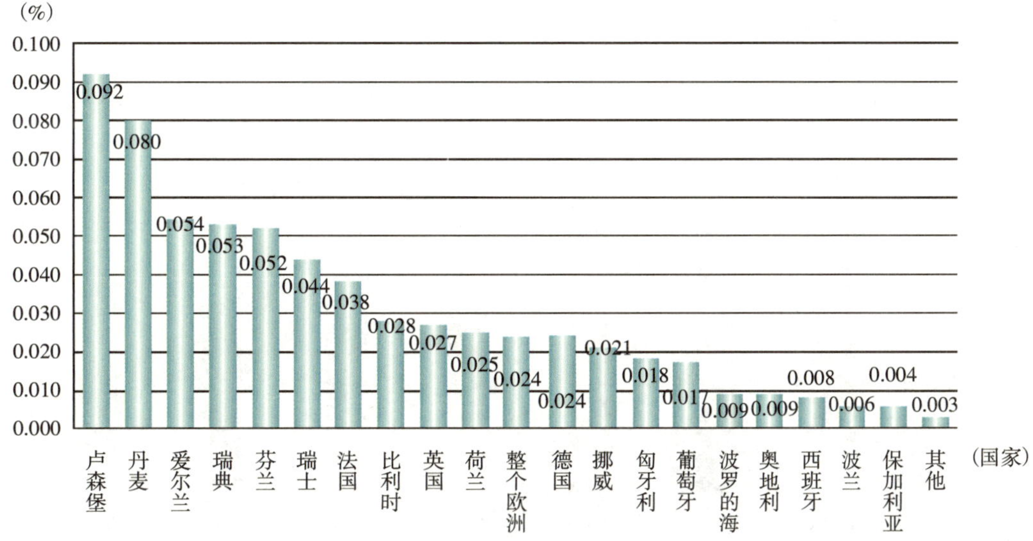

图 5　欧洲主要国家风险投资占 GDP 的比重（2013）

(一）投资阶段分布

其中创业投资的投资额度整体上升 5 个百分点，达到 34 亿欧元。超过 3000 家企业获得了创业投资的资助。无论是从投资金额（占总额的 55%）还是企业数量（占总额的 59%）看，初创期阶段的投资占据了创业投资的绝大多数（见图 6、图 7）。

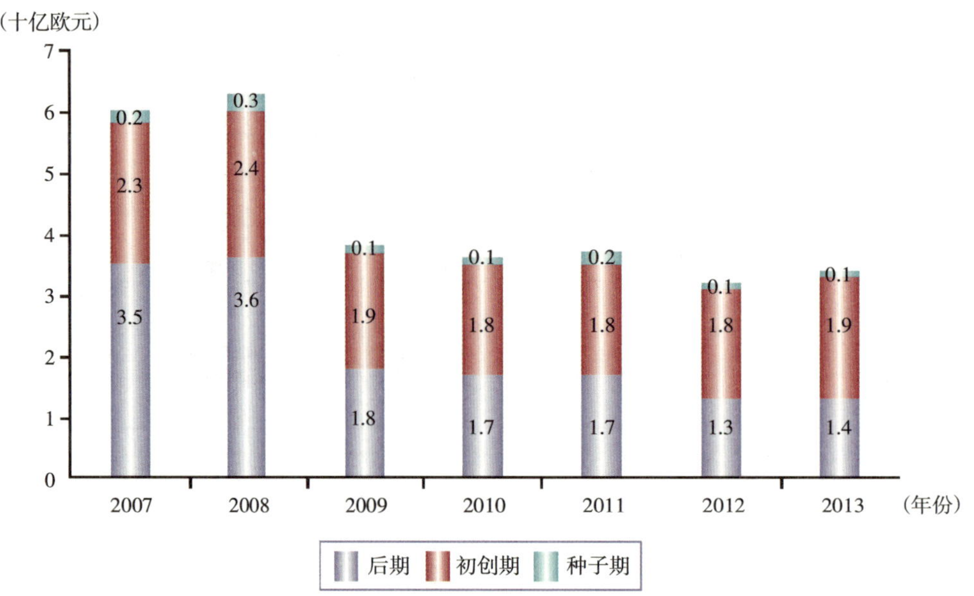

图 6 欧洲创业风险投资基金投资情况（按投资项目）(2007~2013)

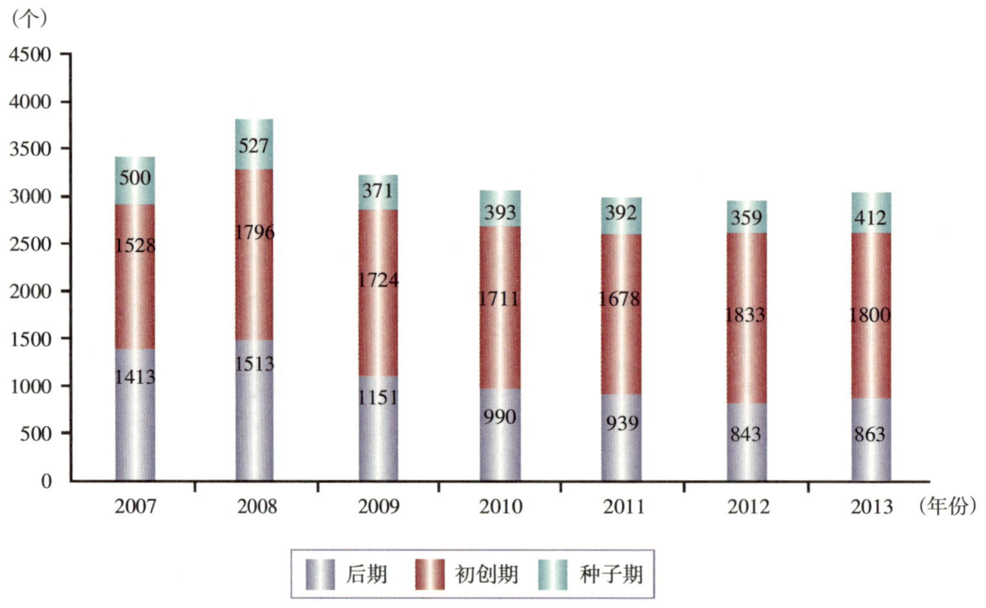

图 7 欧洲创业风险投资基金投资情况（按投资金额）(2007~2013)

(二) 投资行业分布

按风险投资的投资行业划分，生命科学、计算机和消费电子、通讯业和能源环境产业获得了总额中 70%的投资（见图 8、图 9）。

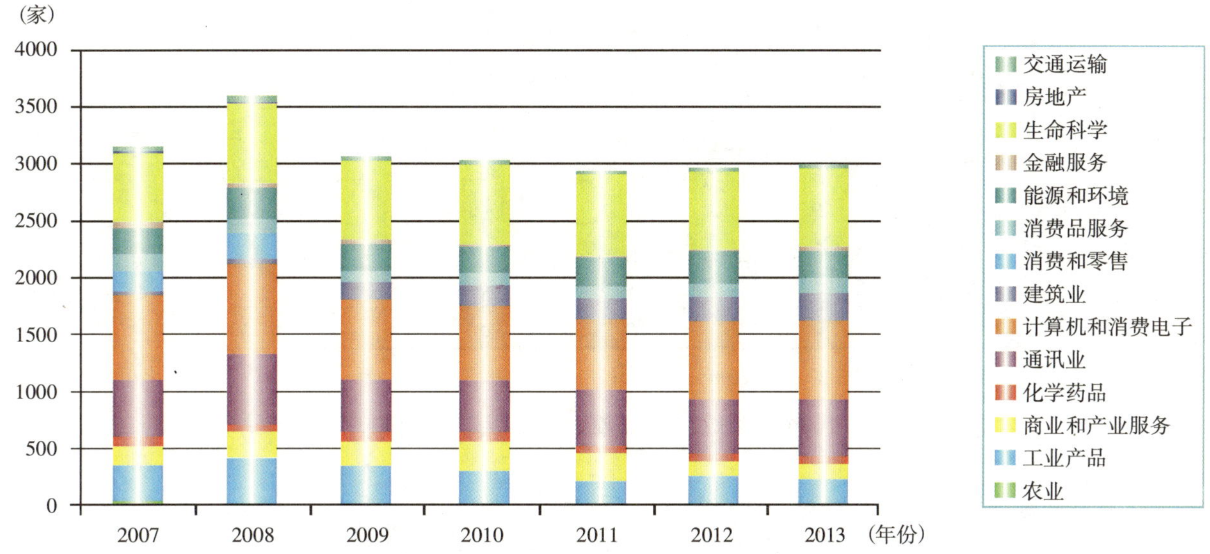

图 8 欧洲创业风险投资基金投资的行业分布（按投资项目）(2007~2013)

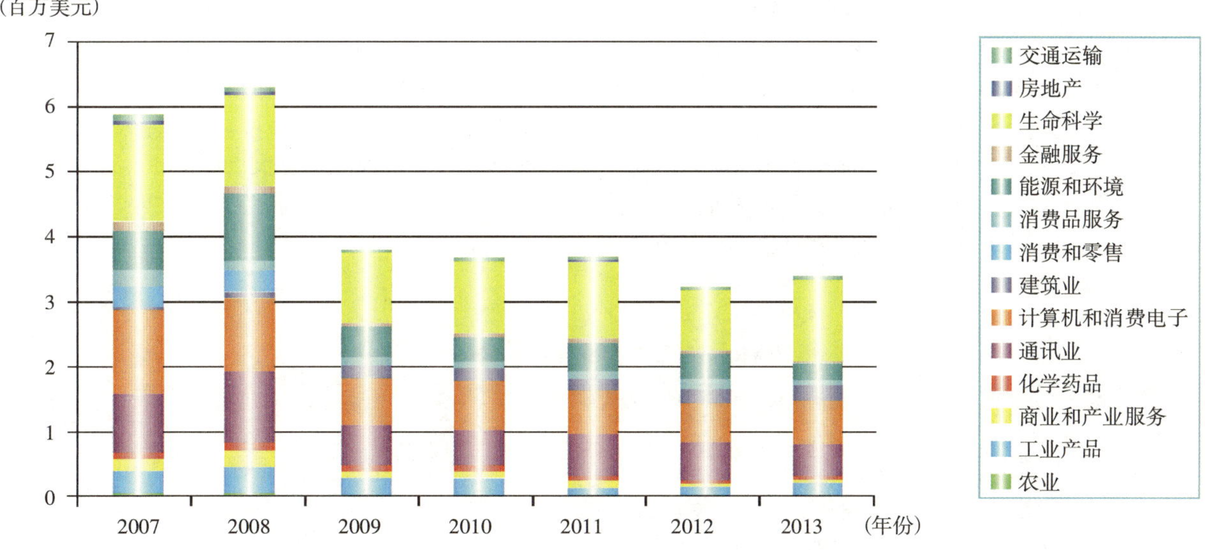

图 9 欧洲创业风险投资基金投资的行业分布（按投资金额）(2007~2013)

(三) 投资轮次分布

从投资轮次分布来看，欧洲股权投资市场的首轮投资与后续投资占比大致持平，但近年来有后续投资增大的趋势。2013 年，首轮投资占 42%，后续投资占 58%（见图 10）。

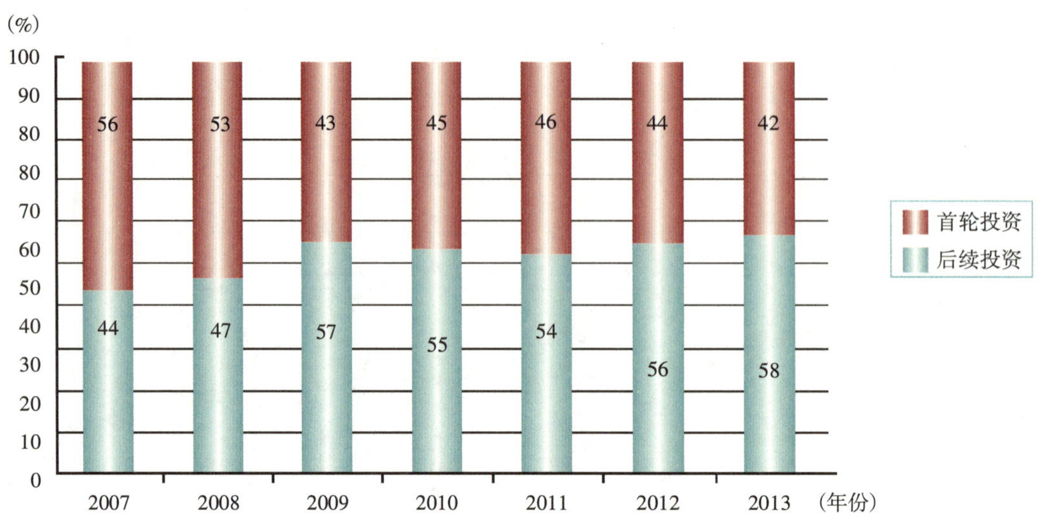

图 10 欧洲股权投资的首轮投资与后续投资（2007~2013）

四、投资退出

2013 年，整个欧洲股权投资市场有 2290 家企业实现退出，金额达 332 亿欧元。与前期相比，数量提升了 10%，但成本也环比上升了 54%。其中，创业风险投资的企业退出占整个市场的近 43%，但退出成本仅占 7%（见表 3）。

2013 年，退出公司的数量几乎增加了 10%，而退出成本则增加了 54%至 18 亿欧元。主要的退出方式依次为贸易销售（27%）、出售给其他 PE 公司（26%）和股权出售（14%）。40%左右的公司都遵循上述退出渠道。2013 年公募市场的力量体现在急剧增加的股票首次公开发行（IPO）上，这种退出方式的成本增加了超过七倍（22 亿欧元），以这种方式退出的公司（23 家）增加了几乎四倍。以股本金形式退出的风险投资退出成本增加 21%，高达 22 亿欧元；以并购形式退出的风险投资退出成本增加 53%至 280 亿欧元。

表 3 欧洲股权投资市场退出活动的主要特征（2013）

2013 年	所有股权类基金	创业投资	并购	成长资本	其他
成本（十亿欧元）	33.2	2.2	28	1.8	1.2
退出项目数（家）	2290	994	688	574	34
涉及的企业数（家）	646	312	332	147	—
涉及的基金数（只）	1133	550	510	221	—

（一）退出方式

按退出方式划分，欧洲风险投资的主要退出方式包括清算、贸易销售，以及偿还合伙人资金等，其中，2013 年，仅有 4 家风险投资资助的企业实现 IPO 退出（见图 11）。

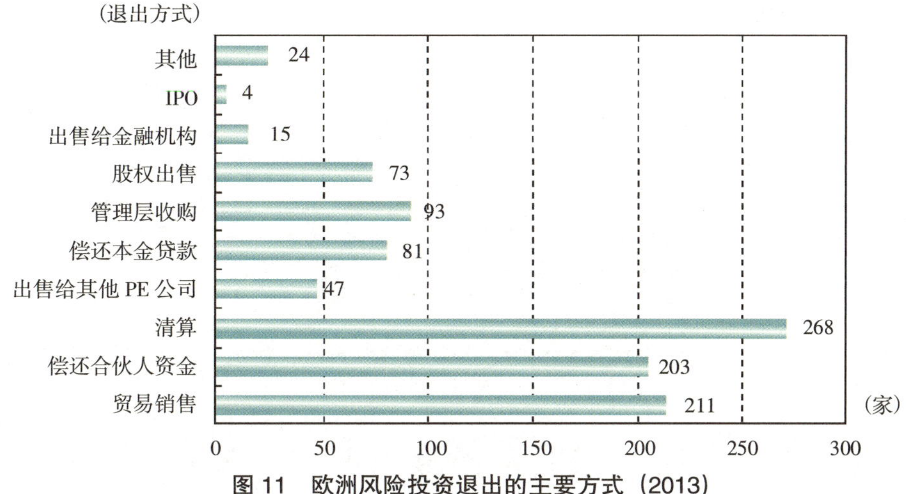

图 11　欧洲风险投资退出的主要方式（2013）

（二）退出的行业划分

按退出行业划分，2012 年当年退出的主要行业包括生命科学、计算机与消费电子、金融服务、通信业，以及能源和环境。其中，生命科学当年退出的金额占总量的 29.4%，项目数占 17.6%（见图 12）。

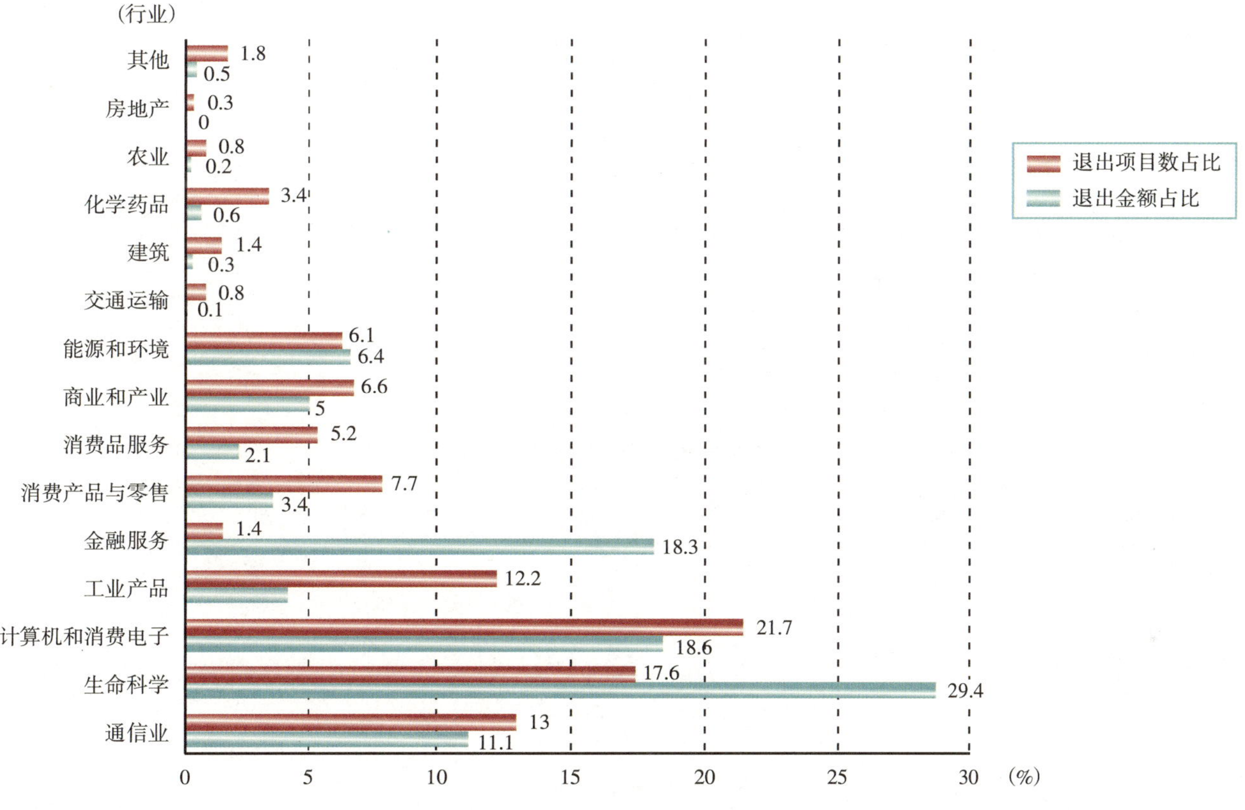

图 12　欧洲风险投资退出的主要行业分布（2013）

资料来源：数据由欧洲私募股权和风险投资协会 European Private Equity and Venture Capital Association 提供。

附录 3 2013 年韩国创业风险投资回顾

一、韩国创业风险投资市场概况

由于近几年韩国政府出台中小企业的支持政策，2013 年的韩国创业风险投资行业伴随着政策红利的逐渐丧失以及国内外经济复苏乏力，韩国创业行业增长趋势有所放缓。2013 年的创业投资公司当年的公司存量微幅下降为 101 家，累积的注册资本金额也有所下降（见表 1）。但是与 2012 年相比，韩国创业风险投资基金注册数以及注册资本金额出现了明显上升，相应地，当年的基金存量以及累计金额出现上升（见表 2）。

截止到 2013 年底，韩国共有 101 家投资公司，431 只风险投资基金（见表 1、表 2、图 1）。

2013 年，创业风险投资公司注册资本为 1397.6 亿韩元，风险投资基金管理资本为 10407.0 亿韩元（见表 1、表 2）。

表 1 韩国创业风险投资公司概况（2005~2013）

项目 \ 年份	2005	2006	2007	2008	2009	2010	2011	2012	2013
当年新注册数（注销数）(家)	0（3）	13（11）	7（10）	5（9）	12（9）	13（10）	9（7）	6（6）	3（7）
当年公司存量（家）	102	104	101	97	100	103	105	105	101
累计注册资本（家）	1536.8	1553.7	1555.8	1475.8	1360.8	1383.8	1398.5	1445.5	1397.6

表 2 韩国创业风险投资基金概况（2005~2013）

项目 \ 年份	2005	2006	2007	2008	2009	2010	2011	2012	2013
当年注册数（只）	46	48	67	51	74	67	67	41	49
金额（十亿韩元）	945.4	861.7	1127.9	975.1	1420.9	1589.9	2286.1	772.7	1537.4
当年注销数（只）	69	98	84	48	44	40	43	45	30
金额（十亿韩元）	433.7	741.8	929.4	406.3	491.7	550.4	440.0	858.6	504.5
当年存量（十亿韩元）	400	350	333	336	366	393	417	431	431
累计金额（十亿韩元）	4757.6	4877.5	5076.0	5644.8	6574.0	7613.5	9460.0	9374.1	10407.0

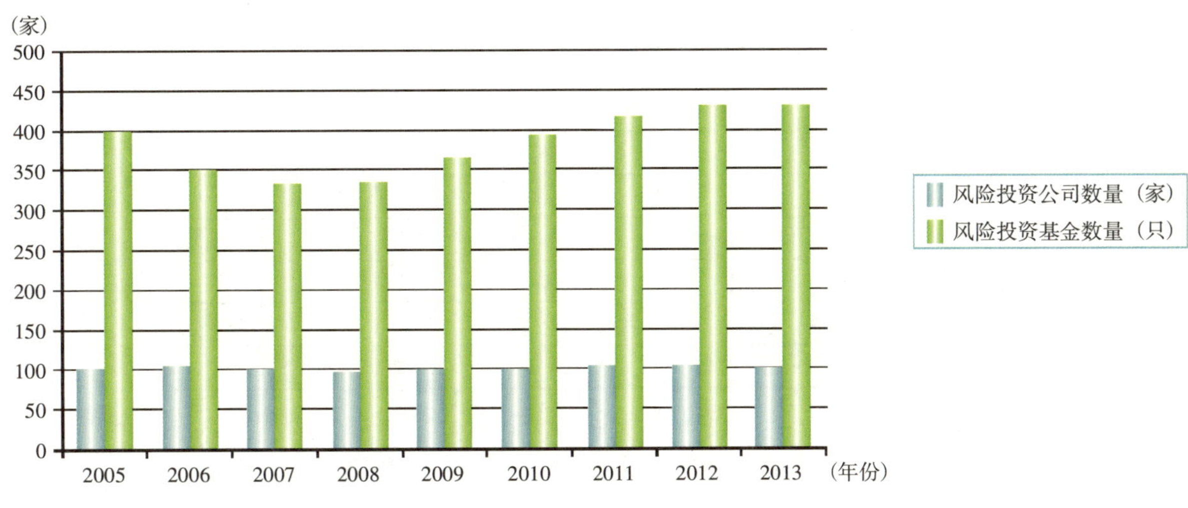

图 1 韩国创业风险投资市场概况（2005~2013）

二、韩国创业风险投资活动

表 3 韩国创业风险投资项目数及金额（2005~2013） 单位：项，十亿韩元

年份 项目	2005	2006	2007	2008	2009	2010	2011	2012	2013
新投资项目数	635	617	615	496	524	560	613	688	755
新投资金额数	757.3	733.3	991.7	724.7	867.1	1091.0	1260.8	1233.3	1384.5
投资强度	1.19	1.19	1.61	1.46	1.65	1.95	2.06	1.79	1.83

三、韩国创业风险投资行业分布

2013 年，韩国创业风险机构的投资仍然集中在文化/娱乐业、IT 以及制造业等行业，从投资项目看，三者占比分别为 28.51%、17.93%、32.25%；从投资金额看，三者占比分别为 35.23%、22.52%、20.63%（见表 4、图 2）。

表 4 韩国创业风险投资行业分布（2013）

行业	IT	制造业	文化/娱乐业	生物技术	服务/教育	零售业	资源回收	其他
项目（项）	229	144	259	68	58	27	6	12
金额（百万韩元）	487.8	311.8	285.6	146.3	59.7	49.6	24.1	19.6

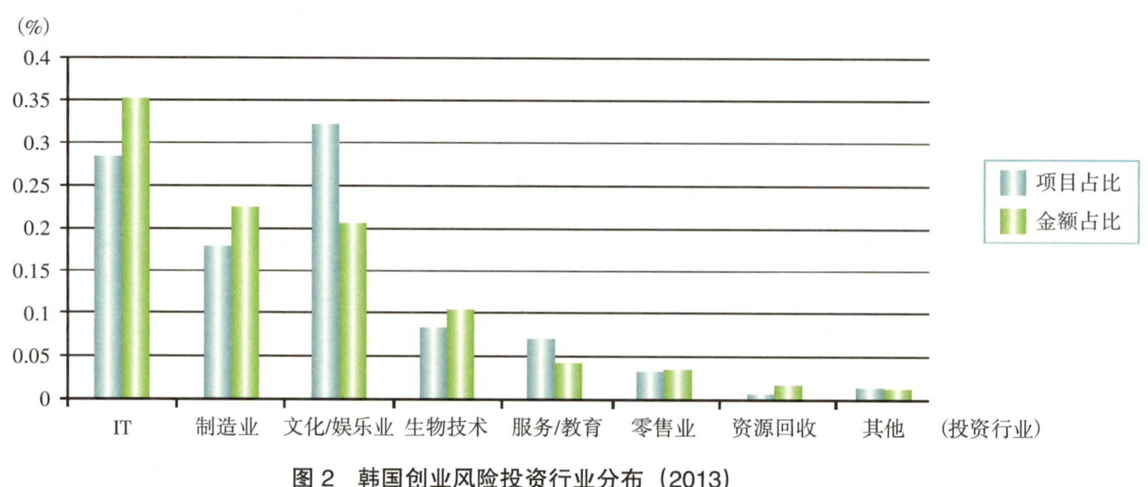

图 2 韩国创业风险投资行业分布（2013）

四、韩国创业风险投资阶段分布

从投资阶段的分布来看，2013 年韩国创业风险投资项目和金额仍然以扩展期为最多，所占比重为 49.74%；从投资项目看，投资于早期和创业期的项目数量比 2012 年均有所增加，投资于扩展期的项目数量有一定下降；然而从投资金额看，投资于创建期和扩展期的金额均比 2012 年有显著增长（见表 5、图 3）。

表 5 韩国创业风险投资阶段分布（2013）

阶段	早期	创建期	扩展期
投资项目（项）	354	212	215
投资金额（百万韩元）	369.9	325.9	688.7

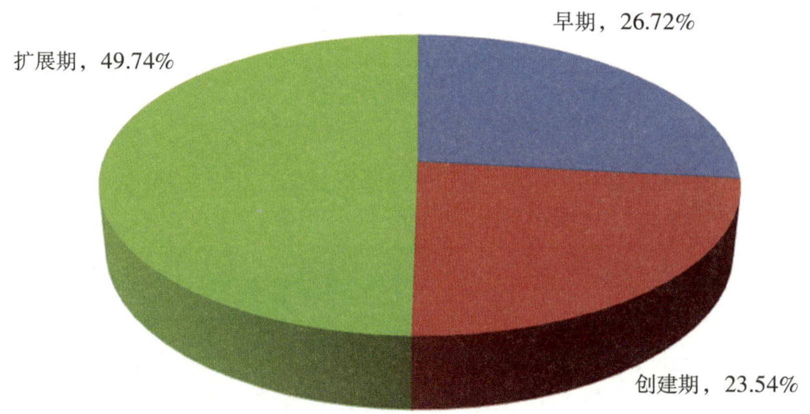

图 3 韩国创业风险投资阶段分布（按金额划分）（2013）

资料来源：数据由韩国风险投资协会 Korean Venture Capital Association 提供。

附录 4 2014 硅谷指数解读

每年一季度，硅谷社区基金会和硅谷合资企业网络公布的权威报告《硅谷指数》都会及时出版。《硅谷指数》自1995 年开始出版，至今已 20 年。《2014 硅谷指数》是一份全面反映 2013 年硅谷发展动态的权威报告，《2014 硅谷指数》主要是从四个方面来反映硅谷的创新创业。

1. 信息行业专利注册量涨幅最大

硅谷的员工人均增加值经过几年的持续增长后，在 2013 年下降了 0.1%，最终进入平稳状态。同年，加利福尼亚州员工人均增加值也略微下降 0.6%，而全美上升了 2.1%。整体上，硅谷的员工增长值平均要比加利福尼亚州的多 40558 美元/人（见图 1）。

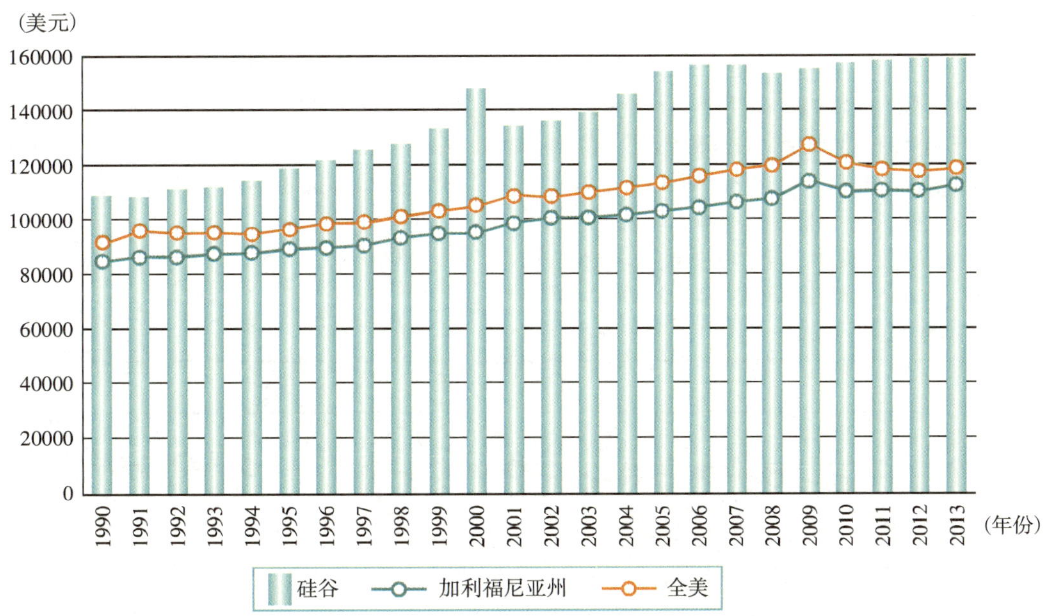

图 1　硅谷、加利福尼亚州及全美员工人均增加值（1990~2013）

尽管硅谷的专利注册数持续增长，但占加利福尼亚州专利注册总数的比例由 2011 年的 48.3%下降至 2012 年的 46.9%。相比而言，硅谷的专利注册数占全美的比例在过去四年里一直保持相对稳定，为 12.4%。2012 年，硅谷专利注册数为 15057 项，比 2011 年增长了 11%。与过去几年类似，计算机、数据处理及信息存储行业的专利所占比例最大，仍占硅谷专利总数的 39%。通信行业的专利注册量在过去一年里涨幅最大，增加了 648 项（占硅谷专利注册总数的比例增长了 2%），累计总数达到了 3572 项。化学和有机材料行业的专利注册数跌幅最大，比 2011 年减少了 105 项，下跌了 18%（见图 2）。

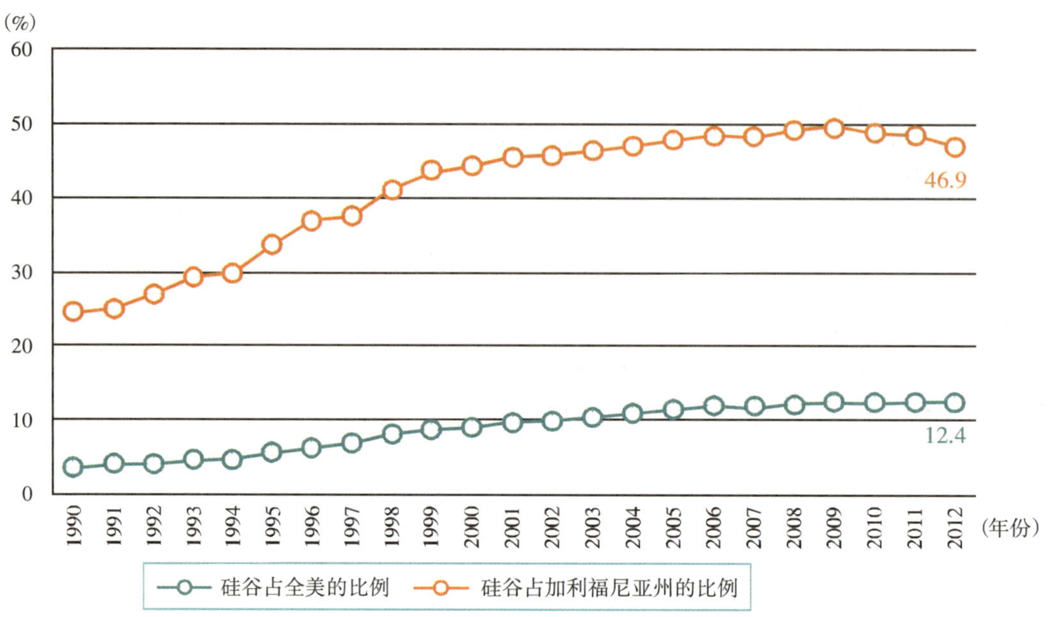

图 2 硅谷专利注册数占加利福尼亚州和全美的比例（1990~2012）

2. 硅谷风险投资青睐生物技术和清洁技术行业

2013 年前三季度的数据显示，硅谷和旧金山地区的风险投资额占加利福尼亚州总额的比例从 2012 年的 70%上升至 77%，占全美风险投资总额的比例也从 37%增加至 39%。按行业分布来看，软件业继续稳步上升，成为吸引风险投资最多的行业，占风险投资总额的 44%，而 2012 年为 38%。生物技术行业吸引的风险投资额占总额的比例也从 2012 年的 8%增加至 11%。相比，能源业所占的比例下跌 5%，占总额的 6%（见图 3）。

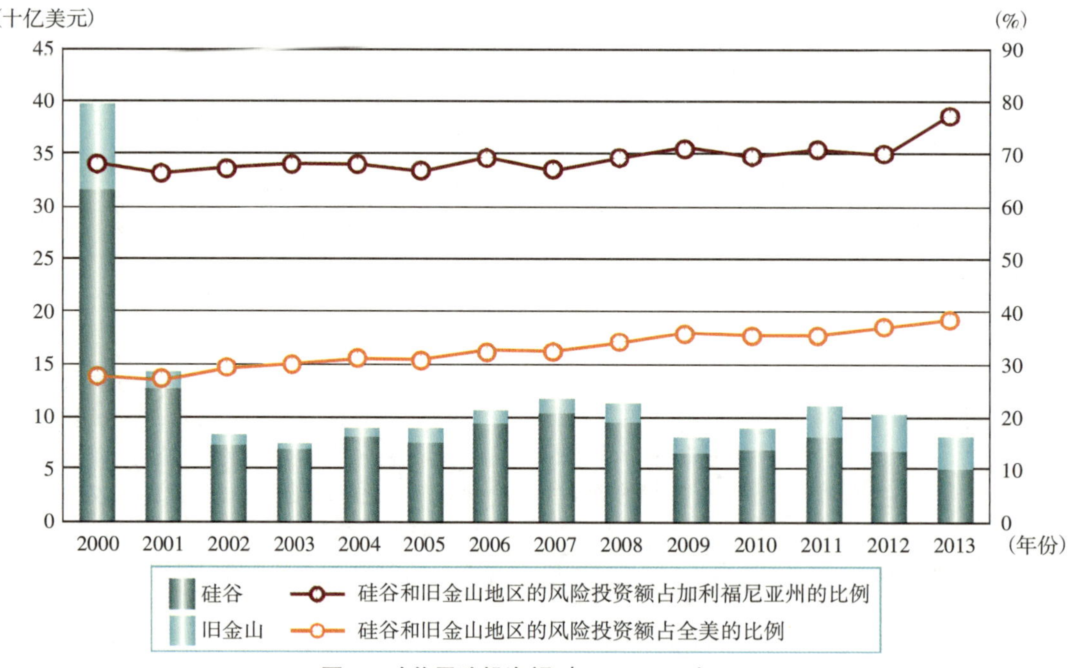

图 3 硅谷风险投资额（2000~2013）

硅谷清洁技术行业的风险投资额有望超过 2012 年，仅 2013 年前三季度的投资额就达到 8.4 亿美元。截至 2013 年 10 月底，旧金山地区的清洁技术行业的投资额已超过 2012 年，达到 4.5 亿美元。这两地区在清洁技术行业的风险投资总额占加利福尼亚州清洁技术行业风险投资总额的比例由 2012 年的 48%迅速增长至 77%。其中，太阳能方面的投资在 2013 年前三季度出现大幅下跌，从 3.32 亿美元跌至 8800 万美元，同比下跌 74%。此外，能源生产，生物燃料及生化药剂，燃料电池及氢能，智能电网及运输行业取得的风险投资有所增长（见图 4）。

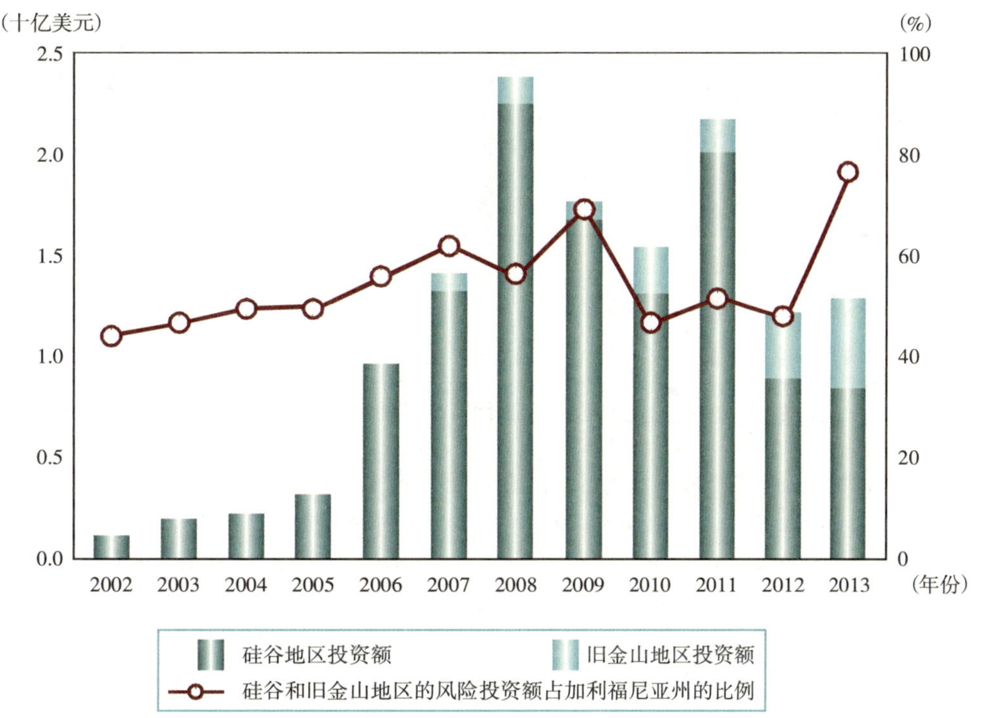

图 4 硅谷清洁技术行业的风险投资情况（2002~2013）

此外，近三年硅谷公开披露的天使投资结构有所变化，A 轮融资投资额逐步增多，2011 年为 4.6 亿美元，2012 年为 7.26 亿美元，2013 年前三季度为 10.28 亿美元。另外，旧金山对于种子期的风险投资稳步增长，从 2011 年的 9600 万美元到 2013 年超过 1.64 亿美元的投资额。然而，A 轮融资的投资额从 2012 年 9.21 亿美元下跌至 2013 年的 5.07 亿美元。整体上，上述两个地区的天使投资占加利福尼亚州天使投资总额的比例较大且不断增长（占 87%）（见图 5）。

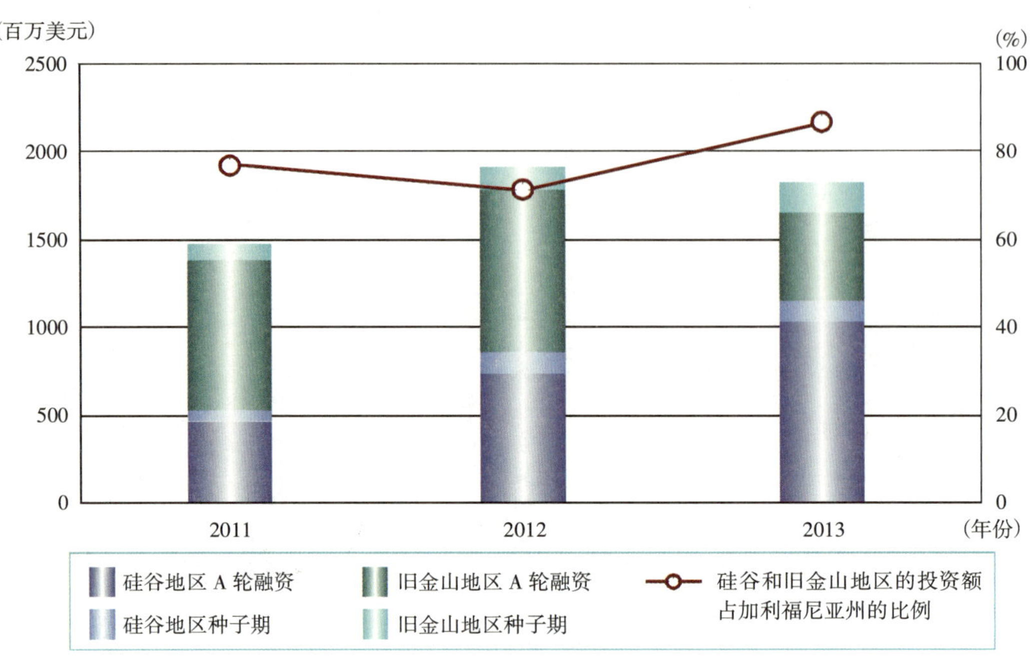

图 5 硅谷、旧金山及加利福尼亚州天使投资情况（2011~2013）

3. IPO 数量和并购数量逐年增多

2013 年，美国 IPO 总数已大大超过前几年。全年全美 IPO 数量为 222 家，比上年增加了 94 家。全美及加利福尼亚州的 IPO 上市数量都高于 2012 年同期水平。硅谷地区 IPO 数量逐年增多，2013 年为 20 家，这比 2009 年仅有 1 家 IPO 的情况大大好转。虽然数量上增多，但是占加利福尼亚州上市总数以及全美总数的比例有所下跌，分别从 51.5%跌至 46.5%、14.8%跌至 10.8%。旧金山 IPO 数量为 4 家，加上硅谷的 20 家，两者占加利福尼亚州和全美 IPO 总数的比例分别为 55.8%和 13%（见图 6）。

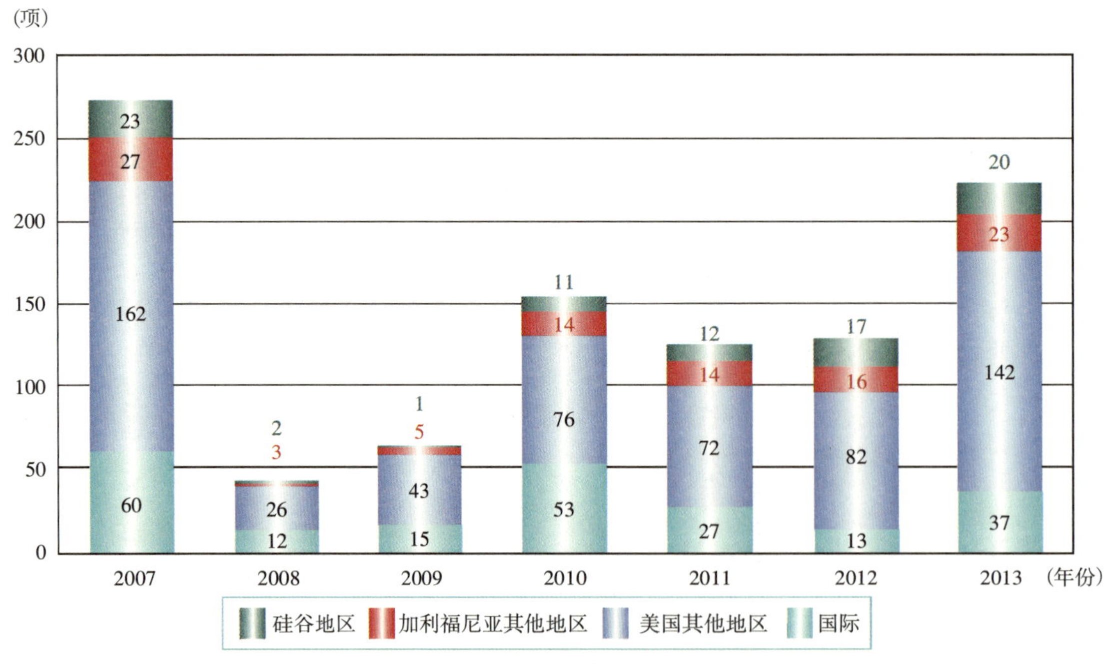

图 6 全美 IPO 总数（2007~2013）

截至 2013 年三季度，硅谷和旧金山占加利福尼亚州、全美并购活动的比例分别从上年的 38%、9%增加至 43%、10%。仅前三季度，硅谷兼并活动数量已经达到 2012 年全年水平。2013 年所有并购交易中，至少有一个并购目标及一个收购方位于硅谷的并购交易数量下降了 3%；而仅有硅谷本地并购对象和仅有本地收购方的交易数分别增长了 2%和 1%。同时，旧金山地区并购活动更多转向仅含本地并购目标的交易（与 2012 年本地并购活动占有率相比，上升了 8%）；而仅有旧金山本地收购方的交易，以及至少有一个旧金山本地并购目标和收购方的交易，分别降低了 7%和 1%（见图 7）。

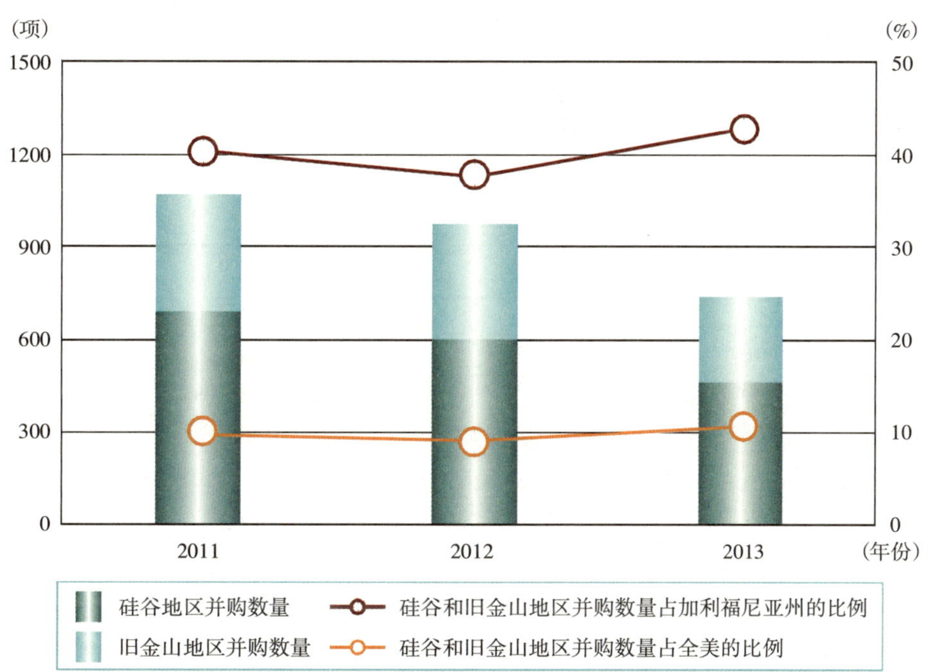

图 7　硅谷、旧金山、加利福尼亚州及全美的并购数量（2011~2013）

4. 非雇主企业数量持续增多

非雇主企业（个人创业，没有员工的企业）数量持续增多。相比 2004 年水平，硅谷增长了 12%，加利福尼亚州和全美均为 15%，旧金山为 16.5%，阿拉米达县为 17%，这意味着有大量的新企业没有员工。2010~2011 年，硅谷注册了 3639 家非雇主企业，比上年增长了 2%。2011 年，硅谷 26%的非雇主企业从事科技和技术服务行业。全美和加利福尼亚州范围内，只有 14%和 18%的非雇主企业从事该行业。这说明硅谷是专业从事科技和技术服务行业（见图 8）。

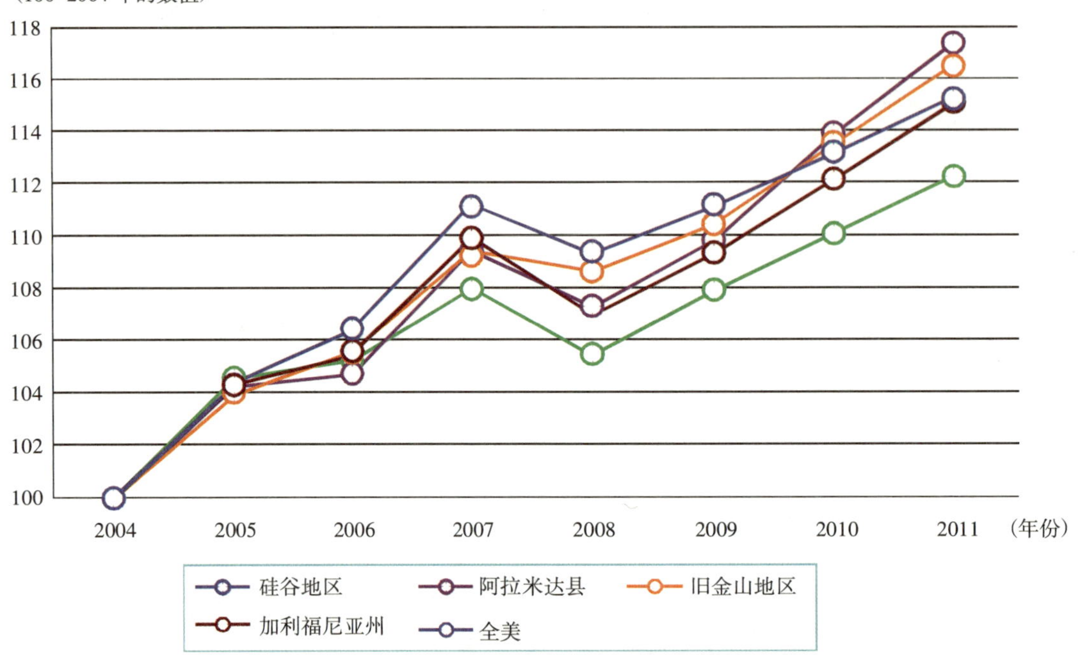

图 8　硅谷、阿拉米达县、旧金山、加利福尼亚州及美国非雇员企业增长情况（2004~2011）

以上数据直观反映了硅谷创新创业在美国有很重要的地位。此外，《2014 硅谷指数》还提供另一组数据，即硅谷各指标占加利福尼亚州比重数据。硅谷土地面积占加利福尼亚州的 1.2%，人口占 7.7%，就业占 9.2%，GDP 占 9.9%，并购占 28.8%，IPO 占 46.5%，专利占 46.9%，风险投资占 47.6%，天使投资占 54.6%（见图 9）。

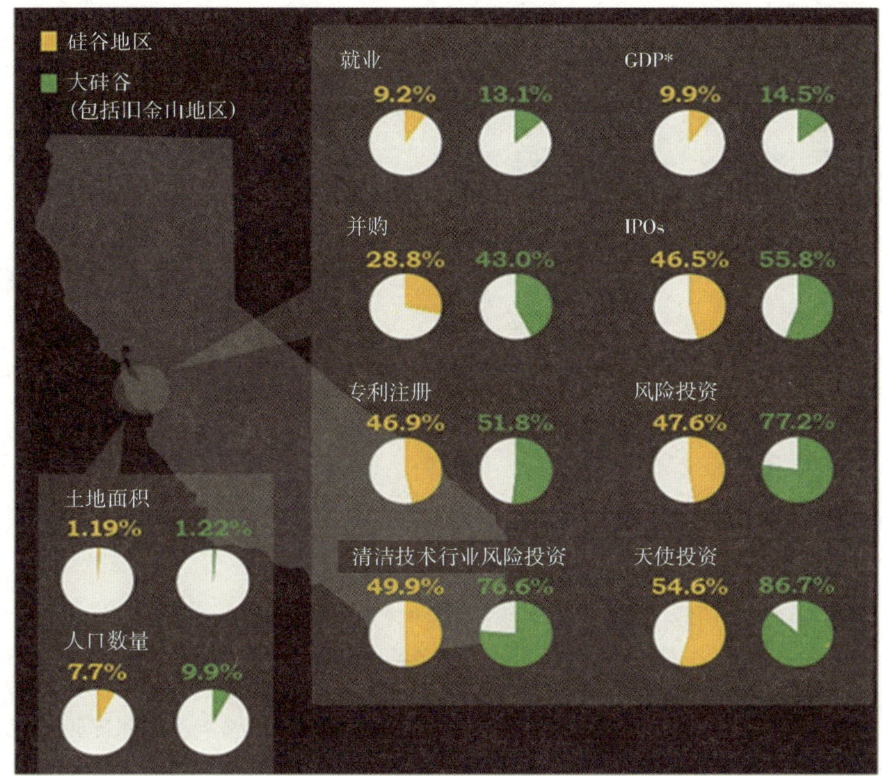

图 9 硅谷各指标占加利福尼亚州比重

数据显示，硅谷专利、风险投资、IPO 和并购等带来的 GDP 产出远远低于加利福尼亚州和美国其他地区，人均 GDP 也仅比加利福尼亚州高 8%左右。

总体上，《2014 硅谷指数》显示出硅谷创新和创业情况因旧金山日益增长的影响较之前有所不同。在并购活动中，硅谷出现更多的收购方，而旧金山出现更多的并购目标。同样，硅谷种子期天使投资出现下降，但是 A 轮融资天使投资有所增长（A 轮融资通常是由机构投资者所投资，例如传统的风险投资公司。而天使基金投资人，通常有机会参与这些投资回合并且投资种子期公司），这与旧金山正好相反。加利福尼亚州创新经济活动最活跃的依旧是硅谷和旧金山地区，两个地区的并购、风险投资、天使投资以及 IPO 总量占了加利福尼亚州总量的大半。综合而言，硅谷的创新引擎正在不断推动整个地区经济的快速发展。

（特别感谢杭州市科技信息研究院吕克斐、钱野、周恺秉供稿）

附录 5 国务院办公厅关于金融支持经济结构调整和转型升级的指导意见

国办发〔2013〕67 号

各省、自治区、直辖市人民政府，国务院各部委、各直属机构：

当前，我国经济运行总体平稳，但结构性矛盾依然突出。金融运行总体是稳健的，但资金分布不合理问题仍然存在，与经济结构调整和转型升级的要求不相适应。为深入贯彻党的十八大、中央经济工作会议和国务院常务会议精神，更好地发挥金融对经济结构调整和转型升级的支持作用，更好地发挥市场配置资源的基础性作用，更好地发挥金融政策、财政政策和产业政策的协同作用，优化社会融资结构，持续加强对重点领域和薄弱环节的金融支持，切实防范化解金融风险，经国务院同意，现提出以下指导意见。

一、继续执行稳健的货币政策，合理保持货币信贷总量

统筹兼顾稳增长、调结构、控通胀、防风险，合理保持货币总量。综合运用数量、价格等多种货币政策工具组合，充分发挥再贷款、再贴现和差别存款准备金动态调整机制的引导作用，盘活存量资金，用好增量资金，加快资金周转速度，提高资金使用效率。对中小金融机构继续实施较低的存款准备金率，增加“三农”、小微企业等薄弱环节的信贷资金来源。稳步推进利率市场化改革，更大程度发挥市场在资金配置中的基础性作用，促进企业根据自身条件选择融资渠道、优化融资结构，提高实体经济特别是小微企业的信贷可获得性，进一步加大金融对实体经济的支持力度。（人民银行牵头，发展改革委、工业和信息化部、财政部、银监会、证监会、保监会、外汇局等参加）

二、引导、推动重点领域与行业转型和调整

坚持有扶有控、有保有压原则，增强资金支持的针对性和有效性。大力支持实施创新驱动发展战略。加大对有市场发展前景的先进制造业、战略性新兴产业、现代信息技术产业和信息消费、劳动密集型产业、服务业、传统产业改造升级以及绿色环保等领域的资金支持力度。保证重点在建续建工程和项目的合理资金需求，积极支持铁路等重大基础设施、城市基础设施、保障性安居工程等民生工程建设，培育新的产业增长点。按照“消化一批、转移一批、整合一批、淘汰一批”的要求，对产能过剩行业区分不同情况实施差别化政策。对产品有竞争力、有市场、有效益的企业，要继续给予资金支持；对合理向境外转移产能的企业，要通过内保外贷、外汇及人民币贷款、债权融资、股权融资等方式，积极支持增强跨境投资经营能力；对实施产能整合的企业，要通过探索发行优先股、定向开展并购贷款、适当延长贷款期限等方式，支持企业兼并重组；对属于淘汰落后产能的企业，要通过保全资产和不良贷款转让、贷款损失核销等方式支持压产退市。严禁对产能严重过剩行业违规建设项目提供任何形式的新增授信和直接融资，防止盲目投资加剧产能过剩。（发展改革委、工业和信息化部、财政部、商务部、人民银行、国资委、银监会、证监会、保监会、外汇局等按职责分工负责）

三、整合金融资源支持小微企业发展

优化小微企业金融服务。支持金融机构向小微企业集中的区域延伸服务网点。根据小微企业不同发展阶段的金

融需求特点，支持金融机构向小微企业提供融资、结算、理财、咨询等综合性金融服务。继续支持符合条件的银行发行小微企业专项金融债，所募集资金发放的小微企业贷款不纳入存贷比考核。逐步推进信贷资产证券化常规化发展，盘活资金支持小微企业发展和经济结构调整。适度放开小额外保内贷业务，扩大小微企业境内融资来源。适当提高对小微企业贷款的不良贷款容忍度。加强对科技型、创新型、创业型小微企业的金融支持力度。力争全年小微企业贷款增速不低于当年各项贷款平均增速，贷款增量不低于上年同期水平。鼓励地方人民政府建立小微企业信贷风险补偿基金，支持小微企业信息整合，加快推进中小企业信用体系建设。支持地方人民政府加强对小额贷款公司、融资性担保公司的监管，对非融资性担保公司进行清理规范。鼓励地方人民政府出资设立或参股融资性担保公司，以及通过奖励、风险补偿等多种方式引导融资性担保公司健康发展，帮助小微企业增信融资，降低小微企业融资成本，提高小微企业贷款覆盖面。推动金融机构完善服务定价管理机制，严格规范收费行为，严格执行不得以贷转存、不得存贷挂钩、不得以贷收费、不得浮利分费、不得借贷搭售、不得一浮到顶、不得转嫁成本，公开收费项目、服务质价、效用功能、优惠政策等规定，切实降低企业融资成本。（发展改革委、科技部、工业和信息化部、财政部、人民银行、工商总局、银监会、证监会、保监会、外汇局等按职责分工负责）

四、加大对“三农”领域的信贷支持力度

优化“三农”金融服务，统筹发挥政策性金融、商业性金融和合作性金融的协同作用，发挥直接融资优势，推动加快农业现代化步伐。鼓励涉农金融机构在金融服务空白乡镇设立服务网点，创新服务方式，努力实现农村基础金融服务全覆盖。支持金融机构开发符合农业农村新型经营主体和农产品批发商特点的金融产品和服务，加大信贷支持力度，力争全年“三农”贷款增速不低于当年各项贷款平均增速，贷款增量不低于上年同期水平。支持符合条件的银行发行“三农”专项金融债。鼓励银行业金融机构扩大林权抵押贷款，探索开展大中型农机具、农村土地承包经营权和宅基地使用权抵押贷款试点。支持农业银行在总结试点经验的基础上，逐步扩大县域“三农金融事业部”试点省份范围。支持经中央批准的农村金融改革试点地区创新农村金融产品和服务。（财政部、国土资源部、农业部、商务部、人民银行、林业局、法制办、银监会等按职责分工负责）

五、进一步发展消费金融促进消费升级

加快完善银行卡消费服务功能，优化刷卡消费环境，扩大城乡居民用卡范围。积极满足居民家庭首套自住购房、大宗耐用消费品、新型消费品以及教育、旅游等服务消费领域的合理信贷需求。逐步扩大消费金融公司的试点城市范围，培育和壮大新的消费增长点。加强个人信用管理。根据城镇化过程中进城务工人员等群体的消费特点，提高金融服务的匹配度和适应性，促进消费升级。（人民银行牵头，发展改革委、工业和信息化部、商务部、银监会等参加）

六、支持企业“走出去”

鼓励政策性银行、商业银行等金融机构大力支持企业“走出去”。以推进贸易投资便利化为重点，进一步推动人民币跨境使用，推进外汇管理简政放权，完善货物贸易和服务贸易外汇管理制度。逐步开展个人境外直接投资试点，进一步推动资本市场对外开放。改进外债管理方式，完善全口径外债管理制度。加强银行间外汇市场净额清算等基础设施建设。创新外汇储备运用，拓展外汇储备委托贷款平台和商业银行转贷款渠道，综合运用多种方式为用汇主体提供融资支持。（人民银行牵头，外交部、发展改革委、财政部、商务部、海关总署、银监会、证监会、保监会、外汇局等参加）

七、加快发展多层次资本市场

进一步优化主板、中小企业板、创业板市场的制度安排，完善发行、定价、并购重组等方面的各项制度。适当放宽创业板对创新型、成长型企业的财务准入标准。将中小企业股份转让系统试点扩大至全国。规范非上市公众公司管理。稳步扩大公司（企业）债、中期票据和中小企业私募债券发行，促进债券市场互联互通。规范发展各类机构投资者，探索发展并购投资基金，鼓励私募股权投资基金、风险投资基金产品创新，促进创新型、创业型中小企业融资发展。加快完善期货市场建设，稳步推进期货市场品种创新，进一步发挥期货市场的定价、分散风险、套期保值和推进经济转型升级的作用。（证监会牵头，发展改革委、科技部、工业和信息化部、财政部、人民银行、工商总局、法制办等参加）

八、进一步发挥保险的保障作用

扩大农业保险覆盖范围，推广菜篮子工程保险、渔业保险、农产品质量保证保险、农房保险等新型险种。建立完善财政支持的农业保险大灾风险分散机制。大力发展出口信用保险，鼓励为企业开展对外贸易和“走出去”提供

投资、运营、劳动用工等方面的一揽子保险服务。深入推进科技保险工作。试点推广小额信贷保证保险，推动发展国内贸易信用保险。拓宽保险覆盖面和保险资金运用范围，进一步发挥保险对经济结构调整和转型升级的积极作用。（保监会牵头，发展改革委、科技部、工业和信息化部、财政部、农业部、商务部、人民银行、林业局、银监会、外汇局等参加）

九、扩大民间资本进入金融业

鼓励民间资本投资入股金融机构和参与金融机构重组改造。允许发展成熟、经营稳健的村镇银行在最低股比要求内，调整主发起行与其他股东持股比例。尝试由民间资本发起设立自担风险的民营银行、金融租赁公司和消费金融公司等金融机构。探索优化银行业分类监管机制，对不同类型银行业金融机构在经营地域和业务范围上实行差异化准入管理，建立相应的考核和评估体系，为实体经济发展提供广覆盖、差异化、高效率的金融服务。（银监会牵头，人民银行、工商总局、法制办等参加）

十、严密防范金融风险

深入排查各类金融风险隐患，适时开展压力测试，动态分析可能存在的风险触点，及时锁定、防控和化解风险，严守不发生系统性区域性金融风险的底线。继续按照总量控制、分类管理、区别对待、逐步化解的原则，防范化解地方政府融资平台贷款等风险。认真执行房地产调控政策，落实差别化住房信贷政策，加强名单制管理，严格防控房地产融资风险。按照理财与信贷业务分离、产品与项目逐一对应、单独建账管理、信息公开透明的原则，规范商业银行理财产品，加强行为监管，严格风险管控。密切关注并积极化解“两高一剩”（高耗能、高污染、产能过剩）行业结构调整时暴露的金融风险。防范跨市场、跨行业经营带来的交叉金融风险，防止民间融资、非法集资、国际资本流动等风险向金融系统传染渗透。支持银行开展不良贷款转让，扩大银行不良贷款自主核销权，及时主动消化吸收风险。稳妥有序处置风险，加强疏导，防止因处置不当等引发新的风险。加快信用立法和社会信用体系建设，培育社会诚信文化，为金融支持经济结构调整和转型升级营造良好环境。（人民银行牵头，发展改革委、工业和信息化部、财政部、住房城乡建设部、法制办、银监会、证监会、保监会、外汇局等参加）

国务院办公厅

2013 年 7 月 1 日

附录 6 国务院办公厅关于金融支持小微企业发展的实施意见

国办发〔2013〕87 号

各省、自治区、直辖市人民政府，国务院各部委、各直属机构：

小微企业是国民经济发展的生力军，在稳定增长、扩大就业、促进创新、繁荣市场和满足人民群众需求等方面，发挥着极为重要的作用。加强小微企业金融服务，是金融支持实体经济和稳定就业、鼓励创业的重要内容，事关经济社会发展全局，具有十分重要的战略意义。为进一步做好小微企业金融服务工作，全力支持小微企业良性发展，经国务院同意，现提出以下意见。

一、确保实现小微企业贷款增速和增量“两个不低于”的目标

继续坚持“两个不低于”的小微企业金融服务目标，在风险总体可控的前提下，确保小微企业贷款增速不低于各项贷款平均水平、增量不低于上年同期水平。在继续实施稳健的货币政策、合理保持全年货币信贷总量的前提下，优化信贷结构，腾挪信贷资源，在盘活存量中扩大小微企业融资增量，在新增信贷中增加小微企业贷款份额。充分发挥再贷款、再贴现和差别准备金动态调整机制的引导作用，对中小金融机构继续实施较低的存款准备金率。进一步细化“两个不低于”的考核措施，对银行业金融机构的小微企业贷款比例、贷款覆盖率、服务覆盖率和申贷获得率等指标，定期考核，按月通报。要求各银行业金融机构在商业可持续和有效控制风险的前提下，单列小微企业信贷计划，合理分解任务，优化绩效考核机制，并由主要负责人推动层层落实。(人民银行、银监会按职责分工负责)

二、加快丰富和创新小微企业金融服务方式

增强服务功能、转变服务方式、创新服务产品，是丰富和创新小微企业金融服务方式的重点内容。进一步引导金融机构增强支小助微的服务理念，动员更多营业网点参与小微企业金融服务，扩大业务范围，加大创新力度，增强服务功能；牢固树立以客户为中心的经营理念，针对不同类型、不同发展阶段小微企业的特点，不断开发特色产品，为小微企业提供量身定做的金融产品和服务。积极鼓励金融机构为小微企业全面提供开户、结算、理财、咨询等基础性、综合性金融服务；大力发展产业链融资、商业圈融资和企业群融资，积极开展知识产权质押、应收账款质押、动产质押、股权质押、订单质押、仓单质押、保单质押等抵质押贷款业务；推动开办商业保理、金融租赁和定向信托等融资服务。鼓励保险机构创新资金运用安排，通过投资企业股权、基金、债权、资产支持计划等多种形式，为小微企业发展提供资金支持。充分利用互联网等新技术、新工具，不断创新网络金融服务模式。(人民银行、银监会、证监会、保监会按职责分工负责)

三、着力强化对小微企业的增信服务和信息服务

加快建立“小微企业—信息和增信服务机构—商业银行”利益共享、风险共担新机制，是破解小微企业缺信息、缺信用导致融资难的关键举措。积极搭建小微企业综合信息共享平台，整合注册登记、生产经营、人才及技术、纳税缴费、劳动用工、用水用电、节能环保等信息资源。加快建立小微企业信用征集体系、评级发布制度和信息通报制度，引导银行业金融机构注重用好人才、技术等“软信息”，建立针对小微企业的信用评审机制。建立健全主要为小微企业服务的融资担保体系，由地方人民政府参股和控股部分担保公司，以省（区、市）为单位建立政府主导的再担保公司，创设小微企业信贷风险补偿基金。指导相关行业协会推进联合增信，加强本行业小微企业的合作互助。充分挖掘保险工具的增信作用，大力发展贷款保

证保险和信用保险业务，稳步扩大出口信用保险对小微企业的服务范围。（发展改革委、工业和信息化部、财政部、商务部、人民银行、工商总局、银监会、证监会、保监会等按职责分工负责）

四、积极发展小型金融机构

积极发展小型金融机构，打通民间资本进入金融业的通道，建立广覆盖、差异化、高效率的小微企业金融服务机构体系，是增加小微企业金融服务有效供给、促进竞争的有效途径。进一步丰富小微企业金融服务机构种类，支持在小微企业集中的地区设立村镇银行、贷款公司等小型金融机构，推动尝试由民间资本发起设立自担风险的民营银行、金融租赁公司和消费金融公司等金融机构。引导地方金融机构坚持立足当地、服务小微的市场定位，向县域和乡镇等小微企业集中的地区延伸网点和业务，进一步做深、做实小微企业金融服务。鼓励大中型银行加快小微企业专营机构建设和向下延伸服务网点，提高小微企业金融服务的批量化、规模化、标准化水平。（银监会牵头）

五、大力拓展小微企业直接融资渠道

加快发展多层次资本市场，是解决小微企业直接融资比例过低、渠道过窄的必由之路。进一步优化中小企业板、创业板市场的制度安排，完善发行、定价、并购重组等方面的政策和措施。适当放宽创业板市场对创新型、成长型企业的财务准入标准，尽快启动上市小微企业再融资。建立完善全国中小企业股份转让系统（以下称“新三板”），加大产品创新力度，增加适合小微企业的融资品种。进一步扩大中小企业私募债券试点，逐步扩大中小企业集合债券和小微企业增信集合债券发行规模，在创业板、“新三板”、公司债、私募债等市场建立服务小微企业的小额、快速、灵活的融资机制。在清理整顿各类交易场所基础上，将区域性股权市场纳入多层次资本市场体系，促进小微企业改制、挂牌、定向转让股份和融资，支持证券公司通过区域性股权市场为小微企业提供挂牌公司推荐、股权代理买卖等服务。进一步建立健全非上市公众公司监管制度，适时出台定向发行、并购重组等具体规定，支持小微企业股本融资、股份转让、资产重组等活动。探索发展并购投资基金，积极引导私募股权投资基金、创业投资企业投资于小微企业，支持符合条件的创业投资企业、股权投资企业等发行企业债券，专项用于投资小微企业，促进创新型、创业型小微企业融资发展。（证监会、发展改革委、科技部等按职责分工负责）

六、切实降低小微企业融资成本

进一步清理规范各类不合理收费，是切实降低小微企业综合融资成本的必然要求。继续对小微企业免征管理类、登记类、证照类行政事业性收费。规范担保公司等中介机构的收费定价行为，通过财政补贴和风险补偿等方式合理降低费率。继续治理金融机构不合理收费和高收费行为，开展对金融机构落实收费政策情况的专项检查，对落实不到位的金融机构要严肃处理。（发展改革委、工业和信息化部、财政部、人民银行、银监会等按职责分工负责）

七、加大对小微企业金融服务的政策支持力度

对小微企业金融服务予以政策倾斜，是做好小微企业金融服务、防范金融风险的必要条件。进一步完善和细化小微企业划型标准，引导各类金融机构和支持政策更好地聚焦小微企业。充分发挥支持性财税政策的引导作用，强化对小微企业金融服务的正向激励；在简化程序、扩大金融机构自主核销权等方面，对小微企业不良贷款核销给予支持。建立科技金融服务体系，进一步细化科技型小微企业标准，完善对各类科技成果的评价机制。在银行业金融机构的业务准入、风险资产权重、存贷比考核等方面实施差异化监管。继续支持符合条件的银行发行小微企业专项金融债，用所募集资金发放的小微企业贷款不纳入存贷比考核。逐步推进信贷资产证券化常规化发展，引导金融机构将盘活的资金主要用于小微企业贷款。鼓励银行业金融机构适度提高小微企业不良贷款容忍度，相应调整绩效考核机制。继续鼓励担保机构加大对小微企业的服务力度，推进完善有关扶持政策。积极争取将保险服务纳入小微企业产业引导政策，不断完善小微企业风险补偿机制。（发展改革委、科技部、工业和信息化部、财政部、人民银行、税务总局、统计局、银监会、证监会、保监会等按职责分工负责）

八、全面营造良好的小微金融发展环境

推进金融环境建设，营造良好的金融环境，是促进小微金融发展的重要基础。地方人民政府要在健全法治、改善公共服务、预警提示风险、完善抵质押登记、宣传普及金融知识等方面，抓紧研究制定支持小微企业金融服务的政策措施；切实落实融资性担保公司、小额贷款公司、典当行、投资（咨询）公司、股权投资企业等机构的监管和风险处置责任，加大对非法集资等非法金融活动的打击惩处力度；减少对金融机构正常经营活动的干预，帮助维护银行债权，打击逃废银行债务行为；化解金融风险，切实维护地方金融市场秩序。有关部门要研究采取有效措施，

积极引导小微企业提高自身素质，改善经营管理，健全财务制度，增强信用意识。（发展改革委、工业和信息化部、公安部、财政部、商务部、人民银行、税务总局、工商总局、银监会、证监会、保监会等按职责分工负责）

各地区、各有关部门和各金融机构要按照国务院的统一部署，进一步提高对小微企业金融服务重要性的认识，明确分工，落实责任，形成合力，真正帮助小微企业解决现实难题。银监会要牵头组织实施督促检查工作，确保各项政策措施落实到位。从 2014 年开始，各省级人民政府、人民银行、银监会、证监会和保监会要将本地区或本领域上一年度小微企业金融服务的情况、成效、问题、下一步打算及政策建议，于每年 1 月底前专题报告国务院。各银行业金融机构有关落实情况及下一步工作和建议，由银监会汇总后报国务院。

国务院办公厅

2013 年 8 月 8 日

附录 7 国务院关于全国中小企业股份转让系统有关问题的决定

国发〔2013〕49 号

各省、自治区、直辖市人民政府，国务院各部委、各直属机构：

为更好地发挥金融对经济结构调整和转型升级的支持作用，进一步拓展民间投资渠道，充分发挥全国中小企业股份转让系统（以下简称全国股份转让系统）的功能，缓解中小微企业融资难，按照党的十八大、十八届三中全会关于多层次资本市场发展的精神和国务院第 13 次常务会议的有关要求，现就全国股份转让系统有关问题作出如下决定。

一、充分发挥全国股份转让系统服务中小微企业发展的功能

全国股份转让系统是经国务院批准，依据证券法设立的全国性证券交易场所，主要为创新型、创业型、成长型中小微企业发展服务。境内符合条件的股份公司均可通过主办券商申请在全国股份转让系统挂牌，公开转让股份，进行股权融资、债权融资、资产重组等。申请挂牌的公司应当业务明确、产权清晰、依法规范经营、公司治理健全，可以尚未盈利，但须履行信息披露义务，所披露的信息应当真实、准确、完整。

二、建立不同层次市场间的有机联系

在全国股份转让系统挂牌的公司，达到股票上市条件的，可以直接向证券交易所申请上市交易。在符合《国务院关于清理整顿各类交易场所切实防范金融风险的决定》（国发〔2011〕38 号）要求的区域性股权转让市场进行股权非公开转让的公司，符合挂牌条件的，可以申请在全国股份转让系统挂牌公开转让股份。

三、简化行政许可程序

挂牌公司依法纳入非上市公众公司监管，股东人数可以超过 200 人。股东人数未超过 200 人的股份公司申请在全国股份转让系统挂牌，证监会豁免核准。挂牌公司向特定对象发行证券，且发行后证券持有人累计不超过 200 人的，证监会豁免核准。依法需要核准的行政许可事项，证监会应当建立简便、快捷、高效的行政许可方式，简化审核流程，提高审核效率，无需再提交证监会发行审核委员会审核。

四、建立和完善投资者适当性管理制度

建立与投资者风险识别和承受能力相适应的投资者适当性管理制度。中小微企业具有业绩波动大、风险较高的特点，应当严格自然人投资者的准入条件。积极培育和发展机构投资者队伍，鼓励证券公司、保险公司、证券投资基金、私募股权投资基金、风险投资基金、合格境外机构投资者、企业年金等机构投资者参与市场，逐步将全国股份转让系统建成以机构投资者为主体的证券交易场所。

五、加强事中、事后监管，保障投资者合法权益

证监会应当比照证券法关于市场主体法律责任的相关规定，严格执法，对虚假披露、内幕交易、操纵市场等违法违规行为采取监管措施，实施行政处罚。全国股份转让系统要制定并完善业务规则体系，建立市场监控系统，完善风险管理制度和设施，保障技术系统和信息安全，切实履行自律监管职责。

六、加强协调配合，为挂牌公司健康发展创造良好环境

国务院有关部门应当加强统筹协调，为中小微企业利用全国股份转让系统发展创造良好的制度环境。市场建设中涉及税收政策的，原则上比照上市公司投资者的税收政策处理；涉及外资政策的，原则上比照交易所市场及上市公司相关规定办理；涉及国有股权监管事项的，应当同时遵守国有资产管理的相关规定。各省（区、市）人民政府要加强组织领导和协调，建立健全挂牌公司风险处置机制，切实维护社会稳定。

国务院

2013 年 12 月 13 日

附录 8 中国人民银行 科技部 银监会 证监会 保监会 知识产权局 关于大力推进体制机制创新扎实做好科技金融服务的意见

银发〔2014〕9 号

为贯彻落实党的十八届三中全会精神和《中共中央 国务院关于深化科技体制改革 加快国家创新体系建设的意见》(中发〔2012〕6 号)等中央文件要求，大力推动体制机制创新，促进科技和金融的深层次结合，支持国家创新体系建设，现提出如下意见：

一、大力培育和发展服务科技创新的金融组织体系

(一) 创新从事科技金融服务的金融组织形式。鼓励银行业金融机构在高新技术产业开发区（以下简称高新区）、国家高新技术产业化基地（以下简称产业化基地）等科技资源集聚地区通过新设或改造部分分（支）行作为从事中小科技企业金融服务的专业分（支）行或特色分（支）行。对银行业金融机构新设或改造部分分（支）行从事科技金融服务的有关申请，优先受理和审核。鼓励银行业金融机构在财务资源、人力资源等方面给予专业分（支）行或特色分（支）行适当倾斜，加强业务指导和管理，提升服务科技创新的专业化水平。在加强监管的前提下，允许具备条件的民间资本依法发起设立中小型银行，为科技创新提供专业化的金融服务。

(二) 积极发展为科技创新服务的非银行金融机构和组织。大力推动金融租赁公司等规范发展，为科技企业、科研院所等开展科技研发和技术改造提供大型设备、精密器材等的租赁服务。支持发展科技小额贷款公司，按照“小额、分散”原则，向小微科技企业提供贷款服务。鼓励符合条件的小额贷款公司、金融租赁公司通过开展资产证券化、发行债券等方式融资。积极推动产融结合，支持符合条件的大型科技企业集团公司按规定设立财务公司，强化其为集团内科技企业提供金融服务的功能。

(三) 培育发展科技金融中介服务体系。指导和推动地方科技部门、国家高新区（或产业化基地）、金融机构和相关中介服务机构建立和培育发展科技金融服务中心等多种形式的服务平台，推动创业投资、银行信贷、科技企业改制服务、融资路演、数据增值服务、科技项目管理、人才引进等方面的联动合作，为科技企业提供全方位、专业化、定制化投融资解决方案。加快发展科技企业孵化、法律会计服务、人力资源管理等机构，为中小科技企业融资提供服务。

二、加快推进科技信贷产品和服务模式创新

(四) 完善科技信贷管理机制。鼓励银行业金融机构完善科技企业贷款利率定价机制，充分利用贷款利率风险定价和浮动计息规则，根据科技企业成长状况，动态分享相关收益。完善科技贷款审批机制，通过建立科技贷款绿色通道等方式，提高科技贷款审批效率；通过借助科技专家咨询服务平台，利用信息科技技术提升评审专业化水平。完善科技信贷风险管理机制，探索设计专门针对科技信贷风险管理的模型，提高科技贷款管理水平。完善内部激励约束机制，建立小微科技企业信贷业务拓展奖励办

法，落实授信尽职免责机制，有效发挥差别风险容忍度对银行开展科技信贷业务的支撑作用。

（五）丰富科技信贷产品体系。在有效防范风险的前提下，支持银行业金融机构与创业投资、证券、保险、信托等机构合作，创新交叉性金融产品，建立和完善金融支持科技创新的信息交流共享机制和风险共控合作机制。全面推动符合科技企业特点的金融产品创新，逐步扩大仓单、订单、应收账款、产业链融资以及股权质押贷款的规模。充分发挥政策性金融功能，支持国家重大科技计划成果的转化和产业化、科技企业并购、国内企业自主创新和引进消化吸收再创新、农业科技创新、科技企业开展国际合作和“走出去”。

（六）创新科技金融服务模式。鼓励银行业金融机构开展还款方式创新，开发和完善适合科技企业融资需求特点的授信模式。积极向科技企业提供开户、结算、融资、理财、咨询、现金管理、国际业务等一站式、系统化的金融服务。加快科技系统改造升级，在符合监管要求的前提下充分利用互联网技术，为科技企业提供高效、便捷的金融服务。

（七）大力发展知识产权质押融资。加强知识产权评估、登记、托管、流转服务能力建设，规范知识产权价值分析和评估标准，简化知识产权质押登记流程，探索建立知识产权质物处置机制，为开展知识产权质押融资提供高效便捷服务。积极推进专利保险工作，有效保障企业、行业、地区的创新发展。

三、拓宽适合科技创新发展规律的多元化融资渠道

（八）支持科技企业上市、再融资和并购重组。推进新股发行体制改革，继续完善和落实促进科技成果转化应用的政策措施，促进科技成果资本化、产业化。适当放宽科技企业的财务准入标准，简化发行条件。建立创业板再融资制度，形成“小额、快速、灵活”的创业板再融资机制，为科技企业提供便捷的再融资渠道。支持符合条件的科技企业在境外上市融资。支持科技上市企业通过并购重组做大做强。推进实施并购重组分道制审核制度，对符合条件的企业申请实行豁免或快速审核。鼓励科技上市企业通过并购基金等方式实施兼并重组，拓宽融资渠道。研究允许科技上市企业发行优先股、定向可转债等作为并购工具的可行性，丰富并购重组工具。

（九）鼓励科技企业利用债券市场融资。支持科技企业通过发行企业债、公司债、短期融资券、中期票据、中小企业集合票据、中小企业集合债券、小微企业增信集合债券、中小企业私募债等产品进行融资。鼓励和支持相关部门通过优化工作流程，提高发行工作效率，为科技企业发行债券提供融资便利。对符合条件的科技企业发行直接债务融资工具的，鼓励中介机构适当降低收费，减轻科技企业的融资成本负担。继续推动并购债、可转债、高收益债等产品发展，支持科技企业滚动融资，行业收购兼并和创投公司、私募基金投资和退出。

（十）推动创业投资发展壮大。发挥政府资金杠杆作用，充分利用现有的创业投资基金，完善创业投资政策环境和退出机制，鼓励更多社会资本进入创业投资领域。推动各级政府部门设立的创业投资机构通过阶段参股、跟进投资等多种方式，引导创业投资资金投向初创期科技企业和科技成果转化项目。完善和落实创业投资机构相关税收政策，推动运用财政税收等优惠政策引导创业投资机构投资科技企业，支持符合条件的创业投资企业、股权投资企业、产业投资基金发行企业债券；支持符合条件的创业投资企业、股权投资企业、产业投资基金的股东或有限合伙人发行企业债券。鼓励发展天使投资。

（十一）鼓励其他各类市场主体支持科技创新。支持科技企业通过在全国中小企业股份转让系统实现股份转让和定向融资。探索研究全国中小企业股份转让系统挂牌公司的并购重组监管制度，规范引导其并购重组活动。探索利用各类产权交易机构为非上市小微科技企业提供股份转让渠道，建立健全未上市科技股份公司股权集中托管、转让、市场监管等配套制度。加快发展统一的区域性技术产权交易市场，推动地方加强省级技术产权交易市场建设，完善创业风险投资退出机制。支持证券公司直投子公司、另类投资子公司、基金管理公司专业子公司等，在风险可控前提下按规定投资非上市科技企业股权、债券类资产、收益权等实体资产，为不同类型、不同发展阶段的科技企业提供资金支持。

四、探索构建符合科技创新特点的保险产品和服务

（十二）建立和完善科技保险体系。按照政府引导、商业保险机构运作、产寿险业务并重的原则，进一步建立和完善科技保险体系。加大对科技保险的财政支持力度，鼓励有条件的地区建立科技保险奖补机制和科技再保险制度，对重点科技和产业领域给予补贴、补偿等奖励和优惠政策，充分发挥财政资金的引导和放大作用，促进科技保险长效发展。支持符合条件的保险公司设立专门服务于科技企业的科技保险专营机构，为科技企业降低风险损失、实现稳健经营提供支持。

（十三）加快创新科技保险产品，提高科技保险服务质量。鼓励保险公司创新科技保险产品，为科技企业、科研项目、科研人员提供全方位保险支持。推广中小科技企业贷款保证保险、贷款担保责任保险、出口信用保险等新型保险产品，为科技企业提供贷款保障。加快制定首台（套）重大技术装备保险机制的指导意见，建立政府引导、市场化运作的首台（套）重大技术装备保险机制和示范应用制度，促进首台（套）重大技术装备项目的推广和科技成果产业化。

（十四）创新保险资金运用方式，为科技创新提供资金支持。根据科技领域需求和保险资金特点，支持保险资金以股权、基金、债权、资产支持计划等形式，为高新区和产业化基地建设、战略性新兴产业的培育与发展以及国家重大科技项目提供长期、稳定的资金支持。探索保险资金投资优先股等新型金融工具，为科技企业提供长期股权投资。推动科技保险综合实验区建设，在更好地服务科技创新方面先行先试，探索建立综合性科技保险支持体系。

五、加快建立健全促进科技创新的信用增进机制

（十五）大力推动科技企业信用示范区建设。鼓励各地依托高新区和产业化基地，因地制宜建设科技企业信用示范区，充分利用金融信用信息基础数据库等信用信息平台，加大对科技企业信用信息的采集，建立和完善科技企业的信用评级和评级结果推介制度，为金融机构推广信用贷款等金融产品提供支持。充分发挥信用促进会等信用自律组织的作用，完善科技企业信用示范区管理机制，逐步建立守信激励、失信惩戒的信用环境。

（十六）积极发挥融资性担保增信作用。建立健全政府资金引导、社会资本参与、市场化运作的科技担保、再担保体系。支持融资性担保机构加大对科技企业的信用增进，提高融资性担保机构服务能力。鼓励科技企业成立联保互助组织，通过建立科技担保互助基金，为协会成员提供融资担保支持。支持融资性担保机构加强信息披露与共享，开展同业合作，集成科技企业资源，进一步增强融资担保能力。

（十七）创新科技资金投入方式。充分发挥国家科技成果转化引导基金的作用，通过设立创业投资子基金、贷款风险补偿等方式，引导金融资本和民间投资向科技成果转化集聚。进一步整合多种资源，综合运用创业投资、风险分担、保费补贴、担保补助、贷款贴息等多种方式，发挥政府资金在信用增进、风险分散、降低成本等方面的作用，引导金融机构加大对科技企业的融资支持。

六、进一步深化科技和金融结合试点

（十八）加快推进科技和金融结合试点工作。完善“促进科技和金融结合试点工作”部际协调机制，总结试点工作的成效和创新实践，研究制定继续深化试点工作的相关措施，适时启动第二批试点工作，将更多地区纳入试点范围。及时宣传和推广试点地区典型经验，发挥试点地区的示范作用。加大资源条件保障和政策扶持力度，进一步调动和发挥地方深化试点工作的积极性与创造性。鼓励地方因地制宜、大胆探索、先行先试，不断拓展科技与金融结合的政策和实践空间，开展具有地方特色的科技和金融结合试点工作建设。

（十九）推动高新区科技与金融的深层次结合。建立完善高新区管委会、金融机构和科技企业之间的信息沟通机制，通过举办多种形式的投融资对接活动，加强科技创新项目和金融产品的宣传、推介，推动高新区项目资源、政策资源与金融资源的有效对接。支持银行业金融机构在风险可控的前提下，在业务范围内综合运用统贷平台、集合授信等多种方式，加大对高新区建设和小微科技企业的融资支持。发挥高新区先行先试的优势，加快构建科技金融服务体系，鼓励金融机构开展各类金融创新实践活动。

七、创新政策协调和组织实施机制

（二十）综合运用多种金融政策工具，拓宽科技创新信贷资金来源。充分运用差别存款准备金动态调整机制，引导地方法人金融机构加大对科技企业的信贷投入。发挥再贴现支持结构调整的作用，对小微科技企业票据优先予以再贴现支持。支持符合条件的银行发行金融债专项用于支持小微科技企业发展，加强对小微科技企业的金融服务。积极稳妥推动信贷资产证券化试点，鼓励金融机构将通过信贷资产证券化业务腾挪出的信贷资金支持科技企业发展。

（二十一）加强科技创新资源与金融资源的有效对接。探索金融资本与国家科技计划项目结合的有效方式和途径，建立科技创新项目贷款的推荐机制，支持国家科技计划项目的成果转化和产业化；建立国家科技成果转化项目库，引导和支持金融资本及民间投资参与科技创新；指导地方科技部门建立中小微科技企业数据库，与金融机构开展投融资需求对接；开展面向中小微科技企业的科技金融培训，培育科技金融复合型人才。

（二十二）建立科技、财政和金融监管部门参加的科技金融服务工作协调机制。健全跨部门、跨层级的协调沟通和分工负责机制，加强科技、财政、税收、金融等政策

的协调，形成推进科技金融发展的政策合力。依托科技部门与金融管理部门、金融机构的合作机制，将科技部门在政策、信息、项目、专家等方面的综合优势与金融机构的产品、服务优势结合起来，实现科技创新与金融创新的相互促进。

（二十三）探索建立科技金融服务监测评估体系。人民银行各分支机构可根据辖区实际情况，按照地方科技部门制定的科技企业认定标准与名录，推动各金融机构研究建立科技金融服务专项统计制度，加强对科技企业贷款的统计与监测分析，并探索建立科技金融服务的专项信贷政策导向效果评估制度。

请人民银行上海总部，各分行、营业管理部、省会（首府）城市中心支行、副省级城市中心支行会同所在省（区、市）科技、知识产权、银监、证监、保监等部门将本意见联合转发至辖区内相关机构，并协调做好本意见的贯彻实施工作。

中国人民银行　科技部　银监会
证监会　保监会　知识产权局
2014 年 1 月 7 日

附录 9 中国创业风险投资机构名录

公司名称	成立时间	网址	传真
安徽鼎信创业投资有限公司	2012-06-05	—	0551-65319112
安徽丰创生物技术产业创业投资有限公司	2013-04-02	—	—
安徽高科创业投资有限公司	2010-01-28	www.ahgoco.com	0551-65319112
安徽国安创业投资有限公司	2010-09-15	—	0551-65732844
安徽国耀创业投资有限公司	2013-11-28	—	—
安徽国元创投有限责任公司	2010-06-13	www.ahgyct.com	0551-63699700
安徽红土创业投资有限公司	2010-08-10	—	0551-65666025
安徽华文创业投资管理有限公司	2003-06-04	—	0551-63533281
安徽徽商产业投资基金管理有限公司	2008-03-18	www.hygcapital.com	0551-5844598
安徽汇智富创业投资有限公司	2013-03-26	—	0551-65383158
安徽火花科技创业投资有限公司	2013-09-01	—	—
安徽昆冈创业股权投资合伙企业（有限合伙）	2011-12-13	—	—
安徽省创投资本基金有限公司	2010-07-27	—	0551-65773880
安徽省创业投资有限公司	2008-07-09	—	0551-63677130
安徽省高新创业投资有限责任公司	2009-12-23	—	—
安徽省科创投资管理咨询有限责任公司	2000-10-31	—	0551-66195765
安徽省科技产业投资有限公司	1999-07	www.ahkjtz.com.cn	0551-65170070
安徽西格玛壹号投资合伙企业（有限合伙）	2013-05-24	—	—
安徽兴皖创业投资有限公司	2010-08-20	—	0551-63677130
安徽亿诚融资理财信息服务有限公司	2012-08-29	www.ahycrzlc.com	0556-5275508
安徽益明投资理财咨询服务有限公司	2013-09-04	www.ahymlc.com	0556-5696657
安庆发投创业投资有限公司	2012-09-28	—	—
蚌埠市科技创业投资有限公司	2008-06-26	—	0552-3186802
蚌埠市远大创新创业投资有限公司	2010-09-28	—	0551-63186678
蚌埠皖北金牛创业投资有限公司	2011-05-17	—	0552-4129773
蚌埠中城创业投资有限公司	2009-03-16	—	0552-3183880
成都盈创动力投资管理有限责任公司	2013-03	—	—

公司名称	成立时间	网址	传真
滁州浚源创业投资中心（有限合伙）	2011-06	jcmchina.cn	010-82661938
合肥高特佳创业投资有限责任公司	2010-04-19	www.szgig.com	0551-65310817
合肥高新科技创业投资有限公司	2012-10-19	gxkt.hfgxjt.com	0551-65326509
合肥广电投资有限责任公司	2003-08-06	www.hfbtv.com	0551-63509205
合肥赛富合元创业投资中心（有限合伙）	2011-01-13	—	—
合肥世纪创新投资有限公司	2002-09-11	—	0551-66195765
合肥市创新科技风险投资有限公司	2000-08-28	www.hfgk.com	0551-62675471
合肥市高科技风险投资有限公司	2000-04-18	—	—
合肥同安创业投资基金行	2010-09	—	0551-63677135
合肥智鼎创业投资管理有限公司	2009-11-10	www.qyzyw.com	0551-64651822
华晟创业投资管理有限公司	2012-05-14	—	0551-63533681
淮南市创业风险投资有限公司	2011-11-26	—	0554-6679199
汇智创业投资有限公司	2009-04-29	—	0551-65321476
六安高科创业投资有限公司	2011-10-20	—	0564-3323933
铜陵天源股权投资集团有限公司	2007-02-01	—	0562-2885077
芜湖达成创业投资中心（有限合伙）	2010-04-28	—	—
芜湖富海浩研创业投资基金	2012-12-27	—	0551-65844598
芜湖奇瑞科技有限公司	2001-11-21	www.mychery.com	0553-5922267
芜湖瑞建汽车产业创业投资有限公司	2010-07-01	—	0553-63823318
芜湖瑞业股权投资基金（有限合伙）	2009-12-21	—	021-64151936
芜湖市科技创业投资有限公司	2004-05-28	www.whkctz.com	0553-5846386
芜湖市世纪江东创业投资中心（有限合伙）	2009-08-18	www.jd-capital.cn	0553-5772022
芜湖远大创业投资有限公司	2009-04-23	—	0553-5992133
中富创业投资（北京）有限公司	2007-09-21	www.zfinvest.com	010-65518503
北京晨光创业投资有限公司	2000-12-25	www.chgvc.com	010-69709488
北京晨光宏盛中小企业创业投资有限公司	2009-03-11	www.bjcghs.com	010-89710922
北京丰图投资有限责任公司	2007-07	www.fundturn.com	010-82604065
北京惠通高创投资管理中心（有限合伙）	2012-06-27	—	0371-86615676
北京新安财富资本投资有限公司	2000-08	www.acvc.com.cn	010-63972281
北京中关村青年科技创业投资有限公司	2000-01	www.bjcvc.com.cn	010-57768020
启迪创业投资管理（北京）有限公司	2001-03	www.tsinghua-vc.com	010-62705209
中发君盛（北京）投资管理有限公司	2009-10-28	www.junsancapital.com	0755-82571198
博楷（福建）创业投资有限公司	2010-04-09	—	0592-5118563
福建红桥创业投资管理有限公司	2007-08-29	hqcapital.com.cn	0592-2278628
福建华兴创业投资有限公司	2000-12-26	www.fjhxvc.com	0591-87858275
福建迅成创业投资有限公司	2007-07-31	www.chancevc.com	0591-22855397
晋江市红桥创业投资有限公司	2008-10-29	www.hqcapital.com.cn	0595-82032092
罗普特（厦门）投资管理有限公司	2013-05-30	—	0592-3662225
南安市红桥创业投资有限公司	2010-08-13	www.hqcapital.com.cn	0595-86392990

公司名称	成立时间	网址	传真
泉州市红桥创业投资有限公司	2010-02-22	www.hqcapital.com.cn	0595-28292990
厦门创翼创业投资有限公司	2008-06-20	—	0592-2360798
厦门创翼德晖股权投资合伙企业（有限合伙）	2011-02-11	www.divinecapital.com.cn	0592-2915616
厦门高新技术创业中心	1996-12	www.xmibi.com	0592-3923999
厦门高新技术风险投资有限公司	1998-12-28	—	0592-2102861
厦门海银投资管理有限公司	2010-12-20	—	0592-6800118
厦门弘信创业工场投资股份有限公司	1996	www.xmhx.com	0592-5627310
厦门红树林高科创业投资有限公司	2012-05-23	—	—
厦门红土创业投资有限公司	2010-06-08	—	0592-5778290
厦门华登创业投资有限公司	2008-08-13	www.xmerqing.com	0592-2219232
厦门京道联萃创业投资管理有限公司	2012-02-24	—	0592-8269533
厦门隆领投资合伙企业（有限合伙）	2011-11-02	www.lognling.com	—
厦门七匹狼创业投资有限公司	2009-07-03	—	0592-5377752
厦门软件产业投资发展有限公司	1998-12-02	www.xsoft.com.cn	0592-3929888
厦门市创业投资有限公司	2011-12-30	—	0592-3502338
厦门松涛风险投资股份有限公司	2000-04-28	www.songtao.com.cn	0592-6093926
厦门永红创业投资有限公司	2006-12-19	—	0592-5058092
甘肃省科技风险投资有限公司	2001-08	—	0931-8537887
兰州高科创业投资担保有限公司	2003	—	0931-8711879
兰州天键投资咨询服务有限公司	2006	—	—
广东德运创业投资有限公司	2013-05-03	—	0757-28399878
广东广弘创业投资有限公司	2011-10-11	—	020-87228300
广东合银创业投资有限公司	2010-06-27	www.gdhyct.com	020-83983566
广东科创投资管理有限公司	2006-04	www.gvcgc.com	020-87683211
广东省科技创业投资公司	1992-05-12	www.gdtvic.com	020-87682766
广东省科技风险投资有限公司	1998-01-08	www.gtvc.com	020-87684955
广东省粤科金融集团有限公司	2000-09-21	www.gvcgc.com	020-87682766
广东粤科钜华创业投资有限公司	2010-10-11	—	0757-23271113
广东粤科润华创业投资有限公司	2012-10-18	—	0750-3882739
广州科技风险投资有限公司	1999-11-25	www.c-vcc.com	020-87556023
广州市粤丰创业投资有限公司	2002-09-28	—	020-87680509
君盛投资管理有限公司	2003-01-13	www.junsancapital.com	0755-82571198
鲁证创业投资有限公司	2010-05-21	—	0755-82798613
融石创业投资管理（深圳）有限公司	2008-02-04	www.rockstead.com	0755-82991769
深圳创富成长创业投资有限公司	2009-05-20	—	0755-26994531
深圳东方赛富投资有限公司	2010-05-06	www.esaif-capital.com	0755-88315925
深圳国成世纪创业投资有限公司	2003-04-16	www.ciamvc.com	0755-82967097
深圳力合创业投资有限公司	1999-08-31	www.leaguer.com.cn	0755-26551372
深圳力合清源创业投资管理有限公司	2010-04-28	www.leaguercapital.com	0755-86363823

公司名称	成立时间	网址	传真
深圳市百禾通顺创业投资有限公司	2008-03-05	—	0755-82876373
深圳市保中太创业投资有限公司	2007-04-06	—	0755-83264501
深圳市博叡创业投资有限公司	2010-03-18	www.boricapital.com	0755-83562711
深圳市创东方投资有限公司	2007-08-21	www.cdf-capital.com	0755-88316231
深圳市创新投资集团有限公司	1999-08-26	www.szvc.com.cn	0755-8291880
深圳市达晨财智创业投资管理有限公司	2008-12-15	—	0755-83515115
深圳市达晨创业投资有限公司	2000-04	www.fortunevc.com	0755-83515115
深圳市大正元股权投资基金管理有限公司	2010-04-16	www.tdrcap.com	0755-33371191
深圳市东方富海投资管理有限公司	2006-10-10	www.ofcapital.com	0755-83475799
深圳市分享投资合伙企业（有限合伙）	2007-08-27	—	0755-86331909
深圳市孚威创业投资有限公司	2007-10-15	—	0755-25771505
深圳市富坤创业投资有限公司	2008-04-11	www.rlequities.com	0755-88311638-8019
深圳市高特佳投资集团有限公司	2001-03-02	www.szgig.com	0755-86332710
深圳市高新投创业投资有限公司	1994-12-29	www.szhti.com.cn	0755-82852555
深圳市国成科技投资有限公司	1997-09-08	www.szgcvc.com	0755-83516944
深圳市华信创业投资有限公司	2011-05-19	—	0755-86410783
深圳市佳利泰创业投资有限公司	2009-07-20	www.jialitai.com	0755-25312056
深圳市君丰创业投资基金管理有限公司	2009-09-30	www.jfamc.com	0755-82823397
深圳市康沃资本创业投资有限公司	2007-04-23	www.careall-vc.com	0755-82912620
深圳市南山区科技创业服务中心	1999-09-01	www.szns.gov.cncyfwzx	0755-33609646
深圳市年利达创业投资有限公司	2007-09-20	—	0755-23993622
深圳市山海创业投资管理有限公司	2005-08-29	www.sunhighvc.com	0755-26077778
深圳市深港产学研创业投资有限公司	1996-09	www.iervc.com.cn	0755-83290622
深圳市松禾资本管理有限公司	2007-04-26	www.pinevc.com.cn	0755-83290622
深圳市天图创业投资有限公司	2002-04-11	www.tiantu.com.cn	0755-36909834
深圳市同创伟业创业投资有限公司	2000-06-26	www.cowincapital.com.cn	0755-82879025
深圳市同威创业投资有限公司	2008-03-02	www.copowerpe.com	0755-26935161
深圳市倚锋创业投资有限公司	2007-08-22	www.efung.cc	0755-88308601
深圳市悦享资本管理有限公司	2010-08-06	www.szyxzbgl.com	0755-23819923
深圳市中安信业创业投资有限公司	2003-10-31	www.zac.cn	0755-83579787
深圳市中金石创业投资有限公司	2009-09-18	—	0755-82876373
深圳市卓佳汇智创业投资有限公司	2006-09-25	www.zhuojiavc.net	0755-82033216
深圳中小企业创业投资有限公司	1997-11-05	www.smevc.com	0755-23982050
盈富泰克创业投资有限公司	2000-04-20	www.infovc.com	0755-82966479
肇庆市粤科金叶创业投资有限公司	2010-10-18	—	0758-2321522
珠海高新技术创业服务中心	2004-08-25	www.zhhbi.com	0756-3629900
珠海红杉资本股权投资中心（有限合伙）	2010-03-26	—	0756-3629900
珠海金控高新创业投资有限公司	2013-11-19	—	0756-2992888
珠海清华科技园创业投资有限公司	2001-07	www.tspz.com	0756-3612000

公司名称	成立时间	网址	传真
珠海招商银科股权投资中心（有限合伙）	2012-01-21	—	0755-26677220
广西海东科技创业投资有限公司	2010-04-14	—	022-59852168
广西中小企业创业投资有限公司	2009-08-12	gxfi.net	0771-5586630
柳州开元创业投资有限公司	2011-12-30	—	0771-5715238
贵阳高科创业投资有限责任公司	2009-09-03	www.guiyanggk.com	0851-8255917
贵阳高新创业投资有限公司	2011-04-27	—	0851-2237948
贵阳花溪技创业投资有限公司	2011-07-19	—	0851-3863159
贵阳市创业投资有限公司	2010-12-28	www.gyiig.com	0851-4757198
贵州鼎信博成投资管理有限公司	2009-09-16	www.gztvc.net	0851-5806514
贵州鼎信卓越创业投资有限公司	2013-12-06	—	—
贵州国喜投资有限公司	2011-09-06	—	0851-2264888
贵州经开创业投资管理有限公司	2012-06-01	—	0851-3890646-804
贵州经开创业投资有限公司	2012-08-01	—	0851-3890646-804
贵州省科技风险投资有限公司	1998-12	www.gztvc.net	0851-5806514
贵州中鼎投资管理有限公司	2004-09-04	www.gzzd.cn	0851-6824648
六盘水科技创业投资有限公司	2011-11-04	—	—
铜仁梵净山科技创业投资有限公司	2009	—	—
遵义科技风险投资有限公司	2010-11-05	—	0852-8922337
海口市创新产业投资有限公司	2008-03-18	www.haikouvc.com	0898-66738612
海南恒星创业投资管理有限公司	2007-09-24	—	0898-66831555
海南华棋科技创业投资管理有限公司	2009-09-09	—	0898-68581383
海南宣辰科技创业投资管理有限公司	2008-09-25	—	0898-66829922
保定高新技术创业服务中心	1994-11-01	—	0312-3326988
保定市创元科技风险投资有限公司	2008-12-22	—	0312-5902519
保定市科锐特创业投资有限公司	2006-02-27	www.krtvc.com	0312-3371336
河北金冀达创业投资有限公司	2009-08-31	—	0311-85961613
河北科技投资集团有限公司	2001-02-15	www.hebvc.com	0311-85961613
河北天鑫创业投资有限公司	2011-07-04	—	—
河北兴石创业投资有限公司	2009-12-21	—	—
廊坊市高科创新创业投资有限公司	2006-10-19	—	0316-2235613
秦皇岛市科技投资公司	2000-02-18	www.qhdktgs.com	0335-3639739
荣盛创业投资有限公司	2007-09-08	—	010-59772531
石家庄高新建设投资有限公司	2010-03-11	—	0311-66685155
石家庄高新区科发投资有限公司	2010-03-23	—	0311-66699013
石家庄科技创业投资有限公司	2002-09-19	—	0311-66685160
石家庄石以创业投资管理有限公司	2009-11-30	—	0311-66699011
唐山高新创业投资有限公司	2007-07-02	—	0315-3858385
河南创业投资股份有限公司	2002-08	www.hnvc.cn	0315-67897012
河南德瑞恒通高端装备创业投资基金有限公司	2013-05-15	—	0371-55698755

公司名称	成立时间	网址	传真
河南高科技创业投资股份有限公司	2001-04-29	www.hnvc.com.cn	0371-67895090
河南华祺节能环保创业投资有限公司	2013-06-20	—	0371-86684801
河南华夏海纳创业投资集团有限公司	2009-06-18	www.huaxiahn.com	0371-86068196
焦作通财创业投资有限责任公司	2007-09-24	www.hntcct.com	0391-3903917
许昌市发展创业投资有限公司	2006-06-20	www.xcct.cn	0374-2783269
郑州百瑞创新资本创业投资有限公司	2007-07-30	www.szvc.com.cn	0371-69177638
哈尔滨创新投资有限公司	2002-06-28	—	0451-84686552
哈尔滨创业投资集团有限公司	2009-02-26	www.hrbvc.com.cn	0451-84858002
哈尔滨哈以孵化器管理有限公司	2011-04-07	www.harbin-incubator.com	—
哈尔滨市科技风险投资中心	1998-05	—	0451-84686552
哈尔滨以哈投资管理有限公司	2012-01-06	—	—
黑龙江辰能哈工大高科技风险投资有限公司	2001-08-28	www.hlj-cvc.com	0451-82285700
黑龙江红土科力创业投资有限公司	2011-07-11	—	0451-55553193
黑龙江省科力高科技产业投资有限公司	2003-06-25	www.hljkl.com	0451-82262600
湖北奥信创业投资管理有限公司	2008-09-08	whaoxin.com	027-85750513
湖北楚银投资有限公司	2009-03-12	www.chu-yin.cn	027-85699728
湖北高和创业投资管理有限公司	2009-12-08	—	027-86659549
湖北红土创业投资有限公司	2009-12	www.szvc.com.cn	027-87339809
湖北量科高投创业投资有限公司	2010-11-26	—	027-87440551
湖北盛世高金创业投资有限公司	2011-03-24	—	027-87440849
湖北新能源投资管理有限公司	2010-08-18	—	027-65796340
荆州高新技术产业开发区创业服务中心	2001-10-28	www.jing-chuang.gov.cn	0716-8123550
科华银赛创业投资有限公司	2009-07-30	www.khysct.com	027-59817377
十堰高新技术产业开发区创业服务中心	2000-12-01	www.sychuangye.com	0719-8319883
武汉承胜创业投资有限公司	2012-06-26	—	027-82920839
武汉东湖创新科技投资有限公司	1999-12	—	027-85613636
武汉东湖创新投资管理有限公司	2012-11-08	www.donghu-pe.com	027-87056266-8808
武汉高农生物创业投资有限公司	2010-08-04	—	027-87397836
武汉固德银赛创业投资管理有限公司	2009-04-21	www.gdysct.com	027-59817377
武汉硅谷天堂晨曦创业投资基金合伙企业（有限合伙）	2012-09-07	—	—
武汉华工创业投资有限责任公司	2000-09-11	www.hustvc.com.cn	027-81338733
武汉华工科技企业孵化器有限责任公司	2003-04-09	www.whbi.com.cn	027-87522800
武汉科技投资有限公司	1992-05-06	—	027-65692512
武汉市洪山科技创业种子资金管理有限公司	2002-10-16	—	027-87526590
武汉天一医药科技投资有限公司	2002-06-11	—	027-87291037
武汉武大创新投资有限公司	2002-02-09	www.wusp.com.cn	027-87055289
武汉一道创业投资有限公司	2009-03-16	—	027-87056266
武汉中部发展创业投资中心（普通合伙）	2008-09	www.c-capital.cn	027-51488302
武汉中科信创业投资管理有限公司	2010-04-09	—	027-87896979

公司名称	成立时间	网址	传真
襄阳博润股权投资基金中心	2012-07-08	—	—
襄阳创新资本创业投资有限公司	2008-09-18	—	—
襄阳中广股权投资有限公司	2012-04-15	—	—
长沙高新技术创业投资管理有限公司	2000-09-09	www.cshvc.com	0731-88286898
长沙市科技风险投资管理有限公司	2000-05-18	www.csvcc.cn	0731-88286892
长沙先导创业投资有限公司	2009-05-15	www.cpih.cn	0731-88768823
常德中科芙蓉创业投资有限责任公司	2011-01-12	—	0736-7703079
郴州汉红股权投资基金管理有限公司	2012-03-27	—	0731-88917899
湖南财信创业投资有限责任公司	2001-01-17	www.hncxvc.com	0731-5196822
湖南达晨财鑫创业投资有限公司	2011-03-28	—	0736-7133995
湖南德源高新创业投资有限公司	2010-12-31	—	0731-85165395
湖南高新创业投资管理有限公司	2011-03-10	www.hhtvcm.com	0731-85165395
湖南红马智信投资管理有限公司	2010-04-08	—	0731-89952611
湖南华友融资担保有限责任公司	2011-11-11	www.hyrzdb.com	0731-28529777
湖南金科投资担保有限公司	2003-11-27	www.hnkt.cn	0731-82768669
湖南瑞驰丰和创业投资管理有限公司	2008-02-28	www.hnrichfund.com	0731-82768320
湖南省广信创业投资基金有限公司	2012-06-05	—	0731-88737722
湖南新能源创业投资基金企业（有限合伙）	2010-05-14	—	0731-82768320
湖南兆富投资控股（集团）有限公司	2009-08-24	www.zaffer.cn	0731-88737722
湖南浙商恒硕创业投资有限公司	2010-08-06	—	0731-85696978
株洲广信兆富投资管理有限公司	2012-02-28	—	0731-88737722
株洲南车时代高新投资担保有限责任公司	2003-05-21	www.timesinvest.cn	0731-28498055
株洲市世富投资有限公司	2009-12-14	—	0731-22727013
株洲兆富成长企业创业投资有限公司	2010-10-13	—	0731-88737722
长春经开科技风险投资有限公司	2000-11-20	www.jlsme.com	0431-86711708
长春科技风险投资有限公司	2000-04-10	www.chinacvc.com	0431-85188007
长春市科技发展中心	1997-06-06	www.ccfengxian.com	0431-88777258
吉林省高新技术创业投资有限公司	2009-12-10	—	0431-89684088
苏州深蓝创业投资有限公司	2007-09-04	—	0512-67871667
北极光创业投资企业	2009	—	010-59696185
滨海沿海创业投资有限公司	2010-03	—	—
博辰创业投资管理（苏州）有限公司	2007-11-26	—	0512-66969661
长汉共同合作基金	2007-09-18	—	025-66009900
长三角创业投资企业	2008-01-07	—	0512-66969677
常创（常州）创业投资合伙企业（有限公司）	2013-09-03	—	0519-85220338
常春藤（昆山）产业投资中心（有限合伙）	2011-01	www.ivycapital.com	021-61908988
常熟博瀚创业投资有限公司	2009-11-23	—	0512-52351556
常熟经济开发区高新技术创业投资有限公司	2009-06	—	0512-52292926
常熟科华创业投资中心（有限合伙）	2011	www.nypcapital.com	—

公司名称	成立时间	网址	传真
常熟市国发创业投资有限公司	2010-11-25	—	0512-52876487
常州常荣创业投资有限公司	2009-09-08	—	—
常州常以创业投资中心（有限合伙）	2011-01-26	—	0519-89629972-804
常州德丰杰清洁技术创业投资中心（有限合伙）	2009-12	www.dfjcompass.com	0519-89182227
常州德丰杰投资管理有限公司	2009-12	www.dfjcompass.com	0519-89182227
常州德丰杰正道创业投资中心（有限合伙）	2012-03	www.dfjcompass.com	0519-89182227
常州德丰杰正道投资管理有限公司	2012-02-20	www.dfjcompass.com	0519-89182227
常州蜂鸟创业投资合伙企业（有限合伙）	2012-06-21	—	0519-81231818
常州高睿创业投资管理有限公司	2007-09-24	—	0519-85150557
常州高投创业投资有限公司	2008-07-22	—	0519-85150557
常州高新创业投资有限公司	2012-01-18	www.czhti.com.cn	0519-81235008
常州高新技术风险投资有限公司	2000-12-22	www.cz-vc.com	0519-85150557
常州和泰股权投资有限公司	2001-10-29	—	0519-85170301
常州和裕创业投资有限公司	2011-04	—	0519-85176186
常州金陵华软创业投资合伙企业（有限合伙）	2010-08-05	—	—
常州金码创业投资管理合伙企业（有限合伙）	2011-11-30	www.jolmo.net	025-84730211
常州金茂经信创业投资管理企业（有限合伙）	2013-12-31	www.jolmo.net	025-84730211
常州金茂新兴产业创业投资合伙企业（有限合伙）	2011-09	www.jolmo.net	025-84730211
常州力合创业投资有限公司	2008-10-10	www.leaguer.com.cn	0519-86220118
常州力合投资管理有限公司	2008-08	www.leaguercapital.com	0519-86220118
常州牡丹江南创业投资有限责任公司	2010-03-15	—	0519-68866908
常州青年创业投资中心（有限合伙）	2012-12-20	—	0519-85220338
常州青企联合创业投资合伙企业（有限合伙）	2013-01-05	—	0519-85220338
常州睿泰创业投资中心（有限合伙）	2012	—	—
常州赛富高新创业投资中心（有限合伙）	2009-12	www.sbaif.com	0519-89606122
常州市久益股权投资中心（有限合伙）	2010-07-30	www.nd-invest.cn	0519-89816672
常州市巨凝创业投资有限公司	2008-04	—	—
常州市民生投资中心（有限合伙）	2007-11-15	—	0519-85164197
常州武进红土创业投资有限公司	2008-08-19	www.szvc.com.cn	0519-86318682
常州武岳峰创业投资管理有限公司	2011-03-03	www.summitviewcapital.com	0519-86621006
常州武岳峰创业投资合伙企业（有限合伙）	2011-03-23	www.summitviewcapital.com	0519-86621006
常州信辉创业投资有限公司	2007-05-11	—	0519-88129306
丹阳市高新技术创业投资有限公司	2010-12-01	—	0511-86922610
德丰杰（无锡）创业投资企业	2010-05-23	www.dfj.com	0510-81156560-807
高投名力成长创业投资有限公司	2007-04-29	www.mcgf.com.cn	021-62889166
高瞻（无锡）创业投资有限公司	2011-04	www.tallwoodvc.com	0510-81814997
高瞻（无锡）企业管理有限公司	2011-05	www.tallwoodvc.com	0510-81814997
光控（海门）创业投资有限公司	2012-11-30	—	—
国科瑞祺物联网创业投资有限公司	2010-07-22	www.casim.cn	010-82607629-802

公司名称	成立时间	网址	传真
国润创业投资（苏州）管理有限公司	2008-05	www.guorun.com	0512-62998663
海得汇金创业投资江阴有限公司	2011-03-03	www.head-capital.com	0510-81602235
海门东翔创业投资有限公司	2012-12-19	—	—
海门市东洲创业投资有限公司	2011-12-28	—	0513-82212931
红塔创新（昆山）创业投资有限公司	2008-07-09	—	010-58555666
洪泽英飞尼迪创业投资中心（有限合伙）	2011-05	—	0517-83361705
华软创业投资无锡合伙企业（有限合伙）	2009-08	www.csinvestmentgroup.com	010-82525169
华穗食品创业投资企业	2009-04-13	—	021-62476800
华映光辉投资管理（苏州）有限公司	2010	www.meridiancapital.com.cn	0512-68327950
淮安平衡股权投资基金中心（有限合伙）	2013-10-25	—	025-51889757
建湖县建科创业投资有限公司	2010-12	—	—
江苏艾利克斯投资有限公司	2006-01-19	—	0511-86900801
江苏滨海高石创业投资有限公司	2011-08	—	—
江苏博硕高新技术产业投资发展有限公司	2011-09-18	—	0512-88880863
江苏昌盛阜创业投资有限公司	2008-08-22	—	0512-69560268
江苏大丰众成科技创业投资有限公司	2010-04	—	0515-83855826
江苏大行临港产业投资有限公司	2012-12-26	—	0511-88224055
江苏鼎鸿创业投资有限公司	2008-03	—	0513-85159991
江苏鼎信咨询有限公司	1998-04-27	www.do-think.com	025-86586939
江苏东恒空港高新技术产业园有限公司	2011-08-26	—	025-52327675
江苏多良创业投资有限公司	2008-03-31	—	0519-83872660
江苏高鼎科技创业投资有限公司	2007-08-31	www.js-vc.com	025-51889757
江苏高弘投资管理有限公司	2006-09	—	025-52313062
江苏高晋创业投资有限公司	2008-06-12	—	0519-85150557
江苏高科技投资集团有限公司	1992-07	www.js-vc.com	025-66009900
江苏高胜科技创业投资有限公司	2006-12-27	www.js-vc.com	025-51889757
江苏高投成长创业投资有限公司	2008-01	—	025-66009900
江苏高投成长价值股权投资合伙企业（有限合伙）	2011-05	—	025-66009900
江苏高投创新价值创业投资合伙企业（有限合伙）	2011-05	—	025-66009900
江苏高投创新科技创业投资合伙企业（有限合伙）	2011-04	—	025-66009900
江苏高投创新天使创业投资合伙企业（有限合伙）	2013-11-30	—	025-66009900
江苏高投创业投资管理有限公司	1999-01-29	—	025-66009900
江苏高投发展创业投资有限公司	2010-07-16	—	025-66009900
江苏高投科贷创业投资合伙企业（有限合伙）	2013-12-31	—	025-66009900-9651
江苏高投宁泰创业投资合伙企业（有限合伙）	2012-01-30	—	025-66009900-9651
江苏高投润泰创业投资合伙企业（有限合伙）	2012-02-14	—	025-66009900-9651
江苏高投鑫海创业投资有限公司	2011-04	—	0514-87876609
江苏高投中小企业创业投资有限公司	2009-05	—	025-66009900
江苏高新创业投资管理有限公司	2005-01-14	www.js-vc.com	025-51889757

公司名称	成立时间	网址	传真
江苏高新创业投资有限公司	2005-08-15	www.js-vc.com	025-51889757
江苏格瑞石墨烯创业投资有限公司	2012-04-10	—	0519-81085951
江苏国投衡盈创业投资中心（有限合伙）	2010-11-22	—	021-62785808
江苏海为创业投资有限公司	2010-12-03	—	0523-86239598
江苏昊海投资发展集团有限公司	2012-11-26	www.hhco.cc	0518-85917545
江苏弘瑞科技创业投资有限公司	2002-09	—	025-52313062
江苏华成华利创业投资有限公司	2009-10-21	—	0512-67161932
江苏华创医药研发平台管理有限公司	2007-06	—	—
江苏华工创业投资有限公司	2010-06	—	0514-89785833
江苏华控创业投资有限公司	2008-07	www.huakongpe.com	025-87716620-801
江苏华控投资管理有限公司	2008-01	—	025-87716220-801
江苏华厦创业投资有限公司	2006-09-30	—	0514-86569000
江苏汇和新材料科技集团有限公司	2010-03-23	www.huihe.com.cn	0516-85803888
江苏汇鸿创业投资有限公司	2004-07-06	—	025-86586939
江苏火炬创业投资有限公司	2010-10-19	www.huojujijin.com	0510-81813907
江苏金茂低碳产业创投有限公司	2010-10	www.jolmo.net	025-84730211
江苏金茂环保产业创业投资有限公司	2010-12-17	www.jolmo.net	025-84730211
江苏金炻创业投资有限公司	2012-05-25	—	0515-82342000
江苏津通创业投资有限公司	2007-06-25	www.jinton.com	0519-86226016
江苏九洲投资集团创业投资有限公司	2007-09-19	www.jiuzhouinvest.com	0519-85220338
江苏聚融创业投资有限公司	2011-11-16	—	0511-87899196
江苏科泉高新创业投资有限公司	2012-10-31	—	025-85589174
江苏旷达创业投资有限公司	2007-06	—	0519-86546893
江苏昆山高特佳创业投资有限公司	2007-05-16	www.ksgig.com	0512-57118196
江苏蓝色动力投资管理有限公司	2010-09-26	—	0517-80850098
江苏联发创业投资有限公司	2011-12-13	—	0513-88869069
江苏领域创业投资有限公司	2010-07	—	0512-69172355-8023
江苏隆鑫创业投资有限公司	2006-06	—	025-84401201
江苏迈新创业投资有限公司	2009-08-17	—	0519-87195666
江苏乾融资本管理有限公司	2011-06-02	—	025-62998656
江苏瑞明创业投资管理有限公司	2009-12-30	—	025-83172132
江苏瑞庭投资管理有限公司	2013-09-01	—	0513-85158550
江苏桑夏投资有限公司	2010-04-28	—	—
江苏省高科技产业投资有限公司	1997	www.jsvc.com.cn	025-83317551
江苏省高新技术创业服务中心	1996-10	www.jsbi.cn	025-83232021
江苏省苏港创业投资有限公司	2010-08	www.sgct.com.cn	0515-83289299
江苏省苏高新风险投资股份有限公司	2000-03-31	www.sz-vc.com	0512-68243439
江苏省无锡江大大学科技园有限公司	2001-12-30	www.j-park.jiangnan.edu.cn	0510-85189107
江苏晟华创业投资有限公司	2008	—	—

公司名称	成立时间	网址	传真
江苏盛泉创业投资有限公司	2007-06	www.vc-century.com	025-58071508
江苏盛宇丹昇创业投资有限公司	2008-10-28	—	0511-86929333
江苏苏大投资有限公司	2001-02	—	0512-67504016
江苏天氏创业投资有限公司	2005	—	025-87752270
江苏通顺创业投资有限公司	2009-08-25	—	0512-69560268
江苏同兴财富投资管理有限公司	2008-05	—	0512-69560268
江苏拓达创业投资有限责任公司	2012-11-26	—	0516-68005601
江苏新材料产业创业投资企业（有限合伙）	2013-11-13	www.jolomo.net	025-84730211
江苏新创投资有限公司	2007-10-17	—	0523-84623002
江苏新海连创业投资有限公司	2010-04-27	—	—
江苏信泉创业投资管理有限公司	2006-12-30	—	025-58071508
江苏兴科创业投资有限公司	2007-08-20	www.jsxinkect.com	0519-86302628
江苏学府科技创业园有限公司	2010-06-08	—	0511-84405258
江苏鹰能创业投资有限公司	2007-08-28	—	025-66009900
江苏中科华艺创业投资有限公司	2007-03-30	—	0513-88869883
江苏中科物联网科技创业投资有限公司	2010-07-14	www.casiot.com	0510-85380859
江苏中欧投资股份有限公司	2009-12-23	—	0512-68079590
江苏卓创创业投资有限公司	2013-12-13	—	0513-80559909
江苏紫金文化产业发展基金（有限合伙）	2010-03-15	—	025-66009900
江阴市高新技术创业投资有限公司	2007-02-06	—	0510-81602090
金沙江联合创业投资企业	2009-09	—	010-57069899
靖江市高新技术创业投资有限公司	2010-03	—	0523-89181480
句容市高新技术创业服务中心	2013-04-01	—	0511-87272670
凯风创业投资有限公司	2006-10-30	—	0512-66969533
昆山高特佳创业投资管理有限公司	2007-06-27	www.ksgig.com	0512-57118196
昆山红土创业投资管理有限公司	2012-08-08	—	0512-36607933
昆山红土高新创业投资有限公司	2012-07-13	—	0512-3660732
昆山市国科创业投资有限公司	2001-08-31	—	0512-57305458
昆山市昆鹏创业投资合伙企业（有限合伙）	2011-05-30	—	0512-55119138
昆山源晟投资管理有限公司	2011-09-22	—	0512-55112955
昆山源泰创业投资有限公司	2011-04-29	—	0512-55112955
昆山源泰股权投资企业（有限合伙）	2011-04-29	—	0512-55112955
昆山中科昆开创业投资有限公司	2011-05	—	0512-36821078
连云港金海创业投资有限公司	2006-07-19	www.lygjhvc.com	0518-85523512
连云港市润财创业投资发展有限公司	2010-10-22	—	0518-85523920
连云港中科黄海创业投资有限公司	2010-03-22	www.csm-inv.com	0518-85807928
南京创业投资管理有限公司	2008-11-26	www.nj-vc.com	025-86579660
南京高新创业投资有限公司	2012-06-01	—	025-58696594
南京市高新技术风险投资股份有限公司	2001-02-24	www.nj-vc.com	025-86599660

公司名称	成立时间	网址	传真
南京市栖霞区科技创业投资有限公司	2009-07-31	—	025-85566570
南京文化创业投资有限公司	2011-02	—	025-86579660
南京中原创业投资有限公司	2010-12-17	—	025-86579660
南京紫金创投基金管理有限责任公司	2011-09-02	—	025-86579655
南京紫金科技创业投资有限公司	2011-08-08	www.njzjkc.com	025-86579616
南通创源科技园发展有限公司	2013-05-07	www.innospring.cn	0513-55018010
南通创源投资有限公司	2012-09	—	0513-86268555
南通得一投资中心（有限合伙）	2012-08-10	—	021-64178726
南通高胜成长创业投资有限公司	2008-09-10	www.js-vc.com	025-51889757
南通高特佳汇金投资合伙企业（有限合伙）	2013-05-24	—	—
南通国泰创业投资有限公司	2006-10-20	www.ntgtvc.com	0513-85288204
南通恒富创业投资合伙企业（有限合伙）	2013-12-16	—	0513-86126133
南通金谷投资有限公司	2013-06-28	—	0513-88695186
南通科创创业投资管理有限公司	2013-04-23	—	0513-85728713
南通科技创业投资有限公司	2011-04-22	—	0513-81500791
南通磊泽投资有限公司	2011-09-07	—	0513-80112053
南通杉杉创业投资中心（有限合伙）	2012-06-08	—	021-51561587
南通松禾创业投资合伙企业（有限合伙）	2009-01	—	0513-85507237
南通松禾创业投资中心（有限合伙）	2011-08-01	—	0513-85517915
南通松禾资本管理有限公司	2009-01-05	—	0513-85507237
南通苏海投资管理中心	2013-11-26	—	0513-88782028
南通五水投资发展有限公司	2013-06-17	—	0513-85609598
日亚创业投资企业	2009-01-06	—	021-61976299
软库博辰创业投资企业	2008-03-03	—	0512-66969661
三角洲创业投资管理（苏州）有限公司	2007-10-16	—	0512-66969677
苏州安固创业投资有限公司	2007-09-30	—	0512-62925311
苏州博韬创业投资管理有限公司	2010-05	—	0512-62535689
苏州创东方富诚投资企业（有限合伙）	2010-09-20	—	0512-68322281
苏州创元高投创业投资管理有限公司	2010-08-27	—	0512-68322738
苏州创元高新创业投资有限公司	2010-11-15	—	0512-68322738
苏州达泰创业投资管理有限公司	2010-05	www.delta-capital.cn	0512-66969677
苏州达泰创业投资中心（有限合伙）	2010-08	www.delta-capital.cn	0512-66969677
苏州德睿亨风创业投资有限公司	2010-04-21	—	0512-66969533
苏州德晟亨风创业投资合伙企业（有限合伙）	2011	—	0512-66969533
苏州鼎融投资管理有限公司	2009-12-10	www.jsqr.com.cn	0512-62998656
苏州东方汇富创业投资企业（有限合伙）	—	—	—
苏州方广创业投资管理合伙企业（有限合伙）	2012-05-28	—	021-54245723
苏州方广创业投资合伙企业（有限合伙）	2012-09-25	—	021-54245723
苏州斐然向风创业投资中心（有限合伙）	2011	—	—

公司名称	成立时间	网址	传真
苏州福马创业投资有限公司	2009-10	—	0512-62821808
苏州富丽东方能源股权投资企业（有限合伙）	2011	www.fuli-capital.com	0512-68322281
苏州富丽高新投资企业（有限合伙）	2010-11-10	—	0512-68322281
苏州富丽明康投资企业（有限合伙）	2011	www.fuli-capital.com	0512-68322281
苏州富丽启康投资企业（有限合伙）	2011	www.fuli-capital.com	0512-68322281
苏州富丽泰泓投资企业（有限合伙）	2010-11-10	www.fuli-capital.com	0512-68322281
苏州富丽投资有限公司	2010-07-29	—	0512-68322281
苏州高华创业投资管理有限公司	2009-09-08	—	0512-68313889
苏州高锦创业投资有限公司	2009-03-27	—	0512-68243439
苏州高铨创业投资企业（有限合伙）	2011-11	—	0512-68243439
苏州高投创业投资管理有限公司	2007-01	—	0512-68059096
苏州高新创业投资集团融联管理有限公司	2012-02-08	—	0512-68081156
苏州高新创业投资集团有限公司	2008-07-30	www.sndvc.com	0512-68311200
苏州高新风投创业投资管理有限公司	2009-02-23	—	0512-68243439
苏州高新国发创业投资有限公司	2009-05-22	—	0512-65126380
苏州高新华富创业投资企业	2010-01-08	—	0512-68313889
苏州高新明鑫创业投资管理有限公司	2010-12-29	www.sndvc.com	0512-68313889
苏州高新启源创业投资有限公司	2011-05	www.sndvc.com	0512-68311200
苏州高新区创业科技投资管理有限公司	2003-03-03	—	0512-68323009
苏州高新新联创业投资管理有限公司	2009-06-24	—	0512-68313585
苏州高新信缘投资管理有限公司	2008-12-04	—	0512-68762955
苏州高新友利创业投资有限公司	2010-04-28	—	0512-68313585
苏州高远创业投资有限公司	2007-03	—	0512-68059096
苏州高钺创业投资管理有限公司	2011	—	0512-68243439
苏州工业园区辰融创业投资有限公司	2008-05-14	www.jsqr.com.cn	0512-62998656
苏州工业园区禾源北极光创业投资合伙企业（有限合伙）	2011	—	010-59696185
苏州工业园区弘丰创业投资有限公司	2010-04	—	0512-69560268
苏州工业园区华穗创业投资管理有限公司	2008-07	—	021-62476800
苏州工业园区科技发展有限公司	2000-04	www.sispark.com.cn	0512-62529777
苏州工业园区南凯创业投资有限公司	2011-03	—	0512-69560268
苏州工业园区启纳创业投资有限公司	2011-07	—	0512-69993999
苏州工业园区易联创业投资基金有限公司	2010-03	—	0512-669669938
苏州工业园区易联投资中心（有限合伙）	2011-10-31	www.easternlinkcapital.com	0512-66969938
苏州工业园区友丰创业投资有限公司	2008-01-30	—	0512-65288822
苏州工业园区元禾顺风股权投资企业（有限合伙）	2013-09-04	—	0512-66969727
苏州工业园区原点创业投资有限公司	2008-03-26	—	0512-66969998
苏州工业园区原点正则壹号创业投资企业（有限合伙）	2013-11-19	—	0512-66969533
苏州国发创富创业投资企业（有限合伙）	2010-07-14	—	0512-65126380
苏州国发创新资本投资有限公司	2007-01-12	—	0512-65168830

公司名称	成立时间	网址	传真
苏州国发创业投资控股有限公司	2008-05-08	www.sidvc.com	0512-65126380
苏州国发东方创业投资管理有限公司	2008-11-14	—	0512-65126380
苏州国发服务业创业投资企业（有限合伙）	2012-04-23	—	0512-65126380
苏州国发高铁文化创业投资管理有限公司	2013-08-19	—	—
苏州国发高铁文化创业投资中心（有限合伙）	2013-09-29	—	—
苏州国发高新创业投资管理有限公司	2008-12-17	—	0512-65126380
苏州国发宏富创业投资企业（有限合伙）	2011-04	—	0512-65126380
苏州国发建富创业投资企业（有限合伙）	2010-06-30	—	0512-65126380
苏州国发聚富创业投资有限公司	2010-03-25	—	0512-65126380
苏州国发黎曼创业投资有限公司	2010-05-19	—	0512-65126380
苏州国发融富创业投资管理企业（有限合伙）	2009-12-28	—	0512-65126380
苏州国发融富创业投资企业（有限合伙）	2010-01-20	—	0512-65126380
苏州国发天使创业投资企业（有限合伙）	2011-06	—	0512-65126380
苏州国发添富创业投资企业（有限合伙）	2012-05-09	—	0512-65126380
苏州国发文化产业创业投资企业（有限合伙）	2012-12-17	—	—
苏州国发涌富创业投资企业（有限合伙）	2011-06	—	0512-65126380
苏州国发源富创业投资企业（有限合伙）	2011-01	—	0512-65126380
苏州国发智富创业投资企业（有限合伙）	2010-03	—	0512-65126380
苏州国发众富创业投资企业（有限合伙）	2010-03-17	—	0512-65126380
苏州国润创业投资发展有限公司	2008-07	—	0512-62998663
苏州国润瑞祺创业投资企业（有限合伙）	2011-07	www.guorunpe.com	0512-62998663
苏州合融创新资本管理有限公司	2007-11	www.jsqr.com.cn	0512-62998656
苏州合盈创业投资管理有限公司	2010	www.renhua.cc	0512-67060338
苏州恒融创业投资有限公司	2007-12	www.jsqr.com.cn	0512-62998656
苏州华创赢达创业投资基金企业（有限合伙）	2012	—	0512-63936955
苏州华慧创业投资中心（有限合伙）	2010-04	—	021-31352499
苏州华慧投资管理有限公司	2010	—	021-31352499
苏州华亿创业投资中心（有限合伙）	2008-12	www.infinity-equity.com	0512-66969503
苏州华亿基金管理有限公司	2008	—	0512-66969503
苏州华映文化产业投资企业（有限合伙）	2010-09-20	www.meridiancapital.com.cn	0512-68327950
苏州辉宏原油股权投资企业（有限合伙）	2011	www.fuli-capital.com	0512-68322281
苏州汇川创业投资中心（有限合伙）	2010-06-08	—	0512-62535689
苏州汇利华创业投资有限公司	2010-08-27	www.js-central.com	0512-68079590
苏州金枫创业投资有限公司	2009	—	0512-66580199
苏州金茂创业投资管理企业（有限合伙）	2011-05	www.jolmo.net	025-84730211
苏州金茂投资管理有限公司	2007-12-27	www.jolmo.net	025-84730211
苏州金茂新兴产业创业投资企业（有限合伙）	2011-06	www.jolmo.net	025-84730211
苏州金沙湖创业投资管理有限公司	2011-03-30	—	010-570669899
苏州金沙江创业投资管理有限公司	2009	—	—

公司名称	成立时间	网址	传真
苏州君玄创业投资中心（有限合伙）	2011	—	—
苏州卡贝高登创业投资中心	2011-01	www.nypcapital.com	0512-69572911
苏州卡贝金牛投资管理有限公司	2011-01	www.nypcapital.com	0512-69572911
苏州凯风进取创业投资有限公司	2009-07-02	www.cowinvc.com	0512-66969533
苏州凯风万盛创业投资合伙企业（有限合伙）	2011	www.cowinvc.com	0512-66969533
苏州凯风正德投资管理有限公司	2010	www.cowinvc.com	0512-66969533
苏州康博沿江创业投资中心（有限合伙）	2010-11-22	—	021-51166899
苏州科技城创业投资有限公司	2007-12-24	—	0512-66899465
苏州科技创业投资公司	1993-07	—	0512-69330076
苏州科嘉创业投资中心	2011-05	www.nypcapital.com	0512-69572911
苏州科荣创业投资中心（有限合伙）	2011-07-04	—	—
苏州科盛投资管理有限公司	2011-09-29	—	—
苏州坤融创业投资有限公司	2010-03-15	—	0512-62998656
苏州蓝贰创业投资有限公司	2010-01	—	0512-52725933
苏州蓝壹创业投资有限公司	2008-03	—	0512-62725933
苏州龙瑞创业投资管理有限公司	2009-12	—	0512-66969306
苏州龙跃投资中心（有限合伙）	2010-01	—	0512-66969306
苏州绿原大成投资管理有限公司	—	—	0512-62990952
苏州镁天创业投资有限公司	2009	—	0512-62993881
苏州明鑫高投创业投资有限公司	2011-02	www.sndvc.com	0512-68313889
苏州农发创业投资中心（有限合伙）	2011-04	—	0512-62990952
苏州磐石杏源创业投资合伙企业（有限合伙）	2012	—	—
苏州启明创智股权投资合伙企业（有限合伙）	2011-10-17	www.qimingvc.com	—
苏州勤云投资中心（有限合伙）	2011-10-12	—	—
苏州青云创业投资管理中心（有限合伙）	2011-09-14	—	—
苏州清商成长创业投资企业（有限合伙）	2011-09	—	0512-62621310
苏州仁华创业投资有限公司	2010-04	www.renhua.cc	0512-67060338
苏州融联创业投资企业（有限合伙）	2012-03-15	—	0512-68081156
苏州瑞璟创业投资企业（有限合伙）	2010-11-17	—	0512-68326637
苏州瑞曼投资管理有限公司	2010-03-17	—	0512-68326637
苏州盛泉百涛创业投资管理有限公司	2010-12-15	—	025-58071508
苏州盛泉万泽创业投资合伙企业（有限合伙）	2011-03-03	—	025-58071508
苏州市澄和创业投资有限公司	2008-08	xcchfof.com	0512-66183052
苏州市吴江创业投资有限公司	2008	—	0512-63493186
苏州市吴中创业投资有限公司	2007-01-12	—	0512-66356670
苏州市吴中科技创业园管理有限公司	2004-06	www.wzcy.cn	0512-65270617
苏州市相城创业投资管理有限责任公司	2009-01-16	—	0512-65808803
苏州市相城创业投资有限责任公司	2008	—	0512-65808803
苏州市相城高新创业投资有限责任公司	2009-03-12	—	0512-65808803

公司名称	成立时间	网址	传真
苏州水木清华资本管理有限公司	2011-09	—	0512-62621310
苏州松禾成长创业投资中心（有限合伙）	2009-11	—	0755-83290622
苏州松禾成长二号创业投资中心（有限合伙）	2011-04	—	0755-83290622
苏州松禾资本管理中心（有限合伙）	2009-12	—	0755-83290622
苏州天图兴苏股权投资中心（有限合伙）	2013-08-07	www.tiantu.com.cn	0755-36909834
苏州通和创业投资合伙企业（有限合伙）	2012-09-12	www.frontlinebioventures.com	021-20287996
苏州蔚蓝投资管理有限公司	2008-03-07	—	0512-62725933
苏州吴中国发创业投资管理有限公司	2008-08-28	—	0512-65126380
苏州吴中国发创业投资有限公司	2008-08-28	—	0512-65126380
苏州吴中科技创业投资有限公司	2012-10-26	—	0512-65855966
苏州羲融创业投资有限公司	2010-02-01	—	0512-62998656
苏州相城经济开发区相发投资有限公司	2011-08	—	0512-66183052
苏州香塘创业投资有限责任公司	2007	—	0512-53560126
苏州协立投资管理有限公司	2011-03	—	—
苏州新麟创业投资有限公司	2009-01-22	—	0512-68762955
苏州新麟二期创业投资企业（有限合伙）	2011-11	—	0512-68762955
苏州新协创业投资有限公司	2006-05	—	0512-62620019
苏州义云创业投资中心（有限合伙）	2011-10-12	—	—
苏州亿和创业投资有限公司	2009-12-29	—	0512-68635705
苏州亿文创新资本管理有限公司	2007-12-03	—	0512-68635705
苏州亿文投资有限公司	2007-12-17	—	0512-68635705
苏州银基创业投资有限公司	2006-05-10	www.chengtai.net	0512-67156968
苏州银基美林创业投资管理有限公司	2012-09-03	—	0512-67156968
苏州银基美林创业投资合伙企业（有限合伙）	2012-10-23	—	0512-67156968
苏州元风创业投资有限公司	2007-04	—	0512-66969998
苏州钟鼎创业二号投资中心（有限合伙）	2011-12-02	www.easternbellvc.com	021-61652669
苏州钟鼎创业投资中心（有限合伙）	2010-01-14	www.easternbellvc.com	021-61652669
宿迁国发创业投资企业（有限合伙）	2011-07-22	—	0527-81686002
宿迁科技创业投资有限公司	2012-03-23	—	0527-87031252
宿迁市开创创业投资有限公司	2010-09-07	—	0527-88859676
睢宁县天使创业投资有限责任公司	2013-03-06	—	0516-88037115
太仓市科技创业投资有限公司	2008-08	—	0512-53739159
泰兴市高新投资有限公司	2010-12-27	—	0523-87627940
泰州华诚高新技术投资发展有限公司	2005	www.tzibi.com	0523-86196007
泰州华健创业投资有限公司	2007-06-08	—	—
泰州华盛投资开发有限公司	2007	—	0523-86200146
泰州健鑫创业投资有限公司	2012-12-14	—	0523-86200146
泰州融众创业投资有限公司	2008-12	—	0523-86999080
泰州市创业风险投资有限公司	2001-08	—	0523-86196199

公司名称	成立时间	网址	传真
泰州市高科创业投资有限公司	2010-08-25	—	0523-86966047
泰州市环晟创业投资有限公司	2011-11	—	—
泰州中国医药城融健达创业投资有限公司	2013-04	—	—
天泉创业投资企业（有限合伙）	2010-02-01	—	—
同利创业投资有限公司	2007-12	—	0512-66969657
无锡 TCL 创动投资有限公司	2009-04	—	0510-82800509
无锡 TCL 创业投资合伙企业（有限合伙）	2010-07	—	—
无锡创业投资集团有限公司	2000-10-26	www.wxvcg.com	0510-82700936
无锡高德创业投资管理有限公司	2006-09-30	—	0510-81813011
无锡高德创业投资有限公司	2006-09-06	—	0510-81813011
无锡高新技术风险投资股份有限公司	2000-08	www.wxvc.com.cn	0510-85226431
无锡国联创业投资有限公司	2006-09-21	www.glgc.com.cn	0510-82830598
无锡国联浚源创业投资中心（有限合伙）	2010-04-16	www.jcmchina.cn	0510-82700340
无锡红杉恒业股权投资合伙企业（有限合伙）	2010-12-03	—	010-84475669
无锡红土创业投资有限公司	2009-04-29	—	0510-82800637
无锡火炬投资管理有限公司	2010-07-23	www.huojujijin.com	0510-81813907
无锡江南大学国家大学科技园有限公司	2009-04-03	www.j-park.jiangnan.edu.cn	0510-85189107
无锡金茂二号新兴产业创业投资企业（有限合伙）	2011-12-21	www.jolmo.net	025-84730211
无锡金茂经信创业投资有限公司	2010-06-17	www.jolmo.net	025-84730211
无锡均衡创业投资有限公司	2007-11-14	—	0510-86216256
无锡浚源资本管理中心（有限合伙）	2010-04-16	www.jcmchina.cn	0510-82700340
无锡凯石尚理投资管理有限公司	2010-03-19	—	0510-85213378
无锡力合创业投资有限公司	2008-11	www.leaguercapital.com	0510-83590286
无锡力合投资管理咨询有限公司	2009-04-17	www.leaguercapital.com	0510-83590296
无锡领峰创业投资有限公司	2009-12-11	—	0510-85213378
无锡瑞明博创业投资有限公司	2010-12-15	—	025-83172132
无锡市锡山创业投资有限公司	2007-08	—	0510-88705868
无锡市新区科技金融创业投资集团有限公司	2008-01-31	www.wxvc.com.cn	0510-85226431
无锡锡山科技创业园有限公司	2005-09-20	—	0510-88218130
无锡新区领航创业投资有限公司	2009-08-03	www.wxvc.com.cn	0510-85226431
无锡源生高科技投资有限责任公司	2006	—	0510-85342727-8102
无锡中科汇盈创业投资有限责任公司	2008-03-07	—	0510-85383122
无锡中科汇盈二期创业投资有限责任公司	2010-04-07	—	0510-85383122
无锡众合投资发展有限公司	2006-12	—	0510-85386981
吴江东方创富创业投资企业（有限合伙）	—	—	—
吴江东方国发创业投资有限公司	2008-11-11	—	0512-65126380
吴江东方融富创业投资管理企业（有限合伙）	—	—	—
吴江东运创业投资有限公司	2008-06-24	www.dyvc.net	0512-63960764
吴江海博科技创业投资有限公司	2010-08-20	www.haiboinvestment.net	0512-63010566

公司名称	成立时间	网址	传真
吴江科祥创业投资中心（有限合伙）	2011	—	—
翔智创业投资企业	2008-02-28	www.idtvc.com.cn	021-63868709
新沂市钟吾股权投资管理有限公司	2012-10	—	0516-81639533
兴化市高新投资有限公司	2010-07-16	—	0523-83242633
星运资本管理（苏州）有限公司	2010-01	—	—
徐州高新创业投资有限公司	2010-02-24	—	0516-85906737
徐州国盛鸿运创业投资有限公司	2014-01-21	—	—
徐州淮海红土创业投资有限公司	2014-01-14	—	—
徐州盛泉创业投资合伙企业（有限合伙）	—	—	—
徐州支点创业投资合伙企业（有限合伙）	2012-11	—	0516-66690376
亚太基金	2007-05-09	www.gvcmc.com	0512-85228930
盐城东南创业投资有限公司	2005-04	—	—
盐城高投创业投资有限公司	2010-08	—	025-66009900
盐城市恒利风险投资有限公司	2002-08-06	—	0515-88580802
盐城市亭湖区财裕创业投资有限公司	2010-12-31	—	—
盐城市中科盐发创业投资企业（有限合伙）	2011-11	—	—
盐城盐龙创业投资有限公司	2011-01	—	0515-88457508
盐城中小企业创业投资实业有限公司	2007-12	—	—
扬中创业投资有限公司	2011-05-01	www.yzgxct.com	0511-88126366
扬中市高新创业投资管理有限公司	2011-05-09	—	0511-88126366
扬中市新坝科技园区开发有限公司	2013-04-02	—	0511-85123406
扬州高投创业投资管理有限公司	2011-01-13	www.js-vc.com	0514-87876609
扬州海圣创业投资中心（有限合伙）	2012-07-09	—	0514-87991537
扬州嘉华创业投资有限公司	2013-12-10	—	010-85698023
扬州经济技术开发区高科创业投资有限公司	2012-11-22	—	0514-87962257
扬州经信新兴产业创业投资中心（有限合伙）	2013-01	www.jolmo.net	025-84730211
扬州市创业投资有限公司	2007-05	—	—
扬州鑫旺创业投资中心（有限合伙）	2011-05-10	—	0514-86299963
扬州英飞尼迪创业投资管理有限公司	2010-11-08	—	0514-87785512
仪征高新技术产业投资发展有限公司	2005	—	0514-80852107
宜兴环保科技创新创业投资有限公司	2010-11-24	—	0510-87061315
宜兴市科技创业投资有限公司	2006-12	—	0510-87929030
英菲尼迪—中新创业投资企业	2005-04-01	—	0512-66969503
镇江高科创业投资有限公司	2012-03-16	—	0511-80822821
镇江高投创业投资有限公司	2008-07	—	025-66009900
镇江高新创业投资有限公司	2010-06-11	—	0511-83175331
镇江国投创业投资有限公司	2011-10-05	—	0511-85213636
镇江红土创业投资有限公司	2011-04-01	—	0511-85988773
镇江金山银河股权投资合伙企业（有限合伙）	2013-08-02	—	—

公司名称	成立时间	网址	传真
镇江君鼎协立创业投资有限公司	2013-02-04	—	025-86816826
镇江康成亨创业投资管理有限公司	2013-07-23	—	—
镇江康成亨创业投资合伙企业（有限合伙）	2013-08-12	—	—
镇江力合天使创业投资企业（有限合伙）	2012-12-13	—	0511-88884035
镇江绿洲创业园发展有限公司	2009-09-28	www.glnenergy.cn	0511-83999880
镇江乾鹏创业投资基金企业（有限合伙）	2012-11-20	—	0511-80896166
镇江市创业风险投资有限责任公司	2001-12-01	www.jszjvc.cn	0511-85015808
镇江市金融产业发展有限公司	2013-03-26	www.zjfdhk.com	0511-81980268
镇江新区高新技术产业投资有限公司	2009-07-16	www.zjxqjf.com	0511-83175331
镇江银河创业投资有限公司	2012-06-11	—	—
镇江中安绿色投资管理有限公司	2013-08-09	—	0511-88890873
镇江中科金山创业投资企业（有限合伙）	2011-08-24	www.csm-inv.com	0510-85383122
镇江中以景润创业投资管理有限公司	2013-10-12	—	—
智龙（苏州）创业投资管理有限公司	2008-01	—	021-63868709
中节能南通合同环境管理投资基金中心（有限合伙）	2013-04-03	—	—
中新苏州工业园区创业投资有限公司	2001-11-28	—	0512-66969998
中宇创业投资管理顾问（无锡）有限公司	2007-05-09	www.gvcmc.com	0510-85228930
钟楼红土创业投资有限公司	2013-08-23	www.szvc.com.cn	0519-86318682
江西高技术产业投资股份有限公司	2002-03	www.jxvc.com.cn	0791-88110252
江西华商股权投资管理有限公司	2012-12-14	—	0791-86573036
江西立达新材料产业创业投资中心（有限合伙）	2011-08-03	www.reitercapital.com	0791-83851565
南昌新世纪创业投资有限责任公司	2009-02-24	www.xsjvc.com	0791-86757668
大连港航产业基金管理有限公司	2011-07-01	www.chnpsf.com	0411-86768576
大连高端装备制造业创业投资基金（有限合伙）	2012-06-20	—	0411-82536160
大连海融高新创业投资管理有限公司	2008-02-18	—	0411-84821325
大连海融高新创业投资基金有限公司	2007-12-29	—	0411-84821325
大连科技风险投资基金有限公司	2000-02	www.dstvc.com.cn	0411-82781352-11
大连万融天使投资有限公司	2010-11-30	—	0411-84821325
大连网信创业投资管理有限公司	1999	—	0411-82859969
大连银信创业投资有限公司	2006-09-13	—	0411-84802259-8001
德晟创业投资有限公司	2011-03-09	—	0411-82779477
联合创业集团有限公司	2005-07-07	—	0411-88009300
辽宁东软创业投资有限公司	2000-04-08	www.neusoft.com	0411-84835058
辽宁和元资产管理有限公司	2010-04	—	0411-82530155
辽宁科技创业投资有限责任公司	2000-02-28	www.lnvc.com.cn	024-23244922
沈阳科技风险开发事业中心（沈阳市中试服务中心）	1992-06-02	—	024-22791108
沈阳科技风险投资有限公司	1998-11-04	—	024-22791108
内蒙古科技风险基金管理办公室	1998	www.fengxianjijin.com	0471-6280827
宁夏银控科技创业投资有限公司	2002	—	0951-6199333

公司名称	成立时间	网址	传真
银川铸龙投资有限公司	2008-12	www.yczlvc.com	0951-6981991
青海国科创业投资基金（有限合伙）	2013-10-23	—	0971-6152307
青海欧瑞科技发展投资基金（有限合伙）	2012-03-27	—	010-59002776
莱芜创业投资有限公司	2009-12-28	—	0634-8891127
美世联合创业投资有限公司	2007-04-04	—	0543-3185686
青岛安芙兰创业投资有限公司	2006-01-12	www.vcpe.hk	0532-88018557
青岛高创投资管理有限公司	2009-12-25	—	0532-88727626
青岛里程碑创业投资管理有限公司	2011-05-20	—	0532-80931757
青岛市科技风险投资有限公司	2000-08-17	www.qdstvc.com	0532-85063780
日照华和科技创业投资有限责任公司	2010-05-28	—	0633-8339288
山东昌润创业投资有限公司	2008-08-22	www.crtz.com	0635-2119616
山东德泰创业投资有限公司	2010-03-29	www,sddetai.cn	18865673765
山东弘利创业投资有限公司	2009-12-31	—	0539-8385619
山东嘉华盛裕创业投资股份有限公司	2009-08-27	www.jhsytz.com	0535-6871999
山东江诣创业投资有限公司	2010-08-12	—	0535-6719638
山东齐星创业投资有限公司	2007-01-30	—	0543-4309019
山东省高新技术创业投资有限公司	2000-06	www.sdvc.com.cn	0531-86969598
山东泰山创业投资股份有限公司	2008-08-27	—	0538-8261790
威海创新投资有限公司	2003-07-16	—	0631-5231709
潍坊万通创业投资有限公司	2009-09-28	—	0536-8101018
烟台华升创业投资有限公司	2007-03-16	—	0535-6663009
烟台市蓝海创业投资有限公司	2011-12	—	0535-6891612
烟台市双兴创业投资有限公司	2010-08-04	—	0535-6662956
山西省高新技术创业中心	1992-07	www.sxbi.net	0351-2209903
山西省科技基金发展总公司（山西省风险投资协会）	1993-06	www.sxstfdc.com	0351-2026370
陕西富晨创业投资管理有限公司	2006-02-28	www.sxfvc.com	029-88377568-94
陕西高端装备高技术创业投资基金（有限合伙）	2013-06-28	—	0917-3322919
陕西金河科技创业投资有限责任公司	2010-07-08	—	029-88606033-6039
陕西科技创业投资管理有限公司	2012-09-18	www.cyzg.net	029-88443083
陕西源丰投资发展有限公司	2009-03-24	—	029-88321218
西安创新投资管理有限公司	2001-07	—	029-88348867
西安高新技术产业风险投资有限公司	1999-02-01	www.capitech.com.cn	029-88356636
西安高新技术产业风险投资有限责任公司	1999-02-01	www.capitech.com.cn	029-88356636
西安国海柏睿投资管理有限公司	2013-08-02	—	0755-83705227
西安国海景恒创业投资有限公司	2013-11-15	—	0755-83705227
西安红土创新投资有限公司	2008-06-24	—	—
西安巨川国际投资有限公司	1995-05-05	—	029-88312715
西安迈朴投资发展有限公司	2002-01-08	—	029-88337228
西安信实投资有限公司	2003-12-26	—	029-88351275

公司名称	成立时间	网址	传真
上海漕河泾创业投资有限公司	2002-05-22	—	021-64951721
上海诚鼎创业投资有限公司	2009-12-10	—	021-66986655
上海德丰杰龙升创业投资合伙企业（有限合伙）	2012-11-01	www.dfjdragon.com	021-62800585
上海鼎嘉创业投资管理有限公司	2003-10-30	www.dj-vc.com	021-50801918
上海复旦创业投资有限公司	2000-11-09	—	021-65642533
上海复星化工医药创业投资有限公司	2003-12-23	—	021-68862467
上海亘元创业投资有限公司	2009-03-02	—	021-67103305
上海硅谷天堂合众创业投资有限公司	2010-06-18	www.ggttvc.com	021-50623593
上海硅谷天堂阳光创业投资有限公司	2009-03-30	www.ggttvc.com	021-50623593
上海国盛古贤创业投资管理有限公司	2012-12-12	—	021-58303168
上海华东理工科技园有限公司	2003-12-15	www.ecustpark.com	021-64960431
上海慧立创业投资有限公司	2000-06-01	www.sjtu-vc.com	021-52989041
上海科技创业投资股份有限公司	1993-06-30	www.sstic.com.cn	021-64330776
上海科技创业有限公司	1999-08-09	—	021-64083607
上海科技投资公司	1992	www.shsti.com.cn	021-64312336
上海力合清源创业投资合伙企业（有限合伙）	2012-8-22	www.leaguercapital.com	021-62370021
上海南风股权投资管理有限公司	2009-09-28	www.southwindequity.com	021-52383372
上海浦东创业投资有限公司	1997-01-09	www.pdvc.com	021-50801728
上海浦东科技投资有限公司	1999-06	www.pdsti.com	021-50276385
上海浦东新星纽士达创业投资有限公司	2009-06-19	—	021-50276385
上海商投创业投资有限公司	2001-06-05	—	021-65650916
上海上创信德投资管理有限公司	2007-11-23	www.shcapital.com.cn	021-60932618
上海时空五星创业投资合伙企业（有限合伙）	2009-12-31	—	021-61218709
上海市北科技创业投资有限公司	2011-11-23	—	021-62505267
上海信息技术创业投资有限公司	2001-09-18	—	021-62720218
上海徐汇科技创业投资有限公司	1998-12-02	www.xhvc.net	021-33680013
上海寅福创业投资有限公司	2010-05-06	—	021-65650817
上海云赛创业投资有限公司	2013-08-02	www.inesavc.com	021-54266376
上海闸北创业投资有限公司	2011-11-09	—	021-62505267
上海张江创业投资有限公司	2000-07-12	www.zj-vc.com	021-50801918
上海张江科技创业投资有限公司	2004-10-09	www.zjventure.com	021-50128827
上海真金高技术服务业创业投资中心（有限合伙）	2012-11-12	—	021-50663716
上海正赛联创业投资有限公司	2010-10-22	www.cacfund.com	021-64275106
成都成创汇智创业投资有限公司	2009-12-16	—	028-85337115
成都创新风险投资有限公司	2001-06-08	www.cd-vc.com.cn	028-85337115
成都创业加速器投资有限公司	2010-07	—	028-85987158
成都创业投资管理有限公司	2003-07	www.cdvc.cn	028-87317097
成都创业投资加速器	2010-08-17	—	—
成都德同银科创业投资合伙企业（有限合伙）	2010-03-03	www.dtcap.com	028-85231897

公司名称	成立时间	网址	传真
成都高特佳银科创业投资合伙企业（有限合伙）	2011-07-01	—	028-86586808
成都高投创业投资有限公司	2004-05-17	www.cdhtgroup.com	028-85335111
成都国泰光华投资管理有限公司	2010-08-16	—	028-86241012
成都宏泰银科创业投资合伙企业（有限合伙）	2011-07-18	www.honorink.net	—
成都凯晟投资管理中心（有限合伙）	2010-11-29	—	—
成都科技创业投资有限公司	2001-06-15	—	028-65575920
成都昆仑投资有限责任公司	2011-12-30	www.kunlunvc.com	028-81713889
成都麦肯锡管理顾问有限公司	2005	www.cdmkx.cn	400-6358835-00483
成都蓉兴创业投资有限公司	2007-12-06	www.cd-tk.com.cn	—
成都晟唐银科创业投资企业（有限合伙）	2011-01-20	—	028-85987150
成都市科技风险开发事业中心	1997-07	www.cdppc.cn	028-65575920
成都天河中西医科技保育有限公司	2001-07-24	www.sc-tianhe.com	028-66070666
成都银科创业投资有限公司	2009-03-18	www.ykvc.cn	—
成都盈创成长股权投资基金合伙企业（有限合伙）	2011-07-29	—	028-65938907-8016
成都涌邦股权投资基金管理有限公司	2011-06-20	—	—
成都招商局银科创业投资有限公司	2010-12-31	—	—
开铂银科（成都）创业投资企业	2010-12-06	—	028-65938829
双流聚源创业投资有限公司	2009-10-28	—	028-85810763
双流英飞尼迪聚源创业投资中心	2010-07	—	028-67066685
四川恒硕投资股份有限公司	2008-06-24	www.hstz.com.cn	028-87421551-801
四川吉亨股权投资基金管理有限公司	2012-06-25	—	028-62037930
天津海达创业投资管理有限公司（成都分公司）	2007	—	022-59852168
天创博盛（天津）股权投资基金合伙企业（有限合伙）	2011-10-18	—	022-58909386
天津滨海财富股权投资基金有限公司	2007-08-21	www.behycapital.com	022-23374077
天津滨海高新技术产业开发区科鑫创业投资有限公司	2012-01-12	—	022-58785820
天津滨海天创众鑫股权投资基金有限公司	2010-02-04	—	022-28408686
天津滨海天使创业投资有限公司	2006-09-11	—	022-58909386
天津创业投资管理有限公司	2003-03-28	www.tjvcm.com	022-58909386
天津创业投资有限公司	2001-03-30	www.tjvc.com.cn	022-58909386
天津迪恩投资管理有限公司	2012-06-13	—	022-83710120
天津东虹科技创业投资发展有限公司	2011-04-28	—	022-58785820
天津海达创业投资管理有限公司	2007-11-29	www.hideavc.com	022-59852168
天津海泰创新投资管理有限公司	2008-05-28	—	022-58357020-8009
天津海泰红土创新投资有限公司	2008-05-28	—	022-58357020-8009
天津海泰科技投资管理有限公司	1997-05-08	www.hitech-investment.com	022-83715773
天津火石信息服务业创业投资合伙企业（有限合伙）	2013-02-06	—	022-8710120
天津开明创业投资发展有限公司	2004-04-16	www.ttkama.com	022-58792370
天津科创天使投资有限公司	2006-06-19	—	022-87890535
天津科技发展投资总公司	1997-12	www.stic.com.cn	022-28455801-8004

公司名称	成立时间	网址	传真
天津锟桥创业投资有限公司	2003-08-07	www.kqvc.com	022-87893441
天津南开区苑鑫创业投资有限公司	2012-10-12	—	022-58785820
天津市武清区信邦科技创业投资发展有限公司	2011-05-23	—	022-58785820
天津水星创业投资有限责任公司	2010-05-10	—	022-59852168
天津泰达科技风险投资股份有限公司	2000-10-13	www.tedavc.com.cn	022-66297288
天津天保成长创业投资有限公司	2007-03-06	—	022-58909386
天津天创华鑫现代服务产业创业投资合伙企业（有限合伙）	2012-12-04	—	022-58909386
天津天创盈讯创业投资合伙企业（有限合伙）	2011-09-26	—	022-58909386
天津天富创业投资有限公司	2007-12-04	—	022-58909386
天津天以生物医药股权投资基金有限公司	2010-11-25	—	022-28408686
天津天英创业投资管理有限公司	2010-06-22	—	022-58909386
天津信石基业投资咨询有限公司	2011-04-13	—	022-87820130
天津浔渡创业投资合伙企业（有限合伙）	2011-04-08	—	0510-87822121
天津燕山科技创业投资有限公司	2011-04-20	—	010-59782234
天津沅渡创业投资合伙企业（有限合伙）	2010-08-11	—	0510-87822121
博汇源创业投资有限合伙企业	2009-05-26	—	0755-27821988
乌鲁木齐高新技术融资担保有限公司	2007-05-09	www.uhdz.gov.cn	0991-3834189
新疆创投资本管理有限责任公司	2010-07-15	www.xjvc.net	0991-3682873
新疆创新投资有限公司	2002-04	www.xjvc.com	0991-2306822
新疆华泰天源股权投资有限合伙企业	2011-02-10	—	0991-8848135
新疆火炬创业投资有限公司	2012-08-09	—	0991-3678085
新疆江之源股权投资合伙企业（有限合伙）	2010-12-02	—	0991-7811089
新疆维吾尔自治区国有资产投资经营有限责任公司	1998-04-23	—	0991-2810861
新疆新科源科技风险投资管理有限公司	2004-08	—	0991-3680756
新疆益通投资有限合伙企业	2011-03-01	—	0571-63431799
新疆中小企业创业投资股份有限公司	2010-01-26	www.xjvc.cn	0991-4583310
红塔创新投资股份有限公司	2000-06-15	—	010-58555666
昆明创业投资有限责任公司	2010-07-07	—	—
云南科技创业投资有限公司	2007-12-19	—	—
云南文产创业投资有限责任公司	2011-12-21	—	0871-63365118
云南越弘创业投资有限公司	2011-05-26	—	0871-65399198
长兴惠宏投资合伙企业（有限合伙）	2012-05-28	—	—
安丰创业投资有限公司	2008-02-28	—	0571-87633580
东方星空创业投资有限公司	2008-10-29	—	0571-85058016
光大金控（浙江）资产管理有限公司	2011-01-06	www.ebasset.com	0571-87361699
海宁海创创新投资合伙企业（有限公司）	2011-09-23	—	0571-87960022
海宁中新力合科金创业投资合伙企业（有限合伙）	2012-12-24	—	—
杭州安丰和众创业投资合伙企业（有限合伙）	2011-03-10	—	0571-87633580
杭州安丰汇群创业投资合伙企业（有限合伙）	2011-08-12	—	0571-87633580

公司名称	成立时间	网址	传真
杭州安丰汇盈创业投资合伙企业（有限合伙）	2011-08-12	—	0571-87633580
杭州安丰领先创业投资合伙企业（有限合伙）	2011-04-26	—	0571-87633580
杭州安丰添富创业投资合伙企业（有限合伙）	2012-07-13	—	0571-87633580
杭州安丰众盈创业投资合伙企业（有限合伙）	2010-04-27	—	0571-87633580
杭州葆光投资管理有限公司	2012-10-18	—	0571-85455412
杭州博润创业投资合伙企业（有限合伙）	2011-01-29	www.broadresources.com	0571-86673771
杭州长江创业投资有限公司	1996-06-05	www.cjvc.cc	0571-86624323
杭州诚和创业投资有限公司	2006-06-01	—	0571-88219849
杭州创东方富邦创业投资企业（有限合伙）	2010-12-19	—	0571-89716640
杭州创业加速器亚盈投资合伙企业（有限合伙）	2011-10-28	—	—
杭州德同创业投资合伙企业（有限合伙）	2010-07-08	—	0571-86690981
杭州德同投资管理有限公司	2010-04-21	—	0571-86690981
杭州敦和创业投资有限公司	2011-04-11	www.dunhevc.com	0571-87789050
杭州飞来投资管理有限公司	2007-06-28	www.flyvc.com	0571-88868827
杭州枫惠投资管理有限公司	2006-07-14	www.fenghuizixun.com	0571-89939631
杭州富海银涛投资管理合伙企业（有限合伙）	2011-07-27	—	0571-28280180
杭州高特佳龙之海脉投资管理合伙企业（有限合伙）	2011-06-15	—	—
杭州高新风险投资有限公司	2005-12-29	—	0571-88212247
杭州高盈创业投资合伙企业	2010-06-28	—	—
杭州高盈蓝驰投资有限公司	2009-08-25	—	0571-87960022
杭州广润创业投资有限公司	2007-11-28	—	0571-86951902
杭州海邦投资管理有限公司	2010-12-10	www.hbvc.com.cn	0571-81022997
杭州杭商宝石创业投资合伙企业（有限合伙）	2011-01-10	—	0571-86586927
杭州浩联创业投资有限公司	2013-02-01	—	—
杭州浩盈创业投资合伙企业（有限合伙）	2010-11-12	—	—
杭州合全投资管理有限公司	2006-11-20	www.hequangroup.com	0571-85300782
杭州恒岩股权投资合伙企业（有限合伙）	2012-04-25	—	021-32585857
杭州红土创业投资有限公司	2009-05-22	www.szvc.com.cn	0571-88861163
杭州宏易创业投资合伙企业（有限合伙）	2011-08-24	—	0571-86945666
杭州吉成创业投资有限公司	2010-04-02	—	0571-87988858
杭州建信诚恒创业投资合伙企业（有限合伙）	2011-12-09	—	021-38571319
杭州金色未来创业投资有限公司	2009-11-25	www.hzjswl.com.cn	0571-87923723
杭州金永信创业投资合伙企业（有限合伙）	2009-12-21	—	—
杭州金永信润禾创业投资合伙企业（有限合伙）	2010-05-04	—	0571-85279925
杭州金永信天时创业投资合伙企业	2010-04-07	—	0571-85279925
杭州经济技术开发区创业投资有限公司	2008-10-09	—	0571-56638083
杭州兰德优势创业投资合伙企业（有限合伙）	2011-07-07	—	—
杭州立元创业投资有限公司	2006-12-08	www.cnlyjt.com	0571-87769018
杭州灵峰赛伯乐创业投资合伙企业（有限合伙）	2008-12-10	—	0571-88085123

公司名称	成立时间	网址	传真
杭州七弦股权投资管理有限公司	2010-05-18	www.china-qixian.com	0571-89980500
杭州钱江浙商创业投资合伙企业（有限合伙）	2009-06-03	—	0571-89922221
杭州钱江中小企业创业投资有限公司	2010-09-25	—	0571-87155993
杭州如山创业投资有限公司	2007-08	—	0571-87896213
杭州赛伯乐晨星投资合伙企业（有限合伙）	2010-09-21	—	0571-88085123
杭州赛智创业投资有限公司	2009-03-13	—	0571-88085123
杭州申尚投资合伙企业（有限合伙）	2013-02-01	—	—
杭州市高科技投资有限公司	2000-08	—	0571-87024904
杭州泰恒股权投资管理有限公司	2010-06-03	—	—
杭州万豪碧扬投资合伙企业（有限合伙）	2012-03-15	—	—
杭州万豪绵汐投资合伙企业（有限合伙）	—	—	—
杭州万豪培汕投资合伙企业（有限合伙）	2012-03-15	—	—
杭州万豪投资管理有限公司	2006-01-09	—	0571-87701437
杭州下城区创业投资有限公司	2008-06-10	www.hzxcgt.com	0571-85383218
杭州英维投资管理有限公司	2007-07-03	—	0571-28280180
杭州盈开投资管理有限公司	2009-06-23	www.incapital.cn	0571-87960022
杭州盈翔创业投资合伙企业（有限合伙）	2011-03-04	—	—
杭州祐康经济开发有限公司	2006-05-09	—	—
杭州浙科汇庆创业投资合伙企业（有限合伙）	2013-04-10	—	—
杭州浙科友业投资管理有限公司	2011-11	—	0571-88869550
杭州正典投资管理有限公司	2009-11-10	—	0571-86945666
湖州市创业投资有限责任公司	2008-09	—	0572-2212918
嘉兴市领汇创业投资管理有限公司	2010-12-21	—	0575-87153786
梦工场传媒有限公司	2012-02-13	www.mediadreamworks.net	—
宁波北远创业投资中心（有限合伙）	2010-08-27	—	0574-27706565
宁波创业风险投资有限公司	1999-05-06	—	0574-86881546
宁波东元创业投资有限公司	2005-05-12	www.nbvc.com.cn	0574-87294001
宁波富博睿祺创业投资中心（有限合伙）	2011-01-07	—	0574-87093878
宁波高新创业资产经营管理有限公司	1999-06-25	—	0755-26935156
宁波杉杉创业投资有限公司	2007-03-30	www.shanshan.com.cn	0574-88133983
宁波杉杉望新科技创业投资有限公司	2009-12-14	—	0574-28833666
宁波天堂硅谷合众股权投资合伙企业（有限合伙）	2012-02-16	—	0571-86483535
宁波新以创业投资管理有限公司	2010-01-13	—	0574-87993884
宁波新以创业投资合伙企业（有限合伙）	2010-01-29	www.infinity-equity.com	0574-87993884
衢州赛伯乐创业投资有限公司	2010-04-06	—	0574-88085123
绍兴凯泰投资管理有限公司	2010-11-26	—	0571-88129634
绍兴龙山赛伯乐创业投资有限公司	2008-09-03	—	0575-85156989
通联创业投资股份有限公司	2000-11	www.tonglianvc.com	0571-87153792
五都投资有限公司	2008-04-03	—	0571-87633677

公司名称	成立时间	网址	传真
浙江安丰进取创业投资有限公司	2009-03-25	—	0571-87633580
浙江安丰稳健创业投资有限公司	2009-07-08	—	0571-87633580
浙江博通创业投资有限公司	2007-07	—	0571-87087810
浙江春晖创业投资有限公司	2007-10-17	—	0575-82150888
浙江大学创业投资有限公司	2001-01-03	—	0571-87382889
浙江大学科技创业投资有限公司	2008-10-29	—	0571-87397929
浙江东翰高投长三角股权投资合伙企业（有限合伙）	2010-09-20	—	025-66009900
浙江富国创新投资有限公司	2010-08-12	—	0571-88068369
浙江富国创业投资有限公司	2007-04-29	—	0571-88068369
浙江富国金溪创业投资合伙企业（有限合伙）	2011-07-25	—	0571-88068369
浙江富国投资管理有限公司	2010-07-13	—	0571-88068369
浙江富鑫创业投资有限公司	2008-02-03	www.zfinvest.com	0571-88352033
浙江国信创业投资有限公司	2003-03	—	0571-85069200
浙江海邦人才创业投资合伙企业（有限合伙）	2011-12	www.hbvc.com.cn	0571-81022997
浙江海洋经济创业投资有限公司	2010-01-19	—	0580-2036865
浙江浩誉创业投资有限公司	2011	—	0571-5689322
浙江合力创业投资有限公司	2011-03-09	—	0571-87988858
浙江恒岚股权投资合伙企业（有限合伙）	2011-11-03	—	021-32585857
浙江红石创业投资有限公司	2007-11-27	—	—
浙江红土创业投资有限公司	2010-04-21	—	0573-83710180
浙江华瓯创业投资有限公司	2007-11-16	www.hovc.cn	0571-87988858
浙江华瓯股权投资管理有限公司	2011-05-17	—	0571-87988858
浙江华睿德银创业投资有限公司	2011-01-24	—	0571-88163180
浙江华睿点金矿业投资有限公司	2009-08-10	—	—
浙江华睿点石投资管理有限公司	2011	—	0571-88163180
浙江华睿富华创业投资合伙企业（有限合伙）	2012-07-03	—	—
浙江华睿海越光电产业创业投资有限公司	2009-12-23	—	—
浙江华睿海越投资有限公司	2009-07-20	—	—
浙江华睿海越现代服务业创业投资有限公司	2010-01-28	—	0571-88163180
浙江华睿弘源智能产业创业投资有限公司	2010-03-22	—	0571-88163180
浙江华睿互联投资有限公司	2010-10-20	—	0571-88163180
浙江华睿庆余创业投资有限公司	2013-12-30	—	—
浙江华睿如山创业投资有限公司	2010-12-07	—	0571-88163180
浙江华睿如山装备投资有限公司	2009-10-13	—	—
浙江华睿睿银创业投资有限公司	2007-03-28	—	—
浙江华睿盛银创业投资有限公司	2009-07-20	—	—
浙江华睿泰信创业投资有限公司	2008-07-21	—	—
浙江华睿投资管理有限公司	2002-08	www.sinowisdom.cn	0571-88163180
浙江华睿祥生环境产业创业投资有限公司	2010-11-15	—	0571-88163180

公司名称	成立时间	网址	传真
浙江华睿兴华股权投资合伙企业（有限合伙）	2012-12-24	—	—
浙江华睿医疗创业投资有限公司	2011-01	—	0571-88163180
浙江华睿中科创业投资有限公司	2011-07	—	0571-88163180
浙江嘉海创业投资有限公司	2010-01-13	—	0571-89922221
浙江嘉庆投资有限公司	2010-06-29	—	0571-86821212
浙江嘉银投资有限公司	2006-05-24	—	0571-88163180
浙江金桥创业投资有限公司	2007-08-14	www.jinqiaojituan.com	0571-89283395
浙江金永信投资管理有限公司	2005-03-24	—	0571-85279925
浙江君亚创业投资合伙企业（有限合伙）	2012-05-21	—	0571-86751630
浙江莱沃创业投资有限公司	2009-07-08	www.uslever.com	0574-82815775
浙江蓝石创业投资有限公司	2008-05-15	—	—
浙江领庆创业投资有限公司	2011-03-14	—	0571-87153787
浙江隆德创业投资管理有限公司	2009-04-01	www.team-china.com	0571-87750989
浙江美林创业投资有限公司	2008-07-11	www.merrillcapital.cn	0571-85455412
浙江瓯联创业投资有限公司	2009-05-12	—	0571-87988858
浙江瓯盛创业投资有限公司	2008-06-03	—	0571-87988858
浙江瓯信创业投资有限公司	2009-04-02	—	0571-87988858
浙江普发科技开发中心	1991-08	—	0571-88911708
浙江普永泽股权投资合伙企业（有限合伙）	2010-08-24	—	021-32585857
浙江如山成长创业投资有限公司	2008-08-18	www.chinadunan.com	0571-87896213
浙江如山高新创业投资有限公司	2010-11-10	www.chinadunan.com	0571-87896213
浙江如山投资管理有限公司	2010-09-26	www.chinadunan.com	0571-87896213
浙江如山新兴创业投资有限公司	2012-09-11	—	0571-87896213
浙江赛伯乐投资管理有限公司	2008-06-16	www.zjcybernaut.com	0571-88085123
浙江赛康创业投资有限公司	2010-04-20	—	0571-88085123
浙江赛康医疗健康创业投资有限公司	2010-04-20	—	0571-88085123
浙江省创业投资集团有限公司	2000-09-30	www.zjvc.cn	0571-88259222
浙江省科技风险投资有限公司	1993-06	www.zvc-zj.com	0571-88869550
浙江省天堂硅谷创业创新投资服务中心有限公司	2008-05	www.vcpes.com	0571-86483535
浙江省浙创启元创业投资有限公司	2012-12-31	—	0571-88259222
浙江泰银创业投资有限公司	2007-10-26	—	—
浙江天堂硅谷长泰股权投资合伙企业（有限合伙）	2011-07-15	—	0571-86483535
浙江天堂硅谷长信投资合伙企业（有限合伙）	2011-03-24	—	0571-86483535
浙江天堂硅谷长盈股权投资合伙企业（有限合伙）	2011-05-11	—	0571-86483535
浙江天堂硅谷朝阳创业投资有限公司	2007-04-16	—	0571-86483535
浙江天堂硅谷晨曦创业投资有限公司	2007-10-16	—	0571-86483535
浙江天堂硅谷大康股权投资合伙企业（有限合伙）	2012-08-21	—	0571-86483535
浙江天堂硅谷海天汇缘创业投资合伙企业（有限合伙）	2013-03-04	—	0571-86483535
浙江天堂硅谷合丰创业投资有限公司	2009-10-13	—	0571-86483535

公司名称	成立时间	网址	传真
浙江天堂硅谷合胜创业投资有限公司	2009-10-20	—	0571-87089718
浙江天堂硅谷合众创业投资有限公司	2007-10-24	—	0571-86483523
浙江天堂硅谷恒通创业投资有限公司	2008-05-26	—	0571-86483535
浙江天堂硅谷恒裕创业投资有限公司	2008-01-03	—	0571-86483535
浙江天堂硅谷汇通股权投资合伙企业（有限合伙）	2011	—	0571-86483535
浙江天堂硅谷久和股权投资合伙企业（有限合伙）	2012-03-01	—	0571-86483535
浙江天堂硅谷久鸿股权投资合伙企业（有限合伙）	2013	—	0571-86483535
浙江天堂硅谷久融股权投资合伙企业（有限合伙）	2011	—	0571-86483535
浙江天堂硅谷久晟股权投资合伙企业（有限合伙）	2011	—	0571-87089718
浙江天堂硅谷久盈股权投资合伙企业（有限合伙）	2012-02-13	—	0571-86483535
浙江天堂硅谷鲲诚创业投资有限公司	2006-12-01	—	0571-86483535
浙江天堂硅谷鲲鹏创业投资有限公司	2009-06-26	—	0571-86483535
浙江天堂硅谷七弦股权投资合伙企业（有限合伙）	2011	—	0571-86483535
浙江天堂硅谷台州合盈股权投资有限公司	2011	—	0571-86483535
浙江天堂硅谷阳光创业投资有限公司	2006-06-20	—	0571-86483535
浙江天堂硅谷银嘉股权投资合伙企业（有限合伙）	2010-11-16	—	0571-86483523
浙江天堂硅谷银泽股权投资合伙企业（有限合伙）	2010-10-19	—	0571-86483523
浙江天堂硅谷盈丰股权投资合伙企业（有限合伙）	2010-07-30	—	0571-87089718
浙江天堂硅谷盈通创业投资有限公司	2010-06-01	—	0571-86483535
浙江天堂硅谷元金创业投资合伙企业（有限合伙）	2013-03-20	—	0571-86483535
浙江天堂硅谷资产管理集团有限公司	2000-11-11	www.ttgg.com.cn	0571-86483535
浙江维科创业投资有限公司	2008-02-28	—	0571-87207613
浙江信达资产管理有限公司	2007-06-01	—	0571-85115715
浙江信德丰创业投资有限公司	2010-05-27	—	0571-87215866
浙江兴科科技发展投资有限公司	2003-12-29	—	0573-82570501
浙江亚欧创业投资有限公司	2010-12-27	—	0571-89880002
浙江亿都创业投资有限公司	2007-11	—	0571-85310949
浙江银泰睿祺创业投资有限公司	2009-11-09	—	0574-87093878
浙江盈瓯创业投资有限公司	2010-11-05	—	0571-87988858
浙江玉泉正合创业投资合伙企业（有限合伙）	2011-10-12	—	0571-88137467
浙江浙大科发股权投资管理有限公司	2003-11-11	www.zdkfcapital.com	—
浙江浙华投资有限公司	2005-06-18	www.zhinvest.com.cn	0573-82582626
浙江浙科汇丰创业投资有限公司	2010-09	—	—
浙江浙科汇利创业投资有限公司	2010-05	—	—
浙江浙科汇涛创业投资合伙企业（有限合伙）	2011-05-09	—	—
浙江浙科汇盈创业投资有限公司	2009-08	—	—
浙江浙科美林创业投资有限公司	2011-04	—	—
浙江浙科升华创业投资有限公司	2010-10	—	—
浙江浙科银江创业投资有限公司	2010-10-14	—	—

公司名称	成立时间	网址	传真
浙江浙商长海创业投资合伙企业（有限合伙）	2010-12-14	—	0571-89922221
浙江浙商创业投资股份有限公司	2007-11	www.zsvc.com.cn	0571-89922221
浙江浙商海鹏创业投资合伙企业（有限合伙）	2008-06-03	—	0571-89922221
浙江浙商诺海创业投资合伙企业（有限合伙）	2010-04-14	—	0571-89922221
浙江支汇股权投资合伙企业（有限合伙）	2010-08-24	—	021-32585857
浙江中大集团投资有限公司	2002-09-19	www.zhongda.com	0571-85777239
浙江中新力合科技金融服务有限责任公司	2011-09-29	—	0571-89939766
中舜投资有限公司	2010-10-14	—	0571-88113118
诸暨鼎信创业投资有限公司	2008-07-29	—	0571-87896213
青海华控科技创业投资基金（有限合伙）	2013-02-21	—	—
瑞旗股权投资管理（重庆）有限公司	2011-06-14	—	023-63877705
深圳大石资本管理有限公司	2013-09-27	www.gemvc.com	023-88653504
英飞尼迪（重庆）股权投资基金合伙企业（有限合伙）	2011-09-29	www.infinity-equity.com	023-63051585
圆基（重庆）股权投资基金管理有限公司	2010-02-05	—	023-63329022
重庆本道投资有限公司	2013-05-16	www.cqbendao.com	023-63053322
重庆博威股权投资基金管理有限公司	2013-11-01	—	—
重庆德同创业投资中心（有限合伙）	2010-04-01	—	023-67889905
重庆富坤创业投资中心（有限合伙）	2009-09-22	www.rlequities.com	023-67030600
重庆高联渝富股权投资管理有限公司	2013-05-08	—	023-63420901
重庆高新创业投资有限公司	2007-08	—	023-68601100
重庆汉能科技创业投资中心(有限合伙)	2011-05-16	www.hinagroup.com.cn	010-85889001
重庆汉能资产管理有限公司	2011-05-16	www.hinagroup.com.cn	023-85889001
重庆恒锐源股权投资基金管理有限公司	2009-12-23	www.chinahry.com	023-86798500
重庆华犇创业投资管理有限公司	2010-04-16	www.chinarunvc.com	023-63318955
重庆华房股权投资基金管理有限公司	2009-10	—	023-68633133
重庆锦道股权投资基金管理有限公司	2011-03-01	—	—
重庆锦道股权投资中心（有限合伙）	2011-03-01	—	—
重庆开创高新技术创业投资有限公司	2005-03-25	—	023-68601100
重庆科技创业风险投资引导基金有限公司	2009-07-17	www.cqvcgf.com	023-67516108
重庆科技风险投资有限公司	1993-01-16	www.cqkjvc.com	023-67516883
重庆科兴乾健股权投资有限公司	2011-12-01	—	—
重庆两江新区创新创业投资发展有限公司	2011-09-26	www.chinaljcapital.com	023-88283537
重庆两江新区创业六环科技发展有限公司	2013-04-24	www.6link.cn	023-88722899-8055
重庆木兰创业投资管理顾问有限公司	2013-06-13	—	—
重庆芃瑞股权投资基金管理有限公司	2013-07-30	www.prpe.cn	023-88601260
重庆起乾点坤创业投资合伙企业（有限合伙）	2013-12-20	www.istartvc.com	023-68535281
重庆软银投资管理有限公司	2008-11-25	—	—
重庆三屋领秀创业投资有限公司	2012-11-22	—	023-62611660
重庆三屋投资有限公司	2009-12-02	www.cqswtz.com	023-62611660

公司名称	成立时间	网址	传真
重庆市大渡口区科技产业创业投资有限公司	2013-01-28	—	—
重庆泰豪晟大股权投资基金管理中心（有限合伙）	2011-08-06	—	023-63022990
重庆泰豪渝晟股权投资基金中心（有限合伙）	2011-08-05	—	023-63022990
重庆天安起乾企业孵化器有限公司	2013-12-12	www.istartvc.com	023-68535281
重庆天使科技创业投资有限公司	2010-01-25	—	023-67516883
重庆西永创新投资有限公司	2007-07-23	www.szvc.com.cn	023-65660566
重庆新天泽股权投资基金管理有限公司	2013-04-17	—	023-61667099-138
重庆新天泽华立股权投资基金合伙企业（有限合伙）	2014-01-09	—	023-61667099-138
重庆鑫山股权投资基金管理有限公司	2011-12-07	www.x-shan.com	023-67517660
重庆兴农资产经营管理有限公司	2013-08-28	—	023-88733896
重庆星光投资有限公司	2007-11-14	www.fucn.com.cn	023-63107366
重庆英飞尼迪创业投资中心（有限合伙）	2011-08-16	www.infinity-equity.com	023-63051585
重庆英飞尼迪投资管理有限公司	2011-11-11	www.infinity-equity.com	023-63051585
重庆永盟股权投资基金管理有限公司	2012-05-25	www.chinavcbi.com	—
重庆圆基新能源创业投资基金合伙企业（有限合伙）	2011-01-27	—	023-63329022
重庆智基股权投资管理有限公司	2010-07	www.idtvc.com	023-88721013